PEREGRINE BOOKS

Y 13

JAMES JOYCE'S *ULYSSES*

STUART GILBERT

JAMES JOYCE'S
ULYSSES

A STUDY BY

STUART GILBERT

*

PENGUIN BOOKS

in association with Faber and Faber

Penguin Books Ltd, Harmondsworth, Middlesex
AUSTRALIA: Penguin Books Pty Ltd, 762 Whitehorse Road,
Mitcham, Victoria

—

First published by Faber & Faber 1930
New revised edition 1952
Published in Peregrine Books 1963

—

Made and printed in Great Britain
by Western Printing Services Ltd
Bristol
Set in Monotype Bembo

CONTENTS

CONTENTS

Preface to the 1952 Edition

TWENTY years have passed since the appearance of the Study of *Ulysses* of which this is a new, revised, and slightly enlarged edition, and amongst the notable events of these two decades one of the most interesting, from the literary point of view, was the lifting of the ban on the admission of *Ulysses* into the English-speaking countries. In the original Preface to my book I said: 'In writing this commentary I have borne in mind the unusual circumstance that, though *Ulysses* is probably the most discussed literary work that has appeared in our time, the book itself is hardly more than a name to many. I have therefore quoted freely from the text, so that those who are unable to make their *voyage à Ithaque*, otherwise to the sign of Shakespeare & Co., Paris, and acquire the original, may, despite the censorial ban, become acquainted with Mr Joyce's epic work.' To the regret of many who are, like the author of this book (and as was Joyce himself during the last twenty years of his life) – to use the fiscal formula – 'domiciled in Paris, France', the sign of Shakespeare no longer hangs in the little rue de l'Odéon. But, on the credit side, we have the fact that *Ulysses* is now accessible to all.

As a result of this happy change I was called on to make a decision regarding the somewhat lengthy excerpts from the text of *Ulysses* prefixed to each of the eighteen chapters of commentary proper. My first plan was to suppress these altogether, as being superfluous, now that *Ulysses* itself was, presumably, in my readers' hands. However, after careful thought, I decided to retain them, for several reasons. For one thing, I have been told by a surprisingly large number of people that they attempted to read *Ulysses* and gave it up, as making too great demands on their attention, memory, and endurance. When, however, they returned to it, after reading this commentary and understanding the thematic structure, the relation of the episodes each to each and the concatenation of the events narrated, they found it relatively easy and usually exhilarating reading. If my book is to be used in this manner, as an introduction to that memorable experience, a first reading of *Ulysses*, it is desirable that this commentary should be complete in itself and give not a mere analysis of the leading themes, Homeric references, etc., but a panoramic view of Joyce's epic as a whole. And, in any case, a commentary sprinkled with page numbers referring the reader back to the original involves him in vexatious huntings up of the passages in question, during which he may well lose the thread of the argument. These are amongst the reasons why I have decided not to change the ground-plan of this book, and have retained the extracts and summaries which precede the analysis of each episode and my comments on it.

Obviously the value of such a work as this depends on its authenticity, and 'authenticity' in the present case implies that the ideas, interpretations, and explanations put forward in these pages are not capricious or speculative, but were endorsed by Joyce himself. Thus it may be of some interest if I describe briefly the circumstances leading up to the writing of this book and those under which it was written. It was when I was assisting MM. Auguste Morel and Valéry Larbaud in the translation of *Ulysses* into French that the project suggested itself to me. In making a translation the first essential is thoroughly to understand what one is translating; any vagueness or uncertainty in this respect must lead to failure. This applies especially when the texture of the work to be translated is intricate, or the meaning elusive. One begins with a close analysis, and only when the implications of the original are fully unravelled does one start looking for approximations in the other language. Thus I made a point of consulting Joyce on every doubtful point, of ascertaining from him the exact associations he had in mind when using proper names, truncated phrases, or peculiar words, and never 'passing' the French text unless I was sure we had the meaning of each word and passage quite clear in our minds. Joyce showed extraordinary patience in bearing with my interrogation which, as I had just returned to Europe after a longish judicial career in the East, must have had much of the tedious persistence so necessary in legal inquiries east of Suez if one is to get reasonably near that coy nymph, Aletheia. But perhaps most valuable of all were the hints thrown out quite casually (this was Joyce's invariable way) as to the sources of *Ulysses*. Needless to say, without any suggestion on his part, I had begun by re-reading much of the *Odyssey* and, though at first I found my knowledge of the Early Ionic sadly rusty after many years' obsolescence, facility came with progress, and, with it, a renewed, and enhanced, pleasure in the greatest of all epics. Indeed the *Odyssey* is quite easy reading; a smattering of Greek (seconded by a good dictionary and W. W. Merry's notes) suffices. No other work of literary art in any language is equally refreshing and rewarding, and if I can persuade any of the readers of *Ulysses* to follow up with a reading of the *Odyssey* in the original – translations are but reflections in a tarnished mirror – I shall have done them a good turn.

'Have you read Victor Bérard's *Les Phéniciens et l'Odyssée*?' Joyce asked me when I mentioned my reading of the *Odyssey*. (This interrogative method of suggestion was characteristic, as I soon came to learn.) I at once procured a copy of that bulky work, and found it fascinating reading. While immensely erudite, Bérard is no pedant, and his reconstruction of the Mediterranean scene in the age of the rhapsodists is not only a triumph of scholarship but also a work of art. On another occasion, when we chanced to be discussing Eliphas Lévi's theories of magic and Mme Blavatsky's entertaining *Isis Unveiled*, he asked me if I had read any of Sinnett's work. (A. P. Sinnett, a cultured and intelligent man, was a member of Mme Blavatsky's circle in India, and her biographer.) Naturally I took the hint and procured his *Esoteric Buddhism* and *Growth of the Soul*, well-written books from which Joyce certainly derived some of his material. He was conversant also with spiritualist literature, I think, but I noticed that, while ready enough to talk about theosophy and occultism, he – perhaps because of his Catholic upbringing – shied off this subject.

I am sometimes asked, 'Did Joyce believe in theosophy, magic, and so forth?' An answer is difficult, owing to the ambiguity of the term 'believe in'. In the meaning the verb has, for example, in the Christian Creed, I doubt if Joyce, though he owned to several deeply rooted superstitions (as they are called), believed in any such doctrines. But he accepted their existence as a fact, on a footing of validity no higher and no lower than that of many of the fashionable and fluctuating 'truths' of science and psychology. He had none of the glib assurance of the late-nineteenth-century rationalist. (I am of course speaking of Joyce as I knew him, in his maturity – when his view of *la condition humaine* was mellower, less dogmatic than that of the astringently young man of the *Portrait*.)

Several of the books Joyce mentioned in the course of our talks together are cited in the footnotes of the pages that follow. All of them can be read to advantage by those who wish to deepen their understanding of *Ulysses*, and as a course of reading 'on the side' – for an appreciation of the aesthetic climate of Joyce's art – I would also recommend the works of Walter Pater (especially the 'Conclusion' of his *Renaissance*), Flaubert, Meredith, and, generally, the writers of the nineties.

Finally, it should be mentioned that in the course of writing this Study I read it out to Joyce, chapter by chapter, and that, though he allowed me the greatest latitude in the presentation of the facts and indeed encouraged me to treat the subject on whatever lines were most congenial to me, it contains nothing (with the exception of Chapter 5 in Part One, written for the new edition) to which he did not give his full approbation; indeed there are several passages which I directly owe to him. Thus the long list of examples of rhetorical forms which concludes my commentary on the 'Aeolus' episode was compiled at his suggestion, and we spent several industrious afternoons collaborating on it. And the opening pages of my commentary on the episode of 'The Sirens' reproduce, word for word, information given me by Joyce.

I have not tried to alleviate the rather pedantic tone of much of the writing in this Study. For one thing, Joyce approved of it; and, for another, we who admired *Ulysses* for its structural, enduring qualities and not for the occasional presence in it of words and descriptive passages which shocked our elders, were on the defensive, and the pedant's cloak is often a convenient protection against the cold blasts of propriety. Moreover, in those early days most readers and many eminent critics regarded *Ulysses* as a violently romantic work, an uncontrolled outpouring of the subconscious mind, powerful but formless. Thus it was necessary to emphasize the 'classical' and formal elements, the carefully planned layout of the book, and the minute attention given by its author to detail, each phrase, indeed each word, being assigned its place with *pointilliste* precision.

*

In the forefront of my acknowledgements I record my indebtedness to James Joyce himself, to whose assistance and encouragement this work owes whatever merit it may possess; also to Victor Bérard, whose *Les Phéniciens et l'Odyssée* proved invaluable for the interpretation of the Homeric correspondences; to the editors of the *Fortnightly Review*, *Transition*, the *Revue de Genève* and *Échanges* for permission to reprint my studies of certain episodes, which appeared in their pages; and to Mr L. M. Irby for his compilation of the Index. In quoting from the *Odyssey* I have used Messrs Butcher and Lang's translation (Messrs

Macmillan & Co., Ltd) which, despite Samuel Butler's gibe at its Wardour Street English, seems better to convey the spirit of the original (couched, even for Greeks of the Classical period, in an exotic dialect) than any of the more modern versions, excellent as some are.

Paris, 1950   S.G.

PART ONE

INTRODUCTION

Chapter 1

THE NARRATIVE OF *ULYSSES*

ULYSSES is the record of a single day, 16 June 1904. That day was very much like any other, unmarked by any important event and, even for the Dubliners who figure in *Ulysses*, exempt from personal disaster or achievement. It was the climax of a long drought and the many public houses of the Irish capital claimed most of the Dubliners' spare time and cash; the former, as usual, abundant, the latter scarce, as usual. In the morning a citizen was buried; a little before midnight a child was born. At about the same hour the weather broke and there was a sudden downpour, accompanied by a violent clap of thunder. In the intervals of imbibing Guinness, Power, or 'J.J. & S.' the Dubliners discoursed with animation on their pet topic, Irish politics, happily bemused themselves by the singing of amorous or patriotic ballads, lost money over the Ascot Gold Cup. At about 4 p.m. an act of adultery was consummated at the residence of one Leopold Bloom, advertisement-canvasser. A perfectly ordinary day, in fact.

The structure of the book as a whole is, like that of all epic narratives, episodic. There are three main divisions, subdivided into chapters or, rather, episodes, each of which differs from the rest not only in subject-matter but also by the style and technique employed.

The first part (three episodes) serves as prelude to the narrative of Mr Bloom's day, the main theme, and may be regarded as a 'bridge-work' between the author's earlier work, the *Portrait of the Artist as a Young Man*[1] and *Ulysses*. The three episodes which compose this part are concerned with Stephen Dedalus, the hero of the *Portrait*, and his doings from 8 a.m. till noon. Stephen is still the arrogant young man who entered in his diary (the concluding lines of the *Portrait*): 'I go to encounter for the millionth time the reality of experience and to forge in

---

[1]. This, Joyce's first full-length novel, is almost entirely autobiographical. In it many of the aesthetic principles on which *Ulysses* is based are expounded by the 'young man', Stephen Dedalus; a careful perusal of the *Portrait* is indispensable for the proper understanding of *Ulysses*.

the smithy of my soul the uncreated conscience of my race. ... Old
father, old artificer, stand me now and ever in good stead.' In the interval between this invocation of the first artist of the Hellenic world,
maker of the labyrinth of Cnossos and the honeycomb of gold, and his
participation in the Odyssey of Mr Bloom, Stephen has passed a year or
so at Paris, but it is evident that his knowledge of the 'reality of experience' has been little enlarged, in so far as such knowledge implies a
capacity for self-adaptation, or acquiescence with one's surroundings.
He is still an intellectual exile, proudly aloof from the mediocrity of his
contemporaries, and he still displays an ironic disdain for their shoddy
enthusiasms, combined with a predilection for the 'abstruosities' in-
culcated by his Jesuit upbringing, the scholastic habit of dialectic and
exact definition.

In the first episode we discover him living in a disused Martello
tower, overlooking Dublin Bay, in the company of Buck Mulligan, a
cynical medical student with a taste for blasphemy, and a somewhat
ridiculous Oxford man named Haines. Next we find him (at 10 a.m.)
giving a Roman History lesson at Mr Deasy's school, where, as Mr
Deasy correctly anticipates, he is not destined to remain very long; and,
finally, we see him walking on the Dublin strand, hear his musings on
things seen and unseen and follow the restless current of his associative
thoughts, symbolized by the upswelling tide. There is, as will be shown
later, an intimate connexion between the personalities of Stephen and
Mr Bloom, the Ulysses of this modern Odyssey; the spiritual relationship of these two, apparently poles apart, is one of the *leitmotifs* of the
book; thus this detailed presentation of Stephen's mental make-up is an
integral part of the psychological background of *Ulysses*.

Mr Bloom's day begins, like Stephen's, at 8 a.m., when he is pre-
paring his wife's morning tea at their house, No. 7 Eccles Street. He
goes out for a few minutes to buy a kidney for breakfast, after having
set the kettle on the fire. On his return he hands his wife her letters in
the bedroom and presently brings up the tray with the tea things. Mrs
Bloom is better known in Dublin as Madame Marion Tweedy, the
singer. An overripe, indolent beauty of a southern type (she is of
mixed Spanish, Jewish, and Irish extraction), this lady is admirably
fitted to the taste of Mr Bloom, who also is of Jewish descent. Unfortunately, however, for him, Marion Bloom is not satisfied by the
exclusive attentions of her mature husband, who tolerantly imputes her

frequent infidelities (which, nevertheless, he deplores) to the call of her 'Spanish blood'. Amongst the letters which Mr Bloom hands her is one from a certain 'Blazes' Boylan, a young Dublin man-about-town, who is acting as her impresario in a coming concert tour and is the most recent of her lovers; in his letter he tells her that he is coming at four that afternoon to show her the programme. Throughout Mr Bloom's day the thought of this interview will weigh on his mind. Each time he encounters Boylan or hears his name mentioned, the comfortable flow of his silent monologue is checked; he tries to concentrate his attention on the first object that meets his eye, but can never wholly rid himself of his obsession.

At 10 o'clock Mr Bloom starts his day's work. He is naturally sociable and anxious to please, and his *métier* of advertisement-canvasser requires that he should keep in touch with many classes of Dubliners, business-men, editors, potential clients of all kinds. For in Dublin, as in most small capitals, bonhomie brings business, and the man who is known as a good fellow, a 'mixer', and cultivates relations with as many of his fellow-citizens as possible, has a pull over an unsociable rival, even though the latter be more competent. His first visit, however, has a romantic object. He obtains from a branch post office a letter addressed to him under the pseudonym of 'Henry Flower' by a trusting typist, Martha Clifford. For Mr Bloom – considering his wife's 'Spanish' ways one can hardly blame him – is himself no model of fidelity, though his sins are rather of intention than of commission. In a meditative mood, hoping to hear some music, he enters All Hallows (St Andrew's) Church to witness the end of a communion service. Then he orders from a chemist a face-lotion for his wife and visits a bathing establish-ment. The next episode describes a funeral attended by Mr Bloom in the company of Mr Dedalus senior and others. The deceased, Dignam, was a friend and when, after the burial, a subscription is opened for the widow, Mr Bloom makes what is, considering his means, a generous donation. At noon he visits a newspaper office to arrange for an adver-tisement. Stephen visits the same office a little after Mr Bloom; he has drawn his salary at the school and so can invite the editor and his cronies to a neighbouring bar for drinks; the invitation, needless to say, proves acceptable. He just misses encountering Mr Bloom. It is now lunch time and Mr Bloom feels the pangs of hunger. He looks into a popular restaurant but is disgusted by the sight of the 'animals feeding'.

'His gorge rose.' Finally he takes the edge off his appetite with a sand-wich and a glass of burgundy at Davy Byrne's public house. The scene now shifts to the National Library where a quasi-Platonic dialogue is engaged between Stephen Dedalus and some literary lights of Dublin. Mr Bloom makes a brief appearance (he has to look up an advertise-ment in a back number of the *Kilkenny People*) but, again, does not encounter Stephen. The next episode consists of eighteen fragmentary scenes of Dublin life, concluding with a coda describing the vice-regal progress through Dublin. Each fragment is thematically linked up with the others and with the book as a whole. It is now four o'clock and Mr Bloom's hunger will no longer be denied. He has a belated lunch at the Ormond Hotel (where Mr Dedalus *père* and others are celebrating the trinity of wine, women, and song) in the company of Richie Goulding, Stephen's uncle. At 5 p.m. we find Mr Bloom at Barney Kiernan's tavern where a charitable errand, on behalf of the late Dignam's widow, has taken him. The xenophobia of an intoxicated nationalist, known as the Citizen, leads to his precipitate retreat from the patriot's den.

Weary and way-worn after incessant peregrination, Mr Bloom now decides to take the air on Sandymount beach. Under the last rays of the setting sun, he yields to the seductions of a precocious Dublin chit, Gerty MacDowell, but does not follow up his conquest. At 10 p.m. he visits the Lying-in Hospital to inquire after a friend, Mrs Purefoy, who is being delivered of a child. Stephen is there, carousing with some medical students, and at last he and Mr Bloom come into contact. Stephen is gradually becoming intoxicated and Mr Bloom, attracted by the young man, decides to take him under his wing. When the band of revellers sally forth and Stephen makes for the Dublin night town, Mr Bloom's paternal instinct prompts him to follow. The next scene, situated in the brothel quarter of Dublin, is one of the most remarkable in *Ulysses*. Stephen, under the influence of drink, and Mr Bloom, exhausted by his daylong Odyssey, are sensitive to the hallucinating *ambiance* and see their most secret desires, their fears, their memories, take form and live and move before their eyes. This scene (correspon-ding to the 'Circe' episode of the *Odyssey*) is usually described as the 'Walpurgisnight' or 'Pandemonium' of *Ulysses*.

The last three episodes describe Mr Bloom's return; he is accompanied by Stephen, who has decided that he will not go back to the Martello tower which he shares with Mulligan. On their way to Eccles Street they halt to take a cup of coffee at a cabman's shelter, where they encounter a marine Munchausen who regales the company with tall yarns of adventure in far lands, and other exotic nightfarers. Later, in Mr Bloom's kitchen, over a cup of cocoa, they compare experiences and, in the catechistic form of question and reply, the personality, antecedents, and past life of Mr Bloom are scientifically dissected. Last of all, when Mr Bloom is asleep beside his wife, we have the long, unpunctuated silent monologue of the latter, the refined quintessence of unrefined femininity. Of this episode Arnold Bennett wrote: 'I have never read anything to surpass it, and I doubt if I have ever read anything to equal it.' *Ulysses* ends, like the marriage service, with 'amazement'.

At a first reading of *Ulysses* the average reader is impressed most of all by the striking psychological realism of the narrative. He is apt to attribute this impression to an (apparently) complete lack of reticence in the self-revelation of the personages and to the presence in the text of words which, if used at all in other novels, are often travestied, like Rudyard Kipling's term of endearment, in a decent disguise, or asterisked out of recognition as in Mr Aldington's *Death of a Hero*. But the realism of *Ulysses* strikes far deeper than the mere exercise of verbal frankness; apart from the author's extreme, almost scientific, precision in his handling of words, there are two factors which place Joyce's work in a class apart from all its predecessors, even the most meticulously realistic: firstly, the creator's standpoint to his theme, the unusual angle from which he views his creatures, and, secondly, his use of the 'silent monologue' as the exponent not only of their inner and hardly conscious psychological reactions but also of the narrative itself.

In most novels the reader's interest is aroused and his attention held by the presentation of dramatic situations, of problems deriving from conduct or character and the reactions of the fictitious personages among themselves. The personages of *Ulysses* are *not* fictitious and its true significance does not lie in problems of conduct or character. After reading *Ulysses* we do not ask ourselves: 'Should Stephen Dedalus have done this? Ought Mr Bloom to have said that? Should Mrs Bloom have refrained?' All these people are as they must be; they act, we see, according to some *lex eterna*, an ineluctable condition of their very existence. Not that they are mere puppets of Necessity or victims, like Tess, of an ironic Olympian. The law of their being is within them, it is a personal heritage, inalienable and autonomous. The meaning of *Ulysses*, for it has a meaning and is not a mere photographic 'slice of life' – far from it – is not to be sought in any analysis of the acts of the protagonist or the mental make-up of the characters; it is, rather, implicit in the technique of the various episodes, in nuances of language, in the thousand and one correspondences and allusions with which the book is studded. Thus *Ulysses* is neither pessimist nor optimist in outlook, neither moral nor immoral in the ordinary sense of these words; its affinity is, rather, with an Einstein formula, a Greek temple, an art that lives the more intensely for its repose. *Ulysses* achieves a coherent and integral interpretation of life, a static beauty according to the definition of Aquinas (as abridged by Joyce): *ad pulchritudinem tria requiruntur: integritas, consonantia, claritas.*[1]

It is curious how few authors in any tongue have written with real detachment and a single eye to the ideal proposed by Aquinas. The novelist can rarely conceal his emotive reactions (often, of course, he does not wish to do so), or his indifference is merely feigned. If, for instance, he has chosen to write on that ever-popular theme, the life of a prostitute, he cannot see her with the clarity and integrity of, for instance, an intelligent business woman; that is to say as the incorrigible sloven she is, a moron, charming maybe but parasitic as the most feckless of mid-Victorian spinsters, or *tout simplement* (as I heard a sensible Frenchwoman describe her) *une bonne manquée*, a tweeny who has missed her vocation. No, he makes of her a Maya, a high-priestess of illusion, a *Dame aux camélias*, or a Thaïs. The unsentimental writer is, in fact, extremely rare. In the fiction and plays of John Galsworthy, under his studied impartiality, a profound pity and sensitive reaction to the sufferings of others is scarcely concealed. Under a more classical form and vestments of more erudite tissue Anatole France shyly enveloped a spiritual affinity with Tolstoy. The contemporary realist and Freudian schools, too, have their axe to grind; they expound the ugly or abnormal in a spate of catharsis – many, of course, being mere merchants of pornography or young people whose joy it is to 'make the bourgeois jump'.

The attitude of the author of *Ulysses* to his personages and their acti-

---

1. See *A Portrait of the Artist as a Young Man*, page 248; Stephen, who aligned his aesthetic views with those of St Thomas Aquinas, translates these words: 'three things are needed for beauty: wholeness, harmony and radiance'.

vities is one of quiet detachment; all is grist to his mill, which, like God's, grinds slowly and exceeding small. When (abruptly to change the metaphor) some divine afflatus begins to swell the creative cyst, till it is distended like the wallet of winds which Aeolus gave to Odysseus, he neatly punctures it with a word, the 'lancet of his art'.[1] Many instances of this deliberate deflation of sentiment will be noticed in the course of this study, notably in the chapter dealing with the doctrine of metempsychosis and a citation of the climax of the 'Circe' episode. Joyce maintained this method in his last work, *Finnegans Wake*, which, despite the difficulties, linguistic and others, of the text, none of the admirers of his previous work should neglect on the ground of its supposed incomprehensibility.

*

All facts of any kind, mental or material, sublime or ludicrous, have an equivalence of value for the artist. But this does not imply that they are meaningless to him or that he is a mere reporter, a literal transcriber of experience. 'The personality of the artist,' as Stephen Dedalus observes, speaking of the epic form of literature, 'passes into the narration itself, flowing round and round the persons and the action like a vital sea.' He is a composer who takes the facts which experience offers and harmonizes them in such a way that, without losing their vitality and integrity, they yet fit together and form a concordant whole. In this detachment, as absolute as the indifference of Nature herself towards her children, we may see one of the causes of the apparent 'realism' of *Ulysses*.

Another of Joyce's innovations is the extended use of the unspoken soliloquy or silent monologue, an exact transcription of the stream of consciousness of the individual, which certainly has the air of an untouched photographic record and has, indeed, been compared to the film of a moving-picture. But, as I show in the next chapter of this introduction, the superficial disorder of Mr Bloom's and Stephen's meditations, the frequent welling up of subconscious memories and the linking together of ideas by assonance or verbal analogy, all in reality

1. *Ulysses*, page 5. (I follow here and elsewhere the pagination of the Bodley Head (1937) *Ulysses*. In 1960 they issued a new edition, entirely re-designed and re-set, but this is provided with an appendix listing the corresponding pages in the old and new editions.)

form part of an elaborate scheme, and the movement, chaotic though
it seem as life itself, is no more disorderly than the composed confusion
of the fair in the ballet *Petrushka*, or the orchestral score of Stravinsky's
Sacre du printemps. The soliloquy is, of course, no new thing; it is part of
the Shakespearian technique and, as will become apparent in the course
of this commentary, the influence of Shakespeare and especially of the
tragical history of Hamlet, noblest soliloquist of them all, is manifest
throughout *Ulysses*. Like Hamlet, of whom Mallarmé wrote, '*Il se
promène, lisant au livre de lui-même*', Mr Bloom and Stephen go their
ways, each 'reading the book of himself'. The technique of the *monologue intérieur* (as M. Valéry Larbaud aptly named this unuttered, un-
dramatized soliloquy) was, as a matter of fact, first exploited in our time
by a French writer, M. Édouard Dujardin, whose admirable tale *Les
Lauriers sont coupés* was originally published in 1887 and re-issued
thirty-seven years later and two years after the publication of *Ulysses*,
with a preface by M. Valéry Larbaud. In this preface the distinguished
French critic and novelist has some interesting remarks to make about
the silent monologue as employed by Dujardin and Joyce.

From March 1918 to August 1920 the *Little Review* (New York), a pioneer
literary periodical, published the greater part of *Ulysses*, the fifth work of the
Irish writer James Joyce, and the influence of this work rapidly made itself felt
among the younger authors writing in the English tongue. Even before James
Joyce's work was complete and published in book form (by Shakespeare & Co.,
Paris), they began to imitate or, rather, to utilize certain of the technical devices
of *Ulysses*. One of these especially attracted attention by its novelty and daring,
and the scope it afforded for the rapid and vigorous presentation of the flow
of those secret and autonomous thoughts which seem to shape themselves beyond the pale of consciousness and to precede in order of time coherent speech.
This device came to be known in France as the *monologue intérieur*. It is easy to
see that this literary device, which enabled a writer to explore the secret places
of the Ego and to capture thoughts at the very moment of their conception, was
destined to fascinate those writers who held that the business of art is to follow
nature; and such, in fact, was the effect produced by *Ulysses* on the younger
generation of writers, whether English-speaking by birth or foreigners acquainted with the English tongue.

In 1920 I read that portion of *Ulysses* which had appeared in the *Little Review*
and soon after I had the privilege of several long conversations about *Ulysses*
with James Joyce himself at the time when he was completing the last episodes.
One day he mentioned to me that the *monologue intérieur* had already been em-

ployed, as a continuous form of narration, in a tale by Édouard Dujardin, *Les Lauriers sont coupés*, published over thirty years before *Ulysses*, at the time when the symbolist movement was at its height. I knew only the title of the book and it was equally unknown to most literary men of my generation; another book of M. Dujardin, *L'Initiation au Péché et à l'amour*, was more widely read, and esteemed his principal contribution to French imaginative literature. 'In *Les Lauriers sont coupés*,' Joyce told me, 'the reader finds himself, from the very first line, posted within the mind of the protagonist, and it is the continuous unfolding of his thoughts which, replacing normal objective narration, depicts to us his acts and experiences. I advise you to read *Les Lauriers sont coupés*.'

I, too, advise the readers of this commentary to follow the suggestion made by Mr Joyce to M. Larbaud, and this they can the more easily do since, as a result of that conversation, the publishers brought out the tale in an easily accessible form.[1] Meanwhile, by way of illustration, I append an extract from the silent monologue of *Les Lauriers sont coupés*. The hero is dining at a restaurant; his attention is divided between the menu and an attractive woman at another table who is with a man, her husband probably, an *avoué* or *notaire*. This passage may be compared with Mr Bloom's silent monologue in Davy Byrne's (the episode of the 'Lestrygonians') or at his musical lunch in the Ormond (the 'Sirens').

'Au poulet; c'est une aile; pas trop dure aujourd'hui; du pain; ce poulet est mangeable; on peut dîner ici; la prochaine fois qu'avec Léa je dînerai chez elle, je commanderai le dîner rue Favart; c'est moins cher que dans les bons restaurants, et c'est meilleur. Ici, seulement, le vin n'est pas remarquable; il faut aller dans les grands restaurants pour avoir du vin. Le vin, le jeu, – le vin, le jeu, les belles, – voilà, voilà ... Quel rapport y a-t-il entre le vin et le jeu, entre le jeu et les belles? je veux bien que des gens aient besoin de se monter pour faire l'amour; mais le jeu? Ce poulet était remarquable, le cresson admirable. Ah! la tranquillité du dîner presque achevé. Mais le jeu ... le vin, le jeu, – le vin, le jeu, les belles ... Les belles chères à Scribe. Ce n'est pas du Châlet, mais de Robert-le-Diable. Allons, c'est de Scribe encore. Et toujours la même triple passion ... Vive le vin, l'amour et le tabac ... Il y a encore le tabac; ça j'admets ... Voilà, voilà le refrain du bivouac ... Faut-il prononcer taba-c et bivoua-c, ou taba et bivoua? Mendès, boulevard des Capucines, disait dom-p-ter; il faut dire dom-ter. L'amour et le taba-c ... le refrain du bivoua-c. ... L'avoué et sa femme s'en vont. C'est insensé, ridicule, grotesque! les laisser partir! ... – Garçon!'

1. Messein, Paris. An English rendering of this remarkable work has been published by *New Directions*.

Various criticisms have been directed against Mr Joyce's use of the silent monologue in *Ulysses*. It was, I think, Mr Wyndham Lewis who suggested that, as thoughts are not always verbal and we can think without words, the technique of the silent monologue is misleading. Against this, however, there is the equally tenable hypothesis that 'without language there can be no thought',[1] and the obvious fact that, even if we do not *think*, we certainly must *write* in words.

Again, there is Professor Curtius's objection (which, however, principally concerns the 'Sirens' episode, q.v.) that the word-fragments of which the silent monologue is largely composed are in themselves meaningless and only become intelligible when related to their objective context. This point will be further discussed in a subsequent chapter (on 'Rhythm'); meanwhile it may suffice to point out that all the *disjecta membra* are ultimately fitted together in the reader's mind and that it is exactly in this fragmentary manner that Nature herself reveals her secrets to the understanding eye of a Darwin or a Newton.

Finally, a distinguished French critic (M. Auguste Bailly, writing in the periodical *Candide*) observed:

Joyce has perceived – a fact that is psychologically correct but no novelty – that our mental life is composed of a continuous monologue within, which, though it generally adjusts itself to the object of our activity or immediate preoccupation, is apt to desert this and wander far afield, to yield to other influences, to distractions, internal or external, and sometimes to be influenced by almost mechanical associations. In fact, we may listen to this inner voice yet be quite unable to control it ... It works by association in much the same way as the children's game of word-chains: *Mouche à miel; miel de Narbonne; bonne à tout faire; fer à cheval; valet de pique.* ... It follows that, if the writer wishes to give a complete and accurate study of the mind of one of his characters, he must no longer employ the classical method of analysing and segregating thoughts, or seek to emphasize the nuances by deliberately ignoring the chaotic turmoil in which they are involved; his object is, rather, to give expression to this turmoil, its fermentation, its stormy nebula of gestation, with all its extensions, contractions and vortices, and even, so to say, its shortcomings. ... But a form of art, if it is to be more than a mere technical experiment, should be judged on its merits, its veracity. As to its merits, let us waive discussion; *de gustibus* ... But

1. Sayce, *Introduction to the Science of Language*. Many philosophers, including Locke, Hegel and Schopenhauer, endorse this view. Cf. the Platonic view (stated in the *Sophist*): 'Is not thought the same as speech with this exception: thought is the unuttered conversation of the soul with herself?'

veracity is another matter, and my opinion is that, though the analytic method may give a partly false or artificial presentation of the stream of consciousness, the silent monologue is just as artificial and just as false. The necessity of recording the flow of consciousness by means of words and phrases compels the writer to depict it as a continuous horizontal line, like a line of melody. But even a casual examination of our inner consciousness shows us that this presentation is essentially false. We do not think on one plane, but on many planes at once. It is wrong to suppose that we follow only one train of thought at a time; there are several trains of thought, one above another. We are generally more aware, more completely conscious, of thoughts which take form on the higher plane; but we are also aware, more or less obscurely, of a stream of thoughts on the lower levels. We attend or own to one series of reflections or images; but we are all the time aware of other series which are unrolling themselves on obscurer planes of consciousness. Sometimes there are interferences, irruptions, unforeseen contacts between these series. A stream of thought from a lower level suddenly usurps the bed of the stream which flowed on the highest plane of consciousness. By an effort of will-power we may be able to divert it; it subsides but does not cease to exist. At every instant of conscious life we are aware of such simultaneity and multiplicity of thought-streams.

The life of the mind is a symphony. It is a mistake or, at best, an arbitrary method, to dissect the chords and set out their components on a single line, on one plane only. Such a method gives an entirely false idea of the complexity of our mental make-up, for it is the way the light falls upon each element, with a greater or a less clarity, that indicates the relative importance for ourselves, our lives and acts, of each of the several thought-streams. But in the silent monologue, as transposed into words by Joyce, each element seems of equal importance, the subsidiary and the essential themes are treated as equivalent and an equal illumination falls upon those parts which were, in reality, brightly lit up, and those which remained in the dark background of thought. I prefer the analytic method, which doubtless eliminates something of reality, but eliminates only the superfluous and neglects only the negligible.

Regarding this searching criticism of the Joycean method, two brief comments suggest themselves. First, that the silent monologues of Stephen and Mr Bloom, though they may seem to involve a confusion of values, are (as I hope to show in the course of this study) in fact laid out according to a logical plan; they are no more incoherent or ill-balanced than the fragments of a picture-puzzle which, fitted together, compose a life-like portrait, and no more irrelevant as to detail than the universe itself. Secondly, that, from the point of view of the author of *Ulysses* (*ipse dixit!*), it hardly matters whether the technique in question is 'veracious' or not; it has served him as a bridge over which to march his eighteen episodes, and, once he has got his troops across, the opposing forces can, for all he cares, blow the bridge sky-high.

*

All the action of *Ulysses* takes place in or about the city of Dublin – the unity of place is as thoroughgoing as that of time – and there are many topical allusions to characteristic sights of Dublin streets, to facts and personalities of the Dublin *milieu* of nearly half a century ago, that are incomprehensible for most English and American readers and may become so, in course of time, even to Dubliners. But without such personal touches, these nuances of evanescent local colour,[1] the realism of the silent monologues would have been impaired; their presence in *Ulysses* was indispensable. It was, rather, a happy accident – if such concatenations can be called 'accidents' – that the creator of *Ulysses* passed his youth in such a town as Dublin, a modern city-state, of almost the Hellenic pattern,[2] neither so small as to be merely parochial in outlook, nor so large as to lack coherency and foster that feeling of inhuman isolation which cools the civic zeal of Londoner or New Yorker. The only resource of such metropolitans is the making of coteries, wherein birds of a feather are warmly cooped, and thus to create a number of little states within the state. This is consoling for the individual, rotary within his narrow orbit, but he loses something by not being obliged to rub shoulders with all sorts of fellow-citizens. Unless he make a hobby of politics he may completely neglect the civic life of his polity and, like a good many Londoners, ignore even the name of his Lord Mayor. In the Dublin of 1904 such ignorance was virtually impossible.[3]

1. Such as the allusions to 'Elvery's elephant house', the 'waxies' Dargle', the 'Old Woman of Prince's Street' and, generally, to the 'Dublin Castle' régime.
2. The key to Joyce's work, as Mr Cyril Connolly observed in an interesting essay (*Life and Letters*, April 1929), 'is in the author's *pietàs* for his native city. ... His life resembles that of the old Greek poets, the youth spent in city politics and local revels, then banishment to foreign places, the publication of a masterpiece after ten years, as Dedalus promised, with his weapons "silence, exile and cunning". Now his whole art is applied to celebrating his native town, though his feeling for Dublin, its squares and stews and beery streets, is as different from the provincial quality of Irish patriotism as it is like to the pagan sentiment of birthplace, to the tag "*dulces moriens reminiscitur Argos*", of Virgil and Theocritus, the feelings of Sophocles for Colonus and Odysseus for Ithaca.'
3. 'Dublin is such a small city, everyone knows everyone else's business.' (*Dubliners*, 'The Boarding House'.)

Man is naturally a political animal (the fact cannot be blinked however much one may sympathize with Mrs Bloom's *cri de cœur*, 'I hate the mention of politics!') and thus the Dubliner had a better right to the device *Homo sum . . .* than the apolitical Londoner. Civic and national politics played a prominent part in Dublin life and hovered in the background of nearly every conversation. Thus, in *A Portrait of the Artist as a Young Man*, Stephen's first Christmas dinner ends in disaster between the clashing rocks of politics and religion. His mother appeals: 'For pity's sake let us have no political discussion on this day of all days of the year.' But, after a mention of Parnell and the treachery of the priests, there is no holding the excited Dubliners. The hostess's appeals are unheeded.

Uncle Charles and Mr Dedalus pulled Mr Casey back into his chair again, talking to him from both sides reasonably. He stared before him out of his dark flaming eyes, repeating:

'Away with God, I say!'

Dante shoved her chair violently aside and left the table, upsetting her napkin-ring which rolled slowly along the carpet and came to rest against the foot of an easychair. Mr Dedalus rose quickly and followed her towards the door. At the door Dante turned round violently and shouted down the room, her cheeks flushed and quivering with rage:

'Devil out of hell! We won! We crushed him to death! Fiend!'

The door slammed behind her.

Mr Casey, freeing his arms from his holders, suddenly bowed his head on his hand with a sob of pain.

'Poor Parnell!' he cried loudly. 'My dead king!'

He sobbed loudly and bitterly.

Stephen, raising his terrorstricken face, saw that his father's eyes were full of tears.

There is, in *Ulysses*, a background of political preoccupations, which is frequently visible behind the texture of the narrative or soliloquies. The betrayal of Parnell is, in fact, one of the themes of the work and there are many allusions to such national leaders as O'Connell, Emmet, Wolfe Tone. But the author of *Ulysses*, in this as in other matters, shows no bias; he introduces political themes because they are inherent in the Dublin scene, and also because they illustrate one of the motifs of *Ulysses*, the betrayal or defeat of the man of mettle by the treachery of the hydra-headed rabble. As far as his own outlook on these matters can be

appraised, it is that of weariness and disgust. 'Ireland is the old sow that
eats her farrow.' 'No honourable and sincere man has given up to you
his life and his youth and his affections from the days of Tone to those
of Parnell but you sold him to the enemy or failed him in need or re-
viled him and left him for another.'

It would, however, be unsafe to draw from the embittered aphorisms of young Stephen Dedalus any absolute inference regarding his
creator's subsequent attitude to politics. The title of the work whence
these quotations are made is *A Portrait of the Artist as a Young Man*; in
Ulysses, young Dedalus is but a year older and has not yet outgrown
his rancour and disillusionment. In 1904 he is only twenty-two years of
age; *Ulysses* was written in Trieste-Zürich-Paris between the years 1914
and 1921, when its author was remote both in time and place from the
experiences of his adolescence and could exercise the detachment which
remoteness gives. This ironical indifference is well illustrated by the
'Cyclops' episode (q.v.) where, by a technique of exaggeration, chauvinism of all kinds is distended to bursting-point and beyond, till,
exploding, it betrays the void within. Moreover, by way of counterpoise to the fanaticism of most of the Dubliners and the bitterness of
young Stephen, who cannot forgive his church or country for his loss
of faith in them, we have the placid commentary of sensible Mr Bloom,
whose considered opinion seems to be that one government is, in
general, as good or bad as another.

So much has been written and said about the 'obscenity' of *Ulysses*
since the far-off day when a favourite racing journal made England
blush with its denunciatory placard[1]

THE SCANDAL OF ULYSSES

that it is, perhaps, desirable briefly to comment on the author's attitude
to such matters, in which the Anglo-American public, both readers and
critics, seem often to take an interest disproportionate, as it appears to
me, to their real importance. This obsession has, in the case of *Ulysses*,

---

1. This fact has been curiously enshrined in a sentence of *Finnegans Wake*. 'Let
manner and matter of this for these our sporting times be cloaked up in the
language of blushfed porpurates that an Anglican ordinal, not reading his own
dunsky tunga, may ever behold the brand of scarlet on the brow of her of Babylon
and feel not the pink one in his own damned cheek.'

led to singularly unfortunate results, for the significance of the work as
an exact portrayal of life, realistic in form but with the facts situated
and disposed according to a subtle rhythm which gives them an esoteric and symbolic universality, has been obscured for many readers by
the occasional passages where narrative or language is conventionally
ineffable.

Ulysses is the story of a day in the life of a Dubliner undistinguished
by any particular virtue or vice, a kind-hearted, moderately educated,
mildly sensual, not even really vulgar, small-business man, who in the
course of this day comes across a certain number of foul-mouthed persons, whose tongues have been loosened by drink, generally in public
houses whither his business or a need for refreshment has taken him.
Towards midnight he finds himself in a brothel, where he has gone to
protect the young man for whom he feels a paternal solicitude. There
both he and Stephen, the former rendered suggestible by fatigue, the
latter by intoxication, yield themselves to the *ambiance* and, like the
Homeric wanderers, temporarily partake of the bestial atmosphere of
Circe's den. In this episode there are passages, appropriate to the cadre
and to the partial collapse of inhibitions, in which the animal nature of
man is laid bare in a manner never before attempted in literature. Still
there is nothing 'indecent' in it, if the framers of the Irish Censorship
Bill correctly construed indecency as 'anything calculated to excite
sexual passion'. These passages are, in fact, cathartic and calculated to
allay rather than to excite the sexual instincts. In the last episode of all
we hear, through the mouth of Mrs Bloom, the voice of Gea-Tellus,
the Great Mother, speaking – the goddess whom the Romans invoked
by sinking their arms downward to the Earth. Her function is what
Hermes Trismegistus styled 'the duty of procreation, which the God of
Universal Nature has imposed for ever on all beings, and to which He
has attributed the supremest charity, joy, delight, longing and divinest
love',[1] and to her nothing is common or unclean. As for Hamlet 'there
is nothing either good or bad but thinking makes it so', so Mrs Bloom
makes short work of such cerebral distinctions. She is a creator of life,
not of codes; she fashions the players of the game but does not impose
on them the rules of their evolution, nor respect categorical imperatives,

1. Cf. *Ulysses*, page 366. '... that evangel simultaneously command and promise
which on all mortals with prophecy of abundance or with diminution's menace
that exalted of reiteratedly procreating function ever irrevocably enjoined.'

aetiological speculations. 'I fear those big words,' Stephen says, 'which make us so unhappy.' Mrs Bloom, too, loathes such big words, 'jaw-breakers'; she prefers monosyllables, curt, crude, obscene. It is, of course, no defence of obscenity to say that nature is obscene. The life according to nature would be as intolerable to civilized man as the perpetual parade of nudity must be nauseating in continental 'schools of nature'. However, obscenity has its niche in the scheme of things and a picture of life in which this element was ignored or suppressed would be incomplete, like the home without Plumtree's Potted Meat.[1]

> *What is home without*
> *Plumtree's Potted Meat?*
> *Incomplete.*

In practice we find that nearly all great works, from the Bible onwards, which treat of the universe as a whole and discover a coherence in all God's works, have to include some obscenity in their presentation of the phenomena of life.

It cannot be too strongly emphasized that the object of the author of *Ulysses* was to present an *aesthetic* image of the world, a sublimation of that *cri de cœur* in which the art of creation begins.

The personality of the artist, at first a cry or a cadence or a mood and then a fluent and lambent narrative, finally refines itself out of existence, impersonalizes itself so to speak.... The mystery of the aesthetic like that of material creation is accomplished. The artist, like the God of creation, remains within or behind or beyond or above his handiwork, invisible, refined out of existence, indifferent, paring his fingernails.[2]

Aesthetic emotion is *static*. 'The mind is arrested and raised above desire and loathing.' 'The feelings excited by improper art are kinetic, desire and loathing. Desire urges us to possess, to go to something; loathing urges us to abandon, to go from something. The arts which excite them, pornographical or didactic, are therefore improper arts.' Such a conception of the function of the artist presided over the creation of *Ulysses*. The instant when the supreme quality of beauty, the clear radiance of the aesthetic image,

is apprehended luminously by the mind which has been arrested by its wholeness and fascinated by its harmony is the luminous silent stasis of aesthetic

---

1. *Ulysses*, page 67.   2. *A Portrait of the Artist as a Young Man*, page 252.

pleasure, a spiritual state very like to that cardiac condition which the Italian physiologist Luigi Galvani, using a phrase almost as beautiful as Shelley's, called the enchantment of the heart.

The artist's aim, then, is to ban kinetic feelings from his readers' minds, and in *Ulysses* we find the ideal silent stasis of the artist nearly realized, his personality almost impersonalized. Nearly – but not entirely. The feeling of desire, which urges us to possess, is absent; there is not the least pornographical appeal; but the loathing, which urges us to abandon – that aversion from the sordid which made of Stephen Dedalus an exile in his own country – is, one can but feel, active in certain passages. One of the influences which may be discerned in *Ulysses* is that of Swift, 'the great hater of his kind', to whom there are many allusions. In those passages where certain physical processes or sensual appetites are minutely described a *rapprochement* with the Swiftian attitude may probably be made, that point of disgust which has been admirably depicted by a French biographer of the Dean of St Patrick's.

The sensualist's leer is foreign to his work save as an object of sarcasm when he sees it on another's face. 'Erotic' subjects take on a purely coprologic form and he purposely presents them in a disgusting light, devoid of any sensual appeal, like a rich essential manure. This can be seen most clearly in the last page of his *Discourse concerning the Mechanical Operation*, where a lover's affections and emotions are described with a realism and a serene indecency that only utter contempt could inspire. Thus, too, the licentious passages of the *Digression* are simply studies in exact realism and admirably subserve the satirical effectiveness of the work as a whole, for they add the nausea of disgust to the force of its invective.[1]

The conflict of deliberate indifference (*stasis*) with the loathing of disgust (*kinesis*) is apparent throughout *Ulysses*.

Of this conflict in the mind of Stephen Dedalus the author of *Ulysses* is fully aware, and though, as has already been pointed out, the assimilation of their personalities must not be pressed too far, it is noteworthy that Stephen is referred to as a 'morbid-minded esthete and embryo philosopher' and, after a characteristic homily by Stephen (at the Lying-in Hospital; the style here is in the manner of Walter Pater) on the unseemly ways of Divine Providence, Mr Bloom 'regarded on

1. Émile Pons, *Swift, les années de jeunesse.*

the face before him a slow recession of that false calm there, imposed, as it seemed, by habit or some studied trick, upon words so embittered as to accuse in their speaker an unhealthiness, a flair for the cruder things of life.' Here doubtless the mind of Stephen Dedalus is being viewed from the outside, a Bloomish view, and the passages, being parodic, are not to be taken too seriously, but a study of Stephen's character as depicted both in the *Portrait* and *Ulysses* makes it clear that, though his ambition was to regard the world with the detachment of the artist, M. Benda's *clerc*, the shock of religious and material disillusion had somewhat impaired the wholeness, harmony, and radiance of his vision. Despite the ubiquity of humour 'wet and dry', despite the perpetual deflation of sentiment and the negation of values which we find in *Ulysses*, there is an undertone of despair, the failure of an Icarus soaring sunwards to hold his flight. And, perhaps, the author of *Ulysses* had not yet quite outgrown the rancours of the young protagonist of the *Portrait* and the still immaturer hero of his 'schoolboy's production', *Stephen Hero*. Yet it may be that to this very disharmony is due the seething vitality of the Dublin epic; the stream of its life is fed by the waters of bitterness.

Chapter 2

THE RHYTHM OF *ULYSSES*

IN his earlier, autobiographic novel, *A Portrait of the Artist as a Young Man*, James Joyce, through the mouth of Stephen Dedalus, defines the qualities which, in his view, give aesthetic beauty to a work of art.

'It awakens, or ought to awaken, or induces, or ought to induce, an aesthetic stasis, an ideal pity or an ideal terror, a stasis called forth, prolonged and at last dissolved by what I call the rhythm of beauty.'

'What is that exactly?' asked Lynch.

'Rhythm', said Stephen, 'is the first formal aesthetic relation of part to part in any aesthetic whole or of an aesthetic whole to its part or parts or of any part to the aesthetic whole of which it is a part.'[1]

Ulysses is a complex of such relations; at a first and casual reading these are perceived vaguely, as a misty nebula of light; in the course of a more attentive perusal their number and permeance will gradually become apparent, 'as', to quote the admirable metaphor of M. Valéry Larbaud, 'at night, after one has been contemplating the sky for a little while, the number of stars seems to have increased'.

One of the simpler aspects of this technique – a device which, for all its apparent artificiality, exactly resembles Nature's method – is the presentation of fragments of a theme or allusion in different parts of the work; these fragments have to be assimilated in the reader's mind for him to arrive at complete understanding. 'It is a truth perpetually,' as Herbert Spencer remarked, 'that accumulated facts, lying in disorder, begin to assume some order when an hypothesis is thrown among them.' Several such hypotheses are not so much 'thrown' as disposed with artfully concealed art amid the welter of accumulated

1. Cf. Coleridge's *Essay on the Principles of Genial Criticism*. 'The sense of beauty subsists in simultaneous intuition of the relation of parts, each to each, and of all to a whole: exciting an immediate and absolute complacency, without intervention, therefore, of any interest, sensual or intellectual.' This is a paraphrase of Pythagoras's definition of Beauty as 'the reduction of many to one' which Aquinas probably had in mind when making the dictum *ad pulchritudinem tria requiruntur* etc., from which Stephen deduced his theory of aesthetics.

facts in *Ulysses*. Moreover, again following Nature's method, Joyce depicts only the present time and place of the times and places that are passing, a rapid flux of images. 'Hold to the now, the here, through which all future plunges into the past.'[1] It is for the reader to assemble the fragments and join the images into a band.

Sometimes the thought of the moment, rising to the surface of the mind under the impact of some external stimulus, is merely the echo of a name or fragment of a phrase. That, then, is all Joyce sets down. But, sooner or later, the reader will come upon a circumstance or thought which will explain the allusion implicit in the name or broken sentence.

Thus, before setting out on his day's wanderings, Mr Bloom examines his hat.[2]

The sweated legend in the crown of his hat told him mutely: Plasto's high grade ha. He peeped quickly inside the leather headband. White slip of paper. Quite safe.

On the doorstep he felt in his hip pocket for the latchkey. Not there. In the trousers I left off. Must get it. Potato I have.

The explanation of the 'white slip of paper' comes only in a subsequent episode. 'His right hand came down into the bowl of his hat. His fingers found quickly a card behind the headband and transferred it to his waistcoat pocket.' Presently Mr Bloom visits a post office.

He handed the card through the brass grill.
'Are there any letters for me?' he asked.

The card, we learn, is inscribed 'Henry Flower', the name adopted by Mr Bloom for his correspondence with Martha Clifford. In a later episode[3] Mr Bloom is taking leave of Richie Goulding: 'Well, so long. High grade. Card inside, yes.' These fragments would seem meaningless to a reader who had forgotten the earlier passages; the broken phrases assume an order only when 'an hypothesis is thrown among them'. In the same way the allusion in 'Potato I have' becomes clear only when the reader arrives at the 'Circe' episode and learns that it is 'a relic of poor mamma', a 'Potato Preservative against Plague and Pestilence', a talisman, in fact.

Similarly, after lunch,[4] Mr Bloom thinks: 'That wonder-worker if I

1. *Ulysses*, page 175.   2. page 49.   3. page 272.   4. page 275.

had.' This cryptic regret is explained many pages later[1] where we find that the *Wonderworker* is a 'thaumaturgic remedy' designed to 'insure instant relief' from postprandial disorders.

But, besides such small isolated correspondences, there are a number of themes, generally stated in the early episodes (those dealing with the morning hours of Stephen and Mr Bloom), which recur more or less frequently throughout *Ulysses*. Some of these relate to esoteric theories, which will be dealt with later; a few are shared by both Stephen and Mr Bloom (several instances of this persistent, though unconscious, exchange of thoughts and impressions between them will be commented on in the course of this study); the majority are concerned with their personal experiences, remarks, or events which have left an impress on the mind of each. Thereafter, a chance word, the glimpse of some apparently irrelevant object, a sudden eddy of the stream of consciousness, will suffice to evoke the associated memory. The occasional obscurities in passages recording the silent monologue of Stephen and Mr Bloom are partly due to the brusqueness and brevity of such allusions. Thus, in the episode (constructed on a musical pattern and dominated from beginning to end by musical forms and rhythms) which describes Mr Bloom's belated lunch at the Ormond Restaurant, we find a fragment of silent monologue which, to a reader who has forgotten or 'skipped' the relevant passages in earlier episodes, may well seem almost meaningless. While Mr Bloom is having his meal in the restaurant, Mr Dedalus (Stephen's father) is singing at the hotel piano the operatic ballad, *When first I saw that form endearing*.

Tenors get women by the score. Increase their flow. Throw flower at his feet when will we meet? My head it simply. Jingle all delighted. He can't sing for tall hats. Your head it simply swurls. Perfumed for him. What perfume does your wife? I want to know. Jing. Stop. Knock. Last look at mirror always before she answers the door. The hall. There? How do you? I do well. There? What? Or? Phila of cachous, kissing comfits, in her satchel. Yes? Hands felt for the opulent.

In the broken phrases of this monologue of Mr Bloom there are several indirect allusions to Blazes Boylan, Mrs Bloom's lover, who has an appointment with her for four o'clock. Mr Bloom, as usual, refrains from mentioning the name of Boylan, his *bête noir*. It is a little past four

1. *Ulysses*, page 682.

o'clock and the latter, after some badinage with the bar-sirens ('Has
he forgotten?' Mr Bloom asks himself) has just driven off in a jingling
jaunting-car to his rendezvous. The jingle of the car continues to echo
in Mr Bloom's brain, mingled with the voice of the singer warbling
amoroso 'Full of hope and all delighted'. Mr Bloom thinks of the *bonnes
fortunes* of tenors (the Dubliners' remarkable cult of the operatic singer
is discussed in the opening passage of my commentary on the 'Sirens');
Boylan is by way of being a singer as well as an impresario, though 'he
can't sing for tall hats'. They get women *by the score* (the musical word-
play is characteristically Joycean). A singer, Bartell d'Arcy, was, it
happens, one of Mrs Bloom's earliest admirers; 'he commenced kissing
me on the choir stairs'.[1] 'My head it simply.' Mr Bloom has received
by the morning post a letter from his young daughter Milly. 'There is a
young student comes here ... he sings Boylan's (I was on the pop of
writing Blazes Boylan's) song about those seaside girls.' After reading
the letter Mr Bloom hums the refrain of 'Boylan's song'.

> *All dimpled cheeks and curls,*
> *Your head it simply swirls.*

Seaside girls. Torn envelope. Hands stuck in his trousers' pockets, jarvey off
for the day, singing. Friend of the family. Swurls, he says....

> *Those girls, those girls,*
> *Those lovely seaside girls.*[2]

His thought of women's infatuation for tenors has evoked Mr
Bloom's bugbear – *via* Milly's allusion and a memory of the torn envelope on the bed (Boylan's letter). 'Jingle all delighted.' The words Mr
Dedalus is singing blend with the vision of a gay don Juan on his jingling car. 'Your head it simply swurls' ('swurls, he says'). 'Perfumed
for him.' In the course of the morning Mr Bloom has procured for his
wife, who likes that kind of literature, an erotic work entitled *Sweets of
Sin*. Glancing through its pages he has read: 'All the dollarbills her
husband gave her were spent in the stores on wondrous gowns and
costliest frillies. For him! For Raoul! ... Her mouth glued on his in a
luscious voluptuous kiss while his hands felt for the opulent curves....'
The 'for him' of Mr Bloom's soliloquy is a recall of this masterpiece of

1. *Ulysses*, page 705.   2. page 59.

the luscious-voluptuous. 'Perfumed' (a reference to Mrs Bloom's phil-aromatic disposition: her husband, too, has a keen nose for odours) evokes another train of thought – his own mild counterpart of Marion's infidelity, a letter he has received from the typist, Martha Clifford. (Moreover, the song Mr Dedalus is singing is from the opera *Martha*. 'Martha it is. Coincidence. Just going to write.') She wrote: 'Do tell me what kind of perfume does your wife use. I want to know.' Mr Bloom recalls her letter almost verbatim. 'What perfume does your wife? I want to know.' The car stops with a jingling jerk before Mr Bloom's house. 'Jing. Stop. Knock.' Here, as elsewhere, a *martellato* rhythm emphasizes Boylan's masterful hammering on the lady's door. In imagination, irrepressible now, Bloom visualizes his wife's reception of Boylan, and his evocation of their eager greeting in the hall ends, appropriately enough, on an afterclang of the *Sweets of Sin*.

Hundreds of other instances of the manner in which the eighteen episodes of *Ulysses* are interlocked, how a knowledge of each part is necessary for the understanding of the whole, will be found in the course of this study, and other reasons which led the author to adopt this unusual method of exposition will, it is hoped, become manifest. For the purposes of the present chapter a brief description of the formal symmetry of the work may suffice, stating but not discussing the Homeric correspondences.

Each episode of *Ulysses* has its Scene and Hour of the Day, is (with the exception of the first three episodes) associated with a given Organ of the human body,[1] relates to a certain Art, has its appropriate Symbol and a specific Technic. Each episode has also a title, corresponding to a personage or episode of the *Odyssey*. Certain episodes have also their appropriate colour (a reference, as M. Larbaud has pointed out, to Catholic liturgy). The references are given in the table of the episodes on the next page.

It will be observed that there is no corresponding 'Organ of the Body' for the first three episodes. The explanation of this is probably that these episodes deal exclusively with the acts and thoughts of Stephen Dedalus, who, of the trinity of major personages appearing in

---

1. Together these compose the whole body, which is thus a symbol of the structure of *Ulysses*, a living organism, and of the natural interdependence of the parts between themselves. Blake uses a like symbolism in *Jerusalem*, where (as Mr Foster Damon points out) 'Judah, Issachar and Zebulun represent the head, heart and loins of Luvah' and Great Britain is similarly divided.

TITLE	SCENE	HOUR	ORGAN	ART	COLOUR	SYMBOL	TECHNIC
1. Telemachus	The Tower	8 a.m.		Theology	White, gold	Heir	Narrative (young)
2. Nestor	The School	10 a.m.		History	Brown	Horse	Catechism (personal)
3. Proteus	The Strand	11 a.m.		Philology	Green	Tide	Monologue (male)
4. Calypso	The House	8 a.m.	Kidney	Economics	Orange	Nymph	Narrative (mature)
5. Lotus-eaters	The Bath	10 a.m.	Genitals	Botany, Chemistry		Eucharist	Narcissism
6. Hades	The Graveyard	11 a.m.	Heart	Religion	White, black	Caretaker	Incubism
7. Aeolus	The Newspaper	12 noon	Lungs	Rhetoric	Red	Editor	Enthymemic
8. Lestrygonians	The Lunch	1 p.m.	Esophagus	Architecture		Constables	Peristaltic
9. Scylla and Charybdis	The Library	2 p.m.	Brain	Literature		Stratford, London	Dialectic
10. Wandering Rocks	The Streets	3 p.m.	Blood	Mechanics		Citizens	Labyrinth
11. Sirens	The Concert Room	4 p.m.	Ear	Music		Barmaids	*Fuga per canonem*
12. Cyclops	The Tavern	5 p.m.	Muscle	Politics		Fenian	Gigantism
13. Nausicaa	The Rocks	8 p.m.	Eye, Nose	Painting	Grey, blue	Virgin	Tumescence, detumescence
14. Oxen of the Sun	The Hospital	10 p.m.	Womb	Medicine	White	Mothers	Embryonic development
15. Circe	The Brothel	12 midnight	Locomotor Apparatus	Magic		Whore	Hallucination
16. Eumaeus	The Shelter	1 a.m.	Nerves	Navigation		Sailors	Narrative (old)
17. Ithaca	The House	2 a.m.	Skeleton	Science		Comets	Catechism (impersonal)
18. Penelope	The Bed		Flesh			Earth	Monologue (female)

Ulysses (Mr Bloom, his wife, and Stephen), represents the spiritual element; in the same way, for the last episode, which is wholly devoted to
the meditation of Marian Bloom (whose symbol is the Earth), there is
no corresponding Art for she is a manifestation of Nature herself, the
antithesis of art. The manner in which the appropriate symbols, arts,
etc., are associated with the subject and technic of the episodes will be
apparent when I come to discuss each episode individually. For the present it is sufficient to point out the symmetry of the technical structure:
a prelude (corresponding to the *Telemachia* of the Odyssey) of three
episodes – (1) Narrative (young), (2) Catechism (personal), (3) Monologue (male); a central section (the Odyssey proper) of thematic development ending in the brothel scene, written in the dramatic form, the
climax of the work; and a finale (the '*Nostos*' or 'Return') in three
episodes balancing the prelude – (1) Narrative (old), (2) Catechism
(impersonal), (3) Monologue (female). The central episode (the 'Wandering Rocks') is itself divided into eighteen short parts differing in
theme and treatment, all interlocked by a curious technical device; thus
reproducing in miniature the structure of the whole.

Each episode, taken independently, has its internal rhythm; in one
of the most remarkable in this respect, the episode of the 'Sirens',
there is a specific musical analogy, the fugue; in the episode of the
'Oxen of the Sun', where the style is a linguistic counterpart of the
development of the embryo, there is a continuously increasing flow of
vitality which ends in a word-dance of clipped phrases, *argot*, oaths,
and ejaculations; a veritable *locus classicus* of Impolite Conversation,
which would have delighted the Dean of St Patrick's.

There could be no greater error than to confuse the work of James
Joyce with that of the harum-scarum school or the *surréaliste* group (to
which some of the most brilliant of the younger French writers belong,
or once belonged) whose particular *trouvaille* was a sort of automatic
writing, no revision being allowed. To suppose that the subconscious
can best be portrayed by direct action of the subconscious – that effectively to depict the state of drunkenness one should oneself be drunk – is
mere *naïveté*. It is your thin young man who best can drive fat oxen
along the rocky road to Dublin, and the 'subconscious', elusive as an
Indian snipe (but less appetizing), will fall only to the aim of an expert
shikari. As for 'free verse' – surely the words are incompatibles, like the
juvenile slogan of free love – at its best it is no less artful and intricate

in its rhythms than an ode of Pindar, at its worst a mere spate of ver-
biage. With the work of the modernist school may be contrasted one
of Joyce's poems of the *Ulysses* period.

ALONE

> The moon's greygolden meshes make
> All night a veil,
> The shorelamps in the sleeping lake
> Laburnum tendrils trail.
>
> The sly reeds whisper to the night
> A name – her name –
> And all my soul is a delight,
> A swoon of shame.

Zürich, 1916

The touch of irony in the second stanza, the allusion to an ancient
myth (the sly reeds which betrayed Midas's shame to the world), is
characteristic.

James Joyce is, in fact, in the great tradition which begins with
Homer; like his precursors he subjects his work, for all its wild vitality
and seeming disorder, to a rule of discipline as severe as that of the
Greek dramatists; indeed, the unities of *Ulysses* go far beyond the
classic triad, they are as manifold and yet symmetrical as the daedal
network of nerves and bloodstreams which pervade the living organism.

Chapter 3

1. 'MET-HIM-PIKE-HOSES'

IN the first episode of Mr Bloom's day ('Calypso') several themes are
stated which will recur frequently throughout *Ulysses*, and it is characteristic of the Joycean method that one of the most important of these
leitmotifs should be presented in a casual manner and a ludicrous context. Mrs Bloom has been reading in bed *Ruby: the Pride of the Ring*, a
decidedly 'kinetic' work of art. She asks her husband what that word
in the book means – 'met him pike hoses'.

> He leaned downward and read near her polished thumbnail.
> 'Metempsychosis?'
> 'Yes. Who's he when he's at home?'
> 'Metempsychosis,' he said, frowning. 'It's Greek: from the Greek. That
> means the transmigration of souls.'
> 'O, rocks!' she said. 'Tell us in plain words.'

Mr Bloom explains. 'Some people believe that we go on living in
another body after death, that we lived before. They call it reincarnation. That we all lived before on the earth thousands of years ago or
on some other planet. They say we have forgotten it. Some say they
remember their past lives.'
Later in the morning, when he is observing the timeball on the Ballast Office, the word 'parallax' ('I never exactly understood') comes into
his mind – it is one of the dozen or so words which haunt him throughout the day – and his own ignorance reminds him of her 'met him pike
hoses she called it till I told her about the transmigration. O rocks!
She's right after all. Only big words for ordinary things on account of
the sound.' There are several other allusions to this big word: for example, in the 'Sirens' episode: 'Met him pike hoses. Philosophy. O
rocks!' and in a later episode ('Nausicaa'): 'Metempsychosis. They believed you could be changed into a tree from grief. Weeping willow.'
In the scene at the Lying-in Hospital Mr Bloom ponders on 'the won-
derfully unequal faculty of metempsychosis' possessed by medical
students, and is amazed 'that the mere acquisition of academic titles

should suffice to transform in a pinch of time these votaries of levity into exemplary practitioners.' In the 'Circe' episode the spectre of Paddy Dignam appears to Mr Bloom, who exclaims, 'The voice is the voice of Esau', and, to the question 'How is that possible?' the defunct Dignam answers 'By metempsychosis. Spooks.'

The passages indicate the persistence of the idea, or, rather, word 'metempsychosis', in Mr Bloom's memory.[1] But it is not only as one of Mr Bloom's possessions that the doctrine of reincarnation is mentioned in *Ulysses*. Allusions, direct or indirect, to it are frequent, and as this is, in fact, one of the directive themes of the work, it seems desirable briefly to set out certain relevant aspects of this ancient and widely accepted intimation of immortality.

We start with a soul in physical life, we follow it through the experiences of life which develop all those innumerable memories and affections and associations of thought which make up the person or personality in question (a something quite distinct, of course, from the body which is its vehicle). We perceive that personality proceeding next to enjoy a spiritual existence (for periods enormously outrunning the span of physical life) and then we find it returning to a new earth life to gather in fresh experience.[2]

For many people it will perhaps remain irrational to say that any person now living, with his recollections bound by the years of his childhood, is the same individual as some one of quite a different nationality and epoch who lived thousands of years ago, or the same that will reappear after a similar lapse of time under some entirely new conditions in the future. But the feeling 'I am I' is the same through the three lives and through all the hundreds; for that feeling is more deeply seated than the feeling 'I am John Smith, so high, so heavy, with such and such property and relations'. Is it inconceivable – as a notion in the mind – that John Smith, inheriting the gift of Tithonus, changing his name from time to time, marrying afresh every other generation or so, losing property here, coming into possession of property there, and getting interested as time went on in a great variety of pursuits – is it inconceivable that such a person in a few thousand years should forget all circumstances connected with the present life of John Smith, just as if the incidents of that life for him had never taken place? And yet the Ego would be the same. If this is conceivable in the imagination, what can be inconceivable in the individual continuity of an *intermittent*

1. Another persistent motif is the phrase (invented by Tom Kernan, one of the minor characters) 'harking' or 'looking back in a kind of retrospective arrangement', which has an obvious affinity with the 'metempsychosis' theme.

2. A. P. Sinnett, *The Growth of the Soul*, page 56. Cf. Stephen's epilogue in the *Portrait*: 'I go to encounter for the millionth time the reality of experience ...'

life, interrupted and renewed at regular intervals, and varied with passages through a purer existence?[1]

Thus forgetfulness of past existences, a partial or complete loss of concrete knowledge acquired in them, is explained by the periods of 'repose' which the soul enjoys between mundane existences, periods which may extend over thousands of years.

Moreover, just as the soul passes through a rhythmic series of what theosophists, employing those 'big words' which Mrs Bloom so much detested, style *manvantara* and *pralaya*, the days and nights of Brahma, alternate periods of activity and repose,[2] so nations and civilizations are born, die, reappear, and disappear. 'There is a geometry that applies to nations an equation of their curve of advance.' The life of an individual is reflected in a nation's life and, as the individual soul, so the spirit of a people may accomplish reincarnation in new conditions, a new habitat. (There is also, of course, the axiom that, if time and the universe are limitless, every finite set of conditions – ours today, for instance, on our own little planet – must somewhere, somewhen, be exactly reproduced. Mr Bloom may be alluding to this when he says, 'We all lived before on the earth thousands of years ago *or on some other planet.*')

That these conceptions and their corollaries have an important place in the highly complex structure of *Ulysses* will become apparent when I come to deal with the Homeric correspondences and historical analogies.[3] References to the eternal recurrence of personalities and things abound in *Ulysses* and many of the obscurer passages can be readily understood if this fact be borne in mind. Indeed, the book itself, the record of a day in a man's life, is a synthetic illustration of 'life's little day', the interval between two periods of darkness and repose. It is a commonplace of esoteric thought that in sleep we are in communication with that higher plane where, after death, the Ego reposes and renews itself before a new descent into the flesh. In fact, the correspondence between the waking state and life, between sleep and death, may be more than a poetic analogy (*pace tua*, Dr Freud), for, if the time and space categories be excluded, we find that all phases of consciousness are coexistent. 'Time and change are merely conducive to the

1. A. P. Sinnett, *Esoteric Buddhism*, page 209.
2. Both *manvantara* and *pralaya* are mentioned in the course of *Ulysses*. Further reference to them will be found in my commentary on the 'Proteus' episode.
3. See Chapter 4 of this Introduction.

advance of knowledge *qua* any given centre of consciousness localized at one point of space at the moment under consideration.'

Stephen, in his silent monologue, frequently alludes to such beliefs, often with characteristic irony, as when he parodies the theosophic practice of using initials for names. 'Dunlop, Judge, the noblest Roman of them all, A.E., Arval, the Name Ineffable, in heaven hight, K.H., their master,[1] whose identity is no secret to adepts.... The life esoteric is not for ordinary person. O.P. must work off bad karma first.' Elsewhere there is a burlesque description of a spiritualistic seance and the droning Pali polysyllables of the adepts.

He stated that he was now on the path of pralaya or return.... Their abodes were equipped with every modern home comfort such as tālāfānā, ālāvātār, hatākāldā, watāklāsāt. ... He exhorted all who were still at the wrong side of Maya to acknowledge the true path, for it was reported in devanic circles that Mars and Jupiter were out for mischief on the eastern angle where the ram has power....

Yogibogeybox in Dawson chambers. *Isis Unveiled.* Their Pali book we tried to pawn. Crosslegged under an umbrel umbershoot he thrones an Aztec logos, functioning on astral levels, their oversoul, mahamahatma.

Tradition, the Deity, esoterism – all these 'abstruosities' are roughly, mockingly handled by Stephen; yet, behind the mockery, there is a latent fear. Thus, in discussing the Eucharist with Cranly,[2] he says, wholly sincere for once: 'I imagine that there is a malevolent reality behind those things I say I fear.' He admits to Cranly that he can be shocked by blasphemy; and it is because his faith persists (once a Catholic always a Catholic) that the Black Mass of 'Circe' has such tragic virulence and Stephen's blasphemies such intensity. 'History', Stephen says, 'is a nightmare from which I am trying to awake.' God is for him 'a noise in the street', the hammer-hurler, the ineffable 'Citizen' of the 'Cyclops' episode[3] hypostasized. Of 'the imp hypostasis', too, Stephen is wary. From all these perils of the soul, theocratic, esoteric, historical, he would insulate himself by a mail of silken scorn. The transcendental casts a comic image in his 'mocking mirrors',[4] troubled pools of bathos; the greater the theme, the greater the parody.

1. K.H. is Koot Hoomi, Mme Blavatsky's invisible mentor and Mahatma.
2. *A Portrait of the Artist*, page 287.
3. The 'Citizen' was champion of all Ireland at putting the shot.
4. See *Ulysses*, pages 28 and 539. 'Averroes and Moses Maimonides flashing in their mocking mirrors the obscure soul of the world.' Thus, too, another Irish-

Stephen watches the tidal flow on the Dublin foreshore: 'Under the upswelling tide he saw the writhing weeds lift languidly and sway reluctant arms, hising up their petticoats, in whispering water swaying and upturning coy silver fronds. .... Lord, they are weary and, whispered to, they sigh. Saint Ambrose heard it, sigh of leaves and waves ....' In this passage there is a deliberate 'false note', a fragment from the ribald refrain rasped out by Buck Mulligan as he hewed the breakfast bread:

> *For old Mary Ann*
> *She doesn't care a damn,*
> *But, hising up her petticoats ...*

Similar discrepancies of sentiment inform another passage, this time in the de Quincey manner,[1] where a fragment from 'Boylan's song' (about the pretty little seaside girls) and the red triangle on Bass's beer are worked into a celestial vision of the 'wonder of metempsychosis, the everlasting bride', the constellation Virgo, shining from the deserted heavens.

Stephen is aware of the continuity of his self under the modality of temporal forms. 'I, entelechy, form of forms, am I by memory because under everchanging forms.' He leaves the sentence unfinished, but it is clear that he is alluding to the theory expounded by Mr Sinnett: 'the feeling "I am I" is the same ... through all the hundreds (of lives).'

It must not be forgotten that Joyce regarded aesthetic beauty as a *stasis*; kinetic art, pornographical or didactic, is, for him, improper art. The artist does not, like the rhetorician, seek to convince, to instruct, or to disgust. He treats his subject-matter, grotesque or transcendental (or both at once), as he finds it. The value, for him, of facts or theories has little or no relation to their moral implications or their ultimate validity (if any). *Ulysses* is not a theosophic tract.

In the 'Shakespeare' episode A.E. 'oracles out of his shadow: "Art has to reveal to us ideas, formless spiritual essences. The supreme question about a work of art is out of how deep a life does it spring."' Mr Russell's oracular dictum is at the opposite pole from James Joyce's conception of aesthetic beauty. Wilde's 'All art is perfectly useless' is probably nearer Joyce's standpoint. If, therefore, we find that the esoteric

---

man, Bernard Shaw, was probably at his most serious when he seemed to play the mountebank; Oscar Wilde, perhaps, too, in his paradoxes.

1. *Ulysses*, page 396.

framework on which *Ulysses* is based should at times be exposed to derision or alluded to in a comic context, the explanation of this seeming incongruity may be found in aesthetic necessity. The author has no philosophical axe to grind, and he has a strong sense of humour; Truth is not necessarily Beauty (often as not she is, as the Bishop said of the lady in the street, an eyesore), nor should an artist, by seeking to persuade, usurp the propagandist's role.

Shakespeare, like the author of *Ulysses*, rendered ample justice to the comic spirit; the toe of the peasant, as Hamlet knew, comes near the heel of the courtier and the 'understanding gentlemen o' the ground' insisted on their rights – quite as valid, indeed, as a Gregers Werle's 'claim of the ideal'. Besides the aesthetic reasons which account for the deliberate bathos of certain passages in *Ulysses*, there is the absolute justification for the ludicrous and the obscene (the two are, and always have been, closely allied) that symbolically these are no whit less significant than the noble emotions of, for instance, that Celtic twilight in which so many Irish bards and reviewers delight to 'dream their dreamy dreams'. The idea of reincarnation may be symbolized as well by the digestive processes as by the universal cycles of *pralaya* and *manvantara* of our vegetative universe, which 'opens like a flower from the earth's centre, In which is Eternity'.

But the theory of recurrence in the affairs of men and nations is not peculiar to mystical thinkers; it appears as an empirical deduction from the facts of history, rather than as an *a priori* dogma, in the works of the Italian philosopher Vico (that 'practical roundheaded Neapolitan', as Mr Samuel Beckett describes him), whose *Scienza nuova* appeared some two hundred years ago. The Viconian theory is of special interest to those who follow Joyce beyond *Ulysses* to his last work, *Finnegans Wake*, which is partly based on the historical speculations of Vico. Briefly, that theory is an extended and almost literal application of the saying: 'history repeats itself', and the Ecclesiast's words:

Is there anything whereof it may be said, See, this is new? It hath been already of old time, which was before us. ...

The wind goeth toward the south, and turneth about unto the north; it whirleth about continually, and the wind returneth again according to his circuits.

All the rivers run into the sea; yet the sea is not full: unto the place whence the rivers come, thither they return again.

Vico held that there is a recurrent cycle in human 'progress', as in the movement of the stars. Societies begin, continue, and have an end according to fixed and universal laws. Every nation passes through three ages – the divine, the heroic, and the human. The prelude and aftermath of each cycle is complete disintegration, brought about by the indiscipline and egoism of the concluding stages of a 'human' régime. The discoveries of the preceding civilized epoch are almost obliterated and man reverts to a brutish state, till once again he hears the voice of God, the hammer-hurler, speaking in the thunder and relearns the beginning of wisdom. The goal of human effort is a resolution of the conflict between good and evil; after each epoch of dissolution and reconstruction, a fragment of the advance gained by the spent wave is conserved, for there is a slowly rising tide in human history and the struggle is not naught availing.[1] Vico contemplated the writing of an 'ideal and timeless history, in which all the actual histories of all nations should be embodied'. (The *Wake* is, in one of its many aspects, a realization of Vico's project.) National heroes were, for him, not so much pre-eminent individuals, accidentally born out of their due time, as the embodiment of actual tendencies of their nations as a whole. They were led rather than leaders. Thus, as the past renews itself and civilizations rise and wane, the figures of antiquity will, *mutatis mutandis*, be reproduced. It does not, of course, follow that each avatar of a hero of legendary times will attain equal eminence. A Nestor may reappear as an elderly pedagogue, a Circe as the 'Madam' of a one-horse brothel. As the cycle of history turns the light of fame may touch now one, now another, facet of the whole. But there will always be a substantially exact reproduction, a recall, of a set of circumstances which have already existed and of those personalities who, in a remote past, expressed better than their fellows the spirit of their age. It will be seen in the following chapter, which deals with the early history of Ireland and the Homeric era, that in *Ulysses* may be found, associated with the metempsychosis motif, the germ of that ultimate application of the Viconian hypothesis which lies at the root of *Finnegans Wake*.

1. I doubt if the author of *Ulysses* endorsed Vico's optimistic belief in 'progress', though Mr Bloom, promoter of 'improvement all round', and wishful thinker, would certainly approve.

2. THE SEAL OF SOLOMON

It has been suggested that the presentation of the mind of each personage in *Ulysses* and its past history by the Joycean method of fragmentary revelation corresponds to the manner in which Nature herself dis-
poses the clues to her discovery. The consequences of universal law lie
scattered before our eyes in apparent confusion. Most of us, limiting
our interest to the immediately practical, make little attempt to arrange
these facts or discover the secret of their disposition: *primum vivere....*
Only the curious philosopher observes and records them on the tablets
of memory or, for greater surety, in ample notebooks. It is possible to
read *Ulysses* as most of us read the book of life, uncritically, forgetfully,
following the line of least resistance; and, though a greater vigilance
would afford a richer pleasure in perusal, the casual reader will reap a
reward proportionate to his effort. The gourmand who cannot distin-
guish a venerable Yquem from a rough, unchronicled Graves, may yet
enjoy his repast and rise from it pleasantly elated. But the bliss of ignorance is a short and sorry affair beside the subtle delectation of the con-
noisseur. The slow ascent of the tree of knowledge is not labour lost;
it is from the topmost branches, unseen by followers of the beaten
track, that its choicest fruits depend.

Ulysses is a book of life, a microcosm which is a small-scale replica of
the universe, and the methods which lead to an understanding of the
latter will provide a solution of the obscurities in *Ulysses*. It may be
assumed that our knowledge of the macrocosm is based on the association of ideas; in fact, the syllogism is no more than that. In their
crudest form such associations, used as the basis of a cosmogony, lead
on to magic. Indeed, all knowledge is ultimately magical, for it derives
from inexplicable facts, the laws of uniformity and causation. Early
observers saw a connexion between the tides and the movement of the
moon, 'the moist star upon whose influence Neptune's empire stands',
and inferred a magic sympathy between moon-goddess and sea-lord.
Later, according to the materialistic method of explaining *obscurum per
obscurius*, that 'sympathy' is described as an 'attraction'.[1] But, whatever

---

1. 'We are ready enough to detect the verbalism of medieval theologians, yet
personification and deification are in reality as rife today as ever. "Forces" now
play the part of the *qualitates occultae*.' Mauthner, *Kritik der Sprache*.

explanation may find favour with the mages of the moment, it will always be based on the miracle of recurrence and an empirical induction from the apparent uniformity of experience.

Our belief that the miracle will eternally renew itself depends largely on the greatest of inductions, the law of causation. That law and its corollaries are the averred basis of mystical philosophy, from the teachings of esoteric Buddhism and the medieval mystics to their modern development in the theosophical school. It is impossible to grasp the meaning of *Ulysses*, its symbolism and the significance of its *leitmotifs* without an understanding of the esoteric theories which underlie the work. We must look beneath the surface realism, the minutiae of local colour, the vulgarity and occasional obscenity of its characters, if we are to find a clue to the mystery, a thread of Ariadne to guide a modern Theseus through its labyrinth.[1]

A hint of the direction in which we must look to find the hidden trend of the long soliloquies of the Jew, Mr Bloom, and his spiritual son, Stephen Dedalus, may be found in their frequent references to the East, its occult sciences and the oriental sources of all religion. At a dramatic moment, when Mr Bloom is being taunted by a nationalist with his Jewish descent, the usually prudent hero is goaded to retaliation.

'Mendelssohn was a jew and Karl Marx and Mercadante and Spinoza. And the Saviour was a jew and his father was a jew. Your God.'

'He had no father,' says Martin. 'That'll do now ...'

'Whose God?' says the citizen.

'Well, his uncle was a jew,' says he. 'Your God was a jew. Christ was a jew like me.'

In the first episode where Mr Bloom appears, his thoughts are directed by a perpetual *Drang nach Osten*. Walking the Dublin streets he pictures himself 'somewhere in the east: early morning: set off at dawn, travel round in front of the sun'. Later in the morning he muses: 'the far east. Lovely spot it must be: the garden of the world, big lazy leaves to float on. ... Flowers of idleness ... Water-lilies.' This episode (the second

1. 'It must not be thought that interpretations of this kind are forced, and nothing more than the conjectures of ingenious men; when we consider the great wisdom of antiquity and how much Homer excelled in intellectual prudence, and in an accurate knowledge of every virtue, it must not be denied that he has obscurely indicated the images of things of a more divine nature in the fiction of a fable.' Porphyry, *On the Cave of the Nymphs* (trans. Thomas Taylor).

of Mr Bloom's Odyssey) is entitled the 'Lotus-eaters', and its texture is infused with a sense of the symbolical, narcotic, religious significance of the lotus flower.

The lotus, the sacred flower of the Egyptians, as well as the Hindus, is the symbol of Horus as it is that of Brahma. No temples in Tibet or Nepaul are found without it; and the meaning of this symbol is extremely suggestive. The sprig of lilies placed in the hand of the archangel who offers them to the Virgin Mary, in the pictures of the Annunciation, have in their esoteric symbolism precisely the same meaning.[1]

The peculiarity of the lotus is that its seeds contain, even before germination, perfectly formed leaves, the miniature of the perfected plant. Thus the lotus[2] is the natural emblem of the saying of Paracelsus: 'all colours and all elements are present in everything', and Shelley's 'All is contained in each'.

Many other illustrations of the eastering trend of Mr Bloom's thoughts will be found in the course of this study. Stephen Dedalus, whose intellect is always awake, watchful for associations (unlike Mr Bloom, who rarely pauses to analyse the content of his thoughts), is aware that the 'call of the east' is the voice of Godhead; the east is the birthplace of 'a lore of drugs', of Averroes and Moses Maimonides, the site of that garden city 'Edenville', home of Heva, naked Eve, 'belly without blemish, bulging big, a buckler of taut vellum, no, white-heaped corn, orient and immortal, standing from everlasting to everlasting'.[3]

The tapestry of *Ulysses* is woven in strands of mystical religion and, for readers who would explore the maze of this 'chaffering allincluding most farraginous chronicle' (as the author, speaking for the nonce with the voice of Carlyle, describes his work) and appreciate the subtleties of its pattern, some acquaintance with the cosmology on which it is based seems indispensable.

The Smaragdine Table of Hermes Trismegistus is one of the most ancient and authoritative records of occultism. The inscription begins:

1. Blavatsky, *Isis Unveiled*, vol. I, page 91.
2. I refer here to the lotus-lily. In my commentary on the 'Lotus-eaters' episode (q.v.) I discuss the ambiguity of the word 'lotus' as used by Homer and the Greeks.
3. Stephen echoes a passage in the 'Third Century' of that noblest and perhaps sincerest of English mystics, Thomas Traherne. The passage is quoted *in extenso* in § 3 of this chapter.

It is truest and most certain of all things.

That which is above is as that which is below, and that which is below is as that which is above, to accomplish the one thing of all most wonderful. ...

In diagrammatic form this axiom is shown as two triangles interlocked, the one pointing upwards, the other downwards: the figure known as Solomon's Seal. 'This means that all that exists, from the smallest imaginable atom, contains within itself all the elements, the entire processus of the whole universe.'[1] 'There is no line to be drawn in Nature between important things that it is worthwhile for her laws to pay attention to, and others which are insignificant and fit to be left to chance. The earth's attraction operates equally on a microbe and a mastodon, and the chemical affinity that holds together the elements of the ocean is not permitted to neglect those of the smallest drop of dew.'[2] 'Human affairs are so intensely entangled that it looks as if we must say – all or nothing; either every act, to the smallest, must be automatic and inevitable, or there is no prearranged course of events and no regular working out of Karma at all.'[3] The law of destiny, an application of the law of causation, is an axiom of esoteric doctrine. Similarly, the associated law of the conservation of energy on the physical plane has its counterpart in a law of the conservation of spiritual forces or personalities. For mind, like matter, is indestructible. All that exists has already existed and will always exist; creation and destruction are both impossible; a flux of transformation pervades the universe but nothing can ever be added to it or taken away from it. Admitting, then, that human personality, the soul, exists, since *ex nihilo nihil fit*, it must have always existed, it can never cease to exist. As Stephen Dedalus remarks (page 35), 'From before the ages He willed me and now may not will me away for ever. A *lex eterna* stays about Him.' This *lex eterna* is, for esoteric thinkers, the law of Karma.

It is the keystone of the edifice, the explanation and justification of the mystery of life. What, then, is this law of Karma? *The* Law, without exception, which rules the whole universe, from the invisible, imponderable atom to the suns; from the infusoria to the highest gods of the celestial hierarchy or evolution, macrocosm of our human hierarchy and evolution; and this law is that *every cause produces its effect*, without any possibility of delaying or annulling

1. A. Arnould, *Les Croyances fondamentales du Bouddhisme*, page 42.
2. A. P. Sinnett, *The Growth of the Soul*, page 125.
3. ibid., page 137.

that effect, once the cause begins to operate. The law of causation is everywhere supreme. This is the law of Karma; Karma is the inevitable link between cause and effect; applied to human destiny, this means that every man reaps what he has sown, neither more nor less, and, in his passage through earthly life, will reap every grain of that harvest – tares or corn, nettles or roses. ... We may acclaim the notion of a God, kind-hearted, indulgent, who is touched by our tears and prayers, who will forgive us our sins or fulfil our desires, if we will but humour Him. But there is no such God. ... For better or for worse no man may escape his Karma.[1]

This doctrine does not necessarily involve the acceptance of a personal fatality, or determinism, for in our present life we may, by an effort towards amelioration, by our personal *attitude towards* the Karma which we cannot escape, build up merit for subsequent existences. Thus, if the just man suffer in his present life, the causes of his misery lie in a past existence, and his merit in this life will assuredly produce its effect in his next incarnation. The theory of reincarnation and Karma, it may be noted, makes a strong appeal to the human ideal of justice; an 'eternity of woe' seems an altogether excessive penalty for even the worst malefactors, and permanent bliss a reward out of proportion to a brief life of virtue. If we are to assume any sort of fair play in the scheme of things, it is difficult to see any other solution which will bring eternity to terms with the allotted three score years and ten wherein man shapes his destiny.

Stress is laid by initiates on the omnipotence and ubiquity of the law of causation. Not a sparrow falls to the ground. ... 'Nothing', Eliphas Lévi has observed, in allusion to the claims of astrology, 'is indifferent in Nature; a pebble more or less upon a road may crush or profoundly alter the fortunes of the greatest men and even of the greatest empires; much more, then, the position of a particular star cannot be indifferent to the destinies of the child who is being born, and who enters by the fact of his birth into the universal harmony of the sidereal world.' This dictum is quoted not to justify the pretensions of astrologists but to illustrate the extreme view of certain occult thinkers respecting so-called 'accidents'. More plausible is the hypothesis of a fixed relation between the micro- and macro-cosm, Blake's 'grain of sand'[2] and the universe,

---

1. A. Arnould, *Les Croyances fondamentales du Bouddhisme.*

2. There is a remarkable anticipation of Blake's famous couplet in the 'Second Century' of Thomas Traherne: 'Suppose a river, or a drop of water, an apple or a sand, an ear of corn, or an herb; God knoweth infinite excellencies in it more than

or Eckhart's 'The meanest thing that one knows in God – for instance, if one could understand a flower as it has its being in God – this would be a higher thing than the whole world!'

> Dans une mort d'insecte on voit tous les désastres,
> Un rond d'azur suffit pour voir passer les astres.[1]

'That which is below is as that which is above.' Nothing is common or unclean but thinking makes it so.[2] *Ulysses* is like a great net let down from heaven including in the infinite variety of its take the magnificent and the petty, the holy and the obscene, interrelated, mutually symbolic. In this story of a Dublin day we have an epic of mankind. For such exact and scientific use of symbolism the nearest parallel to *Ulysses* is in the prophetic books of Blake. All truth, indeed, as Count Keyserling has pointed out, is ultimately symbolic. This must not be taken to mean merely that the artist is justified in fixing an arbitrary set of symbols to give life to his cosmology; it implies that, like the seed of the lotus or the grain of sand, the smallest particle of creation bears within it the secret of the whole. The same laws of causation, evolution, metempsychosis, are valid throughout. The part is a paradigm of the whole and the growth of an embryo illustrates the evolution of the race. 'We must find out and examine the vertues of things by way of similitude.' Resemblances are *not* accidental, and what we term accidents are part of the activity of cosmic growth, and as essential as its normal processes. Thus, speaking of the 'errors' of Shakespeare, 'the greatest creator after God', Stephen Dedalus remarks: 'A man of genius makes no mistakes. His errors are volitional and are the portals of discovery.'[3] Thus it is that in variations from the normal we may often

---

we: He seeth how it relateth to angels and men; how it representeth all His attributes; how it conduceth in its place, by the best of means to the best of ends: and for this cause it cannot be beloved too much. God the Author and God the End is to be beloved in it: Angels and men are to be beloved in it; and it is highly to be esteemed for all their sakes. O what a treasure in every sand when truly understood!'

1. Rostand, *Chantecler*.

2. Cf. Blake's view that 'Everything that lives is holy'. 'Man has no body distinct from his soul; for that called Body is a portion of the Soul discern'd by the five Senses, the chief inlets of Soul in this age.' Contempt of the carnal, exaggerated 'soul-consciousness', is the mark of the moral snob; Blake knew better than to regard the Body as an unruly servant to be 'kept in its place'.

3.   'The Errors of a Wise Man make your Rule
      Rather than the Perfections of a Fool.'

detect the trend of creative evolution. The interpretation of what seems arbitrary, erroneous, or haphazard and the scientific use of so-called unscientific methods are, in fact, portals of discovery.

Again, speaking of Shakespeare, Stephen remarks:

He returns after a life of absence to that spot of earth where he was born, where he has always been, man and boy, a silent witness. ... Maeterlinck says: *If Socrates leave his house today he will find the sage seated on his doorstep. If Judas go forth tonight it is to Judas his steps will tend.* Every life is many days, day after day. We walk through ourselves, meeting robbers, ghosts, giants, old men, young men, wives, widows, brothers-in-love. But always meeting ourselves.[1]

Thus Mr Bloom: 'So it returns. Think you're escaping and run into yourself. Longest way round is the shortest way home.' Later (in the 'Circe' episode) Stephen, partially intoxicated, playing 'a series of empty fifths' on the brothel piano, expounds the ritual perfection of the fifth.

The reason is because the fundamental and the dominant are separated by the greatest possible interval which ... is the greatest possible ellipse. Consistent with. The ultimate return. The Octave. Which ... What went forth to the ends of the world to traverse not itself. God, the sun, Shakespeare, a commercial traveller, having itself traversed in reality itself becomes that self. Wait a moment. Wait a second. Damn that fellow's noise in the street.[2] Self which it itself was ineluctably preconditioned to become. *Ecco!*

The longest way round is the shortest way home. To find ourselves we must first lose our way. The road of excess ...

Thus the growth of the soul, the process of self-realization, may be ultimately due to the 'errors' of the individual, his growing-pains. Friction between the self and its surroundings generates thought; indeed consciousness itself is a consequence of non-adaptation – a view which has been admirably resumed by M. Paul Valéry in a sequence of aphorisms.

L'homme a tiré tout ce qui le fait *homme*, des défectuosités de son système.

L'insuffisance d'adaptation, les troubles de son accommodation, l'obligation de subir ce qu'il a appelé irrationnel.

1. 'The soul is called a circle because it seeks itself, and is itself sought, finds itself and is itself found. But the irrational soul imitates a straight line, since it does not revert to itself like a circle.' *Olympiodorus.*

2. 'Noise in the street' – a formula applied by Stephen Dedalus to describe the voice of God: *Jupiter tonans.*

Il les a sacrés, il y a vu la 'mélancolie', l'indice d'un âge d'or disparu ou le pressentiment de la divinité et la promesse.

Toute émotion, tout sentiment est une marque de défaut de construction ou d'adaptation. Choc non compensé. Manque de ressorts ou leur altération.

Ajouter à cela l'adaptation artificielle – développement de la conscience et de l'intelligence.

Quelle étrange conséquence. La recherche de l'émotion, la fabrication de l'émotion; chercher à faire perdre la tête, à troubler, à renverser ...

Et encore: pourquoi y a-t-il des émotions physiologiques (sans quoi la nature se perdrait)? Nécessité de perdre l'esprit, ou de voir partiellement, ou de former un monde fantastique – sans quoi le monde finirait! – Amour.

Les fonctions finies conscientes contre la vie.

La non-adaptation finale. ...

Nothing in creation is irrelevant; our 'errors' are more than the blundering gestures of some instinctive desire; they are part of the scheme of things, incidents on the long way round which we must travel to meet ourselves; they are – to use one of Stephen's favourite words – ineluctable. Some critics of *Ulysses*, while accepting the work as a whole, accuse defects in this passage or that, in the technique of one episode or another, and blame the author for leading us round unnecessary detours; it is often (as will be demonstrated in the course of this commentary) precisely in the offending passages that the text is at its most significant. For no passage, no phrase in *Ulysses* is irrelevant; in this grain of sand, this banal day in the life of an inglorious Dubliner, we have a complete picture of the human situation, and a clinical analysis of that skin-disease of Gaea Tellus (heroine of the concluding episode) which we call Life.

3. THE *OMPHALOS*

'The Ancients placed the astral soul of man, the ψυχή or his self-consciousness, in the pit of the stomach. The Brahmans shared this belief with Plato and other philosophers. ... The navel was regarded as 'the circle of the sun', the seat of internal divine light.'[1] Similarly, Hermes Trismegistus held that the midst of the world's body is exactly beneath the centre of heaven, and Robert Fludd has written: *Mundi circularis cen-*

1. *Isis Unveiled*, xlv.

trum est terra: humana vero rotunditas punctum centrale est secundum quosdam in umbilico. This portion of the body, the navel, has, partly for symbolic reasons, been associated by esoteric writers with the source of prophetic inspiration, as when the Pythia was styled *ventriloqua vates.* In *Ulysses* the fact of birth, a link in the chain of lives, and its attendant circumstances play an important part, for these are held to symbolize the return to consciousness of the individual soul at reincarnation. The question of heredity will be discussed under the heading 'Paternity'; for the present it is sufficient to point out that the fact of physical parentage does not create any authentic spiritual link between father and son – a point which is insisted on in several passages of *Ulysses*. The soul reborn is spiritually distinct from both father and mother of the child; it is linked up by a bond, closer than that of birth or atavism, with its preincarnations, and an uninterrupted chain of existences on the immaterial plane.

In what is for an understanding of the esoteric side of *Ulysses* perhaps the most important episode of all, 'Proteus', we find the following passage in Stephen's silent monologue.

The cords of all link back, strandentwining cable of all flesh. That is why mystic monks. Will you be as gods? Gaze in your omphalos. Hello. Kinch here. Put me on to Edenville. Aleph, alpha: nought, nought, one.

Spouse and helpmate of Adam Kadmon: Heva, naked Eve. She had no navel. Gaze. Belly without blemish, bulging big, a buckler of taut vellum, no, white-heaped[1] corn, orient and immortal, standing from everlasting to everlasting.

The tone of this passage, half mocking, half intense, is characteristic of the conversation and soliloquies of Stephen Dedalus, 'Kinch, the knifeblade', sceptical even of his scepticism. It is illustrative also of the way in which his train of thought proceeds, by associations rather than by inferences (though Stephen, when he chooses, can bandy dialectic with the best). The reflections which I have cited were inspired by the sight of two midwives ambling seawards; Stephen's sequence of thought is: navel, umbilical-cord, cable, telephone. The umbilical telephone[2] extends back to Eden, to Eve the navelless and her spouse, Adam Kadmon (the kabalistic first man). The image of the 'buckler of taut

---

1. Stephen is probably thinking of: 'Thy belly is like a heap of wheat set about with lilies', *Solomon's Song*, vii: 2.

2. This 'anastomosis of navelcords' is again mentioned at page 374.

vellum' is derived from a Homeric association, for the Achaean shields were adorned with 'white-heaped' *omphaloi* (bosses).

ἐν δέ οἱ ὀμφαλοὶ ἦσαν ἐείκοσι κασσιτέροιο
λευκοί, ἐν δέ μέσοισιν ἔην μέλανος κυάνοιο[1]

The reference to the first Paradise evokes in Stephen's mind a memorable description from the 'Third Century' of that silver-tongued mystic, Thomas Traherne:

> The corn was orient and immortal wheat, which never should be reaped, nor was ever sown. I thought it had stood from everlasting to everlasting. The dust and stones of the street were as precious as gold: the gates were at first the end of the world. The green trees when I saw them first through one of the gates transported and ravished me, their sweetness and unusual beauty made my heart leap, and almost mad with ecstasy, they were such strange and wonderful things. ... Boys and girls tumbling in the street, and playing, were moving jewels. I knew not that they were born or should die; but all things abided eternally as they were in their proper places. Eternity was manifest in the Light of the Day, and something infinite behind everything appeared: which talked with my expectation and moved my desire. The city seemed to stand in Eden, or to be built in Heaven.

In the 'Proteus' episode Stephen has like moments of ecstasy, when, not in entire forgetfulness, he is 'almosting' the 'something infinite behind everything'.

Stephen's grotesque conception of an umbilical telephone-line from Dublin Bay to 001 Edenville is a characteristic modernization of the oriental belief that the navel is the seat of prophetic power. Thus we find in an Indian hymn: 'Hear, O sons of the gods, one who speaks through his navel, for he hails you in his dwellings!' Modern Parsees are said to maintain that adepts have a mystic flame in their navel which lights up for them the spiritual world; this flame is called the Light of the Initiate.

The idea of a 'cable', a cord linking up the generations of mankind, is familiar to esoteric thinkers. 'Though personalities ever shift, the one line of life along which they are strung like beads, runs unbroken.'[2] 'The end or goal of this earthly life is not within this life, which is but one link in a chain that, like all creation, extends in both directions into

---

1. *Iliad*, XI: 34.
2. A. P. Sinnett, *Esoteric Buddhism.*

the eternal, absolute and infinite, whence all has emanated, wherein all
things move and evolve in a sequence of transformations.'[1]

In his interesting analysis of the structure of *Ulysses*,[2] Professor E. R.
Curtius observed that the persistence of the 'Omphalos-Complex' in
Ulysses indicates that 'nativity' is one of the main themes of the work.
The first use of the word[3] is in Stephen's broken soliloquy (suggested
by a remark of Mulligan that he and Stephen between them might
'hellenize' Ireland, and a reference to Matthew Arnold): 'To ourselves[4]
... new paganism ... Omphalos.' Stephen conjures up an association
between the Martello tower where he and Mulligan are living and the
seat of the Delphic oracle, the world's *omphalos*. Mulligan, a few pages
later, explicitly describes the tower as the authentic *omphalos* of all the
towers set up by 'Billy Pitt', and, in another context, ribaldly proposes
to found and manage on his own account a 'fertilising farm, called
Omphalos with an obelisk hewn and erected after the fashion of Egypt',
thus combining the 'tower' and 'navel' motifs.

Mr Bloom, too, starts out from an *omphalos*, for, in the first scene of
his Odyssey, entitled *Calypso*, his home at No. 7 Eccles Street is (as
indicated in my commentary on that episode) a replica, *mutatis mutandis*, of the isle of Ogygia, where Calypso dwelt; a 'navel of the sea', as
Homer calls it.

Victor Bérard's theory as to the Homeric use of the word explains,
perhaps, the at first rather surprising association of the Martello tower
with the 'omphalos motif' in *Ulysses*.

I translate [M. Bérard says] ὀμφαλός by *highest point*, and νήσῳ ἀμφιρύτῃ
ὅθι τ' ὀμφαλός ἐστι θαλάσσης by *isle set in the waters, whence there rises a navel
of the sea*. The usual translation of ὀμφαλός is *central point* and it is thought that
the poet's conception of the island of Calypso is that it was a navel, a central
point of the sea, as, later, Delphi became, for the Greeks, the navel of the earth.
This is not the place to discuss the reasons which led the Hellenes thus to describe
Delphi or their interpretation of the word 'navel'. That nomenclature and
interpretation belong to a period later than Homer's. In the *Iliad* and *Odyssey*
'omphalos' merely signifies a round protuberance, a swelling. [Compare the
Joycean phrase: *bulging big, a buckler of taut vellum*.] The Homeric shields have
not one 'omphalos' but ten or twenty, scattered over their surface. Crete had

1. A. Arnould, *Les Croyances fondamentales du Bouddhisme*.
2. *Neue Schweizer Rundschau*, Heft I, 1929.
3. *Ulysses*, page 5.   4. The Sinn Fein motto.

on its upper plateau the City of the Navel. The Bible speaks of peoples who come down from the mountains, navels of the earth.[1]

The 'tower' allusions in *Ulysses* should therefore be directly associated with the navel motif and need not necessarily be held to refer to that favourite quarry of the symbol-hunter, the phallic emblem. The motif of the 'tower' is usually allied with the idea of birth or reincarnation. Thus Mr Bloom muses on the endless and monotonous chain of human generations.

One born every second somewhere. Other dying every second. ... Cityful passing away, another cityful coming, passing away too: other coming on, passing on. Houses, lines of houses, streets, miles of pavements, piled up bricks, stones. Changing hands. This owner, that. Landlord never dies they say. ... Slaves Chinese wall. Babylon. Big stones left. Round towers[2] ... mushroom houses, built of breeze. Shelter for the night.

The landlord who never dies may be compared with the soul which, ever changing its mortal tenement, endures immortal from everlasting to everlasting, and it is significant that Mr Bloom visualizes 'round towers' in this context.

In the 'Circe' episode, where the most secret thoughts of Stephen and Mr Bloom are endowed with a spectral life, the culminating moment of the pandemonium is followed by a fantastic Black Mass. The stage-directions are: *On an eminence, the centre of the earth, rises the field altar of Saint Barbara.*[3] *Black candles rise from its gospel and epistle horns. From the high barbicans of the tower two shafts of light fall on the smoke-palled altarstone. On the altarstone Mrs Mina Purefoy, goddess of unreason,*

1. *Les Phéniciens et l'Odyssée*, vol. I, page 190.
2. The round towers of Ireland, which were built as a refuge for the monks at the time of the Viking inroads, were, however, slender, obelisk-like erections and different in shape from the squat Martello towers which (as Mulligan says) were built by Pitt 'when the French were on the sea'. (Mulligan is quoting from the song 'Oh the French are on the sea, Says the Sean Bhean Bhocht'. The last three words mean 'the poor old woman', Ireland; she has just appeared to the young men in the Martello tower in the guise of a poor old milkwoman.) Both kinds of tower, however, were circular, and Mr Bloom's reference to 'round towers' is probably an allusion to the *omphalos*. This allusion is, of course, unconscious; Mr Bloom has not read the esoteric tracts from which I quote in this introduction. But he has an uncanny flair for the esoteric, and there are many curious correspondences between his thoughts and Stephen's.
3. Saint Barbara is the patron of gunsmiths; the powder-room on Italian ships is called the Santa Barbara (cf. the French *Ste-Barbe*). The altar of the *omphalos* is a powder-magazine, womb of dynamic outburst.

lies naked, fettered, a chalice resting on her swollen belly. In this passage all the ramifications of the *omphalos* theme are anastomosed; naked Eve, 'belly without blemish, bulging big', is personified by Mrs Purefoy, that prolific mother, who has just (as described in the preceding episode, the 'Oxen of the Sun') given birth to yet another child. The vision of the 'high barbicans of the tower' whence 'two shafts of light fall on the smokepalled altarstone' is an exact recall of the scene at the Martello tower where Stephen took his breakfast (described in the first episode: 'Telemachus'). 'Two shafts of soft daylight fell across the flagged floor from the high barbicans: at the meeting of their rays a cloud of coal-smoke and fumes of fried grease floated, turning.' The 'chalice' which rests on the body of the naked woman is a transmutation of the shaving-bowl which Buck Mulligan mockingly elevated, standing on the plat-form of the Tower,[1] blessing gravely thrice the surrounding country and awaking mountains and chanting *Introibo ad altare Dei.*

The *omphalos* is thus at once a symbol of birth (the explosion of white, fecund grain, orient and immortal), of the strand that links back generation to generation and of a legendary eastern isle embossed on a smooth shield of sea, a lost paradise, the uncorrupted Eden of Traherne's ecstasy.

4. PATERNITY

One of the most interesting and, at the same time, most baffling of problems in the interpretation of *Ulysses* is the relation between young Stephen Dedalus and mature Mr Bloom. It is obvious that throughout the flux of events which is observed and recorded by the author from hour to hour of that memorable day, 16 June 1904, there is a continu-ous movement towards a preordained event, the meeting of Stephen and Bloom, and that, after they have met, the movement slows down and its force is gradually dissipated in the sleepy, retrospective atmo-sphere of the cabman's shelter ('Eumaeus'), the disintegrative analysis of 'Ithaca', and the drone of Mrs Bloom's slumber-song. In a flash the circuit has been closed and the energy has spent itself. Stephen's ges-ture in the brothel symbolizes the finality of that moment. 'He lifts his ashplant high with both hands and smashes the chandelier. Time's

1. See my commentary on the 'Telemachus' episode, where the rhythmic recurrence of allusions to a 'bowl', of lather, of bile, of sea, is discussed.

livid final flame leaps and, in the following darkness, ruin of all space, shattered glass and toppling masonry.' There have been many pre-monitions of this 'catastrophe' (the 'Circe' scene, where it takes place, is in dramatic form, and, as often in Hellenic drama, it follows a 'recog-nition') in earlier episodes.[1] As I have already noted, there is an inter-mittent telepathic communication, a seepage of the current, so to speak, between Stephen and Mr Bloom, even before they meet each other; after that event they seem to be using different languages – the accumu-lated energy has run down in a 'livid final flame'.

What exactly is the relation[2] between these two complementary types, the intellectual and the instinctive, and what was the author's intention in his treatment of Mr Bloom (a fact often pointed out by commentators of *Ulysses*) as the spiritual father of Stephen Dedalus?

First of all it is necessary to establish an absolute distinction between parenthood, in the ordinary sense of the word, and the spiritual 'here-dity' of the new-born soul. 'Physical parents cannot be the progenitors of the spiritual germ of the child, that germ is the product of a previous spiritual evolution.'[3] That evolution is governed, down to the smallest detail, by the law of Merit.

The diversities of human lot are not the sport of brainless chance – the out-come of what by an absurd phrase we sometimes call the accident of birth. There is no 'accident'. ... With the same inevitable certainty that force on the material plane governs the combination of molecules of matter – though the be-wildering complexity of even that aspect of force dazzles the mind as we attempt to follow out its workings – so does the far more exalted force which gives effect to the primary laws of nature in the moral world operate with an exacti-tude that no chemical reactions can eclipse.[4]

Physical forms are transmitted on the plane of physical evolution from father to son with sometimes remarkable resemblances; in such cases heredity is not the cause but the concomitant of the attributes manifested by the son. His inde-pendent soul Karma has required such a vehicle as the man who becomes his father was physically qualified to engender. Many illustrations might be taken

1. See *Ulysses*, pages 21 ('I hear the ruin of all space'), 40 ('Shattered glass and toppling masonry'), 374 ('time's ruins build eternity's mansions'), 409 ('even now that day is at hand when he shall come to judge the world by fire'), 480 ('they say the last day is coming this summer').
2. *Der Komplex des Vater-Sohn Problems*, as Professor Curtius has described it (*Neue Schweizer Rundschau*, January 1929).
3. Hartmann, *Magic*, page 70.
4. A. P. Sinnett, *The Growth of the Soul*, page 66.

from Nature to show her various forces and powers playing in this way into one another's hands.[1]

If such a thing as a 'mistake' were possible in the ordered progress of the soul, an instance would be the case of infant mortality. As Mr Bloom is following Dignam's remains to the cemetery, he sees 'a tiny coffin flash by'. 'A dwarf's face mauve and wrinkled like little Rudy's was. Dwarf's body, weak as putty, in a whitelined deal box. Burial friendly society pays. Penny a week for a sod of turf. Our. Little. Beggar. Baby. Meant nothing. Mistake of nature.'

Even as a schoolboy Stephen recognized his spiritual independence of his 'consubstantial father' and of his father's friends. 'An abyss of fortune or temperament sundered him from them. His mind seemed older than theirs: it shone coldly on their strifes and happiness and regrets like a moon upon a younger earth.'[2] All through *Ulysses* we find passages indicating that Stephen has definitely renounced the 'fiction' of fatherhood. 'Wombed in sin darkness I was too, made not begotten.' 'I moved among them on the frozen Liffey, that I, a changeling, among the spluttering resin fires.' 'He saw clearly, too, his own futile isolation. ... He felt that he was hardly of the one blood with them, but stood to them rather in the mystical kinship of fosterage, fosterchild and fosterbrother.'[3] 'Paternity may be a legal fiction. Who is the father of any son that any son should love him or he any son?' 'A father is a necessary evil.' 'Fatherhood, in the sense of conscious begetting, is unknown to man. It is a mystical estate, an apostolic succession, from only begetter to only begotten.'[4]

A passage in the 'Sirens' episode shows that even Mr Dedalus was dimly conscious of the 'abyss' that sundered them, and that Stephen was a 'changeling'.

He[5] greeted Mr Dedalus and got a nod.
'Greetings from the famous son of a famous father.'
'Who may he be?' Mr Dedalus asked.
Lenehan opened most genial arms. Who?
'Who may he be?' he asked. 'Can you ask? Stephen, the youthful bard.'
Dry.
Mr Dedalus, famous father, laid by his dry filled pipe.
'I see,' he said. 'I didn't recognize him for the moment.'

1. ibid., page 57.   2. *A Portrait of the Artist as a Young Man*, page 107.
3. ibid., page 111.   4. *Ulysses*, page 195.   5. Lenehan.

It is clear that paternity, in the physical meaning of the word, would be incompatible with the central theme of *Ulysses*, the 'atonement' of Stephen, eternal naysayer, and positivist Mr Bloom: the discharge (symbolized by the flash of lightning which plays upon their encounter at the House of Birth) of a high-tension current between negative and positive poles. But 'all truth is ultimately symbolic.' 'What is nature?' Novalis asks, and replies: 'An exact, encyclopaedic index, or plan, of our spirit.' Above and beyond the physical fact of fatherhood, there is a mystic relationship which, like the birth motif, enters into nearly every religion, popular or esoteric, catholic or pagan. In *Ulysses* we find recalls of the great controversies concerning the relations of Father, Son, and Holy Ghost which sundered the unity of the Early Church, the moot 'procession' *filioque*.[1]

The proud potent titles clanged over Stephen's memory the triumph of their brazen bells: *et unam sanctam catholicam et apostolicam ecclesiam*: the slow growth and change of rite and dogma like his own rare thoughts, a chemistry of stars. Symbol of the apostles in the mass for pope Marcellus, the voices blended, singing alone loud in affirmation: and behind their chant the vigilant angel of the church militant disarmed and menaced her heresiarchs. A horde of heresies fleeing with mitres awry: Photius and the brood of mockers of whom Mulligan was one, and Arius, warring his life long upon the consubstantiality of the Son with the Father, and Valentine, spurning Christ's terrene body, and the subtle African heresiarch Sabellius who held that the Father was Himself His own Son.[2]

They[3] clasped and sundered, did the coupler's will. From before the ages He willed me and now may not will me away or ever. A *lex eterna* stays about Him. Is that then the divine substance wherein Father and Son are consubstantial? Where is poor dear Arius to try conclusions? Warring his life long on the contransmagnificandjewbangtantiality. Illstarred heresiarch. In a Greek watercloset he breathed his last: euthanasia.[4]

Stephen, 'the son striving to be atoned with the father', is the second

1. This theme is dealt with, in characteristic fashion, in the fable of the Mookse and the Gripes (*Finnegans Wake*, page 156). '... the loggerthuds of his sakellaries were fond at variance with the synodals of his somepoolium and his babskissed nepogreasymost got the hoof from his philioquus.' The pope of Rome (whose slipper or 'baboosh' is kissed by the faithful) gets 'the hoof' from the *filioque*, here presented as some queer kind of horse!

2. *Ulysses*, page 18.   3. i.e. Stephen's parents.
4. *Ulysses*, page 35.

person of the trinity of Ulysses.[1] Though the analogy suggested by these words may sound blasphemous to orthodox ears, such an idea contains nothing offensive to the mystic.

The whole story of the crucifixion is enacted afresh in the case of every human soul that attains spiritual exaltation. It is the allegory of the soul's progress. It is the only process by which redemption can be accomplished – and it is vividly appreciated as soon as we understand the occult teaching concerning the lower and higher self.[2]

The growth of the soul is a process towards at-onement, a return, the octave. In the 'Circe' episode the Reverend Elijah Dowie harangues the company at the brothel.[3] 'Are you a god or a doggone clod? If the second advent came to Coney Island are we ready? Florry Christ, Stephen Christ, Zoe Christ, Bloom Christ, Kitty Christ, Lynch Christ, it's up to you to sense that cosmic force.' The Christ-Stephen correspondence is clearly hinted at in certain passages of the episodes 'Scylla and Charybdis' and the 'Oxen of the Sun' (q.v.). The personality of Stephen, it may be noted, fits better the Blakean than the orthodox conception of the Second Person of the Trinity.

> Was Jesus gentle, or did he
> Give any marks of Gentility?
> When twelve years old he ran away
> And left his Parents in dismay.
> When after three days' sorrow found,
> Loud as Sinai's trumpet sound:
> 'No Earthly Parents I confess. ...'
>
> I am sure this Jesus will not do
> Either for Englishman or Jew.

Human life is a process of adjustment, a striving after at-onement with a sublime father; achieved adjustment would involve personal extinction, yet it is the end to which all creation moves. There is a

1. In *Ulysses*, as in certain ancient cults, the third person is the female element. 'The trinity of the Egyptians and that of the mythological Greeks', H. P. Blavatsky observes in *Isis Unveiled*, 'were alike representations of the first triple emanation containing two male principles and one female. It is the union of the male Logos, or wisdom, the revealed Deity, with the female *Aura* or *Anima Mundi* – the "holy *Pneuma*", which is the *Sephira* of the Kabalists and the *Sophia* of the refined Gnostics – that produced all things visible and invisible.'

2. A. P. Sinnett, *The Growth of the Soul*, page 48.   3. *Ulysses*, page 482.

perpetual levelling in the universe, a crumbling of individualities, which, like mountains, are slowly eroded, silted down, into the plain of uniformity, towards amalgamation in a 'perfect round'. 'But where are we going?' Novalis asks, and answers: 'Always home.'[1] That return is symbolized in the tale of Odysseus, in a thousand and one legends of all races, and its biblical paradigm is the homecoming of the Prodigal Son. Thus Stephen, in the brothel, chides himself: 'Filling my belly with the husks of swine. Too much of this. I will arise and go to my.' (He does not pronounce the word 'father', perhaps because the meeting with his 'spiritual father' has already taken place; 'the motion is ended' – as Stephen says of Shakespeare's return 'after a life of absence to that spot of earth where he was born', to die.) Stephen sees himself condemned to eat the husks left over by the prosperous Mulligan and Haines. 'You have eaten all we left,' Mulligan says to him after breakfast. Stephen later[2] recalls this remark. 'Come, Kinch, you have eaten all we left. Ay. I will serve you your orts and offals.' Towards the close of Ulysses, Bloom asks Stephen, 'Why did you leave your father's house?' and, watching him carouse in the company of the medical students, pities him 'for that he lived riotously with those wastrels and murdered his goods with whores'. Bloom, the Jew, recalls (in an early episode) a similar theme in a play adapted from the Old Testament, the scene where the old blind Abraham recognizes Nathan's voice and puts his fingers on his face. 'Nathan's voice! His son's voice! I hear the voice of Nathan who left his father to die of grief and misery in my arms, who left the house of his father and left the God of his father.'

It has been suggested by a distinguished critic that Stephen's attitude to his consubstantial father is contemptuous (whereas he respects his mother). It is true that what he sees of maternity is its tragic aspect, what he sees of paternity is its comic side. But as for the Italians who in anger adjure the *putana madonna*[2] and yet are the race who have imposed her cult on Europe, so for Stephen familiarity does not imply contempt. In the 'Circe' episode even Shakespeare, who to Stephen seems 'the greatest creator after God', takes on a grotesque aspect – his brothel self – and stammers inane gibberish. Even in the tragic apparition of Stephen's dead mother (in the same episode) there are touches of the ridiculous – that deflation of sentiment to which I have already referred. Mr Dedalus *père* is really one of the most likeable characters of

1. page 202.   2. See Ulysses, page 583.

Ulysses and Stephen deeply feels his own 'futile isolation'. And, after all, he is equally (indeed, more) aloof from, and ironic towards, his 'spiritual father', the Jew who boldly defied the Citizen and 'told him his God, I mean Christ, was a jew too, and all his family like me'.

'*Ex quibus*,' Stephen mumbled in a noncommittal accent, their two or four eyes conversing, '*Christus* or Bloom his name is, or, after all, any other, *secundum carnem*.'

The last pages of the *Portrait of the Artist as a Young Man* are clearly an invocation to fatherhood – but to what father, whether to the artificer Daedalus, or to a heavenly or an earthly father, it is difficult to say, perhaps Stephen himself hardly knows. Even the meeting with Bloom is, for him, no release from his hopeless quest, no remedy for his futile isolation. Stephen's attitude is really one of despair; he has not lost a father, like Telemachus, but he can never find one.

Chapter 4

1. DUBLINERS-VIKINGS-ACHAEANS

THE Book of Ballymote is one of the earliest documents dealing with Irish history which we possess; it was compiled by several scribes from earlier records at Ballymote, in Sligo, about the year 1391. Amongst its contents are genealogies of all the principal Irish families, tales of the Irish kings, the translation of an *Argonautica*, and a history of the War of Troy.[1] In the list of the peoples described as having fought at Troy appears the name Trapcharla, an authenticated Irish place-name (Co. Limerick), whose derivation is said to be either *torf-karl*, a turf-cutter, or *thorp-karl*, a small farmer.

But the legendary association of the early Irish with the Achaeans or their neighbours is far from being limited to a casual reference in the Book of Ballymote. The following extracts from P. W. Joyce's *Concise History of Ireland* indicate that Irish chroniclers had a strongly rooted belief in the Grecian origins of the Irish race. The manuscripts describe a series of five colonizations. (1) '*The Parthalonians*, the first colony, A.M. 2520. The first man that led a colony to Ireland after the flood was a chief named Parthalon, who came from Greece with his wife, three sons and 1,000 followers.' (2) *The Nemedians*, the second colony, A.M. 2850. These were the followers of one Nemed who came from Scythia. Both they and the Parthalonians succumbed in large numbers to a plague. (3) '*The Firbolgs*, the third colony, A.M. 3266, came from Greece under the leadership of the five sons of Dela, who led them to Ireland. Those brothers partitioned the country into five provinces. Ulster, Leinster, Connaught, and the two Munsters.' (4) '*The Dedannans*, the fourth colony, A.M. 3303, also came from Greece, and were celebrated for their skill in magic.... The Dedannans were in subsequent ages deified and became *Side* (Shee) or fairies, whom the ancient Irish worshipped.' (5) *The Milesians*, the fifth colony, A.M. 3500.

From Scythia, their original home, they began their long pilgrimage. Their first migration was to Egypt, where they were sojourning at the time that

1. P. W. Joyce, *A Concise History of Ireland*.

Pharaoh and his host were drowned in the Red Sea; and after wandering through Europe for many generations they arrived in Spain. Here they abode for a long time, and at last they came to Ireland with a fleet of thirty ships under the command of the eight sons of the hero Miléd or Milesius.

Five of the eight brothers perished; of the remaining three, one, Eremon, established himself as sole king in Ireland.

Milesius is referred to in *Ulysses*[1] where the valiant Sinn Feiner speaks of the ancient Irish flag, 'the oldest flag afloat, three crowns on a blue field, the three sons of Milesius'. Again[2] we read: 'Return Clan Milly: forget me not, O Milesian.'

It is noteworthy that the Milesians made a long stay in Spain before proceeding northwards; of the trinity of personages who dominate Ulysses, one, Mrs Bloom, is, on her mother's side, of Spanish descent, and was born at Gibraltar. 'Pride of Calpe's rocky mount [Gibraltar], the ravenhaired daughter of Tweedy. There she grew to peerless beauty where loquat and almond scent the air. The gardens of Alameda knew her step: the garths of olives knew and bowed.' In a characteristic outburst the Citizen asks: 'Where are the Greek merchants that came through the Pillars of Hercules, the Gibraltar now grabbed by the foe of mankind, with gold and Tyrian purple to sell in Wexford at the fair of Carmen?' Later, he refers to 'our trade with Spain.... Spanish ale in Galway, the winebark on the winedark waterway'.

A curious incident, connecting the early inhabitants of Ireland with Spain and the opposite African coast, is recorded in one of the *Three Fragments of Annals* preserved in the Burgundian library at Brussels. It appears that in the early ninth century a party of the Lochlanns[3]

---

1. *Ulysses*, page 312.   2. page 376.

3. Stephen sees himself (page 42), in retrospect, one of the 'noble race of Lochlanns' (as an old Irish chronicle describes them), yet, in that life as in this, a changeling, a son for ever banished from his father. 'Galleys of the Lochlanns ran here to beach, in quest of prey, their bloodbeaked prows riding low on a molten pewter surf. Dane vikings, torcs of tomahawks aglitter on their breasts when Malachi wore the collar of gold. A school of turlhide whales stranded in hot noon spouting, hobbling in the shallows. Then from the starving cagework city a horde of jerkined dwarfs, my people, with flayers' knives, running, scaling, hacking in green blubbery whalemeat. Famine, plague and slaughters. Their blood is in me, their lusts my waves. I moved among them on the frozen Liffey, that I, a changeling, among the spluttering resin fires. I spoke to no one: none to me.' With this may be compared a similar passage in the *Portrait*. 'He heard a confused music within him as of memories and names which he was almost conscious of but could not capture even for an instant; then the music seemed to recede, to recede,

rowed forward across the Cantabrian Sea until they reached Spain, and they in-flicted many evils in Spain, both by killing and plundering. They afterwards crossed the Gaditanian Straits [the Straits of Cadiz] and fought a battle with the Mauritani [Moors]. ... They carried off a great host of the Moors as captives to Erin and these are the blue men of Erin. Long indeed were these blue men in Erin.

Speaking of this expedition, Depping (*Histoire des expéditions maritimes des Normans*) records that the Scandinavians sailed up the Guadalquivir and, having defeated the Moors who opposed their attack on Seville, pillaged the city and retired to their ships 'bringing with them much booty and a crowd of prisoners, who perhaps never again beheld the beautiful sky of Andalusia'.

The name of the 'blue men' given to these Moors is borrowed from the Scandinavian Vikings for whom Africa was the 'Blauland hit Mikla' or Great Blueland.[1] In my notes on the 'Calypso' episode the theory that attributes an African original to the Homeric Ogygia, Calypso's isle, and its bearing on the structure of that episode, will be discussed. There are many references to the Moors in *Ulysses*, to the Moor Othello, to 'morrice' (Moorish) dances, 'imps of fancy of the Moors', 'the nine men's morrice with caps of indices',[2] and to Mrs Bloom's 'Moorish'

---

to recede: and from each receding trail of nebulous music there fell always one long-drawn calling note, piercing like a star the dusk of silence. Again! Again! Again! A voice from beyond the world was calling. ... Now, as never before, his strange name seemed to him a prophecy. So timeless seemed the grey warm air, so fluid and impersonal his own mood, that all ages were as one to him. A moment before the ghost of the ancient kingdom of the Danes had looked forth through the vesture of the hazewrapped city. ...'

1. C. Haliday, *The Scandinavian Kingdom of Dublin*, page 116.

2. The importance and influence of numbers have been recognized by many schools of mystics, the most important of which was probably the Pythagorean. 'Since of all things numbers are the first,' Aristotle tells us, 'in numbers they [the Pythagoreans] thought they perceived many analogies to things that exist ... they supposed the elements of numbers to be the elements of all things.' Numbers play an important part in *Ulysses*. As Mr Bloom remarks, 'Do anything you like with figures juggling', and the number of his house in Eccles Street (to which I shall refer later) is a 'mystic number'. The 'nine men's morrice' (the name of an old English game) is an allusion to the Arabic origin of the decimal system, which replaced the quinary or five-finger method of calculation. Readers of the *Wake* will have noticed that it contains a fantasia on the quinary scale. There is probably an allusion to this scale in Stephen's 'hollow fifths', 'the greatest possible interval' between the notes of the octave, already mentioned; here, too, we find, doubtless, the recall of a Pythagorean dogma, the treatment of the *octave* as the reconciliation of the *unlimited* and the *limiting*.

eyes which, after her marriage with Leopold Bloom, never again beheld the beautiful sky of Andalusia.

Such is a brief outline of the legendary connexion between ancient Ireland and the Mediterranean; less precise, though perhaps more authentic, is the analogy which can be drawn between the history of Dublin and the conditions of the Homeric age, as described in the *Odyssey*.

That Dublin owes its importance, if not its origin, to the Norsemen may be inferred from the almost total silence of the historians and annalists regarding it in the years preceding the Scandinavian inroads. It is probable that there was a fort to guard the hurdle-ford (the old name for Dublin was *Baile-atha-Cliath*, the town of the hurdle ford) where the great road from Tara to Wicklow, Arklow and Wexford crossed the Liffey, but it seems to have played no great part in history before the Norsemen fortified it in 840. During the ninth and tenth centuries the Kingdom of Dublin – known to the Scandinavians as Dyflinarski – became one of the most powerful in the west. The Dublin kings intermarried with royal families in Ireland, England and Scotland, and between the years 919 and 950 ruled, though in somewhat broken succession, as Kings of York.[1]

The early growth of Dublin was due to a series of waves of invaders from the north. The Ostmen (or *Danes*, as the Irish called them) intermarried freely with the natives, and so intimate was the intermixture of races that 'it is doubtful whether the kings of Dublin during the eleventh century should be called Irish or Scandinavian'. In the ninth and tenth centuries the invaders frequently married the women they had taken as captives, and the ruling classes of both nations confirmed their alliances by intermarriages. The first coins used in Ireland were minted during the reign of Sitric Silken-Beard, who was of mixed descent. Many of the place-names mentioned in *Ulysses* – Howth (O.N. *hofuth*, a head), Ireland's Eye (O.N. *ey*, an island), Leixlip (O.N. *Laxhleypa*, salmon-leap) are of Norse provenience.

The humanizing effects of Saint Patrick's mission to Ireland continued long after his death and, before the incursions of the Norsemen mentioned above, a long succession of saints and scholars had won for Ireland the proud title: *insula sanctorum et doctorum*. From all parts of

1. A. Walsh, *Scandinavian Relations with Ireland*, page 22. The action of *Ulysses* takes place entirely within the Dyflinarski (which is not only the Ostmen's pale but is also coincident with the ecclesiastical jurisdiction of the Bishops of Dublin and Glendalough). The unity of place is thus confirmed by both civil and religious authority.

Europe, even, it is recorded, from Egypt, students flocked to Ireland to profit by the wisdom of the Irish ollavs. 'There were ollavs of the several professions, just as we have doctors of Law, Medicine, Philosophy, Literature, etc.' An ollav sat at table next the king or chief. If the Viking inroads disturbed the progress of scholastic culture, they stimulated by way of compensation the cult of the *saga*. 'At the close of the tenth century story-telling was in high favour in Ireland, and the professional story-teller was able not only to recite any one of the great historical tales, but to improvise, if the occasion arose.'[1] 'The importance of Dublin as a Scandinavian colony is ... strongly marked in its connexion with other colonies of the Norsemen. Of these one of the most celebrated was Iceland.'[2] Of all the makers of sagas the Icelanders were the most expert. 'Icelandic poets were received with favour not only in Norway, but elsewhere, for instance in England and Ireland.'[3] 'After their settlement in Iceland the Norsemen, their sons and descendants, brought thither fresh tales of the old country, acquired in their yearly voyages to Norway as traders or otherwise. These they put into sagas or tales; or the skalds, the professional oral chroniclers, recited them at banquets and public meetings, interspersing in their recitals fragments of ancient verse to adorn and enliven them, a practice they probably learned in Ireland.' And it is significant that 'Irish names were borne by some of the foremost characters of the heroic age in Iceland, especially the poets, of whom it was also remarked that most of them were dark men'. A connexion between the Irish ollavs and the Icelandic or Scandinavian bards is well established. According to the *Book of Leinster*, 'the poet who had attained the rank of ollav was bound to know for recital to kings and chieftains two hundred and fifty tales of prime importance and one hundred secondary ones' – the exact accomplishments, in fact, of a Norwegian or Icelandic skald. It seems likely that, considering the rapid advance in culture of the Irish nation soon after the mission of Saint Patrick, and the intimate relations which existed between Iceland and Ireland even before the Viking inroads, the northern epic was in reality a development of the primitive Irish saga. That is, in fact, the hypothesis put forward by the two learned authors from whose works I have quoted above.

1. ibid., page 69.
2. *The Scandinavian Kingdom of Dublin*, page 98.
3. *Scandinavian Relations with Ireland*, page 66.

It is interesting to note that the Irish sagas came, at an early stage, to be written in *prose*; such orally preserved prose sagas were recited by the *file* or professional minstrels in Ireland as early as the seventh century, whereas in Iceland the prose saga only 'appears to have developed in the course of the tenth century'.[1] These prose narratives were 'detailed and elaborate', and the minstrels of the period must have possessed remarkable powers of memory, far exceeding those necessary for the reciters of epic poems. It is significant that *Ulysses* is both detailed and elaborate in its narration of facts and its numerous historical and literary echoes. Like his predecessors Joyce was gifted with a prodigious memory, and had none of the modern aversion from elaboration and a detailed treatment of narrative.

Two thousand years before the Irish age of ollavs, the rhapsodists of the Greek colonies on the Asia Minor coast were 'stringing together' their epics, and the blind father of poetry creating (or collating) his immortal hexameters. There are many striking resemblances between that period of Greek civilization and the early history of Dublin, and the links between the epic of Mr Bloom and the adventures of the Achaean heroes are at once stronger and subtler than the vague racial legend which I have mentioned above.[2]

According to an ancient tradition the Trojan War covered the period 1220–1210 B.C. After the latter date, Victor Bérard tells us, the Phoenician thalassocracy, which had lasted in the Eastern Mediterranean for about three centuries, 'began to decline and lost its commercial monopoly before the incursions, successes and settlement in the archipelago of the Peoples of the Sea, whom the Egyptian records have described to us. That the Achaeans are the best-known of these Peoples is the work of the Homeric epics, principally the Odyssey.' Before the arrival of these relatively barbarous peoples from the north, all the Eastern Mediterranean was occupied by an Aegaeo-Levantine civilization, 'whose origin the Hellenes attributed to Minos, son of Europa, the Phoenician, to Cadmos the Tyrian and to Danaos, the Egyptian, bringers of the alphabet, of written laws, the horse, the chariot and the fifty-oared ship.'

1. *Scandinavian Relations with Ireland*, page 74.
2. For the brief outline of Viking-Achaean parallelism which follows and of the conditions under which the Homeric poems were composed, I am largely indebted to the researches of the eminent Hellenist, Victor Bérard, the results of which are embodied in his *Les Phéniciens et l'Odyssée*.

The Achaeans of the Homeric epic are these barbarians from the north;[1] tradition places their descent several generations before the Trojan war. ... The heroes of the epics, settled in Pelasgian territory, are the 'sons of the Achaeans', υἷες Ἀχαιῶν; this title they proudly claim as an honorific, for in their eyes it confers on them a nobility of divine succession and the privileges of a caste; and these blond 'peers of the gods', 'of the long locks (καρηκομόωντες)', 'fosterchildren of Zeus', and their 'divine' wives established in the land they conquered, over a population of slaves or vassals, a feudal domination or rule of *chivalry* – if we interpret this latter term according to epic usage, that is to say, not regarding the horse as a beast of burden or mount, but as the animal that draws the chariot.

Thus the Achaean oarsmen of the Homeric ship were all free men, 'knights of the oar', ἐσθλοί, who claimed to be of kingly, if not divine descent. Theoretically there is perfect equality between all these 'comrades', ἑταῖροι, *Gessellen*, free associates whose royal blood ennobled hard labour at the oar.

Amongst the Vikings 'the number of persons who bore the name of king was almost uncountable'.[2] *Fuit hoc inter pirates more receptum, si regibus nati exercitui praeessent, ut hi reges appellarentur, etsi nullas haberent terras ditioni suae subjectas.*[3] The Irish claim to be 'all kings' sons' is mentioned many times in *Ulysses*, generally in a context suggesting pathos or irony. Stephen Dedalus thinks of famous pretenders; 'Thomas Fitzgerald, silken knight ... Lambert Simnel a scullion crowned. All king's sons. Paradise of pretenders then and now.' 'Steak, kidney, liver, mashed at meat fit for princes sat princes Bloom and Goulding. Princes at meat they raised and drank Power and cider.' Two 'commercials' stand fizz in Jammet's. 'Like princes, faith.' 'And heroes voyage from afar to woo them, from Eblana to Slievemargy, the peerless princes of unfettered Munster and of Connacht the just and of smooth sleek Leinster and of Cruachan's land and of Armagh the splendid and of the noble district of Boyle, princes, the sons of kings.'

Like the Vikings, the Achaean princes, 'lovers of the oar', φιλήρετμοι, were both 'commercials' and pirates. Generally, Bérard observes, they were both at once. Thus the Cyclops, questioning Odysseus on his

---

1. Like the Viking berserks who conquered the Irish 'saints and sages', the Achaeans were far less cultured than the aborigines, educated by Phoenician intercourse, whom they ousted. In fact, Helen was quite excusable for preferring the *savoir vivre* of Paris to the Nordic crudity of the austere Menelaus.

2. F. Keary, *The Vikings.*　　3. *Script. Hist. Island*, I, page 120.

occupation, asks: 'Whence sail ye over the wet ways? On some trading enterprise or at adventure do ye rove, even as sea-robbers over the brine, for they wander at hazard of their lives, bringing bale to alien men?' Nestor[1] asks the same question of Telemachus. Indeed, the very first adventure of Odysseus after leaving Ilios was an act of piracy. 'The wind that bare me from Ilios brought me nigh to the Cicones, even to Ismarus, whereupon I sacked their city and slew the people. But from out the city we took their wives and much substance, and divided them between us, that none through me might go lacking his proper share.' Thus the Vikings, on their first landing on the Irish coast (in A.D. 795), sacked the city of Recru, or Lambay Island, near Dublin. For both Achaeans and Vikings piracy was an honourable profession in the practice of which a young man acquired the advantages of a liberal education. The Icelandic records speak of a certain Thorer: '*piraticam facere consuevit; interdum vero mercaturam per varias regiones exercebat; hinc magnam multis in locis rerum hominumque notitiam habuit.*' 'Thus he acquired a wide knowledge of things and men in many places.' The similarity of this passage with the opening of the *Odyssey* is striking. '... that man of many a shift, who wandered far and wide... many were the men whose towns he saw and whose mind he learnt.' An occasional act of piracy was, in fact, indispensable for an Achaean or Viking who wished to acquire a wide knowledge of foreign men and minds. Travellers' cheques were not placed at his disposal by obliging agencies, a polite request for food and lodging was often of no avail; thus the prudent voyager (unless he knew that he had to deal with a civilized people like the Phaeacians) usually helped himself to whatever ship's stores he needed and re-embarked with all speed on his 'gallant ship'.

Like the Vikings, the Homeric heroes were subject to fits of berserk rage.

He fastened the cable of a dark-prowed ship about a pillar of the great kitchen dome, and stretched it high aloft, that none might touch the ground with her feet. And even as when thrushes, long of wing, or doves fall into a net that is set in a thicket, as they seek to their roosting-place, and a hateful bed harbours them, even so the women held their heads all in a row, and about all their necks nooses were cast, that they might die by the most pitiful death. And they writhed with their feet for a little space, but for no long while.

Then they led out Melanthius through the gateway and the court, and cut off

1. *Odyssey*, III: 71–4.

his nostrils and his ears with the pitiless sword, and drew forth his vitals for the dogs to devour raw, and cut off his hands and feet in their cruel anger.

At the end of the eleventh century Eric, King of Denmark, was a model of piety and wisdom. He made the pilgrimage to Rome, to the Apostles' Tomb.... He built churches, founded monasteries and maintained obedience to the laws of God.

One evening after his return from Rome,

King Eric took his dinner in the open; a famous minstrel arrived, who vaunted his power of exciting the guests to berserk rage by the strains of his harp. ... As a measure of prudence, all weapons were removed from the palace. The minstrel began to play, and, little by little, all were seized by a strange madness and raised a great clamour. The bodyguard sought in vain to restrain the King. With his mighty hands he crushed four of his most faithful knights and was only mastered when half suffocated beneath a pile of cushions!

The sons of Arngrim, King of Helgeland, in their rages 'slew their followers, smashed their ships, and vented their rage on the trees and rocks'.

In the 'Cyclops' episode of *Ulysses* Mr Bloom encounters one of these berserks.

'By Jesus,' says he, 'I'll brain that bloody jewman ... I'll crucify him so I will. ...'
'Where is he till I murder him?'
Begob he drew his hand and made a swipe and let fly. Mercy of God the sun was in his eyes or he'd have left him for dead.

As the narrator of this episode, speaking from much knowledge of the forgatherings of Dubliners, remarks, 'there's always some bloody clown or other kicking up a bloody murder about bloody nothing'.

Among the Norsemen, as among the Achaeans, the gift of eloquence was highly esteemed; the great man was almost invariably a great orator. The part played by eloquence in the making of Irish history is considerable. It is hardly possible to find a better example of typical Irish 'blarney' than the speech of Odysseus to Nausicaa, beginning: 'I supplicate thee, O queen, whether thou art some goddess or a mortal! If indeed thou art a goddess of them that keep the wide heaven, to Artemis, then, the daughter of great Zeus, I mainly liken thee, for beauty and stature and shapeliness. ...' No wonder Nausicaa confessed to her

fair-tressed maidens, 'Would that such a one might be called my husband, dwelling here!' The Achaeans

prized the good runner, who could pace or outpace a swift chariot. ... They
preferred city to country life; they were men of the *agora*, of the *place publique*,
of the market, orators, lovers of noise, of debates and fine words. ... They
admired above all a talent for the invention of songs, fiction, well-turned
phrases. Ingenuity, though carried to the point of deceit, ever delighted them;
they had every indulgence for ruse and blandishment such as that whereby
Ulysses won Athene's heart for ever.

The reader of *Ulysses* will see all these qualities in the Dubliners described by Joyce; Mr Dedalus, Stephen's father, is, perhaps, the noblest
'Achaean' of them all.

2. *ULYSSES* AND THE *ODYSSEY*

A Neapolitan critic has said of *Ulysses* that its true protagonist is neither
Mr Bloom nor Stephen but the *language*. Joyce's virtuosity in the mani-
pulation of words is such that, especially since the appearance of *Finnegans Wake*, a tendency has grown up to regard 'Words for Words'
Sake' as his aesthetic creed and sole preoccupation. A casual reading of
Ulysses may well seem to justify this view. There are many characteristic
passages which contain echoes of writers of all races, of all times; there
is a whole episode which has been dubbed a 'chapter of parodies',
another written, for the most part, in the language of *Every Girl's Magazine*, and in the 'Cyclops' episode frequent slices of Whitechapel, Wardour or Fleet Street English are spatchcocked into the main narrative,
which is recorded in the demotic idiom of a Dublin loafer. In another
episode ('Ithaca') where the catechistic structure is employed, questions
and answers are as dryly precise and *ad nauseam* explicit as the Aristotelian hair-splitting of an early theologian. In every instance, for valid
and specific reasons, the author has chosen a style appropriate to the
subject; *le style c'est le thème*.

The presence of numerous 'echoes' in the text is, of course, due to the
necessities of the silent monologue. Stephen Dedalus is a young man
who has read much and forgotten nothing, and the stream of his
thoughts is copiously fed from literary sources. Like the antiquarian,

Hugh C. Love, who walks the Dublin streets 'attended by Geraldines tall and personable', Stephen has ever with him his attendant ghosts, Swift, Shakespeare, Blake, Thomas Aquinas, and a motley horde of medieval philosophers. Mr Bloom's soliloquies, too, are coloured by his literary habits; they are a jumble of bits of advertisements, popular science, music-hall refrains. Moreover, each change of mood, every allusion, leaves an imprint on the plastic prose of the narrative. The episode ('Eumaeus'), for instance, which describes the return of Mr Bloom and Stephen after the orgy at the Lying-in Hospital and Burke's public house, and the pandemonium at the brothel, is written in a style which exactly reflects the half-fuddled exhaustion of Mr Bloom.

The guarded glance of half solicitude, half curiosity, augmented by friendliness which he gave at Stephen's at present morose expression of features did not throw a flood of light, none at all in fact, on the problem as to whether he had let himself be badly bamboozled, to judge by two or three low spirited remarks he let drop, or, the other way about, saw through the affair, and, for some reason or other best known to himself, allowed matters to more or less. ... Grinding poverty did have that effect and he more than conjectured that, high educational abilities though he possessed, he experienced no little difficulty in making both ends meet.

Ulysses contains examples of almost every known dialect and patois of the English tongue, Irish forms being, naturally, the most frequent. There are abrupt transitions from literary idiom to the colloquial, from patristic gravity to the slang of a speak-easy. 'Monkwords, marybeads jabber on their girdles: rogue-words, tough nuggets patter in their packets.'

Homer's vocabulary presents some astonishing anomalies. Recent discoveries have added considerably to our knowledge of the various Greek dialects, but nowhere has an example of the Homeric dialect been detected. In it we find Ionian, Aeolian, Cyprian and even Attic elements; the philologist is bewildered by its phonetic variability and the diversity of grammatical forms employed. Various theories have been proposed to explain these anomalies. It has been suggested that the rhapsodist varied the dialect in which he recited to suit that of his hearers, and that in the final redaction were embodied elements of the various transpositions which the poem had undergone. The theory is plausible. But we must assume that this habit of transposing the dialect of the poem to suit the audience was a very ancient one and had led to the creation of a mixed epic language from whose variable vocabulary the rhapsodists could borrow to suit the audience of the moment. This mixed dialect became the accepted language of the epos, and epic poets conformed to this convention. In much the same way, during two centuries, the troubadours composed their poems in a mixed dialect, Limousine, with an admixture of Provençal, Catalonian and Italian forms.[1]

It was on the Asia Minor coast [M. Bérard remarks] where members of different races found themselves in close contact and whither merchant-adventurers from overseas imported the idioms of their countries, that such a fusion of dialects would most naturally take place. I can see no other part of the Greek world where such a mixed tongue, triumphing over the opposition of local purists, would succeed in making its way and establishing itself.

The birthplace of the Homeric poems was, M. Bérard suggests, Miletus in Asia Minor.

Miletus was certainly a frequent port of call for the Levantine merchant-ships and Phoenician, Cilician, Egyptian and other traders established depots there or even demarcated settlements – 'camps' as they were then called.[2]

Like the Memphis described by Herodotus, Miletus had its Tyrian or Sidonian 'camp'. These Phoenicians, who had partially lost their maritime and commercial supremacy, continued their *métier* of middlemen. They had a permanent establishment in the 'camp', with a national temple in the midst: περιοικέουσι δε τὸ τέμενος τοῦτο Φοίνικες, Τύριοι· καλέεται δὲ ὁ χῶρος οὗτος ὁ συνάπας Τυρίων Στρατόπεδον.[3]

There they maintained their religious cults and customs, spoke their mother tongue and read or sang their national poems. The Cadmeans were marked out to serve as intermediaries between the Phoenicians of the Camp and the Hellenes of the City. These Cadmeans, who boasted of their Phoenician origin, would teach the latter to admire the products, customs, art and science of the superior race, the 'divine' race, whose sons they claimed to be; perhaps they even spoke the 'tongue of the gods', alluded to by the poet of the *Odyssey*. ... It was, I think it more than probable, at the court of the Neleid kings, under the patronage of a Cadmean aristocracy, that, about 900 or 850 B.C., there was composed this magnificent poem, the masterpiece of a great artist, that learned and skilful writer on whom the ages have bestowed the name of Homer.

1. M. Bréal, *Revue de Paris* (15 February 1903).
2. Or '*pales*', as such reserved areas were styled in Ireland. Dublin, too, was an important commercial centre in Viking times. 'Plundering in one country, these "merchant princes" sold the produce of their piracy in another, and Dublin was frequently their place of sale. Hence we find that Thorer, who had long been on Viking expeditions, went on a merchant voyage to Dublin, "as many were in the habit of doing".' Haliday (quoting the *Olaf Tryggv. Saga*).
3. Herodotus, II: 112.

This great artist was not, as a superficial judgement of his works
might lead us to believe, a mere inventor of enchanting fairy-tales, 'the
idle singer of an empty day'. 'A vain teratology, built from fables,'
Strabo tells us, 'would be contrary to the Homeric spirit.'[1] 'Homer's
tales are more accurate than those of his successors,' Strabo continues.
He was no miracle-monger, but subordinated his allegories, artifices,
and the popular appeal of his verse, to the advancement of knowledge,
especially in his account of the wanderings of Odysseus.

The *Odyssey* [M. Bérard observes] is not a mere collection of tales; it is a
geographical authority, depicting in a poetic form, but without any falsification,
a Mediterranean world which had its own maritime customs, its own geodesy
and theory of navigation, a language, commerce and '*Instructions Nautiques*'.
Once we have explored this inner sea of the Phoenicians, we can understand
both the general outline of the Odyssean adventure and its episodes; Ulysses
ceases to be a mythical figure wandering in the mist of legend, in fantastic fairy-
lands; he is a merchant-adventurer visiting shores familiar to the traders of
Sidon. The monsters he encounters – such as the hideous Scylla, who, from the
recesses of her cave, preys upon all who enter a narrow strait – were known to
the Phoenicians and noted in their pilots' manuals, as to our sailors of today (*vide
Instructions Nautiques*, No. 731, page 249) is known a certain cavern overlooking
the strait of Messina: 'Behind the cape stands Mount Scuderi, 1,250 metres in
height. Near the blunt summit of this mountain there is a cave from whose
mouth the wind issues, violently roaring.'

One of the most striking features of *Ulysses* is its extreme *accuracy*;
most, if not all, the characters are drawn from the life, some, indeed,
being mentioned under their real names. There is no falsification of
facts for the sake of effect, no 'vain teratology'.

In the course of his long study of Homeric origins M. Bérard demon-
strates that the poet of the *Odyssey* must have had access to, and carefully studied, some Phoenician record of voyages in the eastern and
western Mediterranean, a pre-Achaean 'Mirror of the Sea'. A very large
number of the Odyssean place-names are of Semitic origin; these were
the names under which the places came to be known to the earliest
Greek navigators. The latter translated the names into their own tongue,
and so each place had a pair of names – the Phoenician and the Greek.
For instance (*Odyssey* X: 135) Circe's island is named *Aiaie*. The 'island

1. Strabo, I: 2, 9. ἐκ μηδενὸς δὲ ἀληθοῦς ἀνάπτειν κενὴν τερατολογίαν οὐχ
ὁμερικόν.

of Circe' is an exact translation of the Semitic compound *Ai-aie*, the island of the hawk (Circe). The Hebrew word for 'hawk', *ai'a*, is, it may be noted, invariably feminine; the Greek κίρκος is a masculine form, used for both the male and the female hawk. The poet, meticulously accurate, has given a feminine termination to κίρκος. Again, the name 'Scylla' (Σκύλλη) is the hellenized form of the Semitic root *s-k-l* (*skoula*), meaning the rock. The poet has given his translation of the Semitic original in the form of an epithet 'Scylla the rocky' (Σκύλλην πετραίην, *Odyssey*, XII: 231). Other illustrations of the manner in which the Greek poet adapted to his purposes the Semitic names or words which he found in the Phoenician records on which he based his narrative will be observed in the course of my commentaries on the various episodes of *Ulysses*. Space does not permit me to set out at length the multifarious data from which M. Bérard infers the Phoenician origin of the *Odyssey*. It is clear, however, that in referring to his Homeric paradigm the author of *Ulysses* has had regard to this oriental background, and, though the data must be omitted, a brief résumé of M. Bérard's conclusions is necessary.

The *Ulysseid* (Ὀδύσσεια) appears to be a Phoenician *periplous* (log-book) transposed into Greek verse and a poetic legend according to certain very simple and typically hellenic principles: anthropomorphic personification of objects, humanization of natural forces, *hellenization*[1] of the raw material. By these methods, to which the Greeks owe so many of their myths and legends, was woven on to a stout, if coarse, Semitic canvas that typically Greek masterpiece, the *Odyssey*.

In the *Odyssey* imagination and fantasy play but a small part. Arrangement and logic were the poet's part in the work; he borrows his themes but shapes them in the Greek manner, endowing them with an anthropomorphic life; above all, he is at the greatest pains to compose and weld together his information in such a manner as to create a uniform whole. The Hellene is, first and foremost, a skilled arranger.

The poet invents nothing. He utilizes the facts given in the 'log'.... From a series of sketches he composes a picture, and this picture is an accurate copy of nature, though some parts of it are left in shadow and others placed in a high light. The picture is complete; the poet omits none of the facts which the records have described to him.

1. Cf. Mulligan's appeal to Stephen. 'If you and I could only work together we might do something for the island. Hellenize it.'

James Joyce's picture of Mr Bloom's day was composed, if for 'records' be substituted 'the author's memory', in exactly this manner.

The poem is obviously the work of a Hellene, while the 'log' is clearly the record of a Semitic traveller. The poet – Homer, if you will – was a Greek; the seafarer – Ulysses, as we known him – was Phoenician.

The author of *Ulysses* – James Joyce – is an Irishman; his wandering hero – Leopold Bloom – is a Jew.

In 'hellenizing' the log-book of Mr Bloom's journey through Dublin, the author has not only followed the Homeric precedent of carefully arranging his data (by the devices of rhythm and interlocking elements) and imposing on them the rule of a severe logic (the western man's way of synthesizing the runes of oriental intuition), but has also freely employed the anthropomorphic methods of his predecessor. Apart from the fact that in the relations between the principal characters of *Ulysses* we may discover the dramatization of certain theological or metaphysical abstractions and that, as will be seen in my notes on the episodes, abstract ideas are in several instances presented anthropomorphically, one of the peculiarities of Joyce's technique is his treatment of inanimate objects or parts of the body as if they had independent personal life. Mr Bloom watches a newspaper press at work.

Sllt. The nethermost deck of the first machine jogged forward its flyboard with sllt the first batch of quirefolded papers. Sllt. Almost human the way it sllt to call attention. Doing its level best to speak. The door too sllt creaking asking to be shut. Everything speaks in its own way. Sllt.

Stephen, passing the powerhouse, hears the dynamos: 'Beingless beings. Stop! Throb always without you and the throb always within. Your heart you sing of....'

The wobbling disk at the end of its course in a slot-machine 'ogles' the bystanders, a shirt hung on a line is 'crucified', growing hops are serpents entwining themselves on long sticks. This animation of the inert reaches its climax in the 'Circe' episode, where a folded fan stutters a creasy remonstrance, soap sings, a cap cross-examines its owner, and the End of the World turns somersaults.

In the same way the Greeks tended to conceive all nature, even their works of art or common use, in terms of humanity. They described a pillar, for instance, as if it were a living organism, a man; the capital was the *head* and the section joining this to the pedestal was a *neck*; the whole pillar was, according to its kind, *male or female*....

There existed even in antiquity, as Strabo records, two distinct schools of Homeric research. There were those who, like Eratosthenes, asserted that the poet was a mere inventor of fables and that it was idle to seek beneath the superficial beauties of his work a profound or permanent significance. But there was another school, the 'more Homeric' οἵ δ' Ὁμερικώτεροι τοῖς ἔπεσιν ἀκολουθοῦντες, who closely examined the text, 'following the words', and discovered that the poet was 'the pioneer of geographical research', and his narrative veridical. Behind a façade of symbols and anthropomorphism, they discerned the palace of truth, a cosmic apocalypse, justifying for the Homeric epics their proud device, the 'Bible of the Greeks'. If, in this study of *Ulysses*, I prefer the method of the more Homeric students described by Strabo, following the words, and in so doing, risk to share the obloquy of that

> scholiast whose unweary'd pains
> Made Horace dull and humbled Milton's strains

I would take refuge behind the aegis of the ablest of modern Homerists, his epigram: *il n'est jamais inutile de bien comprendre pour mieux admirer.*

Chapter 5

THE CLIMATE OF *ULYSSES*

THE interest shown today in the private lives of eminent men of letters may often seem excessive, even indiscreet, yet for the full appreciation of a writer's work it is often desirable to know something of his background, especially when that background is becoming obscured by the lapse of time. In the case of Joyce this knowledge will grow steadily harder to come by as the generation to which he belonged dies out and the décor of his formative years grows more and more like that of a period play, to which its seeming quaintness, conventions now outmoded, and a manner of living no longer practicable or even acceptable lend the defunctive lustre of a museum-piece. For, though the masterpiece may owe its being primarily to an uprush from the subliminal self (to use the phraseology of F. W. H. Myers in his great work on the *Human Personality*), not only the form – and the form is half the masterpiece – is due to the artist's cultural experience, but also the source from which it springs has been conditioned by his environment. In his *Psychology of Art* André Malraux, examining the conditions under which a work of art emerges, draws attention to a circumstance often overlooked where a greatly original genius is concerned.

A writer [Malraux tells us] traces his vocation back to the reading of a certain poem or a novel (or, perhaps, a visit to the theatre); a musician, to a concert he attended; a painter, to a painting he once saw. Never do we hear of the case of a man who, out of the blue so to speak, feels a compulsion to 'express' some scene or incident. 'I, *too*, will be a painter!' That cry might be the impassioned prelude of all vocations. An old story goes that Cimabue was struck with admiration when he saw the shepherd-boy, Giotto, sketching sheep. But, according to the true biographies, it is never the sheep that inspire a Giotto with the love of painting; but, rather, his first sight of the paintings of such a man as Cimabue. What makes the artist is the circumstance that in his youth he was more deeply moved by the sight of works of art than by that of the things which they portray. ... This [Malraux adds in a later chapter] is why every artist's career begins with the pastiche.

Joyce was no exception. At the age of twenty he published in the Dublin magazine, *St Stephen's*, an essay on that brilliant Irish poet, J. C. Mangan, containing the following passage:

Though even in the best of Mangan the presence of alien emotions is sometimes felt, the presence of an imaginative personality reflecting the light of imaginative beauty is more vividly felt. East and West meet in that personality (we know how): images interweave there like soft luminous scarves and words ring like brilliant mail, and whether the song is of Ireland or of Istambol it has the same refrain, a prayer that peace may come again to her who has lost her peace, the moonwhite pearl of his soul, Ameen. Music and odours and lights are spread about her, and he would search the dews and the sands that he might set another glory near her face. A scenery and a world have grown up about her face, as they will about any face which the eyes have regarded with love. Vittoria Colonna and Laura and Beatrice – even she upon whose face many lives have cast that shadowy delicacy, as of one who broods upon distant terrors and riotous dreams, and that strange stillness before which love is silent, Monna Lisa – embody one chivalrous idea, which is no mortal thing, bearing it bravely above the accidents of lust and faithfulness and weariness: and she whose white and holy hands have the virtue of enchanted hands, his virgin flower, the flower of flowers, is no less than these an embodiment of that idea.

Here the debt to Pater is obvious, and indeed implicitly acknowledged in the 'Monna Lisa' reference. The essay was published in May 1902, and Joyce went to Paris for the first time in the autumn of that year; thus at the time of writing he had not yet seen the picture at the Louvre, and his admiration merely echoes Pater's.

Poetry, Joyce writes elsewhere in this essay (and by poetry he means, I think, all creative writing), 'makes no account of history, which is fabled by the daughters of memory,[1] but sets store by every time less than the pulsation of an artery, the time in which its intuitions start forth, holding it equal in its period and value to six thousand years'. The similarities with the famous 'Conclusion' of Pater's *The Renaissance* (which we of Joyce's generation never tired of reiterating; it was indeed the aesthete's Credo) are obvious.

Not the fruit of experience, but experience itself is the end. A counted number of pulses only is given to us of a variegated, dramatic life. How may we see in them all that is to be seen in them by the finest senses? How shall we press most

1. Cf. *Ulysses*, page 21.

swiftly from point to point, and be present always at the focus where the greatest number of vital forces unite in their purest energy?[1] ... To burn always with this hard, gemlike flame, to maintain this ecstasy, is success in life. ... While all melts under our feet, we may well grasp at any exquisite passion, or any contribution to knowledge that seems by a lifted horizon to set the spirit free for a moment, or any stirring of the senses, strange dyes, strange colours and curious odours, or the work of the artist's hand, or the face of one's friend. Not to discriminate every moment some passionate attitude in those about us, and in the very brilliancy of their gifts some tragic dividing of forces on their ways, is, on this short day of frost and sun, to sleep before evening.

These sharp impressions, exquisite moments, are identical with what Joyce called 'epiphanies'[2] and to which several references are made in the course of Joyce's work. In this connexion Dr Theodore Spencer quotes, in his excellent introduction to *Stephen Hero*, an amusing passage from Dr Gogarty's autobiography, *As I was walking down Sackville Street*. 'Gogarty is spending the evening with Joyce and others; Joyce says "Excuse me" and leaves the room. "I don't mind being reported," Gogarty writes, "but to be an unwilling contributor to one of his Epiphanies is irritating."' (Some illustrations of Epiphanies were on view at the Joyce Exhibitions in Paris and London.)

While in *Chamber Music* the influence of the Elizabethans is evident, what Joyce aimed at above all, and frequently achieved, in his poems was that characteristically Latin elegance which he discerned in Horace's elegant simplicity,[3] in Virgil's jewelled phrases and in the work of certain French poets of the second half of the nineteenth century. Mr Frank Budgen, in *James Joyce and the Making of 'Ulysses'*, his fascinating reminiscences of Joyce during his residence in Zürich (1915–19), quotes a

1. Cf. *Ulysses*, page 175. 'Hold to the now, the here, through which all future plunges into the past.'
2. An illustration of a sharp impression of this order may be found in the episode of 'The Wandering Rocks', when Stephen is gazing at a jeweller's window.
3. It is perhaps significant that Joyce's earliest extant composition is an English version of Horace's Thirteenth Ode, Lib. III, made by him when he was fourteen. The last three lines have a felicity indeed remarkable when we consider their maker's youth:

> 'Be of the noble founts! I sing
> The oak-tree o'er thine echoing
> Crags, thy waters murmuring.'

Compared with Milton's juvenile version of the Fifth Ode, Lib. I, *Ad Pyrrham*, the Joycean rendering outdoes, in all respects, the Miltonic.

remark made by Joyce after a friend had read out to him the opening lines of Verlaine's *Spleen*:

> Les roses étaient toutes rouges,
> Et les lierres étaient tout noirs.
> Chère, pour peu que tu te bouges,
> Renaissent tous mes désespoirs.

'That', Joyce said, 'is perfection. No more beautiful poem has ever been made.'

Joyce sometimes spoke to me with appreciation of the training he received at Belvedere College, a Jesuit school in Dublin, to which he came at the age of eleven and where, besides the thorough grounding in the classics provided at all good schools of the period, he acquired a working knowledge of French and Italian, which served him well in later life. Flaubert is one of the three or four authors whose every line Joyce claimed to have read (he was also a great admirer of some of Tolstoy's shorter works of fiction), and *Dubliners*, published in 1914, a collection of *nouvelles*, while superficially resembling some of Maupassant's and Chehov's tales, has a texture more akin to Flaubert's.

A Portrait of the Artist as a Young Man (1916) is in the tradition of the autobiographical novels of the European romantic movement. In its first version (a fragment of which has been published under the original title, *Stephen Hero*) this affinity is still more apparent. Here again are indications of Pater's influence (Meredith's as well), and indeed the picture given by Joyce of himself in his young days has much in common with that of Pater's Marius the Epicurean, who had

a certain bookish air, the somewhat sombre habitude of the avowed scholar, which though it never interfered with the perfect tone, 'fresh and serenely disposed', of the Roman gentleman, yet qualified it by an interesting oblique trait, and frightened away some of his equals in age and rank. Already he blamed instinctively alike in his work and in himself, as youth so seldom does, all that had not passed a long and liberal process of erasure. The happy phrase or sentence was really modelled upon a closely finished structure of scrupulous thought. The sober discretion of his thoughts, his sustained habit of meditation, the sense of those negative conclusions enabling him to concentrate himself, with an absorption so entire, upon what is immediately here and now, gave him a peculiar manner of intellectual confidence, as of one who had indeed been initiated into a great secret.

This description applies in almost every detail to the personality of

Joyce as a young man, the impression he produced on his friends, and to his methods of work; for it was largely through a long and liberal process of erasure that *Stephen Hero* – that 'schoolboy's production' as Joyce severely called it – attained the stylistic virtuosity of the *Portrait*.

But, apart from these individual influences, there is a more general one, which is apt to be overlooked, though it did much to shape the genius of the author of *Ulysses* and the *Wake*. I have in mind the climate of his formative years: the *fin de siècle* and the opening of the twentieth century. There has been a tendency to overemphasize the Irish element in Joyce's work, because, for obvious reasons, he invariably chose Dublin as the setting of his narratives. But, in reality, he always aimed at being a European writer and, in his major works, linked up the local theme with wider references in Space and Time. And, similarly, the place of *Ulysses* is in the vanguard of English literature; stylistically (and the saying that the style is the man fully applies to Joyce) it has little or nothing in common with the self-consciously Irish literary movement so ably promoted by many of Joyce's Dublin contemporaries. There was, moreover, a much closer similarity than is realized today by many of his readers between Joyce's Dublin and the larger English residential towns – a resemblance for which, as a contemporary of Joyce and one who spent his youth in a fairly large west-country English town, I can personally vouch. The gossip in the pubs, where behind every bar you saw a Miss Douce or Mina Kennedy, was much the same; the repertoire of musical comedy, pantomime, and music-hall songs, and 'drawing-room ballads' (so many of which figure in *Ulysses* and the *Wake*) was identical; I can even remember a faintly sinister (though not aggressively obnoxious) eccentric who used to accost and talk to schoolboys in just the same manner as the chief character in 'An Encounter'. There were also many 'houses of decay' in which worthy but improvident gentlefolk who, as they would have put it, had seen better days were trying to keep up appearances. Yet, on the whole, the period preceding 'Bloomsday', if not a golden age, was a time of mild prosperity and, despite failing fortunes, the milieu in which we spent our early years enjoyed the most precious of freedoms – freedom from the fear of major cataclysms.

Thus in the nineties poets could, and did, fix their attention on their art, and subscribed to Gautier's dictum that perfection of form is beauty. They dreamt of creating the Perfect Lyric – some of them,

Dowson for example, brought it off – much as the detective-story writers of the next generation dreamt of concocting a Perfect Crime. Wilde achieved the Perfect Modern Comedy, and Morris, with his Kelmscott '*Chaucer*', the Perfect Book. For the young men of the time the writers' first duty, like that of the contemporary French painters, was deference to the *matière* of their art, and, much as in painting the artists were discarding the notion that the painter's function is to idealize things seen, to play on sentiments, or to point a moral, the writer aimed at creating in the medium of words something perfect in form and durable because of this perfection.

Needless to say, this care for form did not involve a disregard of content. The young men had much to say and said it boldly. Indeed, as Mr Osbert Burdett pointed out in his *The Beardsley Period* (which of the many books on the nineties shows perhaps the greatest insight into the spirit of the age), they aimed at what was called unflinching realism, one of its chief exponents being the Irishman, George Moore, who made no secret of his 'advanced' ideas. 'The healthy school is played out in England; all that could be said has been said; the successors of Dickens, Thackeray and George Eliot have no ideal, and consequently no language.... The reason of this heaviness of thought is that the avenues are closed, no new subject-matter is introduced, the language of English fiction has therefore run stagnant. But if the Realists should catch favour in England, the English tongue may be saved from dissolution, for with the new subjects they would introduce, new forms of language would arise.' And Mr Burdett, writing a quarter of a century ago, followed up this quotation with the query: 'Has this proved prophetic of *Ulysses*?'

Characteristic, likewise, of the period was its preoccupation with Sin, an entity (or nonentity) which fascinated the younger men as much as it appalled their parents. Writers and artists of that bygone age had the advantage over those of the present generation that there was a citadel of organized propriety on which to drop their incendiaries, and the ensuing blaze filled them and their admirers with mischievous delight. They rejoiced when such epithets as decadent or morbid were applied to their works. Thus, when writing to his publisher Grant Richards to announce the completion of *Dubliners*, Joyce spoke of 'the special odour of corruption which, I hope, floats over my stories'. That 'hope' was typically ninetyish.

Typical, too, of the period was a near-great Catholic writer whose first work appeared in the *Yellow Book*: Fr Rolfe ('Baron Corvo') whose career was the theme of a brilliant 'experiment in biography' by the late A. J. A. Symons, *The Quest for Corvo*. Indeed, had the Fates been kinder, that unhappy genius might have moved parallel, if on a somewhat lower plane, to Joyce's. Nicolas Crabbe, the hero of Rolfe's last novel, *The Desire and Pursuit of the Whole*, had a good deal in common with Stephen Dedalus, and the following description of Crabbe – even, *mutatis mutandis*, the tone of the writing – will have a familiar ring for readers of Joyce's early work.

He was very long-suffering, he hesitated hideously; but, when once he went forth to war, he persisted. Right, wrong, success, failure, expediency, inexpediency, had no significance for him then. He just tenaciously and idiorhythmically persisted. When you smashed his skull, and broke his ferocious pincers, and tore off his feelers and claws, in handfuls or one by one, with deliberately Christian cruelty or charity (the terms are synonymous, the method and effect of both are identical) he lay quite still – if he could, he limped, or dragged his mutilated remains, into some crevice – and grew new armour wherewith relentlessly to continue the affray.

Rolfe's feeling for, and deep knowledge of, ritual (his lifelong ambition was to become a priest) are apparent in that extraordinary and, again, largely autobiographical romance, *Hadrian the Seventh* (Rolfe's Hadrian is an imaginary successor to the famous Hadrian, the only Englishman ever elected Pope, to whom a reference is made in the 'Oxen of the Sun' episode) – of which D. H. Lawrence wrote: 'If some of it is caviare, at least it came out of the belly of a live fish.' Some of Rolfe's cadences and word-patterns are in a Joycean vein; as in this description of a death-bed. 'Already his lips were livid; they disclosed the purity of teeth clenched and continually strident.... Bloomed the abhominable unmistakeable pallor on the brow, where the soft caesarial hair was humid with the dew of the breath of death.' Also, Rolfe shared Joyce's fondness for out-of-the-way words, such as 'contortuplicate' and 'tolutiloquence' (a new coinage derived, through Sir Thomas Browne, from the Latin *tolutim*).

All who are familiar with the literature and art of France and England during this period cannot have failed to trace affinities in Joyce's early technique and in the 'Telemachia' of *Ulysses*. Likewise, that combination of naturalism, symbolism and tectonic precision which we see in, for instance, Seurat's art, has its literary counterpart in *Ulysses* and especially the *Wake*; indeed the texture of the latter work (as was the method of its composition) is *pointilliste* throughout.

Yet, interesting as it would be to linger on the background of *Ulysses* and on the climate of the formative years of its creator – which synchronized with one of the most fertile periods of our literature: the period, to name but one of its great writers, of Henry James – we must be careful not to exaggerate the extent to which Joyce's genius was conditioned by his environment. For genius is necessarily unique, the privilege of an exceptional individual who often seems (like Henry James) born out of his due time; or, more exactly, is not esteemed at his true value by his own generation. No doubt in the early work and in the opening episodes of *Ulysses* we can see *fin de siècle* influences in the handling of the themes and in the style, but these are characteristic of the artist 'as a young man'; once the Odyssey proper gets under way (with Bloom's appearance on the scene) both style and treatment show an unprecedented freedom. That the first three episodes are presented in a manner resembling that of the earlier works should not be taken to mean that here Joyce was using a literary form that was more personal or came more naturally to him. He is merely reflecting in the style the personality of Stephen Dedalus in 1904, the earnest, narcissistic, young aesthete, just as in the 'Cyclops' episode the style mirrors the personality of that engaging vulgarian, the narrator.

Whereas in the case of most great writers maturity brings a crystallization, a *maîtrise* controlling the instinctual drive and guiding it down well-defined channels, Joyce's genius had, right to that amazing climax, *Finnegans Wake*, a flexibility, an inventiveness, a gift of metamorphosis which, though we may see analogies in the work of some great painters (Picasso is an obvious example), must surely be almost unique in literature.

PART TWO

THE EPISODES

1. TELEMACHUS

SCENE	The Tower
HOUR	8 a.m.
ART	Theology
COLOURS	White, gold
SYMBOL	Heir
TECHNIC	Narrative (young)

THE first three episodes of *Ulysses* (corresponding to the Telemachia of the *Odyssey*) serve as a bridge-work between the *Portrait of the Artist as a Young Man* and the record of Mr Bloom's adventures on the memorable date of 16 June 1904. The closing lines of the *Portrait* (extracts from the diary of Stephen Dedalus) not only throw considerable light on Stephen's character but also contain premonitions of certain of the motifs which (as I have suggested in my introduction) are essential to the understanding of *Ulysses*.

April 26. Mother is putting my new secondhand clothes in order. She prays now, she says, that I may learn in my own life and away from home and friends what the heart is and what it feels. Amen. So be it. Welcome, O life! I go to encounter for the millionth time the reality of experience and to forge in the smithy of my soul the uncreated conscience of my race.

April 27. Old father, old artificer, stand me now and ever in good stead.

Thus Stephen invokes the example and patronage of the inventor of the labyrinth, first artificer to adapt the reality of experience to the rite of art,[1] first flying man, teacher of 'transcendental mysteries' and of astrology,[2] in the huge task he has set before him.

A little over a year has passed since Stephen recorded these entries in his diary. During this period he has encountered something of the reality of experience – a taste of Parisian life, the shock of his mother's death, and the hard constraint of earning his living by distasteful work

---

1. 'The period represented by the name of Daedalus was that in which such forms [the conventional forms of art] were first broken through, and the attempt was made to give a natural and lifelike impression to statues, accompanied, as such a development in any branch of art always is, by a great improvement in the mechanics of art.' Smith's *Dictionary of Biography and Mythology*.

2. According to Lucian.

(as teacher in a small school). But most 'realistic' of all, perhaps, is his daily contact with 'Buck' (Malachi) Mulligan, a cynical medical student, deliberately boorish in manners, with an immense repertoire of lewd jests and blasphemous doggerel. Stephen is living with Mulligan in a disused Martello tower, overlooking Dublin Bay; Stephen pays the rent but Mulligan insists on keeping the key.

The opening scene is enacted on the platform of this tower. Mulligan comes forth from the stairhead 'bearing a bowl of lather on which a mirror and razor lay crossed'.

Holding up the bowl he intones:

Introibo ad altare Dei.

(*Ulysses* thus opens on a ritual note, the chant of an *introit* on the summit of a round tower and the elevation of a bowl bearing the holy signature.)

Presently Stephen joins Mulligan who, thrusting a hand into Stephen's upper pocket, says:

'Lend us a loan of your snotrag[1] to wipe my razor.'

Stephen suffered him to pull out and hold up on show by its corner a dirty crumpled handkerchief. Buck Mulligan wiped the razorblade neatly. Then, gazing over the handkerchief, he said:

'The bard's noserag. A new art colour for our Irish poets: snotgreen. You can almost taste it, can't you?'

In sudden Swinburnean mood Mulligan hails the 'great sweet mother'.

'*Thalatta! Thalatta!* She is our great sweet mother. Come and look.'

Stephen stood up and went over to the parapet. Leaning on it he looked down on the water and on the mailboat clearing the harbour mouth of Kingstown.

'Our mighty mother,' Buck Mulligan said.

Abruptly Mulligan swings round and reproaches Stephen for his conduct at his mother's deathbed.

'You could have knelt down, damn it, Kinch,[2] when your dying mother asked you. I'm hypoborean as much as you. But to think of your mother begging you with her last breath to kneel down and pray for her. And you refused. There is something sinister in you. ...'

1. The Oxford Dictionary proscribes the word 'snot' and its adjective as 'not in decent use'; but the latter, anyhow, has been canonized by the pious George Herbert in *Jacula Prudentum*: 'Better a snotty child than his nose wiped off.'
2. 'Kinch the knifeblade' is Mulligan's nickname for Stephen.

They continue talking and presently Mulligan grows aware that Stephen is nursing a grievance against him.

'What is it?' Buck Mulligan asked impatiently. 'Cough it up. I'm quite frank with you. What have you against me now?'

They halted, looking towards the blunt cape of Bray Head that lay on the water like the snout of a sleeping whale. Stephen freed his arm quietly.

'Do you wish me to tell you?' he asked. ...

'You were making tea,' Stephen said, 'and I went across the landing to get more hot water. Your mother and some visitor came out of the drawingroom. She asked you who was in your room.'

'Yes?' Buck Mulligan said. 'What did I say? I forget.'

'You said,' Stephen answered, '*O it's only Dedalus whose mother is beastly dead.*'

A flush which made him seem younger and more engaging rose to Buck Mulligan's cheek.

'Did I say that?' he asked. 'Well? What harm is that?'

He shook his constraint from him nervously.

'And what is death,' he asked, 'your mother's or yours or my own? You saw only your mother die. I see them pop off every day in the Mater and Richmond and cut up into tripes in the dissecting room. It's a beastly thing and nothing else. It simply doesn't matter. You wouldn't kneel down to pray for your mother on her deathbed when she asked you. Why? Because you have the cursed jesuit strain in you, only it's injected the wrong way. To me it's all a mockery and beastly. ... Absurd! I suppose I did say it. I didn't mean to offend the memory of your mother.'

He had spoken himself into boldness. Stephen, shielding the gaping wounds which the words had left in his heart, said very coldly:

'I am not thinking of the offence to my mother.'

'Of what, then?' Buck Mulligan asked.

'Of the offence to me,' Stephen answered.

Buck Mulligan swung round on his heel.

'O, an impossible person!' he exclaimed.

For breakfast in the living-room of the tower they are joined by Haines, a young Englishman who is lodging with them, a literary tourist in quest of Celtic wit and twilight. Mulligan presides at the meal.

'Bless us, O Lord, and these thy gifts. Where's the sugar? O, jay, there's no milk.'

Buck Mulligan sat down in a sudden pet.

'What sort of a kip is this?' he said. 'I told her to come after eight.'

While they are taking breakfast the old milkwoman arrives; Stephen
watched her pour into the measure and thence into the jug rich white milk, not
hers. Old shrunken paps. She poured again a measureful and a tilly. Old and
secret she had entered from a morning world, maybe a messenger. ... Crouching by a patient cow at daybreak in the lush field, a witch on her toadstool, her
wrinkled fingers quick at the squirting dugs. They lowed about her whom they
knew, dewsilky cattle. Silk of the kine and poor old woman, names given her
in old times. A wandering crone, lowly form of an immortal serving her conqueror and her gay betrayer, their common cuckquean, a messenger from the
secret morning. To serve or to upbraid, whether he could not tell: but scorned
to beg her favour.

'Silk of the kine' and 'poor old woman' are old names for Ireland;
in the milkwoman Stephen sees a personification of Ireland and in his
musings we discern his attitude to the 'dark Rosaleen' school of thinkers.
He refuses to cringe to the narrow patriots who surround him and to
exploit the sentimentalism in favour with the Dublin literary group.
Thus, watching Mulligan shave holding up a cracked mirror ('I pinched
it out of the skivvy's room'), Stephen bitterly observed:

It is a symbol of Irish art. The cracked lookingglass[1] of a servant.

Haines, impressed by Stephen's epigram, asks if he may make a collection of his sayings.

'Would I make money by it?' Stephen asked.
Haines laughed and, as he took his soft grey hat from the holdfast of the ham-
mock, said:
'I don't know, I'm sure.'
He strolled out to the doorway. Buck Mulligan bent across to Stephen and
said with coarse vigour:
'You put your hoof in it now. What did you say that for?'
'Well?' Stephen said. 'The problem is to get money. From whom? From the
milkwoman or from him. It's a toss up, I think.'

(Stephen cynically speculates which country is the more exploitable.)
After breakfast they walk to the sea and Mulligan bathes. Haines sits
on a rock, smoking.

Stephen turned away.
'I'm going, Mulligan,' he said.

1. An echo of Oscar Wilde. 'I can quite understand your objection to art being
treated as a mirror. You think it would reduce genius to the position of a cracked
looking-glass.' *Intentions* (1894), page 31.

'Give us that key, Kinch,' Buck Mulligan said, 'to keep my chemise flat.'

Stephen handed him the key. Buck Mulligan laid it across his heaped clothes.

'And twopence,' he said, 'for a pint. Throw it there.'

Stephen threw two pennies on to the soft heap. Dressing, undressing. Buck Mulligan erect, with joined hands before him, said solemnly:

'He who stealeth from the poor lendeth to the Lord. Thus spake Zarathustra.'

His plump body plunged.

'We'll see you again,' Haines said, turning as Stephen walked up the path and smiling at wild Irish.

Horn of a bull, hoof of a horse, smile of a Saxon.

Stephen is the central figure in this episode (as in the two following: 'Nestor', 'Proteus'). Despite the encounters he has had with the reality of experience, he remains the young man we knew in the *Portrait of the Artist*. That book was, doubtless, autobiographical in the main, and, in this episode, too, a personal note is discernible. But Stephen Dedalus represents only one side of the author of *Ulysses*, the juvenile, self-assertive side, unmodified by maturer wisdom. The balance is redressed by the essentially 'prudent' personality of Mr Bloom, who is, indeed, as several critics have pointed out, not merely the protagonist of the book, but a more likeable character than Stephen. The somewhat irritating intransigence of the latter – his insistence on the servility of Ireland, Irish art, all things Irish, and his fanatical refusal to kneel at his mother's deathbed[1] – is a sign of immaturity, far removed from the tolerant indifference (to all but aesthetic problems) of the author. Indeed, Stephen Dedalus, as we see him in the *Portrait* and these early episodes of *Ulysses*, could hardly of himself have created a Leopold Bloom, that lively masterpiece of Rabelaisian, human, and rich earthiness. From what we learn of the hero of *Ulysses*, it is easier to believe that a Leopold Bloom, enlightened and refined by a copious, if eclectic, course of philosophy, logic, rhetoric, metaphysics, and drawing upon the resources of his own prodigious memory, might have been the creator of Stephen Dedalus, his 'spiritual son'.

*

1. Actually this incident, Mr Stanislaus Joyce tells us, 'has been overdramatized'. 'The order (to kneel and pray) was given in a peremptory manner by an uncle, and it was not obeyed; Joyce's mother by then was no longer conscious.' (*Recollections of James Joyce, by his Brother*, The James Joyce Society.) It must be borne in mind that *Ulysses*, like the *Portrait*, is not a mere *reportage* but, supremely, a work of art, stylized as are Byzantine figures, or El Greco's.

We have not yet entered upon the *Odyssey* proper and the Homeric recalls in this and the two following episodes are less precise than those
in later chapters which deal with the adventures of Mr Bloom. Some
general correspondences, however, may be noted between the presentation of Stephen's character and circumstances in this episode and the
Telemachia, or prelude of the *Odyssey*.

The first two Books of the Greek epic describe the plight of Telemachus in his father's palace at Ithaca, where the suitors of his mother
Penelope are in possession, wasting his substance, mocking his helpless-
ness. 'Telemachus,' the suitor Antinous says, 'never may Cronion make
thee king in seagirt Ithaca, which is of inheritance thy right.' Thus, too,
Buck Mulligan lords it in the Martello tower; Stephen pays the rent
but Mulligan keeps the key. The 'Buck' is evidently far wealthier than
Stephen, yet he makes Stephen hand him 'twopence for a pint', and
demands that when Stephen gets his pay from the school that morning
he shall not only lend him 'a quid' but bear the expenses of a 'glorious
drunk to astonish the druidy druids'. In talking with Stephen he usually
adopts the patronizing, bullying tone of Antinous with Telemachus.

Stephen in the *Portrait* declares that he will use for his defence 'the
only arms I allow myself to use, silence, exile and cunning'. Those were
the only arms of Telemachus, defenceless among the overweening
wooers of Penelope.[1] And, like Stephen, 'Japhet in search of a father'
(as Mulligan calls him), Telemachus sets out from Ithaca to Pylos in
quest of his father, Odysseus, ten years absent from home.

Each personage of the *Odyssey* has his appointed epithet and, when
he is about to speak, the passage is generally introduced by a set formula.
(Homer, unlike modern writers, always uses the introductory 'he said',
'he asked', 'he replied', etc., when one of his characters speaks; in this
practice he is followed by Joyce.) The formula for Telemachus is:

$$\text{Τὸν δ' αὖ Τηλέμαχος πεπνυμένος ἀντίον ηὔδα}$$

Butcher and Lang translate: 'Then wise Telemachus answered him
and said …' In this rendering the literal meaning of πεπνυμένος is not
sufficiently brought out. M. Bérard's translation seems more exact:
'*Posément Télémaque le regarda et dit …*' This version also elicits the full

1. Not till Athene gave him heart did Telemachus quit his 'moody brooding',
the silence of despair. When, encouraged by the goddess, he told Penelope that he
was at last going to speak 'like a man', 'in amaze she went back to her chamber.'
(*Odyssey*, I: 360.)

meaning of Homer's ἀντίον. Telemachus, like Hamlet, has a trying part to play. He has acquired, perforce, a wisdom beyond his years and learnt to act and speak *posément*, deliberately, to take thought before he speaks and to hide his thoughts beneath a veil of ambiguity or reticence.

In a brilliant, but (as it seems to me) unjustified diatribe on the personality of the author of *Ulysses* as depicted (or supposed to be depicted) in the character of Stephen Dedalus, a distinguished polemist has ridiculed Stephen's habit (especially noticeable in this episode) of answering people 'quietly', and the languid deliberation of his movements. But it is obvious that these mannerisms are in keeping with his Hamlet-Telemachus role; they are the defences of a character unable to take arms against a sea of troubles, yet determined to preserve his personality in the face of scorn and enmity. Telemachus is one who 'fights from afar', *au-dessus de la mêlée*.

The old milkwoman, 'witch on her toadstool', in whom Stephen saw a personification of Ireland, reappears under the name of Old Gummy Granny in the 'Circe' episode.

[*Old Gummy Granny in sugarloaf hat appears seated on a toadstool, the deathflower of the potato blight on her breast.*]

STEPHEN: Aha! I know you, grammer! Hamlet, revenge! The old sow that eats her farrow![1]

OLD GUMMY GRANNY [*rocking to and fro*]: Ireland's sweetheart, the king of Spain's daughter alanna. Strangers in my house, bad manners to them! [*She keens with banshee woe.*] Ochone! Ochone! Silk of the kine! [*She wails.*] You met with poor old Ireland and how does she stand?

STEPHEN: How do I stand you? The hat trick! Where's the third person of the Blessed Trinity? Soggarth Aroon? The reverend Carrion Crow.[2]

When a drunken British soldier is about to knock Stephen down, Gummy Granny thrusts a dagger towards Stephen's hand.

OLD GUMMY GRANNY: Remove him, acushla. At 8.35 a.m. you will be in heaven and Ireland will be free.

She is a recall of Mentor, or rather of that other 'messenger from the secret morning', Athene, who in the likeness of Mentor in fashion and in voice drew nigh to Telemachus, to serve and to upbraid, and hailed

---

1. 'Ireland is the old sow that eats her farrow.' *A Portrait of the Artist*, page 238.
2. Stephen has a trinity of masters, as he tells Haines: British, Irish and the holy Roman catholic and apostolic church.

him in winged words, bidding him be neither craven nor witless, if he has a drop of his father's blood and a portion of his spirit.

The symbol of this episode is 'heir' (obviously appropriate to 'Telemachus') and in it the themes of maternal love (perhaps, as Stephen says elsewhere, 'the only true thing in life') and of the mystery of paternity[1] are first introduced. Haines speaks of the 'Father and the Son idea. The Son striving to be atoned with the father', and Stephen muses on certain heresies of the Church, concerning the doctrine of consubstantiality.

Like Antinous and the other suitors, Mulligan and his ilk would despoil the son of his heritage or drive him into exile.

A voice,[2] sweettoned and sustained, called to him from the sea. Turning the curve he waved his hand. It called again. A sleek brown head, a seal's far out on the water, round.

Usurper.

Finally, the heir is a link between the past and the generations of the future, as this episode is between the *Portrait* and Mr Bloom's Odyssey which is to follow.

Another theme introduced here is Stephen's remorse for his (averred) refusal to obey the last wish of his mother – Agenbite of Inwit.[3] The vision of his mother's deathbed haunts Stephen's thoughts by day and his dreams by night.

In a dream, silently, she had come to him, her wasted body within its loose graveclothes giving off an odour of wax and rosewood, her breath bent over him with mute secret words, a faint odour of wetted ashes.

Her glazing eyes, staring out of death to shake and bend my soul. On me alone. The ghostcandle to light her agony. Ghostly light on the tortured face. Her hoarse loud breath rattling in horror, while all prayed on their knees. Her eyes on me to strike me down. *Liliata rutilantium te confessorum turma circumdet: iubilantium te virginum chorus excipiat.*

Ghoul! Chewer of corpses!

The last exclamation is characteristic. To Stephen God is the dispenser of death, *dio bòia*, hangman God, as 'the most Roman of catholics' call him. His blasphemy is the cry of a panic fear, fear of the Slayer, whose sword is lightning, which reaches its climax in the episode of the

1. See Chapter 3, § 4, of my Introduction (p. 60).   2. Mulligan's.
3. *Agenbite of Inwit* (remorse of conscience) is the title of a fourteenth-century work by Dan Michel of Northgate.

'Oxen of the Sun' where a black crash of thunder interrupts the festivities at the house of birth.

The sacral bowl of lather, in mockery elevated by Mulligan,[1] becomes a symbol of sacrifice and is linked in Stephen's mind with his mother's death and the round expanse of bay at which he gazes from the summit of the tower. 'The ring of bay and skyline held a dull green mass of liquid. A bowl of white china had stood beside her deathbed holding the green sluggish bile which she had torn up from her rotting liver. ...' And, later, when a cloud begins to cover the sun slowly, shadowing the bay in deeper green, 'it lay behind him, a bowl of bitter waters. Fergus' song: I sang it alone in the house, holding down the long dark chords. Her door was open: she wanted to hear my music. Silent with awe and pity I went to her bedside. She was crying in her wretched bed. For those words, Stephen: love's bitter mystery.'

> *And no more turn aside and brood*
> *Upon love's bitter mystery*
> *For Fergus rules the brazen cars ...*

1. The 'art' of this episode is 'theology': hence the frequent use of religious symbolism. Cf. the theotechny of the first book of the *Odyssey*.

2. NESTOR

SCENE	The School
HOUR	10 a.m.
ART	History
COLOUR	Brown
SYMBOL	Horse
TECHNIC	Catechism (personal)

IT is 10 a.m. and Stephen is engaged in giving a history lesson to his pupils at Mr Deasy's school. The work is distasteful, and *history*, the 'art' of this episode as well as the subject he is teaching, seems to him, as he says, a nightmare – an incubus risen from the charnel-house, like the ghost of murdered Denmark, to suck the lifeblood of the present, the little time man has to be himself.

Stephen is catechizing[1] his inattentive class.

'You, Cochrane, what city sent for him?'

'Tarentum, sir.'

'Very good. Well?'

'There was a battle, sir.'

'Very good. Where?'

The boy's blank face asked the blank window.

Fabled by the daughters of memory. And yet it was in some way if not as memory fabled it. A phrase, then, of impatience, thud of Blake's wings of excess. I hear the ruin of all space, shattered glass and toppling masonry, and time one livid final flame. What's left to us then?

'I forget the place, sir. 279 B.C.'

'Asculum,' Stephen said, glancing at the name and date in the gorescarred book.

'Yes, sir. And he said: *Another victory like that and we are done for.*'

That phrase the world had remembered. ...

Characteristically Stephen poses to himself the problem of the 'ifs' of history and finds solution in the Aristotelian definition of movement.

Had Pyrrhus not fallen by a beldam's hand in Argos or Julius Caesar not been knifed to death. They are not to be thought away. Time has branded them and

1. The technic of this, the second, episode of the prologue, 'catechism (personal)', is balanced by the 'catechism (impersonal)' of the second episode ('Ithaca') of the epilogue.

fettered they are lodged in the room of the infinite possibilities they have ousted. But can those have been possible seeing that they never were? Or was that only possible which came to pass? Weave, weaver of the wind.... It must be a movement then, an actuality of the possible as possible.

There is a call 'Hockey!' and the boys rush out of the classroom to their game. One, Cyril Sargent, remains behind; an awkward, slow-witted boy, he has made a mess of his arithmetic lesson and been ordered by Mr Deasy to do his sums again. As Stephen helps him to solve the problem, thoughts flash through his mind of that eastern world where dark men first probed the mystery of number and coined a magic lore.

Across the page the symbols moved in grave morrice, in the mummery of their letters, wearing quaint caps of squares and cubes. Give hands, traverse, bow to partner: so: imps of fancy of the Moors. Gone too from the world, Averroes and Moses Maimonides, dark men in mien and movement, flashing in their mocking mirrors the obscure soul of the world, a darkness shining in brightness which brightness could not comprehend.

At the same moment Mr Bloom's thoughts too (see the 'Lotus-eaters') are turning eastward and he is about to enter the 'mosque' of the Hammam. The themes of the morrice (Moorish) dance of the *indices* and the mocking mirrors of eastern mystics recur several times in *Ulysses*. Thus, in the 'Circe' episode where so many of the abstractions and symbols of *Ulysses* are materialized, there is a grave, ceremonious morrice dance and Mr Bloom observes his image in a 'mocking mirror'.

Mr Deasy at last releases Sargent and calls Stephen to his study for a 'little financial settlement'. As he hands Stephen his salary he tenders, too, sage counsel on the virtues of economy and airs his views on Anglo-Irish history and the Jewish influence in English affairs.

'Old England [he says] is dying.... Dying ... if not dead by now.'

His words awake a Blakean echo in Stephen's mind.

> *The harlot's cry from street to street*
> *Shall weave old England's winding sheet.*

The very atmosphere of Mr Deasy's study is 'historical' – it bears for Stephen an impress of the 'dingdong round' of cyclical return described by Vico. (It is significant that the name of Vico occurs in this episode, in a reference to Vico Road, Dalkey.)

Stale smoky air hung in the study with the smell of drab abraded leather of its chairs. As on the first day he bargained with me here. As it was in the beginning, is now. On the sideboard the tray of Stuart coins, base treasure of a bog: and ever shall be. And snug in their spooncase of purple plush, faded, the twelve apostles having preached to all the gentiles: world without end.

Mr Deasy has a strong sense of public duty; at present he is much exercised by the outbreak of foot-and-mouth disease in Ireland and, while Stephen waits, he concocts a letter to the papers on this subject, for the publication of which Stephen will, he hopes, move his 'literary friends'.

… In every sense of the word take the bull by the horns. Thanking you for the hospitality of your columns.

Stephen undertakes the commission.

As he is going, Mr Deasy runs after him to put a final question, the last of the catechism.

'Ireland, they say, has the honour of being the only country which never persecuted the Jews. Do you know that? No. And do you know why?'
'Why, sir?' Stephen asked, beginning to smile.
'Because she never let them in,' Mr Deasy said solemnly.

Fourteen hours later, Mr Bloom, 'false Messiah', Hungarian Jew, after suffering persecution at the hands of a patriot Irishman, paternally takes Stephen, drugged in the stews of Circe, under his wing.

*

In this description of the old headmaster, Mr Deasy, there are several recalls of the 'old knight' Nestor whose palace was Telemachus's first halting-place in his search for Odysseus. Nestor, as Athene tells the young man, is one who gives 'unerring answer, for he is very wise'. He is one who 'above all men knows judgement and wisdom'. The Homeric formula γερήνιος ἱππότα Νέστωρ is usually translated 'the knight Nestor of Gerenia', but it seems more probable[1] that γερήνιος is an adjectival form of γέρων, 'the old man'. Mr Deasy, like Nestor, is a rather pompous old gentleman (stress is laid on his age: 'he raised his forefinger and beat the air oldly'; his eyes are dead till, in a sunbeam, they 'come to blue life'), conservative in outlook, who is always ready to dispense sage counsel to the young.

1. See Victor Bérard, *Pénélope*, page 246.

Nestor is a knight, a 'tamer of horses'; they were a horsy stock, the Neleids, his ancestors. Mr Deasy says:

'I am descended from Sir John Blackwood who voted for the union. We are all Irish, all kings' sons. ... *Per vias rectas* was his motto. He voted for it and put on his topboots to ride to Dublin from the Ards of Down to do so.'

He stamps 'on gaitered feet'. His walls are covered with pictures of racehorses.

Framed around the walls images of vanished horses stood in homage, their meek heads poised in air: lord Hastings' Repulse, the duke of Westminster's Shotover, the duke of Beaufort's Ceylon, *prix de Paris*, 1866. Elfin riders sat them, watchful of a sign. He saw their speeds, backing king's colours, and shouted with the shouts of vanished crowds.

The symbol of this episode is the *horse*, noble houyhnhnm, compelled to serve base Yahoos. Stephen, too, is restless beneath the pedagogic yoke.

'I foresee,' Mr Deasy said, 'that you will not remain here very long at this work. You were not born to be a teacher, I think. Perhaps I am wrong.'
'A learner rather,' Stephen said.
And here what will you learn more?
Mr Deasy shook his head.
'Who knows?' he said. 'To learn one must be humble. But life is the great teacher.'

Pylos, 'the stablished castle of Neleus', the 'city of the gate' (the gate of Mr Deasy's school was an imposing affair with 'lions couchant on the pillars'), was situated near the mouth of the river Alpheus. The name of this river has interesting associations. The Semitic root *a-l-p* from which it is derived means 'ox' and is also the root of the first letter of the Hebrew alphabet, *Aleph*, and the corresponding Greek letter *Alpha* – the ox-letter. The river Alpheus figures in many legends which deal with oxen, amongst others, those of the Augean stables, the herds of Apollo and the cattle of Melampus. A famous cattlemarket (βουπράσιον) was held beside the Alpheus. Mr Deasy, true to Neleid tradition, is evidently much interested in cattle: 'Our cattle trade. ... Koch's preparation. Serum and virus. Percentage of salted horses. Rinderpest ... Allimportant question. ...' Allusions to this letter of Mr Deasy crop up frequently in the course of *Ulysses* and Stephen foresees that Mulligan will dub him with a new nickname: the bullockbefriending bard. There are many references elsewhere to bulls, Irish and others, especially in the episode of the 'Oxen of the Sun', where the bull, a symbol of fertility, is associated with the *birth theme*, in which Dr Curtius sees the geometrical point where all the basic motifs of *Ulysses* intersect. Alpha, the beginning of all – Adam's telephone number is, according to Stephen, *Aleph, alpha: nought, nought, one* – is specifically associated with the bull in a mention of the star Alpha: 'it blazes, Alpha, a ruby and triangled sign upon the forehead of Taurus.'[1]

In this episode we have one of the rare occasions in *Ulysses* where an Odyssean personage and the modern counterpart are mentioned side by side. Mr Deasy recalls the fatal women of history.

'A woman brought sin into the world. For a woman who was no better than she should be, Helen, the runaway wife of Menelaus, ten years the Greeks made war on Troy. A faithless wife first brought the strangers to our shore here, MacMurrough's wife and her leman O'Rourke, prince of Breffni. A woman brought Parnell low.'

The Helen–Mrs O'Shea correspondence is here explicit. With this speech we may compare Nestor's long narrative of Clytemnestra's treachery.[2] Mr Deasy mentions another hero of Irish history, the great Daniel O'Connell. 'You think me an old fogey and an old tory. I saw three generations since O'Connell's time. I remember the famine. Do you know that the orange lodges agitated for the repeal of the union twenty years before O'Connell did or before the prelates of your communion denounced him as a demagogue?' Thus Nestor, who is said to have ruled over *three generations* of men (*tria saecula*, as Latin writers record it), had as a friend in his early years the hero Heracles (associated in several legends with the river Alpheus); in a subsequent episode[3] an analogy is established between the strong man of Greece and the strong man of Irish nationalism. Nestor himself was no mean fighter, and even in his advanced years was 'distinguished above all others for drawing up horses and men in battle array'. 'I am a struggler now,' Mr Deasy says, 'at the end of my days. But I will fight for the right till the end.'

Nestor had many sons seated at the feast beside him when Telemachus presented himself, and one of these, Peisistratus, he delegated

1. *Ulysses*, page 395.　　　　　　2. *Odyssey*, III: 239–312.
3. See notes on the 'Hades' episode.

to be Telemachus's companion. Thus, under the headmaster's orders, one of the class of schoolboys, Cyril Sargent, stays behind with Stephen when the others have gone out to hockey.

The shouts of the mimic warfare on the hockey field sound in their ears as Stephen and Mr Deasy, who likes to 'break a lance' with youth, converse in the study.

'They[1] sinned against the light,' Mr Deasy said gravely. 'And you can see the darkness in their eyes. And that is why they are wanderers on the earth till this day.'

'Who has not?' Stephen said.

'What do you mean?' Mr Deasy asked.

He came forward a pace and stood by the table. His underjaw fell sideways open uncertainly. Is this old wisdom? He waits to hear from me.

'History', Stephen said, 'is a nightmare from which I am trying to awake.'

From the playfield the boys raised a shout. A whirring whistle: goal. What if that nightmare gave you a back kick?

'The ways of the Creator are not our ways,' Mr Deasy said. 'All history moves towards one great goal, the manifestation of God.'

Stephen jerked his thumb towards the window, saying:

'That is God.'

Hooray! Ay! Whrrwhee!

'What?' Mr Deasy asked.

'A shout in the street,' Stephen answered.

As in 'Telemachus' there is a rhythmic recurrence of the symbol 'bowl', so here of 'coin-shells'. Mr Deasy is a collector of coins and shells and, while Stephen is waiting to be paid, his (Stephen's) 'embarrassed hand moved over the shells heaped in the cold stone mortar: whelks and money cowries and leopard shells: and this, whorled as an emir's turban, and this, the scallop of Saint James. An old pilgrim's hoard, dead treasure, hollow shells.' Mr Deasy, like most historians (and schoolmasters), loves to keep things in order; he hoards his money in a little savings-box with a compartment for each kind of coin, and advises Stephen to get one for himself. '"Mine would often be empty," Stephen said.' Shells are for Stephen 'symbols of beauty and power'; coins are 'symbols soiled by greed and misery'. As Mr Deasy takes leave of Stephen at his gate and turns back to the school, 'on his wise shoulders through the checkerwork of leaves the sun flung spangles,

1. The Jews.

dancing coins'. References to 'shells' continue in the next episode ('Proteus'), in which certain of the esoteric motifs of *Ulysses* are introduced. Esoterics use the name 'shells' to designate bodies discarded by the soul, tenements emptied of life. The 'facts' of history, its dates, battles, marches and countermarches, alarums and excursions, are shells, hollow shells into which the historian vainly seeks to pour the life of his own quick imagination. Such life as they may seem to gain is fictive; their own has passed on and cannot be recalled. The mêlée of history, 'joust of life',[1] is ever pushing forward to new fronts, leaving on the abandoned field a débris of discarded vehicles, empty shells.

1. 'Again: a goal. I am among them, among their battling bodies in a medley, the joust of life. ... Jousts. Time shocked rebounds, shock by shock. Jousts, slush and uproar of battles, the frozen deathspew of the slain, a shout of spear spikes baited with men's bloodied guts.'

3. PROTEUS

SCENE	The Strand
HOUR	11 a.m.
ART	Philology
COLOUR	Green
SYMBOL	Tide
TECHNIC	Monologue (male)

THIS episode contains practically no action. Nothing happens, and yet in following the trail of Stephen's thoughts, as he idles on the Dublin strand, we encounter a diversity of experience as exciting as any tale of adventure in 'the land of Phenomenon'. In dealing with 'Proteus' I have thought it best to vary my practice of separating narrative from exposition, and to combine the excerpts from the text with a running commentary.

For the appreciation of this intricate episode it is necessary to bear in mind a triad of directive themes that permeate its fabric. First there is the Homeric narrative of the capture of Proteus (as told by Menelaus in the fourth book of the *Odyssey*) and the Egyptian background of that adventure; secondly, certain esoteric doctrines, notably that of metempsychosis (already dealt with in an introductory chapter), here combined with the symbol of the *tide*; lastly, the 'art' of this episode, *philology*, a conscious virtuosity in the handling of language as an end in itself and an exploitation of the affective resonance of words.

The encounter of Menelaus with Proteus, the 'old man of the sea', took place at the island of Pharos 'in the wash of the waves over against Egypt'. The name of this island is undoubtedly a Greek adaptation of the title *Pharaoh*, and *Proteus* is a transcription of the Egyptian title *Prouti*, the 'Sublime Porte', an Egyptian king who, Diodorus Siculus tells us, 'acquired the art of metamorphosis in the company of the astrologers'. An Egyptian legend relates that the prince Noferkephtah, accompanied by his wife Akhouri (like himself, an offspring of the *Prouti*), set out on a voyage to discover the magic Book of Thoth. He constructed a ship, a company of workers, and their tools, and, by reciting an incantation, endowed the puppets with life. With their aid he bored a hole in the waters of the Nile and discovered the Book under a nest of serpents, scorpions, and reptiles. A divine serpent lay coiled on the casket containing the Book. After pronouncing a charm of magic words he was able to slay the serpent which, thrice smitten, came thrice to life again. Thus he obtained the book and Akhouri read out the Words of Power.

Thereupon I bound the sky, earth, nightworld and waters with a spell. I knew all that was said by the birds of heaven, the fishes of the abyss, the animals. ... I saw the fishes of the deep for there was a divine power which made them rise to the surface of the waters.[1]

Thus Eidothea, daughter of Proteus, by her counsel and the gift of ambrosia, enabled Menelaus to capture the seagod and learn the way of his returning.

So often as the sun in his course hath reached the mid heaven, then forth from the brine comes the ancient one of the sea, infallible, before the breath of the West Wind, and the sea's dark ripple covers him. And around him the seals, the brood of the fair daughter of the brine, sleep all in a flock, stolen forth from the grey sea water, and bitter is the scent they breathe of the deeps of the salt sea.

And I will tell thee all the magic arts of that old man. First he will number the seals and go over them; but when he has told their tale and beheld them, he will lay him down in their midst, as a shepherd amid the sheep of his flock. So soon as ever ye shall see him couched, even then mind you of your might and strength, and hold him there, despite his eagerness and striving to be free.

Menelaus and his company accordingly lay in wait for Proteus.

We rushed upon him with a cry, and cast our hands about him, nor did that ancient one forget his cunning. Now behold, at the first, he turned into a bearded lion, and thereafter into a snake, and a pard, and a huge boar; then he took the shape of running water, and of a tall and flowering tree. We the while held him close with steadfast heart.

Conquered, Proteus instructs Menelaus of the way of his returning and the fate of his comrades, and, finally, of the manner of his own end. 'Thou, Menelaus, son of Zeus, art not ordained to die ... but the deathless god will convey thee to the Elysian plain and the world's end, where is Rhadamanthus of the fair hair, where life is easiest for men.'

In esoteric writings the name 'Proteus' has been aptly applied to the primal matter, the Akasa of the Brahmins, the Iliaster of Paracelsus.

---

1. See Victor Bérard, *Les Phéniciens et l'Odyssée*, II: 52.

The nature of the universe [Marcus Antoninus has observed] delights not in anything so much as to alter all things, and present them under another form. This is her conceit to play one game and begin another. Matter is placed before her like a piece of wax and she shapes it to all forms and figures. Now she makes a bird, then out of the bird a beast – now a flower, then a frog, and she is pleased with her own magical performance as men are with their own fancies.

'Ineluctable modality of the visible,' Stephen's monologue begins; 'at least that, if no more, thought through my eyes. Signatures[1] of all things I am here to read, seaspawn and seawrack, the nearing tide, that rusty boot. Snotgreen, blue-silver, rust: coloured signs.' (Surely the 'signature' of Bishop Berkeley is on this passage!) According to the mystics the thumb-marks of the Demiurge are apparent everywhere for him who has eyes to see and the 'might and strength' of a Menelaus to apprehend and hold the slippery object of apperception.

Their (the 'astral influences') signatures may be seen in the book of life belonging to every form, in the shape and size of features and limbs, in the lines of the hands.[2] ... They are the forces by which the Universal Mind puts his mark upon everything and those who are able to read may find the true history of everything written upon the leaves of its soul.[3]

Throughout his self-communings, as recorded in this episode, Stephen is trying to grasp, whether metaphysically or mystically, the eternal ideas that cast their shadow on the wall of the cave. Near the end of the episode he asks himself: 'Now where the blue hell am I bringing her beyond the veil? Into the ineluctable modality of the ineluctable visuality.' She whom Stephen is bringing beyond the veil is here the soul, but, in a flash, Psyche is transformed into 'the virgin at Hodges Figgis' window on Monday morning' who 'lives in Leeson park, with a grief and kickshaws, a lady of letters'.

An association between the plastic primordial matter of the universe

1. Cf. Mr Bloom's comment (page 363) as he, at sunset, contemplates the rock whereon Nausicaa revealed herself to him. 'Tide comes here a pool near her foot. Bend, see my face there, dark mirror, breathe on it, stirs. All these rocks with lines and scars and letters.' 'Scars' are history's sigils. Thus Stephen (page 24) consults a 'gore-scarred' history book to verify the date of the battle of Asculum.

2. In the 'Circe' episode (page 531) the whore Zoe 'reads' Stephen's hand. 'ZOE [examining Stephen's palm]: Woman's hand.
'STEPHEN [murmurs]: Continue. Lie. Hold me. Caress. I never could read His handwriting except His criminal thumbprint on the haddock.'

3. Hartmann, Magic, page 63. This is, of course, the extreme 'magical' view, expressed in magical terminology. Credat Judaeus Apella.

and the 'art' of this episode, 'philology', is suggested in the opening sentences. The interpretation of nature is an act of *reading*; the 'signs' or 'signatures' are there, plain to see, if we will but open our eyes and read them.

Now, by way of experiment, Stephen closes his eyes for a moment and excludes the modality of the visible. He hears his boots 'crush crackling wrack and shells': the 'ineluctable modality of the audible'.

I am getting on nicely in the dark. My ash sword hangs at my side. Tap with it: they do.[1] My two feet in his[2] boots are at the end of his legs, *nebeneinander*. Sounds solid: made by the mallet of *Los Demiurgos*. Am I walking into eternity along Sandymount strand?

Open your eyes now. I will. One moment. Has all vanished since? If I open and am for ever in the black adiaphane. *Basta!* I will see if I can see.

See now. There all the time without you: and ever shall be, world without end.

Two *Frauenzimmer*, midwives, appear in the offing; one of them is carrying a bag. 'What has she in the bag? A misbirth with a trailing navelcord. ... The cords of all link back, strandentwining cable of all flesh.' There follows the passage describing the 'umbilical telephone' to 'Edenville' which I have already discussed under the heading 'The *Omphalos*'. Stephen's vision of the primordial Eden, of Traherne's 'orient and immortal wheat, standing from everlasting to everlasting', is, doubtless, an allusion to the description which Proteus gave to Menelaus of the Elysian plain at the world's end. 'No snow is there, nor yet great storm, nor any rain; but alway oceans sendeth forth the breeze of the shrill West to blow cool on man: yea for thou hast Helen to wife, and thereby they deem thee to be the son of Zeus.' But this nirvanal paradise was, as M. Bérard points out, decidedly ill-suited to the Achaean race, 'that horde of warriors and pirates. There is no fighting there, no slaughter, not even contests of athletic prowess or skill. Such a paradise of silence and peace is singularly unfitted for these garrulous orators of the market-place, these lusty debaters, natural politicians.' The Homeric paradise resembles rather the Egyptian 'garden of Ialou', where the north wind, blowing steadily, softens ever the ardour of the sun, where harvests are rich and abundant and there is no more sorrow

1. A preparation for the rhythmic progress of the blind tuner – *Tap. Tap, tap. Tap, tap, tap* – in the last movement of the 'Sirens'' fugue.
2. Mulligan's.

or death. Never-failing canals ensure the coolth and fertility of that happy land, where 'the wheat is seven cubits in height, whereof two cubits go to the ear alone': orient and immortal. Such another paradise was the island-valley of Avilion,

> Where falls not hail, or rain, or any snow,
> Nor ever wind blows loudly; but it lies
> Deep-meadowed, happy, fair with orchard lawns
> And bowery hollows crown'd with summer sea.

Far removed, farther yet than Ithaca, is the Dublin of *Ulysses* from Avilion, Ialou, the Elysian plain. Yet, at moments, when Stephen stays to enjoy the new air of the morning and quits his 'moody brooding', he can feel the enchantment of that lost primordial paradise around him.

Et vidit Deus. Et erant valde bona. ... He watched through peacocktwittering lashes the southing sun. I am caught in this burning scene. Pan's hour, the faunal noon.[1] Among gumheavy serpentplants, milkoozing fruits, where on the tawny water leaves lie wide. Pain is far.

Stephen's pace slackens and, for a moment, he thinks of going to visit his 'nuncle Richie' (Richie Goulding, brother of Stephen's mother, appears in the flesh in the 'Sirens' episode). He seems to hear the voice of his father, Simon Dedalus, jeering at all the Goulding clan and Richie, that broken-down roisterer, in particular.

My consubstantial father's voice. Did you see anything of your artist brother Stephen lately? No? Sure he's not down in Strasburg terrace with his aunt Sally? Couldn't he fly a bit higher than that, eh? And and and and tell us, Stephen, how is uncle Si? O weeping God, the things I married into. De boys up in de hayloft. The drunken little costdrawer and his brother, the cornet player. Highly respectable gondoliers. And skeweyed Walter sirring his father, no less. Sir. Yes, sir. No, sir.

This passage illustrates one of the difficulties of Stephen's silent monologue; the reader has to reconstruct the scene and identify the speakers from hints thrown out. Stephen, who has left home to live with Mulligan, a 'bloody doubledyed ruffian' as Mr Dedalus calls him, pictures his father's speculations as to the way he spends his time. Mr Dedalus senior parodies Richard Goulding's mannerisms, 'And and and and tell

---

1. It was at this very hour of noon, and in such a 'burning scene', that Proteus was caught by Menelaus.

us ...', and jeers at the way the Goulding children have been brought
up.

House of decay, mine, his and all. You told the Clongowes gentry you had an
uncle a judge and an uncle a general in the army. Come out of them, Stephen.
Beauty is not there. Nor in the stagnant bay of Marsh's library where you read
the fading prophecies of Joachim Abbas. For whom? The hundredheaded rabble
of the cathedral close. A hater of his kind ran from them to the wood of madness, his mane foaming in the moon, his eyeballs stars. Houyhnhnm, horse-
nostrilled.

Here the mention of Marsh's Library (in St Patrick's close) recalls
to Stephen the famous dean of St Patrick's and he sees the houyhnhnm
in the face of its creator and a hydra in the horde of worshippers: Protean metamorphosis. 'Oval equine faces.' 'Abbas father, furious dean
what offence laid fire to their brains? Paff! *Descende, calve, ut ne nimium
decalveris.*' (Stephen quotes a prophecy of Joachim Abbas.) 'A garland
of grey hair on his comminated head see him me clambering down to
the footpace (*descende*), clutching a monstrance, basiliskeyed.' (Another
reptilian allusion. Stephen recalls the priest, 'a blowing red face ... garland of grey hair', whom he saw at the bathing-pool, and, for an instant, imagines himself, metamorphosed, in the priestly role; as we
learnt in the *Portrait*, Stephen was almost persuaded to enter the
Church.) 'Get down, bald poll! A choir gives back menace and echo,
assisting about the altar's horns, the snorted Latin of jackpriests moving
burly in their albs, tonsured and oiled and gelded, fat with the fat of
kidneys of wheat.' He sees himself in the skin of Swift and murmurs,
'Cousin Stephen, you will never be a saint', recalling Dryden's remark
to Swift, 'Cousin, you will never be a poet.'

Stephen once aspired to write 'deep' books, epiphanies, manifestations of Himself, which would be apprehended only after the great
cycle of a *manvantara* had rolled its course.

Books you were going to write with letters for titles. Have you read this F?
O yes, but I prefer Q. Yes, but W is wonderful. O yes, W. Remember your
epiphanies on green[1] oval leaves, deeply deep, copies to be sent if you died to
all the great libraries of the world, including Alexandria? Someone was to read
them there after a few thousand years, a mahamanvantara. Pico della Mirandola

1. The 'colour' of this episode is 'green', of the sea, of moonlight, of absinthe,
of Stephen's epiphanies, etc.

like. Ay very like a whale.[1] When one reads these strange pages of one long
gone one feels that one is at one with one who once. ...

The esoteric doctrines of *Manvantara* and *Pralaya* are, it is significant,
named for the first time in this episode, whose 'symbol' is the 'tide',
never-ceasing flux and reflux.

Man has a manvantara and pralaya every four-and-twenty hours, his periods
of waking and sleeping; vegetation follows the same rule from year to year as it
subsides and revives with the seasons. The world too has its manvantaras and
pralayas, when the tide-wave of humanity approaches its shore, runs through
the evolution of its seven races, and ebbs away again, and such a manvantara
has been treated by most exoteric religions as the whole cycle of eternity.[2]

Stephen walks on, treading a 'damp crackling mast', past unwhole-
some sandflats 'breathing upward sewage breath' (compare the 'deadly
stench' of the seals, Proteus's flock, which 'sorely distressed' Menelaus)
and a stogged porter-bottle. 'A sentinel: isle of dreadful thirst.' (Compare the 'isle of dreadful hunger' of Pharos; such isles of hunger and
thirst were only too familiar to Egyptian and Phoenician mariners.)
A view of the Pigeonhouse and the recall of a French pasquinade on
that holy bird lead his thoughts back to Paris days,[3] his 'latin quarter
hat' and his desperate attempt to get a money-order cashed at a Parisian
post-office which, characteristically enough, has put up the notice
Fermé, two minutes before time. The dramatization of a transient lust
to kill, in this passage, is perhaps a foretaste of the large-scale use of this
technique in the 'Circe' episode.

Proudly walking. Whom were you trying to walk like? Forget: a dispossessed. With mother's money order, eight shillings, the banging door of the
post office slammed in your face by the usher. Hunger toothache. *Encore deux
minutes.* Look clock. Must get. *Fermé.* Hired dog! Shoot him to bloody bits with
a bang shotgun, bits man spattered walls all brass buttons. Bits all khrrrrklak

---

1. *Hamlet*, III: 2.
2. A. P. Sinnett, *Esoteric Buddhism*, page 171.
3. Egypt (the town of Thebes in particular) was to the Achaeans what Paris was
to the Danes and is still to northern and western races, an arbiter of elegance for
certain kinds of apparel and an exponent of the art of *savoir vivre*. An old chronicle
tells that the Danish nobles 'sent their sons to Paris to prepare themselves not only
for the ecclesiastical career, but also to gain a knowledge of mundane affairs'. The
Achaeans adopted from the Egyptians the linen *chiton* and the supple coat of mail
(in lieu of leather garments and rigid armour). Stephen adopted the 'latin quarter
hat' and a taste for 'black' tea.

in place clack back. Not hurt? Oh, that's all right. Shake hands. See what I meant, see? O, that's all right. Shake a shake. O, that's all only all right.

At Paris, amid the matin incense of 'froggreen wormwood', the 'sweet-scented ambrosia' of a Parisian Eidothea, he came to know Kevin Egan, an exiled Irish conspirator, 'loveless, landless, wifeless'.[1] Kevin Egan tells Stephen tales of the revolutionary movement. 'How the head centre got away, authentic version. Got up as a young bride, man, veil, orange-blossoms, drove out the road to Malahide. Did, faith. Of lost leaders, the betrayed, wild escapes. Disguises, clutched at, gone, not here.' There is here an unmistakable allusion to the transformations of Proteus in the ineluctable grip of his captor. The thought of *disguises* recalls to Stephen the pretenders of history. 'For that you are pining, the bark of their applause? Pretenders: live their lives. The Bruce's brother, Thomas Fitzgerald, silken knight, Perkin Warbeck, York's false scion, in breeches of silk of whiterose ivory, wonder of a day, and Lambert Simnel, with a tail of nans and sutlers, a scullion crowned. All king's sons. Paradise of pretenders then and now.'

A woman and man approach, cockle-pickers, with their dog, itself proteiform as the tidal margin of the bay.

The dog yelped running to them, reared up and pawed them, dropping on all fours, again reared up at them with mute bearish fawning. Unheeded he kept by them as they came towards the drier sand, a rag of wolf's tongue red-panting from his jaws. His speckled body ambled ahead of them and then loped off at a calf's gallop. .... He rooted in the sand, dabbling, delving and stopped to listen to the air, scraped up the sand again with a fury of his claws, soon ceasing, a pard, a panther, got in spouse-breach, vulturing the dead.

The word 'panther' recalls to Stephen the Englishman Haines who, in his sleep, 'was raving all night about a black panther', and woke Stephen up.

After he woke me up last night same dream or was it? Wait. Open hallway. Street of harlots. Remember. Haroun al Raschid. I am almosting it. That man led me, spoke. I was not afraid. The melon he had he held against my face.

1. The theme of the exile whose return to his home is forbidden by the gods is common both to the story of Menelaus ('Which of the immortals is it that binds me here?') and the Noferkephtah legend. Thoth complained to Ra of Nofer-kephtah's larceny and Ra sent down from heaven a divine embargo against his return to Memphis, his home.

Smiled: creamfruit smell. That was the rule, said. In. Come. Red carpet spread. You will see who.

This dream, albeit vaguely, portends certain happenings in the course of the day: Mr Bloom's encounter with Stephen, his paternal aid in the street of harlots and his proposal that Stephen should come to stay at Eccles Street. The melon, as will be seen later, is a fruit with sentimental associations for Mr Bloom and the colour *red* (the ruby) is Mr Bloom's characteristic colour, for symbolic reasons.

After watching for a while the movements of the cockle-pickers, Stephen returns to the abstract world of metaphysics, the subjective idealism of the 'good bishop of Cloyne'.

His shadow lay over the rocks as he bent, ending. Why not endless till the farthest star? Darkly they are there behind this light, darkness shining in the brightness, delta of Cassiopeia, worlds. Me sits there with his augur's rod of ash, in borrowed sandals, by day beside a livid sea, unbeheld, in violet night walking beneath a reign of uncouth stars. I throw this ended shadow from me, manshape ineluctable, call it back. Endless, would it be mine, form of my form? Who watches me here? Who ever anywhere will read these written words? Signs on a white field. ... The good bishop of Cloyne took the veil of the temple out of his shovel hat: veil of space with coloured emblems hatched on its field. Hold hard coloured on a flat: yes, that's right. Flat I see, then think distance, near, far, flat I see, east, back. Ah see now: falls back suddenly, frozen in stereoscope. Click does the trick.

The veil, used by Bishop Berkeley for his conjuring trick, behind which Stephen leads Psyche, 'a woman to her lover clinging', is an anticipation of the 'veil' motif which is a leading theme in the episode which follows, 'Calypso'.

It is curious that a poet should have seen in the tide a symbol of encouragement for despondent hearts that hold 'the struggle naught availeth'; *trompe-l'œil*, surely, if picturesque, futile as the macrocosm itself 'founded upon the void', is the labour of the tides.

Under the upswelling tide he saw the writhing weeds lift languidly and sway reluctant arms, hising up their petticoats, in whispering water swaying and upturning coy silver fronds. Day by day: night by night: lifted, flooded and let fall. Lord, they are weary: and whispered to, they sigh. Saint Ambrose heard it, sigh of leaves and waves, waiting, awaiting the fullness of their times, *diebus ac noctibus injurias patiens ingemiscit*. To no end gathered: vainly then released, forth

flowing, wending back: loom of the moon. Weary too in sight of lovers, lasci-
vious men, a naked woman shining in her courts, she draws a toil of waters.

Five fathoms out there. Full fathom five thy father lies. At one he said. Found
drowned. High water at Dublin bar. Driving before it a loose drift of rubble,
fanshoals of fishes, silly shells. A corpse rising saltwhite from the undertow, bobbing landward, a pace a pace a porpoise. ... Sunk though he be beneath the
watery floor. ...

Bag of corpsegas sopping in foul brine. A quiver of minnows, fat of a spongy
titbit, flash through the slits of his buttoned trouserfly. God becomes man becomes fish becomes barnacle goose becomes featherbed mountain. ...

'The sea,' Professor Curtius has remarked, 'the primordial element,
giver and taker of life, beats about the Ulyssean world of life-experi-
ence. As in Mr T. S. Eliot's *Waste Land*, so through the work of Joyce
runs the motif of the Drowned Man.' It is interesting to note that Mr
Eliot's 'Drowned Man' was, like the prototype of Odysseus himself, a
Phoenician trader.

> Phlebas the Phoenician, a fortnight dead,
> Forgot the cry of gulls, and the deep sea swell
> And the profit and the loss.
> > A current under sea
> Picked his bones in whispers. As he rose and fell
> He passed the stages of his age and youth
> Entering the whirlpool.

In the first episode Stephen refers to Mulligan's rescue of a drowning
man[1] and hears a boatman speaking of a drowning case (the corpse was
expected to appear, 'bobbing landward', at about one o'clock). 'It'll
be swept up that way when the tide comes in.' In Mr Deasy's school
Stephen heard his class repeat *Lycidas*.

> For Lycidas, your sorrow, is not dead,
> Sunk though he be beneath the watery floor.

His mother he could not save. 'Waters: bitter death: lost.'
Other recalls of this motif will be observed in later episodes. The

---

1. The drowning man is said to have a flash of insight into 'the vast repository
where the records of every man's life as well as every pulsation of the visible cosmos are stored up for all eternity', that is to say, the 'Akasic records' alluded to by
Stephen in the 'Aeolus' episode. Mr Bloom, avatar of a Phoenician adventurer,
observes: 'drowning they say is pleasantest. See your whole life in a flash. But
being brought back to life no.'

rising of the corpse to the surface, porpoise-like, attended by a retinue of following fish, recalls a passage in the magic Book of Thoth discovered by Noferkephtah. 'I saw the fishes of the deep for there was a divine power which made them rise to the surface of the waters.' (Cf. the powers of the 'deathless Egyptian Proteus, who knows the depth of every sea'.) The last sentence of the passage quoted above ('God becomes man', etc.) is a variant of the kabalistic axiom of metempsychosis (as well as an allusion to the protean ebb and flow of living matter): 'a stone becomes a plant, a plant an animal, an animal a man, a man a spirit, and a spirit a god.'

Come. I thirst. Clouding over. No black clouds anywhere, are there? Thunderstorm. Allbright he falls, proud lightning of the intellect, *Lucifer, dico, qui nescit occasum.* No. My cockle hat and staff and his my sandle shoon. Where? To evening lands. Evening will find itself.

He took the hilt of his ashplant, lunging with it softly, dallying still. Yes evening will find itself in me, without me. All days make their end.

The allusions to the Crucifixion and Hamlet (Ophelia's song; again, death by drowning) are a preparation for certain correspondences which I will discuss in the episode of 'Scylla and Charybdis'; here, too, Stephen has a premonition of the 'black crack' of thunder which marks the climax of the episode of the 'Oxen of the Sun'. It is characteristic of Stephen's pride that he can never forget he is wearing the 'Buck's' cast-off shoes (another 'disguise'); still, on one occasion anyhow, he suffered such disguisement gladly. 'You were delighted when Esther Osvalt's shoe went on you: girl I knew in Paris. *Tiens, quel petit pied!*'

It has already been mentioned that the 'art' of this episode is 'philology', and the analogy between the incessant modifications of human speech and the transformations of Proteus, the movements of the tides, is obvious. Language is always in a flux of becoming, ebb or flow, and any attempt to arrest its trend is the folly of a Canute. Moreover, by the study of language we can often diagnose the processes of change operating in the world about us; for the written signs remain. (Corresponding to philology, we have, on the esoteric plane, the doctrine of 'signatures', already discussed.) In the beginning, as the Abbé Jousse has declared, was the gesture. The earliest language (according to Vico) was that of the gods, of which Homer speaks: 'the gods call this giant Briareus, men call him Egeon', the gods call the river Scamander 'Xanthe', the bird Cyminidis 'Chalcis'. The second language was the heroic – the *semata* of Homer. Last of all came 'popular' speech and the use of an alphabet. (There are several allusions to the alphabet in this episode and perhaps the speech of the giant Sir Lout, quoted hereafter, is a survival of the spoken equivalent of the heroic *semata*.) The 'popular' speech was, Vico suggests, adopted by a free convention of the people (how characteristic of the epoch, this theory of a 'free convention'!), for it is a law of nature that the common speech and script are the people's domain; even the emperor Claudius failed to compel the Romans to adopt three new letters proposed by him.

Coming to more recent times, we find the mutability of language still more apparent; all the academicians have failed – perhaps for want of some fair goddess Eidothea to counsel them – to arrest the transformations of popular, even written, speech. No sooner has the lexicographer completed his colossal task than *tout est à recommencer*; Proteus, inconstant snake, has sloughed his skin.

The monologue of Stephen in this episode is as varied in its linguistic transformations and disguises as the *Ubiquiste* of C. T. Féret.[1]

> L'Ubiquiste, Messieurs, Mesdames, vous salue.
> De douze gens j'habite en même temps la peau.
> Des couleurs de Protée éclate l'oripeau
> Et ma forme ondoyante et diverse évolue.
>
> Toute la Compagnie en un seul. Et chacun
> Peut monter sans façon me toucher sur la scène.
> En bas, en haut, devant, derrière, je suis UN,
> Un seul, et cependant cela fait la douzaine. ...
>
> .   .   .   .   .
>
> Je tiens dans un éclair mille rôles, et seule
> La boîte de mon corps n'est pas à double fond.

In this episode there are fragments of French, German, Latin, Spanish, Italian, Greek, Scandinavian, and other languages. The sea has its own tongue. 'Listen: a four-worded wavespeech: seesoo, hrss, rsseeiss, ooos. Vehement breath of waters amid sea-snakes, rearing horses, rocks. In cups of rocks it slops: flop, slop, slap.' The rough boulders of the strand are 'Sir Lout's toys. Mind you don't get one bang on the ear. I'm the bloody well gigant rolls all them bloody well boulders, bones for my

1. *L'Arc d'Ulysse*. Charles-Théophile Féret.

stepping-stones. Feefawfum. I zmellz de bloodz oldz an Iridzman.'[1]
Often his thoughts are couched in the jargon of heraldry: 'veil of space
with coloured emblems hatched on its field', 'rere regardant', 'on a
field tenney a buck, trippant, proper, unattired'. He 'seehears' sand-
speech. Before him 'the bloated carcass of a dog lolled on bladderwrack
and a boat sunk in sand. *Un coche ensablé*, Louis Veuillot called Gautier's
prose. These heavy sands are language tide and wind have silted here.'

The sight of the two cockle-pickers returning from the sea suggests a
protean sequence of thought and dialect.

Shouldering their bags they trudged, the red Egyptians. His blued feet out of
turnedup trousers slapped the clammy sand, a dull brick muffler strangling his
unshaven neck. With woman steps she followed: the ruffian and his strolling
mort.[2] Spoils slung at her back. Loose sand and shellgrit crusted her bare feet.
About her windraw face her hair trailed. Behind her lord his helpmate, bing
awast, to Romeville. When night hides her body's flaws calling under her brown
shawl from an archway where dogs have mired. ... Buss her, wap in rogues'
rum lingo, for, O, my dimber wapping dell. A shefiend's whiteness under her
rancid rags. Fumbally's lane that night: the tanyard smells.

> White thy fambles, red thy gan
> And thy quarrons dainty is.
> Couch a hogshead with me then.
> In the darkmans clip and kiss.

Morose delectation Aquinas tunbelly calls this, *frate porcospino*. Unfallen

1. Cf. Blake's variation on the *Fa, fe, fi, fo, fum* rhyme in *Jerusalem*.
   'Hark! hear the Giants of Albion cry at night:
   "We smell the blood of the English! we delight in their blood on our Altars.
   The living and the dead shall be ground in our rumbling Mills
   For bread of the Sons of Albion, of the Giants Hand and Scofield." '
2. Here, and in the stanza hereafter quoted by Stephen, the Rogues' or Gipsies'
   Cant language is employed. The Gipsies were known as 'Egyptians'; they were
   described in a proclamation of Henry VIII as 'outlandish people calling themselves
   Egyptians'. (The name 'Gipsy' is, in fact, derived from the Middle English *Gyptian*,
   contracted from 'Egyptian'.) Thus the language of this passage is a natural consequence of Stephen's sight of 'the red Egyptians' (itself, of course, appropriate to
   the Proteus theme). I append a glossary of the Cant terms used here. *Mort:* a 'free
   woman', one for common use among the male Gipsies, appointed according to
   their custom (see *The Slang Dictionary*). *Bing awast to Romeville:* Go away to London (Old Cant: *Bynge a waste*); *Rome,* or *rum,* meant originally *first-rate* or *noted,* as
   in *Rome booze* (used in *Ulysses*), i.e. wine. To *wap:* make love. *Dimber wapping dell:*
   pretty, loving wench. *Fambles:* hands. *Gan:* mouth. *Quarrons:* body. *Couch a hogs-*
   head: lie down and sleep. *Darkmans:* night.

Adam rode and not rutted.[1] Call away let him: *thy quarrons dainty is*. Language no whit worse than his, Monkwords, marybeads jabber on their girdles: rogue-words, tough nuggets patter in their pockets.

Passing now.

A side-eye at my Hamlet hat. If I were suddenly naked here as I sit? I am not. Across the sands of all the world, followed by the sun's flaming sword, to the west, trekking to evening lands. She trudges, schlepps, trains, drags, trascines her load. A tide westering, moondrawn in her wake. Tides, myriad-islanded within her, blood not mine, *oinopa ponton*, a winedark sea. Behold the hand-maid of the moon. In sleep the wet sign calls her hour, bids her rise. Bridebed, childbed, bed of death, ghostcandled. *Omnis caro ad te veniet*. He comes, pale vampire, through storm his eyes, his bat sails bloodying the sea, mouth to her mouth's kiss.

Here. Put a pin in that chap, will you? My tablets. Mouth to her kiss. No. Must be two of them. Glue em well. Mouth to her mouth's kiss.

His lips lipped and mouthed fleshless lips of air: mouth to her womb. Oomb, all wombing tomb.

Here we catch the primal matter of poetry in the very act of meta-morphosis from the particular to the general. The detritus of the city foreshore, the cockle-picker (a Megapenthes: slave's son, child of sor-row) and his ragged companion are transmuted into words of magic, stuff of dreams. The woman who 'schlepps, trains, drags, trascines' her load (in these changes of language, German, French, English, Italian, Stephen is feeling for the perfectly expressive verb) becomes the symbol of all womanhood. She is a handmaid of the moon (the 'wet sign', Hamlet's 'moist star') and at the moon's behest rises from her bed. The word 'bed' evokes bridebed, childbed, bed of death (his mother's deathbed: 'the ghost-candle to light her agony. Ghostly light on the tortured face'). *All flesh shall come to thee*, to Death, a Flying Dutchman

1. Cf. Blake's remark to Crabb Robinson: 'I saw Milton in imagination and he told me to beware of being misled by *Paradise Lost*. In particular he wished me to show the falsehood of his doctrine that the pleasures of sex arose from the fall. The fall could not produce any pleasure.' 'I answered,' Crabb Robinson continues, 'the fall produced a state of evil in which there was a mixture of good or pleasure. And in that sense the fall may be said to produce the pleasure. But he replied that the fall produced only generation and death. And he went off upon a rambling state of a union of sexes in man as in Ovid, an androgynous state, in which I could not follow him.' (Quoted by Mr S. F. Damon, *William Blake*, page 175.) This 'andro-gynous state' is referred to several times in *Ulysses*. Thus, in 'Circe', Mr Bloom is described as 'a finished example of the new womanly man' and feels himself with child, and, in 'Scylla', Stephen avers that 'in the economy of heaven, foretold by Hamlet', glorified man is an androgynous angel.

in a phantom ship. The womb-tomb (birth-death) rhyme has interesting Shakespearian and Blakean associations.

> The earth that's nature's mother is her tomb;
> What is her burying grave, that is her womb.[1]

> The Door of Death I open found
> And the Worm Weaving in the Ground:
> Thou'rt my Mother from the Womb,
> Wife, Sister, Daughter, to the Tomb,
> Weaving to dreams the sexual strife
> And weeping over the Web of Life.[2]

This episode concludes the first part of *Ulysses*, the Telemachia, and
closes with Stephen's sight of a gallant three-masted schooner, the *Rosevean* (as we learn later) 'from Bridgwater with bricks', which is bearing a waveworn wanderer, W. B. Murphy of Carrigaloe, Odysseus
Pseudangelos, to his own native shore.

He turned his face over a shoulder, rere regardant. Moving through the air
high spars of a threemaster, her sails brailed up on the crosstrees, homing, upstream, silently moving, a silent ship.

1. *Romeo and Juliet*, II, iii, 9, 10.
2. Blake, *The Gates of Paradise*.

4. CALYPSO

SCENE	The House
HOUR	8 a.m.
ORGAN	Kidney
ART	Economics
COLOUR	Orange
SYMBOL	Nymph
TECHNIC	Narrative (mature)

WITH this episode Mr Bloom's day begins: 16 June 1904; this date is esteemed, I am told, by certain advocates of a reformed calendar, a holy-day, styled *Bloomsday*. It is 8 a.m. Within the residence of Mr Bloom, 7 Eccles Street, there is still cool twilight, but, outside, the streets are already warming up, and there is a hint of thunder in the air. As Mr Bloom moves softly about the basement kitchen (for Madame Marion Tweedy, that popular soprano, awaits, as usual, her little breakfast in bed) kidneys are 'in his mind', for he eats with relish 'the inner organs of beasts and fowls'. The cat requests and receives milk on a saucer. The cat and Mr Bloom are on excellent terms. There is much of the *ewig weiblich* about the hero of *Ulysses*; he is no servile replica of his Homeric prototype, for he has a cat instead of a dog, and a daughter instead of a son. Before setting out for his marketing Mr Bloom inspects the lining of his hat to see if the pseudonymous card of 'Henry Flower' is safely there, and verifies the presence of the potato mascot in his trouser pocket. Passing Larry O'Rourke's public house he greets the proprietor and indulges in some characteristic speculations about the profits made by Dublin 'curates'.[1]

Where do they got the money? Coming up redheaded curates from the county Leitrim, rinsing empties and old man[2] in the cellar. Then, lo and behold, they blossom out as Adam Findlaters or Dan Tallons. Then think of the competition. General thirst. Good puzzle would be cross Dublin without passing a pub. Save it they can't. Off the drunks perhaps. Put down three and carry five. What is that? A bob here and there, dribs and drabs. On the wholesale orders perhaps. Doing a double shuffle with the town travellers. Square it with the boss and we'll split the job, see?

1. In Ireland public-house employees are known as 'curates'.
2. 'Old man' is the drink a customer leaves in his glass.

He reaches his destination, the butcher's shop of the Hungarian Jew, Dlugacz, to find that only one kidney is left, and passes an anxious moment wondering if the servant of the people next door, who is there before him, will take it. Fortunately, she buys sausages and Bloom gets his kidney. For a moment Dlugacz and Mr Bloom, mutually observant, wonder whether they should hail each other as compatriots. 'No: better not: another time.' The servant walks away, followed by Mr Bloom's regard.

Pleasant to see first thing in the morning. Hurry up, damn it. Make hay while the sun shines. She stood outside the shop in sunlight and sauntered lazily to the right. He sighed down his nose: they never understand. Sodachapped hands. Crusted toenails too. Brown scapulars in tatters, defending her both ways. The sting of disregard glowed to weak pleasure in his breast. For another: a constable off duty cuddled her in Eccles' Lane. They like them sizeable. Prime sausage. O please, Mr Policeman, I'm lost in the wood.

From a pile of cut sheets on the butcher's table he picks up a page: 'the model farm at Kinnereth on the lakeshore of Tiberias'. Already the heat has warmed his latent memory of the East and now the advertisement picture of blurred cattle cropping in silver heat gives form to his daydream. 'Agendath Netaim: planter's company. To purchase vast sandy tracts from Turkish government and plant with eucalyptus trees. ... Orangegroves and immense melonfields.' The melon, as we learn in 'Ithaca',[1] is a fruit for which Mr Bloom has, on *a posteriori* grounds, a marked predilection. And the man whom Stephen met in the 'street of harlots', in his dream, held a melon against his face. Mr Bloom visualizes 'silvered powdered olive-trees. Quiet long days: pruning ripening. ... Citrons too. Wonder is poor Citron still alive in Saint Kevin's parade. And Mastiansky with the old cither. Pleasant evenings we had then. Molly in Citron's basketchair. Nice to hold, cool waxen fruit, hold in the hand, lift it to the nostrils and smell the perfume. Like that, heavy, sweet, wild perfume.'

'A cloud began to cover the sun wholly slowly wholly. Grey. Far.' The cloud that Stephen watched, 'shadowing the bay in deeper green'. Under its shadow Mr Bloom's mood, like Stephen's, is darkened, and he thinks of the Dead Sea: 'no fish, weedless, sunk deep in the earth'. (Compare with this Stephen's thought – 'a bowl of bitter waters'.)

1. *Ulysses*, page 690.

No wind would lift those waves, grey metal, poisonous foggy waters. Brimstone they called it raining down: the cities of the plain; Sodom, Gommorah, Edom. All dead names. A dead sea in a dead land, grey and old. Old now. It bore the oldest, the first race. A bent hag crossed from Cassidy's clutching a naggin bottle by the neck. [The milkwoman of 'Telemachus': 'Old Gummy Granny'.] The oldest people. Wandered far away over all the earth, captivity to captivity, multiplying, dying, being born everywhere. It lay there now. Now it could bear no more. Dead. ...

Grey horror seared his flesh. ... Cold oils slid along his veins, chilling his blood: age crusting him with a salt cloak. Well, I am here now. Morning mouth bad images. Got up wrong side of the bed. Must begin again those Sandow's exercises. On the hands down.

There are two letters and a card lying on the hall floor. On one of the letters, addressed to his wife, he recognizes the handwriting of Boylan ('Blazes Boylan') her impresario and the most recent of her lovers. 'His quick heart slowed at once.' The other letter and card are from his daughter, Milly. He takes both letters and the card upstairs to Marion, who greets him with: 'Hurry up with that tea, I'm parched.' Obedient, he goes down again, sets the tea to draw and his kidney to fry. He carefully lays out his wife's breakfast on a tray – 'Bread and butter, four, sugar, spoon, her cream.' Madam is served. She tells him that Boylan is bringing the programme of the concert at which she is to sing 'Love's Old Sweet Song'.

Mrs Bloom, like many of her sex, is apt when she wants something to revert to the language of gesture. Now Mr Bloom marks her pointing finger and lifts, one by one, various articles of clothing for her to see.

'No: that book.'
Other stocking. Her petticoat.
'It must have fell down,' she said.

She asks her husband to explain *metempsychosis*,[1] 'met-him-pike-hoses'.

'That means the transmigration of souls.'
'O, rocks!' she said. 'Tell us in plain words.'

Mr Bloom glances at the title.

Ruby: the Pride of the Ring. Hello. Illustration. Fierce Italian with carriage whip.

1. See Part One, Chapter 3, § 1, '*Met-him-pike-hoses*'.

Must be Ruby pride of the on the floor naked. Sheet kindly lent. *The monster Maffei desisted and flung his victim from him with an oath.* Cruelty behind it all. Doped animals. Trapeze at Hengler's. Had to look the other way. Mob gaping. Break your neck and we'll break our sides. Families of them. Bone them young so they metempsychosis. That we live after death. Our souls. That a man's soul after he dies. Dignam's soul. ...

Regretfully Mrs Bloom: 'There's nothing smutty in it.'
Mr Bloom, by nature informative, continues to expound to his wife the meaning of metempsychosis.

The *Bath of the Nymph* over the bed. Given away with the Easter number of *Photo Bits*: Splendid masterpiece in art colours. Tea before you put the milk in. Not unlike her with her hair down: slimmer. She said it would look nice over the bed. Naked nymphs: Greece: and for instance all the people that lived then. He turned the pages back.
'Metempsychosis', he said, 'is what the ancient Greeks called it. They used to believe you could be changed into an animal or tree, for instance. What they called nymphs, for example.'
Her spoon ceased to stir the sugar. She gazed straight before her, inhaling through her arched nostrils.
'There's a smell of burn,' she said. 'Did you leave anything on the fire?'

He runs down just in time to save his kidney from incineration. (Several motifs which will frequently recur in the course of *Ulysses* are introduced in this passage: *Ruby, the Pride of the Ring*, metempsychosis, the *Nymph*, the *monster Maffei*.)
Eating his breakfast, Mr Bloom reads Milly's letter. She has just turned fifteen and is apprenticed to a provincial photographer.

There is a young student [she writes] comes here some evenings named Bannon his cousins or something are big swells he sings Boylan's (I was on the pop of writing Blazes Boylan's) song about those seaside girls. Tell him silly Milly sends my best respects. Must now close with fondest love.

The jingling rhymes of 'Boylan's song' run in Mr Bloom's head as he eats the kidney.

> *All dimpled cheeks and curls,*
> *Your head it simply swirls.*
> *Those girls, those girls,*
> *Those lovely seaside girls.*

(We have already heard of this Bannon in 'Telemachus'. 'I got a card from Bannon. Says he found a sweet young thing down there. Photo girl he calls her.')

Milly too [Mr Bloom muses]. Young kisses: the first. Far away now past. Mrs Marion. Reading lying back now, counting the strands of her hair, smiling, braiding.

A soft qualm regret flowed down his backbone, increasing. Will happen, yes. Present. Useless: can't move. Girl's sweet light lips. Will happen too.

Mr Bloom now visits the earth-closet at the end of his garden, where he reads the prize story in *Tit-Bits*, 'Matcham's Masterstroke' by Philip Beaufoy, Playgoers' Club, London, and considers the possibility of himself composing a 'prize titbit'.

Might manage a sketch. By Mr and Mrs L. M. Bloom. Invent a story for some proverb which? Time I used to try jotting down on my cuff what she said dressing. ... Biting her nether lip, hooking the placket of her skirt. Timing her. 9.15. Did Roberts pay you yet? 9.20. What had Gretta Conroy[1] on? 9.23. What possessed me to buy this comb? ...

He recalls that fateful dance at which his wife first met Boylan.

Rubbing smartly in turn each welt against her stocking calf. Morning after the bazaar dance when May's band played Ponchielli's Dance of the Hours. Explain that morning hours, noon, then evening coming on, then night hours. Washing her teeth. That was the first night. Her head dancing. Her fansticks clicking. Is that Boylan well off? He has money. Why? I noticed he had a good smell off his breath dancing. No use humming then. Allude to it. Strange kind of music that last night. The mirror was in shadow. ... Peering into it. Lines in her eyes. It wouldn't pan out somehow.

Evening hours, girls in grey gauze. Night hours then black with daggers and eyemasks. Poetical idea pink, then golden, then grey, then black. Still true to life also. Day, then the night.

The 'Dance of the Hours' is an important theme in *Ulysses*; it suggests symbolically the time-structure of the entire book.

The bells of George's Church toll the hour, reminding Mr Bloom of the funeral he has soon to attend.

> *Heigho! Heigho!*
> *Heigho! Heigho!*
> *Heigho! Heigho!*

1. Gretta Conroy figures in the story 'The Dead' in *Dubliners*.

Quarter to. There again: the overtone following through the air. A third.
Poor Dignam!

*

To Menelaus's inquiry concerning the fate of Odysseus, Proteus made
answer: 'Him I saw on an island shedding plenteous tears in the halls
of the nymph Calypso, who holds him there perforce; so he may not
come to his own country, for he has by him no ships with oars, and
no companions to send him on the way.'

The isle of Ogygia, Calypso's home, was evidently situated far to the
west of the Ionian seas. To return from it Odysseus had to travel seventeen days, keeping the constellation of the Great Bear always on his
left hand. This, according to Dr Merry, proves that he had to sail from
north-west to south-east. It has been suggested by some topographers
that the home of the Atlantid Calypso may have been situated beyond
and north-west of the Strait of Gibraltar and that Ogygia may actually
be identified with Ireland. But, however tempting it might be to apply
this somewhat farfetched hypothesis to the present occasion, the rea-
soned conclusions of M. Bérard (summarized in the following paragraph) as to the habitat of Calypso must prevail. Moreover, as will
be seen, the author of *Ulysses* in narrating, or, rather, indicating by
allusions in Mr Bloom's monologue and elsewhere, the early life of
Marion Bloom, *née* Tweedy, seems to imply his acceptance of M.
Bérard's view.

Calypso lives in a 'navel of the sea', a woodland isle, where there is a
great cave and meadows of violet and parsley. She is the daughter of
the giant Atlas, that living column which, at the world's end, upholds
the sky. The pillar Atlas is (according to Herodotus) beside the pillars
of Hercules; there is a legend that Hercules relieved Atlas for a while at
his task of upholding the firmament. The name of 'Atlas' has been given
in modern times to a range of mountains in the vicinity of the Strait,
but originally Atlas was a single mountain, now known as Apes Hill,
on the African coast facing Gibraltar, the European 'pillar'. Apes Hill
was known to Strabo as 'Abila', a semitic word meaning 'the sup-
porter', the exact equivalent of the Greek 'Atlas'. The Greek name of
Gibraltar was 'Kalpe' (the pitcher, bowl). Viewed, as the Phoenician
adventurers first saw it, from the African coast, against the highlands of
Algeciras, Gibraltar and the recess of the sea which it flanks have exactly
the appearance of a 'cup' set in the coastline. Moreover it was the bay

rather than the Rock that interested a Phoenician trader. The Greeks, coming later, adopted and translated the semitic nomenclature, and continued to call Gibraltar the 'bowl', 'Kalpe'.

On the opposite shore, dominated by Calypso's mountain sire, is a little island named Perejil (Spanish 'parsley') which corresponds in many respects to Homer's description of Ogygia, densewooded and studded with clumps of violets. But, as M. Bérard points out, Homer's description of Calypso's isle is evidently a composite picture. For example, the four Ogygian springs referred to in the Odyssey are not to be found in Perejil. These springs were evidently 'imported' by Homer from the African or Spanish coast. The 'nautical instructions', probably of Phoenician origin, which Homer adapted for his account of Calypso's isle, gave doubtless a general description of the western 'end of the world', including Mauretania, Gibraltar, and the Spanish littoral; these Homer has combined in his description of Ogygia. That island has, therefore, both 'Moorish' and Spanish characteristics.

The name of Calypso is clearly derived from the Greek *kalupto* (I hide, veil). Ogygia seems to be the Greek adaptation of a semitic root which means 'to surround'.[1] The island is low-lying, secret, dominated by the 'columns' of the two coasts, an *omphalos*. Yet, by a curious transference, the name of the obscure islet, Nesos Kalupsous (the island of the hiding-place) was chosen by early seafarers to designate the mainland of Spain. The semitic root s-p-n-i is the exact translation of the Greek *kalupto*. I-spania, Spain, is the *land-of-the-hiding-place*, a mysterious Far West, whose secrets the astute Phoenician traders were too prudent lightly to divulge.

Some three thousand years have passed since Odysseus abode, not without domestic, if spelaean, consolations, in the dark retreat of the veiled nymph. We have now Mr Bloom, wanderer in quest of advertisements, not adventure, a patient captive in the domestic penumbra of No 7 Eccles Street, servant of that inconstant nymph, the daughter of Major Brian Cooper Tweedy (sometime stationed at Gibraltar on service) and a Spanish Jewess, Lunita Laredo ('lovely name she had').

Mrs Bloom was born at Gibraltar. In a lyrical passage of the 'Cyclops'

1. Cf. Kalpe – the ring of sea, the bowl. There is thus a presage of the correspondences Calypso–Mrs Bloom, Ogygia–Dublin, in the first episode, where Stephen watches 'the *ring* of bay and skyline', 'a *bowl* of bitter waters'.

episode she is hailed: 'Pride of Calpe's rocky mount, the ravenhaired daughter of Tweedy. There she grew to peerless beauty where loquat and almond scent the air. The gardens of Alameda knew her step; the garths of olives knew and bowed.' Her father's second christian name 'Cooper' is probably another allusion to 'Calpe' (there is a close etymological affinity between these names), and 'Tweedy' may be a suggestion of Mrs Bloom's Penelope aspect,[1] as a weaver of webs, as well as of the mingled strands of her birth (*tweed*: 'a wool-and-cotton fabric usually with two colours combined in the yarn').[2] She is perhaps only a quarter Spanish, but to her husband she is a typical Spanish beauty. Thus, alluding to the woman who caused Parnell's downfall, he muses: 'she *also* was Spanish or half so, types that wouldn't do things by halves, passionate abandon of the south, casting every shred of decency to the winds.' Sometimes, too, he recognizes a strain of Moorish blood in her.[3] 'That's where Molly can knock spots off them ["homemade Irish beauties"]. It's the blood of the south. Moorish.'

The key-word to the first part of *Ulysses* (the Telemachia) is 'Usurpers'; Stephen was living in a world of usurpers and serving alien powers, spiritual and temporal. Mr Bloom too, though in a different way, the way of the flesh, not of the spirit, is a reluctant exile in Ireland. He is never quite at home amongst the noble Danes of Dublin. 'Denmark's a prison.' A prisoner perforce he languishes – there is no better word for his vague malaise. A secret voice unceasingly urges his return to the warm light and blue shadows of the East.

Somewhere in the east: early morning: set off at dawn, travel round in front of the sun steal a day's march on him. Keep it up for ever never grow a day older technically. Walk along a strand, strange land, come to a city gate, sentry there, old ranker too, old Tweedy's big moustaches, leaning on a long kind of a spear. Wander through awned streets. Turbaned faces going by. Dark caves of carpet shops, big man, Turko the terrible,[4] seated crosslegged smoking a

---

1. This side of Mrs Bloom is discussed in my notes on the last episode, 'Penelope'.
2. In *Ulysses* every detail is significant and we may be sure that none of the names are irrelevant. The importance of names is a canon of esoteric thought: *nomina* are *numina*. '*Imago animi, vitae, vultus nomen est*.' And an analysis of the names used in the *Odyssey* throws a flood of light on Homeric origins. Both considerations are relevant in dealing with the names in *Ulysses*.
3. Cf. the Eurafrican isle of Calypso, and the 'Moorish' allusions in Irish history and *Ulysses* mentioned in an earlier chapter.
4. Cf. Stephen's allusion to 'Turko the terrible' (page 8).

coiled pipe. Cries of sellers in the street. Drink water scented with fennel, sher-
bet. Wander along all day. Might meet a robber or two. Well, meet him. Getting on to sundown. The shadows of the mosques along the pillars: priest with
a scroll rolled up. A shiver of the trees, signal, the evening wind. I pass on.
Fading gold sky. A mother watches from her doorway. She calls her children
home in their dark language. High wall: beyond strings twanged. Night sky
moon, violet, colour of Molly's new garters. Strings. Listen. A girl playing one
of those instruments what do you call them: dulcimers. I pass.

In the next episode, the 'Lotus-eaters', his mind is still steeped in the
languors of this *Orient imaginaire*. For all his brisk activity Mr Bloom's
heart is set on rest. 'Just loll there: let everything rip.' The meeting with
Dlugacz, a reminder of racial affinities, symbolizes the Recall of Odysseus
from the far island of Calypso eastwards to his own country. The sun-
burst, to the Irish a national emblem, is to Bloom a symbol of orient
splendour; grey twilight, a cloud over the sun, of the shadow of death.
Throughout the episode there is a rhythmic interchange of shadow and
sunlight. The 'hollow cave' where Calypso held Odysseus captive has
its counterpart in the 'yellow twilight' of the bedroom presided over
by the Nymph, whence Bloom emerges into the orange brightness
of the streets. 'He crossed to the bright side, avoiding the loose cellar-
flap of number seventyfive.' Here, as so often in *Ulysses*, what seems
meticulous realism is profoundly symbolic. The 'cave' motif reappears in the allusion to 'dark caves' of carpet shops, the gloom of the
privy. 'He pulled back the jerky shaky door and came forth from the
gloom into the air. In the bright light, lightened and cooled of limb,
he carefully eyed his black trousers. ... A dark whirr in the air high up.
... They tolled the hour: loud dark iron.' The same contrast is brought
out in the 'Dance of the Hours'. Darkness is of the prison-house, the
shackles of the flesh, all that withholds Mr Bloom from Zion, Odysseus
from Ithaca.

The domain of the Agendath Netaim company was to be planted with
eucalyptus, the 'well-hidden' flower (perhaps, the 'wide-shading'
tree); the streets seen by Mr Bloom in his day-dream are awned; he
often thinks of his wife (Calypso, the veiled nymph, to him, but Penelope as she sees herself) in oriental dress, wearing a yashmak, as when,
hallucinated, in Circe's den, he beholds her, 'a handsome woman in
Turkish costume' beside her mirage of date palms standing before him.
In Book XXI of the *Odyssey*, when Penelope makes a formal and final

appearance to the suitors carousing in her halls, she 'held up her glistering tire before her face'. Thus in the next episode Mr Bloom pictures
Marion 'looking at me, the sheet up to her eyes, Spanish, smelling
herself, when I was fixing the links in my cuffs'. (It is noteworthy that
each time the reader of *Ulysses* has the privilege of beholding her,
Marion Bloom is between the sheets.)

Again, in the 'Sirens' episode, Mr Bloom wonders: 'Why do they
hide their ears with seaweed hair? And Turks their mouth, why? Her
eyes over the sheet, a yashmak. Find the way in. A cave. No admittance
except on business.'

But, for Mr Bloom, Marion has more affinity with the divine and
'splendid masterpiece' above the bed than with the Ithacan weaver of
veils. Every day a ration of cream is taken in for Marion's exclusive
regalement:[1] ambrosia for the nymph Calypso, to an immortal the
food of immortality. 'The nymph placed beside him all manner of food
to eat and drink, such as is meet for men. As for her she sat over against
divine Odysseus, and the handmaids placed beside her ambrosia and
nectar.'[2] At the climax of the *Nostos* ('Return'), the interview between
Stephen and Mr Bloom, the latter serves 'extraordinarily to his guest ...
the viscous cream ordinarily reserved for the breakfast of his wife
Marion (Molly)'. This serving of ambrosia to his young guest, his son
but not according to the flesh, not consubstantial, has a peculiar significance, coming as the service does from a Jew, sonless, in quest of a son-
father, his Messiah.

Between the darkness of night, the grave, and the golden hours,
domain of Helios the Quickener, there is stretched a gossamer veil of
twilight, 'the shepherd's hour: the hour of holding: hour of tryst'. Thus
the evening hours are lightly veiled in gauze, while the lethal nighthours wear black with daggers and eyemasks. The veil is, indeed, the
instrument of desire, a partial eclipse of beauty, as opposed to the blank
night of a cave, a tomb, the loud dark iron of tolling bells.[3] Oriflamme

1. That is the custom of the house, its 'economics'; the 'art' of this episode is
'economics'.
2. *Odyssey*, v: 196–9.
3. Compare the symbolism of the veil in the famous gesture of Isolde. The
night invoked by Tristan is the love-night of death, of *nie-wiedererwachens*, and in
the fluttering of the veil there is a presage of the
sehnend verlangter
Liebestod.

of *la petite mort*, it is like a *mouche* to set off the white lure of living flesh (since imperfection is a rowel to desire), a dusky yet benign recall of the little time man has to live as the hours dance deathwards.

> Soles occidere et redire possunt:
> Nobis, cum semel occidit brevis lux,
> Nox est perpetua una dormienda.
> Da mi basia mille, deinde centum. ...

5. THE LOTUS-EATERS

SCENE	The Bath
HOUR	10 a.m.
ORGAN	Genitals
ART	Botany, chemistry
SYMBOL	Eucharist
TECHNIC	Narcissism

MR BLOOM sets out for his day's work at about 10 a.m. His first errand is to visit the Westland Row post office where he hands across the counter the card of 'Henry Flower' and receives the homage of a trusting typist to 'Dear Henry's' second blooming. On his way to the post office he passes a tea-merchant's and the sight of the 'finest Ceylon brands' of tea exposed in the window evokes his eternal *Drang nach Osten*.

The far east. Lovely spot it must be: the garden of the world, big lazy leaves to float about on, cactuses, flowery meads, snaky lianas they call them. Wonder is it like that. Those Cinghalese lobbing around in the sun in *dolce far niente*. Not doing a hand's turn all day. Sleep six months out of twelve. Too hot to quarrel. Influence of the climate. Lethargy. Flowers of idleness. The air feeds most. Azotes. Hothouse in Botanic gardens. Sensitive plants. Waterlilies. Petals too tired to. Sleeping sickness in the air. Walk on roseleaves. Imagine trying to eat tripe and cowheel. Where was the chap I saw in that picture somewhere? Ah, in the dead sea, floating on his back, reading a book with a parasol open. Couldn't sink if you tried: so thick with salt. Because the weight of the water, no, the weight of the body in the water is equal to the weight of the. Or is it the volume is equal of the weight? It's a law something like that. Vance in High school cracking his fingerjoints, teaching. The college curriculum. Cracking curriculum. What is weight really when you say the weight? Thirtytwo feet per second, per second. Law of falling bodies: per second, per second. They all fall to the ground. The earth. It's the force of gravity of the earth is the weight.

Leaving the post office he scans and muses on the recruiting posters, 'bearskin caps and hackle plumes'. 'Redcoats. Too showy. That must be why the women go after them. Uniform. Easier to enlist and drill.'

Before he can open his letter he encounters one M'Coy, who figures in the story 'Grace' in *Dubliners*.

Mr M'Coy had been at one time a tenor of some reputation. His wife, who had been a soprano, still taught young children to play the piano at low terms. His line of life had not been the shortest distance between two points and for short periods he had been driven to live by his wits. ... Mr M'Coy had recently made a crusade in search of valises and portmanteaus to enable Mrs M'Coy to fulfil imaginary engagements in the country.

Mr Bloom, aware of this unpleasing habit, detects the usual gambit in M'Coy's opening announcement.

'My missus has just got an engagement. At least it's not settled yet.'
Valise tack again. By the way no harm. I'm off that, thanks.

Mr Bloom effectively checks M'Coy's move by announcing that Mrs Bloom too is shortly starting for a concert tour in the north.

Didn't catch me napping that wheeze. The quick touch. Soft mark. I'd like my job. Valise I have a particular fancy for. Leather. Capped corners, riveted edges, double action lever lock. Bob Cowley lent him his for the Wicklow regatta concert last year and never heard tidings of it from that good day to this.

Mr Bloom, strolling towards Brunswick street, smiled. My missus has just got an. Reedy freckled soprano. Cheeseparing nose. Nice enough in its way: for a little ballad. No guts in it. You and me, don't you know? In the same boat. Softsoaping. Give you the needle that would. Can't he hear the difference? ... Thought that Belfast would fetch him. I hope that smallpox up there doesn't get worse. Suppose she wouldn't let herself be vaccinated again. Your wife and my wife.

M'Coy further annoys him by interfering with his observation of an elegant lady climbing on to an 'outsider' on the opposite side of the road. Tied to the spot by his interlocutor, he has to allow a passing tram to eclipse a promising vision of silk stockings. 'Curse your noisy pugnose' – this for the 'honking' tram-driver.

Escaped from the toils of the valise-hunter, Mr Bloom observes a hoarding which announces that Mrs Bandman Palmer will play *Leah* tonight. 'Like to see her in that again. Hamlet she played last night. Male impersonator. Perhaps he was a woman. Why Ophelia committed suicide?' The thought of suicide recalls his father's end (the memory is amplified in the 'Hades' episode), and the old Jew's fondness for the scene

where the old blind Abraham recognizes the voice and puts his fingers on his face.

'Nathan's voice! His son's voice! I hear the voice of Nathan who left his father to die of grief and misery in my arms, who left the house of his father and left the God of his father.'[1]

Every word is so deep, Leopold.

At last he finds a deserted street where he can open his *poste restante* letter, in which a yellow flower with flattened petals is enclosed. 'What does she say?'

DEAR HENRY,

I got your last letter to me and thank you very much for it. Why did you enclose the stamps? I am awfully angry with you, I do wish I could punish you for that. I called you naughty boy because I do not like that other word. Please tell me what is the real meaning of that word. Are you not happy in your home you poor little naughty boy? ... I often think of the beautiful name you have. Dear Henry, when will we meet? I think of you so often you have no idea. I have never felt myself so drawn to a man as you. I feel so bad about. Please write me a long letter and tell me more. Remember if you do not I will punish you. So now you know what I will do to you, you naughty boy, if you do not wrote (*sic*). ... Henry dear, do not deny my request before my patience are exhausted. Then I will tell you all. Goodbye now, naughty darling. I have such a bad headache today and write *by return* to your longing

MARTHA

P.S. – Do tell me what kind of perfume does your wife use. I want to know.

He tore the flower gravely from its pinhold, smelt its almost no smell and placed it in his heart pocket. Language of flowers. They like it because no-one can hear. Or a poison bouquet to strike him down. Then, walking slowly forward, he read the letter again, murmuring here and there a word.[2] Angry tulips with you darling manflower punish your cactus if you don't please poor forgetmenot how I long violets to dear roses when we soon anemone meet all naughty nightstalk wife Martha's perfume.

Mr Bloom owes this epistolary romance with Martha to an advertisement he inserted in the *Irish Times*: 'Wanted smart lady typist to aid gentleman in literary work.' He chose Martha – it can hardly have been on account of her literary competence – from forty-four aspirants to the post. As he passes under a railway arch he tears up the envelope. 'You could tear up a cheque for a hundred pounds in the same way.'

1. Like Stephen Dedalus.
2. This is one of the rare instances where the author of *Ulysses* explains his technique to the reader.

It reminds him of the million-pound cheque cashed by Lord Iveagh of Guinness's, and he tries to calculate the profits of the famous brewery.

Twopence a pint, fourpence a quart, eightpence a gallon of porter. One and four into twenty: fifteen about. Yes, exactly. Fifteen millions of barrels of porter.

What am I saying barrels? Gallons. About a million barrels all the same.

He passes All Hallows and, after studying the announcement that the very reverend John Conmee, s.j., will preach on Saint Peter Claver and the African mission, enters the church.

Something going on: some sodality. Pity so empty. Nice discreet place to be next some girl. Who is my neighbour? Jammed by the hour to slow music. That woman at midnight mass. Seventh heaven.

As he watches the women receive the Host, Mr Bloom's reflections are in his characteristic vein – irreverent, demotic, yet not without penetration.

There's a big idea behind it, kind of kingdom of God is within you feel. First communicants. Hokypoky penny a lump. Then feel all like one family party, same in the theatre, all in the same swim. They do. I'm sure of that. Not so lonely. In our confraternity. Then come out a bit spreeish. Let off steam. Thing is if you really believe in it. Lourdes cure, waters of oblivion, and the Knock apparition, statues bleeding. Old fellow asleep near that confession box. Hence those snores. Blind faith. Safe in the arms of kingdom come. Lulls all pain. Wake this time next year.

Leaving the church, he remembers that his wife has asked him to get a face-lotion made up for her. 'Where is this? Ah yes, the last time. Sweny's in Lincoln place. Chemists rarely move. Their green and gold beaconjars too heavy to stir.' He orders the lotion at Sweny's, promising to call for it later in the day. But he fails to redeem his promise; history, in the form of Nausicaa, is, it seems, to blame. A lotus-eater, he forgets the hour of his returning. For himself he buys, and pockets, a cake of 'sweet lemony' soap. (We shall hear much of this soap in the course of *Ulysses*; it has a 'little Odyssey' all to itself, to which I shall refer in my notes on the 'Ithaca' episode.) Outside the chemist's Mr Bloom encounters one Bantam Lyons (mentioned in 'The Boarding House' in *Dubliners* as one of 'the Madam's' lodgers at fifteen shillings a week) who borrows his paper to see the runners in the Ascot Gold Cup. Mr

Bloom says to him: 'You can keep it. I was just going to throw it away.' These words act like a charm on Bantam Lyons, who, exclaiming 'I'll risk it', hurries off to a bookmaker's. The significance of Mr Bloom's innocent remark will appear later: it involves the secret of a race and is destined to provoke a partial pogrom later in the day. Mr Bloom strolls on towards the 'mosque of the baths', for the sweet, clean smells of the chemist's shop and the lemony soap have oriented his desire to a 'womb of warmth', the Hammam. As he turns under the shadow of the minarets, he has a brief regret that the quick morning sunlight which 'in slim sandals' ran to meet him in Eccles Street is already passing westwards away.

Heavenly weather really. If life was always like that. Cricket weather. Sit around under sunshades. Over after over. Out. They can't play it here. Duck for six wickets. ... Heatwave. Won't last. Always passing the stream of life, which in the stream of life we trace is dearer than them all.

*

On the tenth day we set foot on the land of the lotus-eaters, who eat a flowery food. So we stepped ashore and drew water, and straightway my company took their midday meal by the swift ships. Now when we had tasted meat and drink I sent forth certain of my company to go and make search what manner of men they were who here live upon the earth by bread, choosing out two of my fellows and sending a third with them as herald. So they went at once, and mixed with the men of the lotus-eaters, and so it was that the lotus-eaters devised not death for our fellows, but gave them of the lotus to taste. Now whosoever of them did eat the honey-sweet fruit of the lotus had no more wish to bring tidings nor to come back, but chose rather to abide there with the lotus-eating men, ever feeding on the lotus, and forgetful of returning. Therefore I led them back to the ships weeping, and sore against their will, and dragged them beneath the benches, and bound them in the hollow barques. But I commanded the rest of my well-loved company to make speed and go on board the swift ships, lest haply any should eat of the lotus and be forgetful of returning. Right soon they embarked and sate upon the benches, and sitting orderly they smote the grey sea water with their oars.

Unlike most of the barbarians encountered by Odysseus on his travels, Cyclopes, Lestrygonians, and the rest, the Lotus-eaters were gentle and friendly folk; aptly enough, the present inhabitants of Djerba (identified with Homer's Lotusland) have received an official encomium from the French Marine, as being *très hospitaliers*.

The name 'lotus' seems to have been applied by the Greeks to several distinct members of the vegetable kingdom, as well as to the plant which we now know as the lotus, the water-lily. Thus Herodotus and Poly-bius see in the lotus a tree which bears fruit like dates or figs (perhaps they mean the mango-tree), 'but much more odorous', and elsewhere Homer seems to mean by 'lotus' some kind of grass or clover, a good fodder for horses.[1] But here lotus is probably a semitic root in the guise of a Greek homonym; it obviously means one of the many opiates for which oriental races have such a predilection. There is a Semitic word *lōt* (it appears in the Old Testament) which signifies a certain kind of perfume, perhaps narcotic. In the episode of the 'Lotus-eaters' the lotus is evidently considered both as a scented flower and an opiate. The scented soap and the odours at Sweny's have already been men-tioned; there are several other references to scents – 'Cochrane's ginger ale (aromatic)', the 'almost no smell' of Martha's yellow flower, the smell of 'fresh printed rag paper'. Martha asks 'what kind of perfume does your wife use?' Mr Bloom visualizes Marion in bed, 'the sheet up to her eyes, smelling herself'.

But it is chiefly by its narcotic virtue that the lotus dominates this episode. The opening passage (already quoted), Mr Bloom's dream of a land – *Kennst du das Land* ...? – where the tea-flowers bloom,[2] places the mood of this chapter: languor and *far niente*. The letter from Martha Clifford recalls to his mind a picture he once saw: *Martha and Mary*.

He[3] is sitting in their house, talking. Mysterious ... Nice kind of evening feel-ing. No more wandering about. Just loll there: quiet dusk: let everything rip. Forget. Tell about places you have been, strange customs. The other one, jar on her head, was getting the supper: fruit, olives, lovely cool water out of the well stonecold like the hole in the wall at Ashtown. Must carry a paper goblet next time I go to the trotting matches. She listens with big dark soft eyes. Tell her: more and more: all. Then a sigh: silence. Long long long rest.

Wideleaved flowers, cool well-water, quiet lakes of lotusland, these

---

1. *Odyssey*, IV: 603, 604.

2. Ceylon is known to Buddhists as 'the ferry to Nirvana'. It was in the 'southern island' that Buddha appeared and taught the law of deliverance from Karma. Only there is the end of the dreary round of reincarnations, desired oblivion, in sight.

3. It is noteworthy that Mr Bloom (except on one occasion, when the 'Cyclops' has provoked him beyond measure) avoids mentioning the name of Jesus – the Jew's aversion from naming the Christian Messiah.

are the stuff of which his daydream is made. Even the thought of the brewery with its million barrels of porter is interwoven with the lore of the lotus. 'The bungholes sprang open and a huge full flood leaked out, flowing together, winding through mudflats all over the level land, a lazy pooling swirl of liquor bearing along wideleaved flowers of its froth.'[1]

The lotus-eaters appear under many aspects in this episode: the cab-horses drooping at the cabrank ('gelded too. ... Might be happy all the same that way'), doped communicants at All Hallows (land of the saints), 'hypnotized-like' soldiers on the recruiting poster, placid eunuchs ('one way out of it'), the watchers of cricket ('sit around under sunshades'), and, finally, Mr Bloom himself, flowerlike, buoyed lightly upward in the bath. There are many references to sleep and nar-cotics. The cabhorses are 'too full for words'. 'A wise tabby, a blinking sphinx, watched from her warm sill. Pity to disturb them. Mahomed cut a piece out of his mantle not to wake her.' Mr Bloom pictures a group of Negro converts listening to their missionary: 'sitting round in a ring[2] with blub lips, entranced, listening. Still life. Lap it up like milk, I suppose.' 'Good idea the Latin. Stupefies them first.'

The eucharist is the symbol of all these anodynes. 'The priest went along by them, murmuring, holding the thing in his hands. He stopped at each, took out a communion, shook a drop or two (are they in water?) off it and put it neatly into her mouth. ... Now I bet it makes them feel happy. Lollipop. It does. Yes, bread of angels it's called. There's a big idea behind it.' 'Same in the theatre, all in the same swim.' For the theatre, too, is a form of 'dope'. The eucharist 'lulls all pain'. The old fellow sleeping in the church will 'wake this time next year'. Thus those who ate of the honey-sweet lotus had no more wish to bring tidings nor to come back, but chose to abide there forgetful of returning.

A water motif also runs through this episode, apposite both to the lotus-flower[3] and to the technic: *narcissism*. 'Lourdes cure, waters of

1. Cf. Stephen's thoughts as, at about the same hour, he watches the flowing tide (one of several instances of the *rapport* between Bloom's mind and Stephen's). 'It flows purling, widely flowing, floating foam-pool, flower unfurling.'

2. If each episode of *Ulysses* had a geometrical correspondence, that for the 'Lotus-eaters' would be the 'circle'. (The smooth chalice roundness of the lotus is distinctive.) Allusions to circles and round objects are frequent in this episode.

3. The poet of the *Odyssey* has, as M. Bérard points out, made a characteristic *jeu de mots* round the Semitic word *lōt*; he has made the lotus the fruit of forgetting, λήθω, λήθη, thus associating it with Lethe, the river of oblivion.

oblivion'; 'a lazy pooling swirl'; 'the low tide of holy water', etc. The metaphor quoted above 'all in the same swim' is another allusion to this motif.

In her letter, which encloses a flower, Martha writes to Mr Bloom ('Henry Flower'): 'I often think of the beautiful name you have.' This chapter of *Ulysses* is a veritable florilegium and it is appropriate that it should contain a passage fixing attention on the name (and pseudonym) of the hero and also a reference to his father. The latter, Rudolph Virag, formerly of Szombathely in the kingdom of Hungary, changed his name to 'Bloom' after settling in Ireland; *virag* in Hungarian means 'flower'.

The technic of this episode, *narcissism*, has obvious affinities with the lotus theme. Much of it is written in the form of the silent monologue and, if the texture here and in other episodes be compared, it will be found that Mr Bloom is even more introspective than usual, is, in fact, watching his own reflections all the time with a tender interest. 'Will you be as gods? Gaze in your omphalos.' (In the last line but two of the episode we see Mr Bloom literally following Stephen's advice, in the bath.) Mr Bloom is something of an adept in the rites of oriental ecstasy and the little language of the hypnotist, passwords to the lotusland of trance. Bent over the mirror of himself, lulled by the echo of his inner voice, drugged by his own perfume, the lotus-eater dreams out enchanted days. 'He took off his hat quietly inhaling his hairoil and sent his right hand with slow grace over his brow and hair.' 'Kind of a placid. No worry.' The sublime indifference of Tennyson's Lotus-eaters.

> Let us swear an oath, and keep it with an equal mind,
> In the hollow Lotus-land to live and lie reclined
> On the hills like Gods together, careless of mankind.
> For they lie beside their nectar, and the bolts are hurled
> Far below them in the valleys, and the clouds are lightly curl'd
> Round their golden houses, girdled with the gleaming world:
> While they smile in secret, looking over wasted lands,
> Blight and famine, plague and earthquake, roaring deeps and fiery sands,
> Clanging fights, and flaming towns, and sinking ships, and praying hands.

But Mr Bloom's spiritual home lies farther east than Attic Olympus; rather, one may surmise, on the flowery slopes of Mount Meru where Devas in dazed contemplation await Nirvana.

The episode as a whole is dominated by two arts (now esteemed sciences): botany and chemistry. Both of these contribute to the paraphernalia of eucharistic glamour: 'flowers, incense, candles', as Mr Bloom observes. The arts of botany and the chemist's are allied; the latter owes much to his precursors, the herbalists. 'Homely recipes', as Mr Bloom remarks, 'are often the best: strawberries for the teeth: nettles and rainwater: oatmeal they say steeped in buttermilk.' 'That orangeflower. Pure curd soap. Water is so fresh. Nice smell these soaps have.'

The chemist turned back page after page. Sandy shrivelled smell he seems to have. Shrunken skull. And old. Quest for the philosopher's stone. The alchemists. Drugs age you after mental excitement. Lethargy then. Why? Reaction. A lifetime in a night. Gradually changes your character. Living all the day among herbs, ointments, disinfectants. All his alabaster lilypots. Mortar and pestle. Aq. Dist. Fol. Laur. Te Virid. Smell almost cure you like the dentist's doorbell. ... Electuary or emulsion. The first fellow that picked an herb to cure himself had a bit of pluck. Simples. Want to be careful. Enough stuff here to chloroform you. Test: turns blue paper red. Chloroform. Overdose of laudanum. Sleeping draughts. Lovephiltres. Paregoric poppysyrup bad for cough. Clogs the pores or the phlegm. Poisons the only cures. Remedy where you least expect it. Clever of nature.

It will be seen that this fragment of Mr Bloom's silent monologue includes a number of the themes of this episode. In the closing sentences the narcissus, water, chemistry, lotus, and eucharist motifs are compounded in the chalice of Mr Bloom's ablution.

'Enjoy a bath now: clean trough of water, cool enamel, the gentle tepid stream. This is my body.'
He foresaw his pale body reclined in it at full, naked, in a womb of warmth, oiled by scented melting soap, softly laved. He saw his trunk and limbs rippled over and sustained, buoyed lightly upward, lemonyellow ... a languid floating flower.

6. HADES

SCENE	The Graveyard
HOUR	11 a.m.
ORGAN	Heart
ART	Religion
COLOURS	White, Black
SYMBOL	Caretaker
TECHNIC	Incubism

AN ancient cab, littered with the crumbs of a departed picnic party, its upholstery mildewed and buttonless, a properly lugubrious vehicle, conveys Messrs Bloom, Power, Simon Dedalus, and Martin Cunningham to the cemetery, behind Dignam's hearse. This is the first appearance in *Ulysses* of Simon Dedalus, Stephen's consubstantial father. He is still the hearty *laudator temporis acti* we came to know in *A Portrait of the Artist.*

'When you kick out for yourself, Stephen – as I daresay you will one of these days – remember, whatever you do, to mix with gentlemen. When I was a young fellow I tell you I enjoyed myself. I mixed with fine decent fellows. Everyone of us could do something. One fellow had a good voice, another fellow was a good actor, another could sing a good comic song, another was a good oarsman or a good racket player, another could tell a good story and so on. We kept the ball rolling anyhow and enjoyed ourselves and saw a bit of life and we were none the worse for it either. But we were all gentlemen, Stephen – at least I hope we were – and bloody good honest Irishmen too. That's the kind of fellows I want you to associate with, fellows of the right kidney. I'm talking to you as a friend, Stephen. I don't believe a son should be afraid of his father. No, I treat you as your grandfather treated me when I was a young chap. We were more like brothers than father and son. I'll never forget the first day he caught me smoking. I was standing at the end of the South Terrace one day with some maneens like myself and sure we thought we were grand fellows because we had pipes stuck in the corners of our mouths. Suddenly the governor passed. He didn't say a word, or stop even. But the next day, Sunday, we were out for a walk together and when we were coming home he took out his cigar case and said: – By the by, Simon, I didn't know you smoked, or something like that. – Of course I tried to carry it off as best I could. – If you want a good

smoke, he said, try one of these cigars. An American captain made me a present
of them last night in Queenstown.'

Stephen heard his father's voice break into a laugh which was almost a sob.

'He was the handsomest man in Cork at that time, by God he was! The
women used to stand to look after him in the street.'

Here is Mr Dedalus talking with some of his cronies in a bar at Cork,
the scene of his youthful exploits.

'We're as old as we feel, Johnny. And just finish what you have there and
we'll have another. Here, Tim or Tom or whatever your name is, give us the
same again here. By God, I don't feel more than eighteen myself. There's that
son of mine there not half my age and I'm a better man than he is any day of the
week.'

'Draw it mild now, Dedalus. I think it's time for you to take a back seat,'
said the gentleman who had spoken before.

'No, by God!' asserted Mr Dedalus. 'I'll sing a tenor song against him or I'll
vault a fivebarred gate against him or I'll run with him after the hounds across
the country as I did thirty years ago along with the Kerry Boy and the best
man for it.'

'But he'll beat you here,' said the little old man, tapping his forehead and
raising his glass to drain it.

'Well, I hope he'll be as good a man as his father. That's all I can say,' said
Mr Dedalus.

It is not surprising that Stephen felt 'an abyss of fortune or of temperament' sunder him from his father and his father's friends, the great
gulf nature has fixed between the types known to modern psychology
as introvert and extravert. Mr Bloom, a mixed type, effusive at moments, yet prudently repressive in general of his own dark thoughts,
was more akin to Stephen, that 'changeling' in his own home.

Martin Cunningham is known to readers of the story 'Grace' (Dubliners) as 'a thoroughly sensible man, influential and intelligent. His
blade of human knowledge, a natural astuteness particularized by long
association with cases in the police courts, had been tempered by brief
immersions in the waters of general philosophy.' He is naturally good-
natured and tolerant, unlike Mr Dedalus who, with all his bonhomie,
has a declared aversion for all that is not decently normal, and for those
who are not of the 'hail-fellow-well-met' persuasion.

The fourth occupant of the cab, a Mr Power, was delineated in the
same story, 'Grace'. 'Mr Power, a much younger man, was employed

in the Royal Irish Constabulary Office in Dublin Castle. His inexplicable debts were a byword in his circle; he was a debonair young man.' He is amiable, rather colourless; Mr Bloom finds him 'a nice fellow'.

As the cab rattles over the cobbled streets, past a patch of ripped-up roadway (the underworld is already appearing), the cortège is saluted on its way by passers-by: 'a fine old custom', Mr Dedalus remarks. They pass 'a lithe young man, clad in mourning, a wide hat': Stephen. Mr Dedalus remarks that Stephen's *fidus Achates*, Mulligan, is a 'bloody doubledyed ruffian', a counterjumper's son. A few drops of rain fall. 'Curious', Mr Bloom thinks, 'like through a colander. I thought it would. My boots were creaking I remember now.'

The conversation of the four men is scrappy and topical; it is clear that the three Irishmen, anyhow, would be the better for a drink, and happier in a bar-parlour. As the washerwoman by the Anna Liffey observes in *Finnegans Wake*: Ireland sober is Ireland stiff. At this hour of the morning, unstimulated, Mr Dedalus's verve is in defect and his temper decidedly 'stiff'; his comments on the passers-by are merely malicious or morose. Mr Bloom is the one whose thoughts are most in keeping with the occasion. The dogs' home they pass reminds him of his dead father's dog Athos, a scion, perhaps, of the longlived Argos stock.[1] 'Poor old Athos. Be good to Athos, Leopold, is my last wish. Thy will be done. We obey them in the grave ... He took it to heart, pined away. Quiet brute. Old men's dogs usually are.' Presently some sententious remarks of the others on the 'disgrace' of the suicide's end turn his thoughts again to his father's tragic death.

They pass Blazes Boylan out 'airing his quiff' and the sight of his wife's latest lover has its usual disquieting effect on Mr Bloom, who, to distract his own attention, meticulously examines his nails.

Mr Bloom reviewed the nails of his left hand, then those of his right hand. The nails, yes. Is there anything more in him that they she sees? Fascination. Worst man in Dublin. That keeps him alive. They sometimes feel what a person is. Instinct. But a type like that. My nails. I am just looking at them: well pared. And after: thinking alone. Body getting a bit softy. I would notice that from remembering. What causes that I suppose the skin can't contract quickly enough when the flesh falls off. But the shape is there. The shape is there still. Shoulders. Hips. Plump. Night of the dance dressing. ...

The sight of the 'tall blackbearded figure' of a well-known Dublin

1. *Odyssey*, XVII: 290–323.

moneylender, Reuben J. Dodd, elicits an imprecation from Mr Dedalus: 'the devil break the hasp of your back!' 'We have all been there,'
Martin Cunningham laments. Mr Bloom, in haste to disclaim confraternity, begins to tell how 'Reuben J.'s' son attempted suicide without success. The youth jumped into the Liffey and was fished out by a
boatman whom 'Reuben J.' rewarded with a florin. 'One and eightpence too much,' is Mr Dedalus's dry comment.

At last they reach Glasnevin cemetery, where some other mourners
have already arrived. The service in the mortuary chapel begins,
accompanied by the silent commentary of Mr Bloom's monologue.

They halted by the bier and the priest began to read out of his book with a
fluent croak. ...

Non intres in judicium cum servo tuo, Domine.

Makes them feel more important to be prayed over in Latin. Requiem mass.
Crape weepers. Black edged notepaper. Your name on the altarlist. Want to
feed well, sitting in there all the morning in the gloom kicking his heels waiting
for the next please. Eyes of a toad too. What swells him up that way? Molly
gets swelled after cabbage. Air of the place maybe. Looks full up of bad gas.
Must be an infernal lot of bad gas round this place. ... Down in the vaults of
saint Werburgh's lovely old organ hundred and fifty they have to bore a hole
in the coffins sometimes to let out the bad gas and burn it. Out it rushes: blue.
One whiff of that and you're a goner. ...

The priest took a stick with a knob at the end of it out of the boy's bucket
and shook it over the coffin. Then he walked to the other end and shook it
again. Then he came back and put it back in the bucket. As you were before
you rested. It's all written down: he has to do it.

Et ne nos inducas in tentationem.

The server piped the answers in the treble. I often thought it would be better
to have boy servants. Up to fifteen or so. After that of course. ...

Holy water that was, I expect. Shaking sleep out of it. He must be fed up with
that job, shaking that thing over all the corpses they trot up. ...

In paradisum.

Said he was going to paradise or is in paradise. Says that over everybody.
Tiresome kind of a job. But he has to say something.

The service ended, the gravediggers come and 'shove the coffin on
their cart'. They walk past the O'Connell circle (an *omphalos*); 'in the
middle of his people, old Dan O'. But his heart is buried at Rome'[1] and,

1. Daniel O'Connell died at Genoa. In accordance with his last wish, his heart
was taken to Rome, his body buried at Glasnevin.

near the grave of Mrs Dedalus, Simon Dedalus breaks down and weeps.
'I'll soon be stretched beside her. Let Him take me whenever He likes.'
The mourners are joined by Mr Kernan (another of the characters in
'Grace'), 'a commercial traveller of the old school, of Protestant stock,
though converted to Catholicism at the time of his marriage. He was
fond of giving side-thrusts at Catholicism.' He makes a characteristic
remark to Mr Bloom.

'The service of the Irish church, used in Mount Jerome, is simpler, more
impressive, I must say.'
  Mr Bloom gave prudent assent. The language of course was another thing.
  Mr Kernan said with solemnity:
'*I am the resurrection and the life.* That touches a man's inmost heart.'

The conservator, John O'Connell, tells them a funny story 'to cheer
a fellow up', as Martin Cunningham points out, 'pure goodheartedness: damn the thing else'.

The coffin dived out of sight, eased down by the men straddled on the grave-
trestles. They struggled up and out: and all uncovered. Twenty.
  Pause.
  If we were all suddenly somebody else.
  Far away a donkey brayed. Rain. No such ass. Never see a dead one, they say.
Shame of death. They hide. Also poor papa went away.
  Gentle sweet air blew round the bared heads in a whisper. Whisper . . . The
gravediggers took up their spades and flung heavy clods of clay in on the coffin.
Mr Bloom turned his face. And if he was alive all the time? Whew! By Jingo,
that would be awful! No, no: he is dead, of course. Of course he is dead.
Monday he died. They ought to have some law to pierce the heart and make
sure or an electric clock or a telephone in the coffin and some kind of a canvas
airhole. Flag of distress. Three days. Rather long to keep them in summer. Just
as well to get shut of them as soon as you're sure there's no.
  The clay fell softer. Begin to be forgotten. Out of sight, out of mind.

Hynes the reporter (a character in 'Ivy Day in the Committee
Room') notes the names of mourners present and suggests they go
round by 'the chief's grave'.

With awe Mr Power's blank voice spoke:
'Some say he is not in that grave at all: That the coffin was filled with stones.
That one day he will come again.'
  Hynes shook his head.

'Parnell will never come again,' he said. 'He's there, all that was mortal of him. Peace to his ashes!'

Passing a statue of the Sacred Heart, Mr Bloom censures the anatomical inaccuracy of the sculptor, but himself boggles at a classical reminiscence. 'The Sacred Heart that is: showing it. Heart on his sleeve. Ought to be sideways and red it should be painted like a real heart. Ireland was dedicated to it or whatever that. Seems anything but pleased. Why this infliction? Would birds come then and peck like the boy with the basket of fruit but he said no because they ought to have been afraid of the boy. Apollo that was.' He watches an obese grey rat wriggle under the plinth of a crypt; the sight of 'the grey alive' crushing itself in under the entrance to the charnel-house fixes itself in his memory and is recalled several times in the course of the day. He remembers that the last time he was here it was to attend the funeral of Mrs Sinico (see 'A Painful Case' in *Dubliners*). As he is leaving the cemetery he encounters the solicitor, John Henry Menton, who has never forgiven Mr Bloom a trivial triumph.

Got his rag out that evening on the bowling green because I sailed inside him. Pure fluke of mine: the bias ... Got a dinge in the side of his hat. Carriage probably.

'Excuse me, sir,' Mr Bloom said beside them.

They stopped.

'Your hat is a little crushed,' Mr Bloom said, pointing.

John Henry Menton stared at him for an instant without moving.

'There,' Martin Cunningham helped, pointing also.

John Henry Menton took off his hat, budged out the dinge and smoothed the nap with care on his coatsleeve. He clapped the hat on his head again.

'It's all right now,' Martin Cunningham said.

John Henry Menton jerked his head down in acknowledgement.

'Thank you,' he said shortly.

They walked on towards the gates. Mr Bloom, chapfallen, drew behind a few paces so as not to overhear. Martin laying down the law. Martin could wind a sappyhead like that round his little finger without his seeing it.

Oyster eyes. Never mind. Be sorry after perhaps when it dawns on him. Get the pull over him that way.

Thank you. How grand we are this morning.

*

There are, in this episode, many recalls of the 'Nekuia.'[1] The four rivers of Hades have their counterparts in the Dodder, the Liffey, and the Grand and Royal Canals of Dublin. Patrick Dignam, deceased, is an avatar of Elpenor who, it will be remembered, broke his neck in a fall from the roof of Circe's house, where he had been sleeping, heavy with wine. The end of Dignam, a 'comical little teetotum always stuck up in some pub corner', as Mrs Bloom describes him, was equally sudden and due to a series of similar indiscretions.[2] There is a direct allusion to the name of Elpenor in Mr Bloom's description of Dignam. 'Blazing face: red-hot. Too much John Barleycorn. Cure for a red nose. Drink like the devil till it turns adelite.'[3] M. Bérard derives the name of El-penor from a Semitic root meaning 'the blazing-face'. The first shade encountered by Odysseus on the shore of Erebus was that of Elpenor. 'At the sight of him I wept and had compassion on him; and uttering my voice spake to him winged words: "Elpenor, how hast thou come beneath the darkness and the shadow? Thou hast come fleeter on foot than I in my black ship."' Thus Bloom, arrived at the graveyard, soliloquizes: 'Coffin now. Got here before us, dead as he is', and, later, at the mortuary chapel, when the coffin is lying on the bier, four tall yellow candles at its corners, 'always in front of us'.

This episode has a number of other Homeric parallels, more easily recognizable, nearer the surface, than the symbolic recalls in other episodes. This comparative directness of allusion may be ascribed to the near affinity of the ancient and modern narratives, each of which records a visit to the abode of the dead – the domain of Hades, Glasnevin cemetery. Thus the amiable Cunningham is doomed to the labour of Sisyphus

pressing a monstrous stone with hands and feet, striving to roll it towards the brow of a hill. But oft as he was about to hurl it over the top, the weight would drive him back, so once again to the plain rolled the stone, the pitiless thing. And he once more kept heaving and straining, and the sweat the while was pouring down his limbs, and the dust rose upwards from his head.

1. The episode of the *Odyssey* which describes the visit of Odysseus to the nether world (Book XI), generally known as the '*Nekuia*', is really a '*Nekuomanteia*', an evocation of the shades, like the calling up of Samuel by the witch of Endor or that of Melissa by Periander's envoys.

2. '*Pareil accident*', as M. Bérard aptly remarks of Elpenor's end, '*n'arrive qu'après une longue beuverie*.'

3. Cf. the reflections of young Patrick Aloysius Dignam (page 241): 'His face got all grey instead of being red like it was.'

The 'pitiless thing' for Cunningham is 'that awful drunkard of a wife of his. Setting up house for her time after time and then pawning the furniture on him every Saturday almost. Wear out the heart of a stone, that. Leading him the life of the damned. Monday morning start afresh. Shoulder to the wheel.' The last words are also, perhaps, an evocation of the doom of Ixion. The toil of the Danaids has its Ulyssean counterpart in the never-ending trouble of an old tramp. 'On the curbstone before Jimmy Geary the sexton's, an old tramp sat, grumbling, emptying the dirt and stones out of his huge dustbrown yawning boot. After life's journey.'

On its way to the cemetery the cab is held up by a drove of branded cattle

lowing, slouching by on padded hoofs, whisking their tails slowly on their clotted bony croups. Outside them and through them ran raddled sheep bleating with fear.

'Emigrants,' Mr Power said.

'Huuuh!' the drover's voice cried, his switch sounding on their flanks. 'Huuuh! out of that!'

Thursday of course. Tomorrow is killing day.

The driver with his switch may be likened to 'the great Orion driving the wild beasts together over the mead of asphodel … with a strong mace all of bronze in his hands, that is ever unbroken'.

Father Coffey wears the mask of Cerberus. 'Father Coffey. I knew his name was like a coffin. *Dominenamine.* Bully about the muzzle he looks. Bosses the show. Muscular christian. Woe betide anyone that looks crooked at him: priest. Thou art Peter. Burst sideways like a sheep in clover Dedalus says he will. With a belly on him like a poisoned pup.' There is another, more direct, allusion to Cerberus, whose name Mr Bloom cannot recall, in his comment on the hawker's barrow of cakes at the entrance to the graveyard: 'Simnel cakes those are, stuck together: cakes for the dead. Dogbiscuits. Who ate them?'

The caretaker, John O'Connell, personifies Hades himself; he was a well-known Dublin character, of a longevity worthy of his prototype. 'John O'Connell. He never forgets a friend.' All the mourners make a point of speaking well of the caretaker – an echo of the Euripidean eulogy of Hades and such euphemisms as the designation of the Eumenides, *la veuve* for the guillotine and so forth. 'Quietly, sure of his ground, he traversed the dismal[1] fields.' There is an epic turn in this phrase, a recall of 'the dank house of Hades' and the Cimmerian land shrouded in clouds and mist. Mr Bloom remembers with surprise that John O'Connell is a married man.

Wonder how he had the gumption to propose to any girl. Come out and live in the graveyard. Dangle that before her. It might thrill her first. Courting death … Shades of night hovering here with all the dead stretched about. The shadows of the tombs when churchyards yawn and Daniel O'Connell must be a descendant I suppose who is this used to say he was a queer breedy man great catholic all the same like a big giant in the dark. Will o' the wisp. Gas of graves. Want to keep her mind off it to conceive at all. Women especially are so touchy.

To Mr Bloom the 'gumption' which got John O'Connell his wife was, perhaps, not unlike that which won Proserpine for her dark lord, most 'catholic'[2] of all the gods; but awe of Hades has stayed the candour normal to his silent monologue.

The mourners pass the monuments of Daniel O'Connell and Parnell, the shades of Heracles and Agamemnon. The latter hero, like Parnell, came to his end through a woman; 'there is no more faith in women'. When Odysseus had greeted these and other heroes 'the soul of Ajax alone stood apart, being still angry for the victory wherein I prevailed against him, in the suit by the ships concerning the arms of Achilles, that his lady mother had set for a prize; and the sons of the Trojans made award and Pallas Athene. Would that I had never prevailed and won such a prize.' The attitude of John Henry Menton and the episode on the bowling green recall the aloofness of Ajax who, like Menton, requited a proffered service with a snub and passed 'grandly' on.

The incident of the man in the mackintosh (which will be recalled by Mr Bloom several times in the course of his day) offers interesting possibilities for Joycean interpretation in the light of Homeric precedent. When the gravediggers are about to lower the coffin to its resting-place, Mr Bloom, looking round, wonders: 'Now who is that lankylooking galoot over there in the macintosh? Now who is he I'd

1. The derivation of 'dismal' is *dies mali*; here the word is, perhaps, a foretaste of the *dies irae* that is to come in the halls of Circe.
2. The etymology of the name 'Hades' is uncertain, but the most plausible of the derivations which have been suggested is from ἅδω or χάδω, so that Hades would mean 'the all-embracer' – the exact equivalent of 'catholic'.

like to know? Now I'd give a trifle to know who he is. Always someone turns up you never dreamt of. A fellow could live on his lonesome
all his life. Yes he could. Still he'd have to get someone to sod him after
he died though he could dig his own grave. ...' When the ceremony is
over, Hynes, the reporter, makes his round recording the names of
those present.

'And tell us,' Hynes said, 'do you know that fellow in the, fellow was over
there in the ...'
He looked around.
'Macintosh. Yes I saw him. Where is he now?'
'M'Intosh,' Hynes said, scribbling. 'I don't know who he is. Is that his name?'
He moved away, looking about him.
'No,' Mr Bloom began, turning and stopping. 'I say, Hynes!'
Didn't hear. What? Where has he disappeared to? Not a sign. Well of all the.
Has anyone here seen? Kay ee double ell. Become invisible. Good Lord, what
became of him?

There is something uncanny about this Burberry's dummy dubbed
M'Intosh, the thirteenth mourner,[1] and Mr Bloom adds the incident
to the growing repertoire of memories whence he aptly draws as
Bloomsday moves on towards Penelope's night. In the 'Eumaeus' episode, when Mr Bloom and Stephen, slowly convalescent from the
drugged ecstasy of the brothel (where M'Intosh has, of course, made
a spectral entry and disappearance), sit talking in the cabman's shelter,
the former, reading the *Telegraph*, finds recorded amongst the mourners
present '*L. Boom, C. P. M'Coy, Dash M'Intosh and several others*'. Mr
Bloom, though nettled by the mutilation of his name, points out to
his companion the names of M'Coy and Stephen 'who were con-
spicuous, needless to say, by their total absence (to say nothing of
M'Intosh)' at Dignam's funeral.

In the *Nekuia* there is a curious passage, unusually ambiguous for the
Odyssey, dealing with the Melampus legend (*Odyssey* XI: 281–98).
This passage (suspected to be an interpolation) seems to have been

1. One sees this M'Intosh as one of those ominous and more-than-unnecessary
persons in an Ibsen play – Gregers Werle in the *Wild Duck*, for instance, which
concludes:

GREGERS [*looking straight before him*]: In that case, I'm glad my destiny is what it is.
RELLING: Excuse me. What is your destiny?
GREGERS [*going*]: To be the thirteenth at table.
RELLING: The devil it is!

introduced to lead up to the longer digression in the fifteenth book of the *Odyssey* (corresponding to the 'Eumaeus' episode in *Ulysses*), relating to Theoclymenos. Telemachus is about to embark from Pylos, on his way back to Ithaca, where he is destined to meet his father at Eumaeus's hut.

Thus he was busy thereat and praying and making burnt-offering to Athene, by the stern of the ship, when a man came nigh him, a stranger, that had slain his man and turned outlaw from Argos. He was a soothsayer, and by his lineage he came of Melampus, who of old time abode in Pylos, mother of flocks, a rich man and one that had an exceeding goodly house among the Pylians, but afterward he had come to the land of strangers, fleeing from his country and from Neleus the great-hearted, proudest of living men, who kept all his goods for a full year by force. All that time Melampus lay bound with hard bonds in the halls of Phylacus, suffering great pains for the sake of the daughter of Neleus, and for the dread blindness of soul which the goddess, the Erinnys of the grievous stroke, had laid on him. Howsoever he escaped his fate, and drave away the lowing kine from Phylace to Pylos and brought the maiden home to his own brother to wife.

There follows a lengthy genealogy tracing the descent of Polypheides from Melampus, and concluding: 'Apollo made the high-souled Polypheides a seer far the chief of human kind, Amphiaraus being now dead. He removed his dwelling to Hypheresia, being angered with his father, and here he abode and prophesied to all men. This man's son it was, Theoclymenos by name, that now drew nigh and stood by Telemachus.' The speculations of M. Bérard as to why this irrelevant personage is introduced and his lineage traced at such length are pertinent to the M'Intosh mystery.

Here, as in other instances, an interpolation is enclosed at both ends by the same line [thus the M'Intosh 'interpolation' is preceded by '*burying him. We come to bury Caesar*' and followed by the words '*Only man buries. … Bury the dead*']; the relevance of this passage is of the slightest when the part played by this Theoclymenos in the *Odyssey* is considered. This famous seer, whose genealogy is given us in thirty almost incomprehensible verses, must have been associated (in some legend which has not survived) with the later life of Ulysses or Telemachus. He figures only in the last books of the *Odyssey* and then merely to repeat the same banal prophecies (Books XV and XVI) and to warn the suitors (Book XX). … In the Epic Cycle the Odyssey was followed by the Telegony; was this Theoclymenos one of the heroes of the Telegony? Did he figure in the first lines of that epic as a compeer of Telemachus and Ulysses?

And was some allusion made in those opening lines to the manner in which Telemachus rescued him at Pylos? Was it in order to explain that allusion that this obscure and pointless passage was intercalated in the *Odyssey*?

M. Bérard goes on to point out the mystery which surrounds the movements of Theoclymenos after his arrival in Ithaca. When Odysseus, disguised as a beggar, arrives at the palace, the suitors discuss where he is to sleep; Theoclymenos they seem to ignore. 'Where did the latter sleep that night? He did not accompany the suitors or Telemachus; he did not stay with Ulysses. It is unlike Homer thus to abandon one of his characters without having assured him bed and shelter. Yet next day he reappeared at the palace when the slaughter of the suitors was about to begin.' There is a strangely modern touch about this MYSTERY MAN FROM PYLOS as a newspaper-man of today would feature him. Indeed, M'Intosh-Theoclymenos is always with us; he is the hunchback one never fails to see in the left-hand corner-seat of the front row of the gallery on every first night, the bearded Russian priest who never misses an international football match, that old woman in a moleskin coat with a packet of peppermint lozenges who is always in evidence in the Nisi Prius court when mixed cases of equity are being heard. The *état civil* of such queer fish is written on their shells, as, to the Romans, Ibsen, when living in their city, were merely the *Cappellone* – the fellow with the big hat.

The ambiguous prophecy of Tiresias is recalled by a mention of Robert Emmet, the text of whose 'last words' is cited at the close of the episode of the 'Sirens'. '*When my country takes her place among the nations of the earth, then and not till then, let my epitaph be written: I Have Done.*' The equivocation of that utterance lies, of course, in the fact that, assuming that Emmet had the normal desire for prolongation of life, he was, in reality, impetrating a long postponement of Ireland's freedom – a double-edged postulate like the oracle's *Ibis redibis nunquam in bello peribis*, and akin to the strange rigmarole, about a wayfarer who takes an oar for a winnowing-fan and death that shall come from the sea, which the Theban seer rendered to Odysseus.

Even though such echoes of the *Nekuia* be disregarded by the reader, the effect of the technic of 'incubism' as applied in this episode is ample in itself to produce – and with, apparently, the most commonplace materials – a mortuary atmosphere at least as intense as that of Homer's 'dank house of Hades' or the Gravediggers' Scene in *Hamlet*. Allusions are expressly made to the latter; the gravediggers, for instance, are numbered, and Mr Bloom, recalling Shakespeare's scene, admires his 'profound knowledge of the human heart'. The air presses down upon the mourners; the very earth seems to open in fissures to receive them. *Facilis descensus* ... 'The carriage, passing the open drains and mounds of rippedup roadway before the tenement houses, lurched round the corner.' The tramp's huge boot 'yawns' as he empties the dirt out of it. 'They follow: dripping into a hole one after the other.' The idea of the bed, 'bed of death ghostcandled' (see 'Proteus'), is woven into Mr Bloom's soliloquy. His father's suicide. 'Thought he was asleep at first. Then saw yellow streaks on his face. Had slipped down to the foot of the bed.' He pictures his own death.

Well it is a long rest. Feel no more. It's the moment you feel. Must be damned unpleasant. Can't believe it at first. Mistake must be: someone else. Try the house opposite. Wait, I wanted to. I haven't yet. Then darkened death-chamber. Light they want. Whispering around you. Would you like to see a priest? Then rambling and wandering. Delirium all you hid all your life. The death struggle. His sleep is not natural. Press his lower eyelid. Watching is his nose pointed is his jaw sinking are the soles of his feet yellow. Pull the pillow away and finish it off on the floor since he's doomed.

There is a downward movement, the stifling pressure of an incubus from beginning to end. Mr Bloom sees a barge in a lock: 'a man stood on his dropping barge between clamps of turf. ... Dropping down, lock by lock, to Dublin.' The horse which draws the hearse has a tight collar 'pressing on a bloodvessel or something'. Various forms of burial, prehistoric positions of inhumation, some of which, perhaps, are allusions to Jewish ritual, are recalled – closing up the orifices, cremation, sea-burial, the Parsee fires, mummification. Mr Bloom has a grotesque inspiration in sepulchral economics: 'Holy fields. More room if they buried them standing.[1] Sitting or kneeling you couldn't. Standing? His head might come up some day above ground in a landslip with his hand pointing. All honeycombed the ground must be: oblong cells.' One of the gravediggers bends to 'pluck from the haft [of his spade] a long tuft of grass' – a ritual gesture. There is a persistent use of mortuary metaphor, apt to deepen the Cimmerian[2] dusk of the charnel-

---

1. Thus kings and warriors were buried in pagan Ireland.
2. The Semitic root *k-m-r* signifies 'darkness'. Thus *Kimeriri* is used in the Bible to describe an eclipse of the daylight, a sudden darkness.

house: 'fellow like that mortified if women are by', 'whole place gone to hell'. 'Every mortal day a fresh batch.' The ghoulish rat serves as a link between the graveyard and the Lestrygonian (esurient) motifs; in Mr Bloom the baser or, rather, basic appetites are rarely dormant. 'One of those chaps would make short work of a fellow. Pick the bones clean no matter who it was. Ordinary meat for them. A corpse is meat gone bad. Well and what's cheese? Corpse of milk.' Mr Bloom lunches frugally off a cheese sandwich (compensated at teatime by a more substantial meal).

The bodily organ related to this episode is the heart.

'*I am the resurrection and the life*. That touches a man's inmost heart.'
'It does,' Mr Bloom said.

Your heart perhaps but what price the fellow in the six feet by two with his toes to the daisies? No touching that. Seat of the affections. Broken heart. A pump after all, pumping thousands of gallons of blood every day. One fine day it gets bunged up and there you are. Lots of them lying around here: lungs, hearts, livers. Old rusty pumps: damn the thing else. The resurrection and the life. Once you are dead you are dead. That last day idea. Knocking them all up out of their graves. Come forth, Lazarus! And he came fifth and lost the job. Get up! Last day! Then every fellow mousing around for his liver and his lights and the rest of his traps. Find damn all of himself that morning. Pennyweight of powder in a skull. Twelve grammes one pennyweight. Troy measure.

The Epic glory reduced to a little dust in a skull, *pulvis et umbra*. ...

Thinking of the suicide's degradation, Mr Bloom muses: 'they have no mercy on that here or infanticide. Refuse christian burial. They used to drive a stake of wood through his heart in the grave. As if it wasn't broken already. ...' Mr Bloom's heart, anyhow, is in the right place.

7. AEOLUS

SCENE	The Newspaper
HOUR	12 noon
ORGAN	Lungs
ART	Rhetoric
COLOUR	Red
SYMBOL	Editor
TECHNIC	Enthymemic

THE scene of this episode is the office of the *Freeman's Journal and National Press*,[1] which Mr Bloom visits in order to arrange for the publication of an advertisement of Alexander Keyes's 'high class licensed premises'. He also hopes to persuade the editor that the *Telegraph*, an evening paper under the same management, should give his client a 'puff' in the 'Saturday pink' edition of that journal. Mr Keyes has had an inspiration which Mr Bloom explains to Councillor Nannetti, business-manager of the *Freeman*. 'Like that, see. Two crossed keys here. A circle. Then here the name of Alexander Keyes, tea, wine and spirit merchant. ... The idea is the house of keys. You know, councillor, the Manx parliament. Innuendo of home rule. Tourists, you know, from the isle of Man. Catches the eye you see. Can you do that?' Mr Bloom undertakes to produce the design in question, which has already appeared in a Kilkenny paper; it is this errand which, in the next episode but one, takes him to the national library.

Besides the business activities of Mr Bloom, this episode depicts the inner life of a daily paper and there are realistic descriptions of the *Telegraph* editor, Myles Crawford, and of a conversation on journalistic topics between him and some of his cronies, Mr Dedalus, Professor MacHugh, Ned Lambert, and others. After Mr Dedalus has left – the eloquence of one Dan Dawson, as reported in the *Freeman* and retailed *viva voce* by Ned Lambert, has given him a thirst – in quest of refreshment, Stephen appears, in his role of 'bullock-befriending bard', escorted by Mr O'Madden Burke. Stephen has come to deliver Mr

---

1. This office was burnt down during the rising of 1916. The paper ceased publication in the twenties, after an existence of a century and a half.

Deasy's letter on the epidemic of foot-and-mouth disease. He is regaled with a symposium of journalistic reminiscence, and profits by his temporary affluence to lead the editorial party to a neighbouring bar. ' "Chip of the old block!" the editor cried, slapping Stephen on the shoulder. "Let us go."'

In this episode Stephen and Mr Bloom come near each other but do not meet. The foreman has insisted that, if Keyes is to get his 'little puff' in the *Telegraph*, the advertisement must be renewed for three months. Mr Bloom hurries off in search of Keyes to arrange the matter. Meanwhile Stephen arrives. When Mr Bloom returns Stephen is already leading his thirsty retinue barwards, walking beside MacHugh. The editor follows, in conversation with O'Molloy. Mr Bloom hurries, breathless, towards the former. 'Just this ad. I spoke with Mr Keyes just now. He'll give a renewal for two months, he says. After he'll see. But he wants a par to call attention in the *Telegraph* too, the Saturday pink. ... What will I tell him, Mr Crawford?'

The editor's reply is terse and rude.

Mr Bloom catches sight of Stephen in front. 'Wonder is that young Dedalus the moving spirit. Has a good pair of boots on him today. Last time I saw him he had his heels in view.'

Thus in this episode, as in the subsequent scene at the national library, Mr Bloom and his spiritual son come within an ace of meeting each other. That meeting and the culminating recognition take place only when Bloomsday nears its climax, in the Maternity Hospital and Brothel scenes; destiny is fulfilled only at the third attempt.

In 'Aeolus' the text is split up into brief sections, each headed with a caption composed in the journalistic manner.[1] An early section in which O'Molloy is described handing round cigarettes is headed: THE CALUMET OF PEACE. A reference to the Nelson Column is headed: HORATIO IS CYNOSURE THIS FAIR JUNE DAY; in a later section Professor MacHugh remarks to Stephen: 'You remind me of Antisthenes, a disciple of Gorgias, the sophist. It is said of him that none could tell if he were bitterer against others or against himself. He was

1. It will be noticed that the style of the captions is gradually modified in the course of the episode; the first are comparatively dignified, or classically allusive, in the Victorian tradition; later captions reproduce, in all its vulgarity, the slickness of the modern press. This historico-literary technique, here inaugurated, is a preparation for the employment of the same method, but on the grand scale, a stylistic *tour de force*, in a later episode, the 'Oxen of the Sun'.

the son of a noble and a bondwoman. And he wrote a book in which he took away the palm of beauty from Argive Helen and handed it to poor Penelope.' This passage is headed:

SOPHIST WALLOPS HAUGHTY HELEN SQUARE ON PROBOSCIS
SPARTANS GNASH MOLARS
ITHACANS VOW PEN IS CHAMP

The conversation in the editorial office turns mainly on journalistic 'shop'. Ned Lambert reads Dan Dawson's speech: '*the transcendent translucent glow of our mild Irish twilight that mantles the vista far and wide till the glowing orb of the moon shines forth to irradiate her silver effulgence*'. 'High falutin stuff,' thinks Mr Bloom. 'Bladderbags.' 'Doughy Daw!' MacHugh cries.

WHAT WETHERUP SAID

All very fine to jeer at it now in cold print but it goes down like hot cake that stuff. He was in the bakery line too wasn't he? Why they call him Doughy Daw. Feathered his nest well anyhow. ... Daughter engaged to that chap in the inland revenue office with the motor. Hooked that nicely. Entertainments open house. Big blow out. Wetherup always said that. Get a grip of them by the stomach.

This Wetherup is mentioned again in *Ulysses* (page 621) in a similar context – a statement of the advantages of keeping a good table and open house. Nothing more is known of this curiously named personage, whose only claim to immortality seems to lie in the phrase quoted above.

Professor MacHugh, in a rhetorical flight, compares the Irish and Greeks, pioneers of spirituality, with materialist empire-builders of past and present times.

'The Greek! *Kyrios!* Shining word! The vowels the Semite and the Saxon know not. *Kyrie!* The radiance of the intellect. I ought to profess Greek, the language of the mind. *Kyrie eleison!* The closet-maker and the cloaca-maker will never be the lords of our spirit. We are liege subjects of the catholic chivalry of Europe that foundered at Trafalgar and of the empire of the spirit, not an *imperium*, that went under with the Athenian fleets at Aegospotami. Yes, yes. They went under. Pyrrhus, misled by an oracle, made a last attempt to retrieve the fortunes of Greece. Loyal to a lost cause. ...'

'They went forth to battle,' Mr O'Madden Burke said greyly, 'but they always fell.'

Myles Crawford tells the tale of 'the great Gallaher' (see the story of this successful journalist in *Dubliners*: 'A Little Cloud'), who brought off a scoop at the time of the Phoenix Park political murders (1881), by telegraphing details of the murderers' movements to the *New York World* in an ingenious code, based on an advertisement in a back number of the *Freeman*.

'History!' Myles Crawford cried. 'The Old Woman of Prince's Street was there first. There was weeping and gnashing of teeth over that. Out of an advertisement. Gregor Grey made the design for it. That gave him the leg up. Then Paddy Hooper worked Tay Pay who took him on the *Star*. Now he's got in with Blumenfield. That's press. That's talent. Pyatt! he was all their daddies.'

'Clamn dever,' Lenehan said to Mr O'Madden Burke.

Lenehan, the practised parasite (see 'Two Gallants' in *Dubliners*), is much in evidence in this episode, and, amongst other witticisms, launches a conundrum which sticks in Mr Bloom's mind and is recalled by him several times in the course of the day.

Q. What opera resembles a railway line?
A. *The Rose of Castille*. See the wheeze? Rows of cast steel. Gee!

MacHugh quotes 'the finest display of oratory he ever heard', an *extempore* speech by John F. Taylor in reply to one 'pouring the proud man's contumely upon the new movement' for the revival of the Irish tongue.

'*Mr chairman, ladies and gentlemen: Great was my admiration in listening to the remarks addressed to the youth of Ireland a moment since by my learned friend. It seemed to me that I had been transported into a country far away from this country, into an age remote from this age, that I stood in ancient Egypt and that I was listening to the speech of some high-priest of that land addressed to the youthful Moses. ... And it seemed to me that I heard the voice of that Egyptian high-priest raised in a tone of like haughtiness and pride. I heard his words and their meaning was revealed to me.*

FROM THE FATHERS

It was revealed to me that those things are good which yet are corrupted which neither if they were supremely good nor unless they were good could be corrupted. Ah, curse you! That's saint Augustine.[1]

1. It is characteristic of this episode that the Father of the Church chosen by Stephen in his citation and expletive should be one of the greatest rhetoricians of all time.

'*Why will you Jews not accept our culture, our religion and our language? You are a tribe of nomad herdsmen; we are a mighty people. You have no cities nor no wealth; our cities are hives of humanity and our galleys, trireme and quadrireme, laden with all manner merchandise, furrow the waters of the known globe. You have but emerged from primitive conditions; we have a literature, a priesthood, an age-long history and a polity. ... You pray to a local and obscure idol; our temples, majestic and mysterious, are the abodes of Isis and Osiris; of Horus and Ammon Ra. Yours serfdom, awe and humbleness; ours thunder and the seas. Israel is weak and few are her children; Egypt is an host and terrible are her arms. Vagrants and daylabourers are you called; the world trembles at our name.*

'*But ladies and gentlemen, had the youthful Moses listened to and accepted that view of life, had he bowed his head and bowed his will and bowed his spirit before that arrogant admonition he would never have brought the chosen people out of their house of bondage nor followed the pillar of cloud by day. He would never have spoken with the Eternal amid lightnings on Sinai's mountaintop nor ever have come down with the light of inspiration shining in his countenance and bearing in his arms the tables of the law, graven in the language of the outlaw.*'[1]

He ceased and looked at them, enjoying silence.

OMINOUS – FOR HIM

J. J. O'Molloy said not without regret:
'And yet he died without having entered the land of promise.'
'A sudden – at – the – moment – though – from – lingering – illness – often – previously – expectorated – demise,' Lenehan said. 'And with a great future behind him.'

The opening passage of this eloquent oration and the oriental comparison involved are suggestive of the transmigration motif discussed in an introductory chapter. The 'Promised Land' theme is further developed in the course of this episode in the anecdote invented by Stephen, entitled *A Pisgah Sight of Palestine or the Parable of the Plums*, an ironic fable of two ancient Dublin vestals who consume twenty-four ripe plums on the summit of Nelson's monument, spitting out the plumstones slowly between the railings on to the panorama of Dublin far below.

Then we came to the isle Aeolian, where dwelt Aeolus ... in a floating island, and all about it is a wall of bronze unbroken and the cliff runs up sheer from the

1. It is significant also that this was the passage from *Ulysses* chosen by Joyce for a gramophone record (H.M.V., Paris) of his voice, as being the most rhetorical passage in the book and thus most easily reproducible (at the time of reading: 1923).

sea. His twelve children too abide there in his halls, six daughters and six lusty sons; and, behold, he gave his daughters to his sons to wife. And the steaming house echoes all around its outer court by day.

Odysseus stayed a whole month with Aeolus and was kindly treated by him. On his departure Aeolus gave him a wallet containing all the noisy winds, closely bound with a silver thong, 'for him Cronos made keeper of the winds, either to lull or to rouse what blasts he will'. Sped by a favouring zephyr, Odysseus arrived within sight of his home and could even perceive his folk tending the beacon fires. But, when he laid him down to sleep, his ship's company, imagining that the wallet was stuffed with treasure, loosed the silver thong. The winds broke out and drove the ship violently back to the isle Aeolian. And now Aeolus's temper had changed; he cursed Odysseus, 'vilest of living men', and bade him begone with all speed.

The characteristic of the palace of the King of the Winds is its noisiness. This is not (as implied in Butcher and Lang's translation) the sound of revelry by day, but a continued roaring of the prisoned winds.

κνισῆεν δὲ τε δῶμα περιστεναχίζεται αὐλῇ

Mr Bloom's approach to the editorial office, lorded over by Myles Crawford, Ruler of the Winds, is attended by a chaos of noises, trams 'right and left parallel clanging ringing', the thud of 'loudly flung sacks of letters' loaded in vermilion mailcars, and a rumble of barrels. 'Grossbooted draymen rolled barrels dullthudding out of Prince's stores and bumped them up on the brewery float.' (The last words are, perhaps, a subsidiary recall of the 'floating island' of Aeolus.) 'He passed in through the sidedoor and along the warm dark stairs and passage, along the now reverberating boards. ... Thumping, thumping. Through a lane of clanking drums he made his way towards Nannetti's reading closet.' All through the opening passage of this episode we hear the surge and thunder of the printing-press and Mr Bloom has difficulty in making himself audible to Nannetti, who, accustomed to this tumult, 'slips his words deftly into the pauses of the clanking'. (This passage indicates that Mr Bloom has a soft voice, excellent in a canvasser as in a woman. No direct description of the hero of *Ulysses* is given in any part of the work and we have to build up our impression of his manner and appearance from such small hints as this.)

This analogy between the daily press and the palace of the winds is

seen to be curiously appropriate if we consider the factual basis of
Homer's anthropomorphic description of the isle of Aeolus, girt with
a wall of bronze, which can be identified, beyond all reasonable doubt,
with the island of Stromboli. Among the volcanic products found on
this island is a metallic ore which adheres in flakes to the surface of the
rocks. This substance is smooth-polished and brilliant as a mirror.
Another volcanic product is pumice-stone; though recently there have
been no such eruptions at Stromboli, ancient deposits of pumice-stone
are found on the island and at certain periods Stromboli may have re-
sembled the isle of Santorin as it was seen by the French traveller,
Thévenot.

Flames suddenly rose from the sea-bed in the harbour and from morning till
evening there was an eruption of pumice-stone, which was hurled up into the
air with the noise of a cannonade. The air was poisoned and many persons died.
The waters of the Archipelago were so thickly strewn with floating blocks of
pumice-stone that, when the wind blew from a certain quarter, the harbours
were blocked and ships could only enter when their company had opened a
way with poles.

This is the most probable explanation of the floating island of Aeolus.
The Aeolian island rose sheer from a wide belt of buoyant pumice-
stone on which it seemed to float.

Zeus made Aeolus keeper of the winds. Thus, speaking of the isle of
Strongule (Stromboli), Martianus Capella observed: 'The smoke and
flames of Strongule announce the direction of the winds; to this very
day the islanders can predict in advance the wind to be expected.' This
belief that by observation of a volcano it is possible to foretell the
direction from which the wind will come is based apparently on the
fact that the winds appear to have some influence on the nature of a
volcanic eruption. Thus Spallanzani in his *Voyages* mentions that on
Stromboli 'when there is a northerly wind, the smoke is white and
thin and there are few explosions; when the wind is southerly the smoke
is thick and black and spreads widely over the island; explosions are
frequent and violent.' This information was given him by the islanders,
who further affirmed that, when the smoke is thick and explosions are
frequent, these phenomena *precede* the coming of a southerly wind by
several days. Spallanzani was, personally, unable to decide whether
there was any truth in the alleged possibility of making meteorological forecasts by observation of the volcano. Strabo's view seems

more rational. 'Observation shows that wind fans the flames of the volcano and calm weather calms them.'

This ancient dispute as to whether the volcano is a meteorological prophet, a 'lord of the winds', or the 'lord' is really a servant, obedient to the winds' caprice, has an obvious journalistic analogy, on which it is needless to insist.

The brazen walls of the palace of Aeolus have, perhaps, their counterpart in the tramlines, 'rows of cast steel', which encircle the office. The episode begins with a description of the trams starting from the terminus, bound for various parts of the city, slowing, shunting, changing trolley, swerving, gliding parallel. Towards the close of the episode we read of a short circuit, the doldrums: 'at various points along the eight lines tramcars with motionless trolleys stood in their tracks, bound for or from Rathmines, Rathfarnham, Blackrock, Kingstown and Dalkey, Sandymount Green, Ringsend and Sandymount tower, Donnybrook, Palmerston Park and Upper Rathmines, all still, becalmed in short circuit.' The idea of 'circulation', in its journalistic as well as its urban application, recurs frequently in this episode and it is relevant that Stromboli was known to the Greeks as Strongule, the circular island.

A buoyant debris, vomited by the printing machines, like pumice from a volcano, litters the offices – 'strewn packing-paper', 'limp galleypages', light 'tissues' which, 'rustling up' in every draught, 'floated softly in the air blue scrawls and under the table came to earth'.

It will be remembered that Aeolus's conduct towards Odysseus displayed that capriciousness which, as sailors know to their cost, is characteristic of the keeper of the winds. After a friendly welcome and generous gifts at his first visit, Aeolus, on the enforced return of his guest, had nothing but harsh words for him. Thus, too, the Editor, when Mr Bloom hurries off to 'fix up' the matter of Keyes's 'ad', genially waves him away.

'Begone!' he said. 'The world is before you.'
'Back in no time,' Mr Bloom said, hurrying out.

But, when Mr Bloom returned, the Editor's mood had changed and he refused to listen to his soft-voiced suppliant. 'A bit nervy. Look out for squalls.' And Mr Bloom, prudent mariner, thought it safer not to insist.

Odysseus had almost reached his destination, Ithaca, and could see the beacons burning on the coast, when the communistic zeal of his men frustrated their homecoming and the tempest drove him back. The theme of undeserved frustration, of a goal nearly, but not quite, attained, recurs under several aspects in this episode. There is, for instance, the case of Moses who 'died without having entered the land of promise', Mr Bloom's eleventh-hour failure to secure the promise of a 'puff' for his client in the evening paper; of J. J. O'Molloy who tries to get a loan from the editor but has to 'take the will for the deed'; who starts to tell a story about chief Baron Palles – 'everything was going swimmingly' – when he is brusquely interrupted by Lenehan, and that is the end of his attempt. J. J. O'Molloy himself, indeed, was one of life's failures: 'cleverest fellow at the junior bar he used to be', but ill-health frustrated the promise of his youth: 'a might-have-been'.

Bushe, K.C., is another who failed to 'arrive'.

'Bushe?' the editor said. 'Well, yes. Bushe, yes. He has a strain of it in his blood. Kendal Bushe or I mean Seymour Bushe.'

'He would have been on the bench long ago,' the professor said, 'only for ... But no matter.'

(The professor's aposiopesis guards its secret; in the cause of Bushe's frustration we have one of the few instances in *Ulysses* of a mystery unresolved.)

The journalist's *métier*, like the wedlock of the children of Aeolus, involves an illicit union, of aspiration and compromise, of literature and opportunism; occasionally, too, the journalist, sensitive to the way the wind is blowing, secures his transfer from conservative to left-wing organs, or vice versa – a party misalliance.[1] 'Bulldosing the public!' the editor exclaims. 'Give them something with a bite in it!' 'Sufficient for the day is the newspaper thereof.'[2] The practice of journalism involves the ancient art of rhetoric; the pressman, in fact, has some of the functions of the orator in a Greek city state. 'Cities are taken', an old adage ran, 'by the ears'; in our times, by the eyes as well. It was therefore fitting that this episode should teem with oratorical effects.

1. The *Freeman* itself (I quote from the *O'Connell Centenary Record*), in the course of its long career, 'passed through strange vicissitudes, at one time for, at another against, Irish interests'.

2. The rendering of this phrase in the French translation may interest; it is seldom that a translation succeeds in being even terser than an epigrammatic original: *À chaque jour suffit son quotidien.* (*Ulysse*, page 156.)

The orator relies on argumentation to produce that conviction which is the object of his art, and, according to Aristotle, the foundation of argumentation is the *enthymeme*, or syllogism with one premise suppressed; the general technique of this episode is, therefore, '*enthymemic*'. The hearer of oratory may be a mere seeker of aesthetic enjoyment, a θεωρός, or one who forms a judgement on what is to come, or on what is past. There are three kinds of oratory (according to Aristotle), appropriate respectively to each of the three kinds of hearer; the deliberative (γένος συμβουλευτικόν), the forensic (γ. δικανικόν), and the expository (γ. ἐπιδεικτικόν). All three kinds are illustrated in this episode. The flowery prose of Dan Dawson is expository; the fragment (quoted hereafter) of a speech by Seymour Bushe, defending an accused person in the Childs murder case (several times mentioned in the course of *Ulysses*) is forensic; Taylor's speech, comparing the arrogance of an Egyptian high-priest with that of Mr Justice Fitzgibbon, 'pouring the proud man's contumely' upon a proposed revival of the Irish tongue, is deliberative.[1] The reference to the Childs murder, a case of fratricide, recalls to Stephen the Ghost's speech in *Hamlet*:

> *And in the porches of my ear did pour ...*

Shakespeare's metaphor returns to Stephen's mind in his evocation of another Irish orator, the great tribune Daniel O'Connell. After listening to MacHugh's declamation of Taylor's speech – 'That is oratory' – Stephen muses: 'Gone with the wind. Hosts at Mullaghmast and Tara of the kings.[2] Miles of ears of porches. The tribune's words howled and

1. This speech is an apt example of the manner in which eloquence aided by the rhetorical device of a far-fetched, not to say false, analogy, can produce conviction in the listener's mind. The resemblance between the movement for a revival of the Irish tongue and the situation of the Chosen People in the land of Egypt was really of the slightest; the question at issue for the latter was not the revival of a dead or moribund tongue, nor is there any reason to believe that the Egyptians sought to impose their culture on the Jews. The speaker uses the *argumentum ad hominem* by comparing his hearers' race with the Chosen People, an *argumentum ad fidem* in exploiting for the purposes of his similitude their belief in the miraculous origin of the tables of the law, and an *argumentum ad passiones* in his description of the brow-beating of a small, inspired race by the arrogant spokesman of a mighty empire. Yet it is impossible to read, *a fortiori* to hear, this speech without being in some measure convinced by the speaker's eloquence.

2. At the Tara political meeting (August 1843) *The Times* estimated that a million Irish assembled to hear O'Connell's oratory; at Mullaghmast (October 1843), at a similar meeting, O'Connell was crowned by the sculptor Hogan.

scattered to the four winds. A people sheltered within his voice. Dead noise. Akasic records of all that ever anywhere wherever was. Love and laud him: me no more.' Stephen's reference to Akasic records (the expression recurs in a subsequent paragraph) is a reminder of the esoteric belief in the indestructibility of thoughts and words. On a higher plane 'consciousness is in indirect relations with the all but infinite memory of Nature, which is preserved with imperishable perfection in the all-embracing medium known to occult science as the *Akasa*.'[1] Each thought, silent or expressed, has its own immortality, an Akasic record. Thus Stephen, remembering his dead mother's trinkets locked away in a drawer and her vanished laughter ('phantasmal mirth, folded away: musk-perfumed'), thought: 'Folded away in the memory of nature with her toys.' It is fitting that this, the only mention of the Akasa in *Ulysses* (in whose structure, however, this theory of the indestructibility of thought has an important place) should occur in the 'Aeolus' episode, for Akasa (Sanskrit for sky) is the invisible sky of the mystics, the propeller or aerial vehicle of immaterial energy as well as its storehouse, just as air in movement is the vehicle of oratory, 'words scattered to the four winds'.

The thirty-two pages of this episode comprise a veritable thesaurus of rhetorical devices and might, indeed, be adopted as a text-book for students of the art of rhetoric. Professor Bain has remarked that in the course of the plays 'Shakespeare exemplifies nearly every rhetorical artifice known'. Doubtless this might be said of any copious writer, such as Miss Braddon or Scott, whose work extends over many decades and scores of volumes, but the gathering together under the pen within the space of thirty-two pages, in the one episode of *Ulysses* which deals exclusively with rhetoric, of nearly all the important, misleading enthymemes elenchated by Quintilian and his successors, and the making out of such elenchation a lively organic part of a very living organism, is a hoax of quite another colour. An enumeration of some of the technical devices employed (the list given hereunder is far from being exhaustive) has more than a merely academic interest, for it shows that the journalist of today has invented nothing; all the tricks of his trade were already known and classified by the Schoolmen.

Only in two instances is the rhetorical artifice employed mentioned by name in the text. One is the passage where J. J. O'Molloy quotes the

1. A. P. Sinnett, *The Growth of the Soul*, page 216.

forensic eloquence of Seymour Bushe, describing the *Moses* of Michelangelo: '*that stone effigy in frozen music, horned and terrible, of the human form divine, that eternal symbol of wisdom and prophecy which, if aught that the imagination or the hand of sculptor has wrought in marble of soultransfigured and of soultransfiguring deserves to live, deserves to live.*' 'His slim hand with a wave graced echo and fall.' Here the terms 'echo' and 'fall' are technically exact. The other instance is Professor MacHugh's comment on Stephen's fable: Two Dublin Vestals.

'Anne Kearns has the lumbago for which she rubs on Lourdes water given her by a lady who got a bottleful from a passionist father. Florence MacCabe takes a crubeen and a bottle of double X for supper every Saturday.'

'Antithesis,' the professor said, nodding twice.

The advertisement of Alexander Keyes with its design of two crossed keys (to illustrate which Mr Bloom 'crossed his fingers at the tip' – a ritual gesture), in imitation of the emblem of the Manx parliament, 'an innuendo [yet another rhetorical allusion is here] of home rule', forms part of the queer assortment of mental flotsam, fragments of which bob up at frequent intervals to the surface of Mr Bloom's consciousness in the course of the day. Seemingly irrelevant, this motif is, nevertheless, associated with one of the 'magical' themes of *Ulysses*, the legend of Mananaan MacLir, the founder of the Manx nation. The Book of Fermoy relates that Mananaan was a necromancer, who had the power of enveloping himself in a mist (cf. the 'steaming home' of Aeolus) to outwit his enemies. The name MacLir means 'son of the sea'; Aeolus, too, is the son of Poseidon, the ocean's ruler; each, from a seagirt palace, controls the air of the multitudinous seas. 'Airs romped around him [Stephen], nipping and eager airs. They are coming, waves … the steeds of Mananaan' ('Proteus' episode, page 35). (The 'nipping airs' – 'waves, steeds of Mananaan' association is perhaps a preparation for the subsequent Aeolus-Mananaan analogy.) Later, a mention of *King Lear* (page 177), that stormiest of plays, recalls to Stephen the lines:

Flow over them with your waves and with your waters, Mananaan, Mananaan MacLir …

Mananaan is mentioned in a 'mystical' context in the episode of the 'Oxen of the Sun', and, finally, in the 'Circe' episode, makes a grotesque entry in person. *In the cone of the searchlight behind the coalscuttle, ollave, holyeyed, the bearded figure of Mananaan MacLir broods, chin on*

knees. A cold seawind blows from his druid mantle. About his head writhe
eels and elvers. ... He roars 'with a voice of waves'; wails 'with a voice
of whistling seawind'. (Here Stephen's vision of the god of Man is
combined, by the chemistry of dreams, with a memory of A. E. (Mr
Russell), 'ollave, holyeyed', whom he has seen earlier in the day at the
National Library.) The first word uttered by Mananaan is the mystic
monosyllable AUM, which is held by some occultists to be 'a *résumé*
of every science, contained in the three letters A (creation), U (conservation), M (transformation)'. The knowledge of this word was the first
step, according to mystics of the east, to knowledge of that still higher
word, which rendered him who came to possess its key nearly the
equal of Brahmâtma himself. That ultimate word was engraved in a
golden triangle and preserved in a sanctuary of which Brahmâtma
alone held the keys. Thus Brahmâtma 'bore on his tiara *two crossed keys*,
symbol of the precious deposit of which he had the keeping'.[1] Crossed
keys are, therefore, an emblem of the ultimate word of existence as well
as of Mananaan, lord of spirits of the air, and Alexander Keyes, spirit
merchant. This linking up of the vulgar with the esoteric, as here in the
sequence: Alexander Keyes's 'ad' – Keys – Isle of Man – Mananaan –
AUM – Brahmâtma's secret word, is characteristic of the Joycean method
and it is appropriate that several items of the series should be named in
the 'Aeolus' episode, for Mananaan MacLir, that northern 'paynim,
who at his pleasure kept by necromancy the land of Man in mists', is own
brother to Poseidon's son, ruler of the fog-girt[2] isle of Aeolia.

A gale of wind is blowing through this episode, literally and meta-
phorically. Doors are flung open violently, Myles Crawford blows violent puffs from his cigarette, the barefoot newsboys, scampering in,
create a hurricane which lifts the rustling tissues in to the air; swing-doors
draughtily flicker to and fro. 'They always build one door opposite
another for the wind to. Way in. Way out.' Mr Bloom describes the
ways of journalists and the decline of O'Molloy in windy metaphors.

Practice dwindling. Losing heart. Gambling. Debts of honour. Reaping the
whirlwind. ... Believe he does some literary work for the *Express*. Wellread
fellow. Myles Crawford began on the *Independent*. Funny the way those newspaper men veer about when they get wind of a new opening. Weathercocks.

1. *Isis Unveiled*, II: 31.
2. '*Il arrive souvent que la fumée se répand sur l'île entière et l'obscurcit comme un
brouillard pluvieux.*' Spallanzani.

Hot and cold in the same breath. Wouldn't know which to believe. One story good till you hear the next. Go for one another baldheaded in the papers and then all blows over. Hailfellow well met the next moment.

As Swift observes, 'some maintain these Aeolists to have been very ancient in the world'. (I have already noted that all the artifices exploited by the modern pressman were the stock-in-trade of the rhetor in the Agora.) The source of the Aeolists' inflatus, Swift tells us, was

in a certain region well known to the Greeks, by them called Σκοτία, or the land of darkness. And although many controversies have arisen upon that matter, yet so much is undisputed, that from a region of the like denomination the most refined Aeolists have borrowed their original, from whence in every age the zealous among their priesthood have brought over their choicest inspiration, fetching it in their own hands from the fountain head in certain bladders, and disploding it among the sectaries in all nations, who did, and do, and ever will, daily gasp and pant after it.[1]

Not otherwise do our modern Aeolists ensure with punctual emphasis our daily gasp, relayed on wings of wind from a land of darkness, or loose on us a wallet of *canards* bound with a silver thong.

Professor MacHugh recalls an Aeolian epithet of classical times. '*Fuit Ilium*. The sack of windy Troy. Kingdoms of the world. The masters of the Mediterranean are fellaheen today.' 'Aeolisms' abound in the course of the episode; 'big blow out', 'the vent of his jacket', 'windfall when he kicks out', 'the moving spirit', 'if I could raise the wind', 'a cure for flatulence', etc. Mr Bloom, when he leaves the noisy isle, has a file of 'capering newsboys in his wake, the last zigzagging white on the breeze a mocking kite, a tail of white bowknots'.

'Red' is the colour associated with this episode; its appropriateness to the theme, the blood-warming, flag-wagging, red-ragging stunts of newsmongers, out to stimulate their circulation, is obvious. There are no crimes described in *Ulysses* and few allusions to such subjects, but in this episode we hear of two cases of murder. In the first pages we find references to red mail-vans, to the 'rougy cheeks' of the tenor Mario, and to 'Red Murray', a *Freeman* employee. Stephen's blood is 'wooed by grace of language' and he blushes. Crawford, the editor, has a 'scarlet-beaked face, crested by a comb of feathery hair'; his straw hat 'aureoles his scarlet face'. This Aeolus-Crawford, lord of the air,

1. *A Tale of a Tub*, section VIII.

has much of the bird in his appearance; like the librarian, he is a 'bird-god, moony-crowned'. When he reappears in the 'Circe' episode he 'strides jerkily, a quill between his teeth. His scarlet beak blazes within the aureole of his straw hat. ... His cock's wattles wag.' He walks in jerks, gawkily, like a long-legged bird, apt symbol of the rhetoric art, spindle-necked, heavy-billed, a scarlet flamingo.

EXAMPLES OF RHETORICAL FORMS
IN THE 'AEOLUS' EPISODE

PAGE	DEVICE
108 THE WEARER OF THE CROWN	*Metonymy*
Grossbooted draymen rolled barrels dullthudding out of Prince's stores and bumped them up on the brewery float. On the brewery float bumped dull-thudding barrels rolled by grossbooted draymen out of Prince's stores.	*Chiasmus* (a sentence in which the terms of the second of two parallel phrases reverse the order of the first)
109 steered by an umbrella.	*Metaphor*
All his brains are in the nape of his neck.	*Diasyrm* ('a pulling to pieces': mild sarcasm)
Fat folds of neck, fat, neck, fat, neck.	*Anaphora*
Co-ome thou lost one, *Co-ome thou dear one.*	*Diaeresis*
THE CROZIER AND THE PEN	*Concrete Synecdoche*
They watched the knees, legs, boots vanish.	*Asyndeton*
110 Working away, tearing away.	*Epiphora*
111 More Irish than the Irish.	*Ploce* (the using of a name, in the same phrase, both as a name and to signify the qualities of the person or persons to whom it is applied)
If you want to draw the cashier is just going to lunch.	*Enthymeme*
Hell of a racket they make.	*Hyperbaton* (transposition – as in *Silver and gold have I none*)
Maybe he understands what I.	*Anacoluthon*
113 Sllt ... Almost human the way it sllt to call attention.	*Onomatopoeia*
Doing its level best to speak.	*Prosopopoeia*
114 mangiD, kcirtaP.	*Metathesis*

PAGE	DEVICE
And then the lamb and the cat and the dog and the stick and the water ...	*Polysyndeton* (plethora of conjunctions)
Citronlemon.	*Idiotism* ('Bloomism')
115 'The ghost walks.'	*Hypotyposis* (vision). The classical example of this visionary imagination of things not present as being before the eyes is a passage from Pope's 'Elegy to an Unfortunate Young Lady':
	'What beckoning ghost along the moonlight glade
	Invites my steps, and points to yonder shade?
	'Tis she; but why that bleeding bosom gored,
	Why dimly gleams the visionary sword?'
	Another example of *hypotyposis* is Stephen's vision of Dante's three rhymes as 'three by three, approaching girls'.
Agonizing Christ, wouldn't it give you a heartburn ...?	*Apostrophe*
tho' quarrelling ...	*Apocope*
'neath the shadows ...	*Aphaeresis*
o'er	*Syncope*
pensive bosom	*Solecism*
overarching ... overarsing	*Paradiastole*
'A recently discovered fragment of Cicero's.'	*Irony* (Professor MacHugh is referring to Dan Dawson's high-falutin speech)
117 *Peaks towering high on high*	*Paregmenon*
Blessed and eternal God!	*Ecphonesis*
'The moon,' professor MacHugh said. 'He forgot Hamlet.'	*Prolepsis* (anticipation: sure enough, in his next words Dan Dawson 'features' the glowing orb of the moon)
the vista far and wide	*Synonomy*
'Doughy Daw!' he cried.	*Hypochorisma*
118 'North Cork militia! We won every time! North Cork and Spanish officers!'	*Paralogism*
O, HARP EOLIAN!	*Synaeresis*
119 'That'll be all right,' Myles Crawford said more calmly. 'Never you fret. That's all right.'	*Exergasia* (use of different phrases to express the same idea)
'I hear feetstoops.'	*Anagram*

PAGE   DEVICE

'It wasn't me, sir. It was the big fellow shoved me, sir.' — *Epanaphora* (combined use of *Anaphora* and *Epiphora*)

120 'The accumulation of the *anno Domini*.' — *Metalepsis* (one trope under another)

121 'Steal upon larks.' — Truncated *simile*

'Seems to be,' J. J. O'Molloy said ... 'but it is not always as it seems.' — *Epanalepsis* (beginning a clause with a word that is made to end the next clause)

THE CALUMET OF PEACE — *Xenia*

'Twas rank and fame that tempted thee, ... — *Synoeceiosis*

'Twas empire charmed thy heart.

122 'We haven't got the chance of a snowball in hell.' — *Catachresis* (metaphor bold to a degree of impropriety)

'Vast, I allow: but vile.' — *Synchoresis* (concession, a rhetorical device for enlisting sympathy before a tirade)

'The Roman ... brought to every new shore on which he set his foot (on our shore he never set it) only his cloacal obsession.' — *Parenthesis*

'Our old ancient ancestors ...' — *Tautology*

'Youth led by Experience visits Notoriety.' — *Abstract Synecdoche and Allegory*

123 'That old pelters.' — *Topika*

'Was he short taken?' — *Anastrophe* (word, that usually comes first, placed last)

'By Jesus, she had the foot and mouth disease and no mistake! That night she threw the soup in the waiter's face in the Star and Garter. Oho!' — *Parataxis*

124 *Dominus!* Lord! — *Metaphrase*

'They went forth to battle but they always fell.' — *Litotes*

'Boohoo!' Lenehan wept. — *Mimesis* (he mimics the grief of Pyrrhus's followers)

125 *I can't see the Joe Miller* — *Antinomasia* (use of a proper for a common name: here 'Joe Miller' for *joke*)

'*The Rose of Castille.* ... Rows of cast steel. Gee!' — *Paranomasia*

'I feel a strong weakness.' — *Oxymoron*

'The turf,' Lenehan put in. — *Synathroesmus* (accumulation by enumeration)

'Literature, the press ...'

PAGE		DEVICE

'... the gentle art of advertisement.'

'The vocal muse.'

'Dublin's prime favourite.' — *Pleonasm*

126 'I caught a cold in the park. The gate was open.' — *Auxesis*

'See it in your face. See it in your eye. — *Anaphora* (redundant repetition of same words at the beginning of clauses)

127 'Look at here. What did Ignatius Gallaher do? (*et seqq.*).' — *Anacoenesis* ('communication': the *put-yourself-in-his-place* method, used by the editor to explain Gallaher's 'stunt')

CLEVER, VERY — *Hysteron Proteron*

128 'Madam, I'm Adam. And Able was I ere I saw Elba.' — *Palindrome* (reversible sentences)

'That's press.' — *Professional Jargon*

'father of scare journalism and brother-in-law of Chris Callinan.' — *Zeugma*

'Clamn dever.' — *Metathesis*

Would anyone wish that mouth for her kiss? How do you know? — *Apostrophe*

129 Underdarkneath — *Anastomosis*

mouth south: tomb womb — *Homoioteleuton*

'I hold no brief, as at present advised, for the third profession but ...' — *Epitrope* (permission – a form of *concession*)

'your Cork legs are running away with you.' — *Hibernicism*

'Sufficient for the day is the newspaper thereof.' — *Epigram*

'He would have been on the bench long ago only for ... But no matter.' — *Aposiopesis*

130 Muchibus thankbus. — *Parody*

131 'The speech of a finished orator ... pouring in chastened diction, I will not say the vials of his wrath but pouring the proud man's contumely on the new movement.' — *Paraleipsis* (omission of a possible argument, which, however, is stated)

132 'He looked (though he was not) a dying man.' — *Epanorthosis* (correction of a possible misunderstanding)

I heard his words and their meaning was revealed to me. — *Epanalepsis* (taking up the last words of a previous clause)

PAGE	DEVICE
FROM THE FATHERS	
It was revealed to me that those things are good, etc.	
'Ah, curse you!'	*Sarcasm* (the speaker 'shows his teeth' in *rictus*: Cf. Gk. *Sarcos*)
You are a tribe of nomad herdsmen ...	*Incrementum* (a piling-up of points in an argument)
You have no cities nor no wealth ...	
You have but emerged from primitive conditions ...	
all manner merchandise	*Archaeism*
had the youthful Moses ... bowed his head and bowed his will and bowed his spirit. ...	*Anabasis* (gradation)
133 'A sudden - at - the - moment - though - from - lingering - illness - often - previously - ex- pectorated - demise.'	*Polyhyphenation* *Periphrasis*
expectorated (for 'expected')	*Paragoge*
134 We will certainly refuse to partake of strong waters, will we not?'	*Tapinosis*
'I hope you will live to see it pub- lished.'	*Charientism* (mild sarcasm)
135 DEAR DIRTY DUBLIN	The passage which follows is a *Parable*
'They had no idea it was that high.'	*Oratio recta-obliqua* (giving, by quota- tion of a vulgar form, vivacity to the flatness of a third-personal report)
136 A newsboy cried:	
'Terrible tragedy in Rathmines! A child bit by a bellows!'	*Anticlimax*
K. M. A.	*Abbreviation*
137 'With a heart and a half if I could ...'	*Hyperbole*
138 SPEEDPILLS VELOCITOUS AEROLITHS	*Neologism*
Poor Penelope. Penelope Rich.	*Epanodos* (repetition in inverted order; here combined with *antithesis*)
Hackney cars, cabs, delivery wag- gons, mailvans, etc.	*Aparithmesis* (enumeration in detail of things in corresponding words of the same grammatical character)
139 'Call it, wait,' the professor said, opening his long lips to reflect. 'Call it. let me see ...'	*Aporia* (dubitation)
ANNE WIMBLES	*Hapax Legomenon*

8. THE LESTRYGONIANS

SCENE	The Lunch
HOUR	1 p.m.
ORGAN	Esophagus
ART	Architecture
SYMBOL	Constables
TECHNIC	Peristaltic

THOUGHTS of luncheon are never far from Mr Bloom's mind through-out this episode. The only immediate business he has in hand is a visit to the national library to trace, in a back number of the *Kilkenny People*, an advertisement which he has promised one of his customers to get republished. Meanwhile he profits by the empty hour to indulge his 'wanderlust', his hobby of seeing the habitations of many men and observing their various minds. 'A sombre Y.M.C.A. young man, watchful among the warm sweet fumes of Graham Lemon's, placed a throwaway in a hand of Mr Bloom. ... Elijah is coming. Dr John Alexander Dowie, restorer of the church in Zion, is coming.' Dilly Dedalus, 'lobbing about' outside Dillon's auction-rooms, excites Mr Bloom's compassion. 'Must be selling off some old furniture. ... Good Lord, that poor child's dress is in flitters. Underfed she looks too. Potatoes and marge, marge and potatoes. It's after they feel it. Proof of the pudding. Undermines the constitution.' Crossing a bridge, he watches a brewery barge puff its way seawards, the gulls flapping strongly about it. 'Wait. Those poor birds.' Compassionate, he buys two Banbury cakes.

He broke the brittle paste and threw its fragments down into the Liffey. ... They wheeled, flapping weakly. I'm not going to throw any more. Penny quite enough. Lot of thanks I get. Not even a caw. They spread foot and mouth disease too. If you cram a turkey, say, on chestnut meal it tastes like that. Eat pig like pig. But then why is it that saltwater fish are not salty? How is that?

The timeball on the Ballast Office reminds him of Sir Robert Ball's *Story of the Heavens*, and the cryptic word 'parallax' enters his mind. 'I never exactly understood.' That is perhaps why this word so fascinates Mr Bloom – for we have not heard the last of 'parallax' by any means.

The oriental in Mr Bloom is ever in quest of the Word, and, just as any son may be the Messiah, so any word of mystery – why not 'parallax'? – might be the Word Ineffable. But common sense asserts itself, the earth-sense of Mrs Bloom, who has a short way with such 'abstruosities' as parallax or metempsychosis: 'met him pike hoses she called it. ... She's right after all. Only big words for ordinary things.'

A procession of whitesmocked men marched slowly towards him along the gutter, scarlet sashes across their boards. Bargains. Like that priest they are this morning: we have sinned: we have suffered. He read the scarlet letters on their five tall white hats: H.E.L.Y.S. Wisdom Hely's. Y lagging behind drew a chunk of bread from under his foreboard, crammed it into his mouth and munched as he walked.

He remembers the time when he worked for Hely and how he disliked the *corvée* of collecting debts at a convent. 'A nice nun there, really sweet face. ... It was a nun they say invented barbed wire.' Days when Milly was a kiddy. Her tubbing night.

American soap I bought: elderflower. Cosy smell of her bathwater. Funny she looked soaped all over. Shapely too. Now photography. Poor papa's daguerreotype atelier he told me of. Hereditary taste.
He walked along the curbstone.
Stream of life ...

Those were good times, halcyon days, when Marion was gentle yet. 'Swish and soft flop her stays made on the bed. Always warm from her. Always liked to let herself out. Sitting there after till near two, taking out her hairpins. Milly tucked up in beddyhouse. Happy. Happy. That was the night. ...'
His musing are interrupted by the greetings of Mrs Breen, an old flame, now married to an 'old mosey lunatic'.

'There must be a new moon out,' she said. 'He's always bad then. Do you know what he did last night?'
Her hand ceased to rummage. Her eyes fixed themselves on him, wide in alarm, yet smiling.
'What?' Mr Bloom said.
Let her speak. Look straight in her eyes. I believe you. Trust me.
'Woke me up in the night,' she said. 'Dream he had, a nightmare.'
Indiges.
'Said the ace of spades was walking up the stairs.'
'The ace of spades!' Mr Bloom said.

She took a folded postcard from her handbag.

'Read that,' she said. 'He got it this morning.'

'What is it?' Mr Bloom asked, taking the card. 'U.P.?'

'U.P.: up,' she said. 'Someone taking a rise out of him. It's a great shame for them whoever he is.'

'Indeed it is,' Mr Bloom said.

She took back the card, sighing.

'And now he's going round to Mr Menton's office. He's going to take an action for ten thousand pounds, he says.'

She folded the card into her untidy bag and snapped the catch.

Same blue serge dress she had two years ago, the nap bleaching. Seen its best days. Wispish hair over her ears. And that dowdy toque, three old grapes to take the harm out of it. Shabby genteel. She used to be a tasty dresser. Lines round her mouth. Only a year or so older than Molly.

See the eye that woman gave her, passing. Cruel. The unfair sex.

Mr Bloom learns from Mrs Breen that their friend Mina Purefoy is in the lying-in hospital, Holles Street. 'She's three days bad now.' As he walks on, undecided where to take his lunch, he inwardly condoles with the unfortunate Mrs Purefoy.

Sss. Dth, dth, dth! Three days imagine groaning on a bed with a vinegared handkerchief round her forehead, her belly swollen out! Phew! Dreadful simply! Child's head too big: forceps. Doubled up inside her trying to butt its way out blindly, groping for the way out. Kill me that would. Lucky Molly got over hers lightly. They ought to invent something to stop that. Life with hard labour. Twilightsleep idea. ...

The sight of a squad of constables reminds him how he got involved in a crowd of young medicals demonstrating against the Boer War. 'Silly billies: mob of young cubs yelling their guts out.' Mr Bloom has little sympathy with political fanatics, though he takes an academic interest in the technique of conspiracy, James Stephens's 'circles of ten', for instance. (This James Stephens, a conspirator, who escaped from jail with the aid of the turnkey's daughter, must not be confused with the eminent writer of the same name.)

A heavy cloud hides the sun, and his mood is darkened by a sense of the endless, futile routine of things, trams passing one another, ingoing, outgoing, ceaselessly clanging along grooved circuits.

Useless words. Things go on the same; day after day; squads of police marching out, back; trams in, out. Dignam carted off. Mina Purefoy on a bed groaning to have a child tugged out of her. One born every second somewhere. Other dying every second. Since I fed the birds five minutes. Three hundred kicked the bucket.

Cityful passing away, other cityful coming, passing away too: other coming on, passing on. Houses, lines of houses, streets, miles of pavements, piledup bricks, stones. Changing hands. This owner, that. Landlord never dies they say. Other steps into his shoes when he gets his notice to quit. They buy the place up with gold and still they have all the gold. Swindle in it somewhere. Piled up in cities, worn away age after age. Pyramids in sand. Built on bread and onions. Slaves Chinese wall. Babylon. Big stones left. Round towers. Rest rubble, sprawling suburbs, jerrybuilt, Kerwan's mushroom houses, built of breeze. Shelter for the night.

No one is anything.

This is the very worst hour of the day. Vitality. Dull, gloomy: hate this hour. Feel as if I had been eaten and spewed.

He sees A. E. (Mr Geo. Russell) in conversation with a young woman and wonders if she is Lizzie Twigg, one of the numerous Dublin girls who answered his advertisement for a typist 'to aid gentleman in literary work'. 'My literary efforts have had the good fortune to meet with the approval of the eminent poet A.E.,' she wrote.

His eyes followed the high figure in homespun, beard and bicycle, a listening woman at his side. Coming from the vegetarian. Only weggebobbles and fruit. Don't eat a beefsteak. If you do the eyes of that cow will pursue you through all eternity. They say its healthier. Wind and watery though. Tried it. Keep you on the run all day. Bad as a bloater. Dreams all night. Why do they call that thing they gave me nutsteak? Nutarians. Fruitarians. To give you the idea you are eating rumpsteak. Absurd.

Mr Bloom enters a restaurant but the sight of the carnivores at their feed revolts him.

Men, men, men.

Perched on high stools by the bar, hats shoved back, at the tables calling for more bread no charge, swilling, wolfing gobfuls of sloppy food, their eyes bulging, wiping wetted moustaches. A pallid suetfaced young man polished his tumbler knife fork and spoon with his napkin. New set of microbes. A man with an infant's saucestained napkin tucked round him shovelled gurgling soup down his gullet. A man spitting back on his plate halfmasticated gristle: no teeth to chewchewchew it.

Nauseated, Mr Bloom backs out. 'Couldn't eat a morsel here. ... Out. I hate dirty eaters.'

He remembers the time when he was employed in the cattle-market.

Wretched brutes waiting for the poleaxe to split their skulls open. Moo. Poor trembling calves. Meh. Staggering bob. Bubble and squeak. Butchers' buckets wobble lights. Give us that brisket off the hook. Plup. Rawhead and bloody bones. Flayed glasseyed sheep hung from their haunches, sheepsnouts bloodypapered snivelling nosejam on sawdust. Top and lashers going out. Don't maul them pieces, young one.

('Top' and 'lashers' are butcher's terms for certain parts of the slaughtered animal. The butcher is addressing an assistant who checks the meat as it is carried out.)

It is not surprising that Mr Bloom, after his reminiscence of the variegated massacre of the slaughter-house, considers, almost approvingly, the daintier diet of the cannibal. The realism of such passages may seem repulsive to some of the omnivores who read them, but civilized man is apt to forget that as he dies so he lives 'beastly' (to quote Buck Mulligan) and, but for his soul, if any, has little to brag about. ...

At last, in Davy Byrne's,[1] after a cheese sandwich and a glass of Burgundy, Mr Bloom finds that his dark mood is passing and yields to an evocation of remembered beauty.

Stuck on the pane two flies buzzed, stuck.

Glowing wine on his palate lingered swallowed. Crushing in the winepress grapes of Burgundy. Sun's heat it is. Seems to a secret touch telling me memory. Touched his sense moistened remembered. Hidden under wild ferns on Howth. Below us bay sleeping sky. No sound. The sky. The bay purple by the Lion's head. Green by Drumleck. Yellow-green towards Sutton. Fields of undersea, the lines faint brown in grass, buried cities. Pillowed on my coat she had her hair, earwigs in the heather scrub, my hand under her nape, you'll toss me all. O wonder! Coolsoft with ointments her hand touched me, caressed: her eyes upon me did not turn away. Ravished over her I lay, full lips full open, kissed her mouth. Yum. Softly she gave me in my mouth seed-cake warm and chewed. Mawkish pulp her mouth had mumbled sweet and sour with spittle.

1. I am indebted to Mr Roger McHugh for permission to quote from a letter of his, describing 'Davy Byrne's' which, like one of the liquors it supplies, is still going strong. 'Chromium, steel, murals, initialled barman whom Joyce would have appreciated like the HELY'S troupe. I saw an old man gazing mournfully into his glass and murmuring, "This used to be a bloody lovely pub. A Bloody ... Lovely ... Pub!" ' Tears, idle tears. ...

Joy: I ate it: joy. Young life, her lips that gave me pouting. Soft, warm, sticky gumjelly lips. Flowers her eyes were, take me, willing eyes. ... All yielding she tossed my hair. Kissed, she kissed me.

Me. And me now.

Stuck, the flies buzzed.

His downcast eyes followed the silent veining of the oaken slab. Beauty: it curves: curves are beauty. Shapely goddesses, Venus, Juno: curves the world admires ... naked goddesses. Aids to digestion. They don't care what man looks. All to see. Never speaking. I mean to say to fellows like Flynn. Suppose she did Pygmalion and Galatea what would she say first? Mortal! Put you in your proper place. Quaffing nectar at mess with gods, golden dishes, all ambrosial. Not like a tanner lunch we have, boiled mutton, carrots and turnips, bottle of Allsop. Nectar, imagine it drinking electricity: god's food. Lovely forms of woman sculped Junonian. Immortal lovely. And we stuffing food in one hole and out behind: food, chyle, blood, dung, earth, food: have to feed it like stoking an engine.

Meanwhile the other customers at Davy Byrne's are discussing the runners for the Ascot Gold Cup; Bantam Lyons tells Paddy Leonard that Mr Bloom has given him a tip for the race – a lie which is destined to land Mr Bloom later in the day in trouble with a Cyclops. On his way to the Museum (to examine the anatomy of the Greek goddesses there exhibited) he plays the Good Samaritan to a blind piano-tuner.

Poor fellow! Quite a boy. Terrible. Really terrible. What dreams would he have, not seeing. Life a dream for him. Where is the justice being born that way? All these women and children excursion beanfeast burned and drowned in New York. Holocaust. Karma they call that transmigration for sins you did in a past life the reincarnation met him pikehoses.

Approaching the museum, he espies Blazes Boylan in the offing; as before (see the 'Hades' episode) on the occasion of a similar glimpse of his wife's lover, Mr Bloom's perturbation is indicated by a breaking up of the silent monologue and a self-deluding attention to something about his person. The comedy is played to himself, not for the benefit of possible onlookers. Anything to get over this *mauvais moment*!

Look for something I.

His hasty hand went quick into a pocket, took out, read unfolded Agendath Netaim. Where did I?

Afternoon she said.

I am looking for that. Yes, that. Try all pockets. Handker. *Freeman.* Where did I? Ah, yes. Trousers. Purse. Potato. Where did I?

Hurry. Walk quietly. Moment more. My heart.

His hand looking for the where did I put found in his hip pocket soap lotion have to call tepid paper stuck. Ah, soap there! Yes. Gate.

Safe!

*

One of the preoccupations of the Homeric heroes as they landed at each unknown isle was to discover the kind of food on which the inhabitants lived. The Odyssean formula 'men who live upon this earth by bread' is not an empty periphrasis for 'human beings'; the food a nation eats is, to a certain extent, the criterion of its civilization, just as the library of an educated man is usually the index of his mental make-up. Pausanias speaks contemptuously of the Arcadians as eaters of acorns and wearers of pigskins and there can be little doubt that Odysseus and his companions would have ranked the Arcadians lower in the scale than 'men who live by bread'. Dr Merry's suggestion that the expression σῖτον ἔδοντες (bread-eaters) merely 'distinguishes mortals from Gods and brutes, if it be anything more than a fixed epithet', seems hardly to go far enough. It was expedient for wandering Greeks to ascertain the table-manners of the folk whose land they had made – whether they were to encounter the charm of kindly lotus-eaters, the culture of the breadline, or – most urgent problem of all – the periods of cannibal hospitality.[1] Had Odysseus known the diet of the 'strong Lestrygonians', he would certainly have dissuaded his companions from mooring their ships between the jutting cliffs of the port of Lamos. The decoy, 'noble daughter of Lestrygonian Antiphates', inveigled them to the hall of her father, where 'they found his wife, huge of bulk as a mountain peak and loathly in their sight'. She called renowned Antiphates who forthwith 'clutched up one of the company and made ready his midday meal'. Then he raised the warcry and the huge Lestrygonians cast at the ships of Odysseus with great rocks 'and anon there

1. Thus early Mediterranean travellers were less interested in the nationality and language of the peoples they encountered than in the kind of food they ate. There were fish-eaters (ἰχθυοφάγοι), eaters of elephants, of grasshoppers (still used as an ingredient of an appetizing far-eastern curry), and galactophages who lived on mare's milk. The wandering epicure of those days had a vast choice of *plats régionaux*, far surpassing that of any Parisian restaurant; but he ran the risk of having to furnish in his person the *pièce de résistance*.

rose from the fleet an evil din of men dying and ships shattered withal. And like men spearing fishes they bare home their hideous meal.'

As in the *Odyssey*, so in the record of Bloomsday the pangs of hunger and rites of refection have their appointed place. The persistence of the 'hunger motif' in the *Odyssey* is noteworthy; it makes itself heard in season and out of season, as, for instance, when Odysseus is making an impassioned appeal to King Alcinous (Book VII) or, again, at the dramatic moment when Odysseus is about to re-enter his palace (Book XVII). The preoccupation when, where, and how to procure the next meal is ever with the wandering man, be he Greek or Jew. In the 'Lestrygonian' episode, however, the esurient theme dominates all others and is developed to a climax of disgust, followed by a quiet close – Mr Bloom's frugal collation of a sandwich and glass of wine.

The technic of the episode is based on a process of nutrition: *peristalsis*, 'the automatic muscular movement consisting of wavelike contractions in successive circles by which nutritive matter is propelled along the alimentary canal'. This process is symbolized by Mr Bloom's pauses before various places of refreshment, the incomplete movements he makes towards satisfaction of the pangs of hunger which spasmodically urge him onward, and their ultimate appeasement. A direct reference to the movement of alimentation is apparent in Mr Bloom's scheme for watching some coloured food ('spinach say') wind its way through the human body. 'Then with those Röntgen rays searchlight you could. ... Watch it all the way down, swallow a pin sometimes come out of the ribs years after, tour round the body, changing biliary duct, spleen squirting liver, gastric juice coils of intestines like pipes.' Peristaltic, too, are the movements of 'Lamppost' Farrell, the eccentric pedestrian who zigzags along the Dublin streets, looping round the lamp-posts. There is, perhaps, another illustration of this technic in Mr Bloom's reflections on the appearance of pregnant women. 'Funny sight two of them together. ... Molly and Mrs Moisel. Mother's meeting. Phthisis retires for the time being, then returns. How flat they look after all of a sudden! Peaceful eyes. Weight off their minds.' The rise and fall of cities, rising again, falling again; the 'same old ding-dong always' of nature: increase, decay; the philosophies of each epoch, minced, chewed up ('never know whose thoughts you're chewing'), re-formed into tissue seemingly new for a next generation, hashed again and served up as the *plat du jour* to admiring modernists – everything happens again, and again, and again. Yet, as Mr Bloom, despite his passing nausea, is aware, we come back to the banquet with appetite renewed, like the 'ravenous terrier' he watches in Duke's Lane, which, choking up a 'sick knuckly cud', returns to its vomit with new zest.

Here, as in the preceding episodes, the metaphors employed are in harmony with the theme, and alimentary allusions add their pungency to the heavy noonreek of Dublin's luncheon-hour. Thus the pro-Boers are 'young cubs yelling their guts out', sentimental verse is 'creamy dreamy stuff', Mrs Bloom is 'well nourished', judges are 'crusty old topers', Paddy Leonard adjures Bantam Lyons if he is 'worth his salt' to give him the straight tip for the Gold Cup. The art of architecture, which is one of the subjects treated in this episode (the references to buildings range from the pyramids and the Chinese wall to the Dublin Museum, designed by Sir Thomas Deane), is blended with the nutritive theme in Mr Bloom's allusion to 'cream curves of stone'. Joyce's method of selective terminology is further illustrated by the nomenclature of persons or places seen or mentioned by Mr Bloom in his silent monologue. Thus he pauses at Butler's monument house corner, remembers how he 'played the monkey' at Goose Green, recalls Vinegar Hill and the 'Butter Exchange Band', passes the Provost's House, occupied by the reverend Dr Salmon.

There are some direct recalls of the Homeric description of the disaster which befell Odysseus's companions at Lamos. 'The gulls swooped silently two, then all, from their heights, pouncing on prey. Gone. Every morsel. Aware of their greed and cunning he shook the powdery crumb from his hands. They never expected that.' Mr Bloom pictures a communal kitchen with a 'soup pot as big as the Phoenix Park. Harpooning flitches and hindquarters out of it.' The descent of the gulls, pouncing on prey, recalls the onslaught of the Lestrygonians, swooping down from their cliffs upon the unexpected quarry, and the soup pot may be likened to the ring of the harbour, where the crews of all the Achaean ships save that of Odysseus (who had prudently moored without) were drowned or harpooned by the cannibals. Lestrygonian, too, is the theme of Mr Bloom's limerick on the sad end of a worthy missionary, Mr MacTrigger, who was eaten up with zeal, and his dyspeptic 'feel as if I had been eaten and spewed'.

The callous king Antiphates is symbolized by Mr Bloom's imperious hunger; the sight and reek of food are the decoy, his daughter, and the horde of the Lestrygonians, may be likened to the teeth, Homer's 'hedge of teeth', a palisade of hungry sentinels. Famine, in fact, that greatest tyrant of all, has launched more ships and burnt more towers than Beauty herself, ruin of cities. Hunger could worst even the loyalty of Irish catholics, as Mr Bloom observes. '*Why I left the church of Rome? Bird's Nest.*' (A society for the 'conversion' of catholics.) 'They say they used to give pauper children soup to change to protestants in the time of the potato blight. Society over the way papa went to for the conversion of poor jews. Same bait. Why we left the church of Rome?' The converts during the potato blight (1847) were known as 'soupers' and the term 'boiled protestants' which the Irish sometimes use for boiled potatoes may owe its origin to this conversion *à la Wetherup*.[1] In this connexion it is interesting to observe the Ulyssean word technique carried a stage further in Joyce's later work, the mastication of food and its disintegration being reflected in a congruous treatment of language, as in the following description of a heavy meal. 'All the vitalmines is beginning to sozzle in chewn, fudgem, kates and epas and naboc and erics and oinnos on kingclud and xoxxoxo and xooxox xxoxoxxoxxx till I'm fustfed like fungstif.' Here the 'masticated' words can easily be reconstructed by the reader: *kates* being 'steak', *kingclud* 'duckling', *oinnos* 'onions' (with, obviously, a tang of Greek wine) and so on. In the final stages of this metabolism alphabetic differences are reduced to a minimum, letters becoming mere noughts and crosses (vowels and consonants) and a mess of cabbage (*xoxxoxo*), followed by boiled protestants *en purée* (with a dash of beef extract), completes the bellyful.

1. See *Ulysses*, page 117, 'WHAT WETHERUP SAID'.

9. SCYLLA AND CHARYBDIS

SCENE	The Library
HOUR	2 p.m.
ORGAN	Brain
ART	Literature
SYMBOL	Stratford, London
TECHNIC	Dialectic

In the first episode of *Ulysses*, Haines, the Englishman, his curiosity aroused by a hint from Buck Mulligan, asks Stephen Dedalus what is his idea of Hamlet.

'No, no,' Buck Mulligan shouted in pain. 'I'm not equal to Thomas Aquinas and the fifty-five reasons he has made to prop it up. Wait till I have a few pints in me first.'

Nothing daunted, Haines persists in asking what Stephen's theory is.

It's quite simple [Buck Mulligan explains]. He proves by algebra that Hamlet's grandson is Shakespeare's grandfather and that he is himself the ghost of his own father.

Haines, baffled by Mulligan's Hibernian exuberance, murmurs vaguely: 'I read a theological interpretation of it somewhere. The Father and Son idea. The Son striving to be atoned with the Father.'

The 'paternity motif', one of the leading themes of *Ulysses*, parodied by Mulligan, misunderstood by Haines, has a prominent place in the structure of the 'Scylla and Charybdis' episode. It is, perhaps, on account of the dominance of this theme, which, applied to the mystery of Godhead, has been so fruitful a cause of misunderstanding and dissension in the Christian Church, that this episode is the subtlest and hardest to epitomize of all the eighteen episodes of *Ulysses*.

'Scylla and Charybdis' deals almost entirely with Shakespearian criticism and especially with the personality of Hamlet, and records a long Platonic dialogue in the Dublin National Library between Stephen Dedalus, Mr Best, John Eglinton (Magee), Mr George Russell (A.E.), and 'Quakerlyster' (the librarian) on these matters; it includes some lyrics, a short passage in blank verse and another in dramatic form. Thus the three forms of literature defined by Stephen in *A Portrait of the Artist* (page 251) – lyrical, epic, and dramatic – are all represented in this episode, whose 'art' is *literature*. There are innumerable Elizabethan echoes and Shakespearian idioms, and all the speakers at times tend to imitate the poet's various styles and borrow his rhythms. Synge, too, figures in the brief parodic speech put in the mouth of Buck Mulligan, when he is complaining that, while he and Haines were waiting thirsty in a tavern for the arrival of Stephen with funds for the purchase of drinks, he had merely received a sententious telegram from the latter.

'It's what I'm telling you, mister honey, it's queer and sick we were, Haines and myself, the time himself brought it in. 'Twas murmur we did for a gallus potion would rouse a friar, I'm thinking, and he limp with leching. And we one hour and two hours and three hours in Connery's sitting civil waiting for pints apiece.'
He wailed.
'And we to be there, mavrone, and you to be unbeknownst sending us your conglomerations the way we to have our tongues out a yard long like the drouthy clerics do be fainting for a pussful.'

The episode abounds in abrupt contrasts, formal speeches alternating with clownery, argot with metaphysics. Each of the speakers in the dialogue has his appropiate tempo; thus there is a choppy curtness about Stephen's remarks, Mr Russell's have a sinuous and studied smoothness, John Eglinton is shrewdly matter of fact.

Mr Bloom makes a brief visit to the Library to consult the *Kilkenny People* (about Keyes's advertisement) and leaves about the same time as Stephen, passing out between him and Buck Mulligan.

A man passed out between them, bowing, greeting.
'Good day again,' Buck Mulligan said.
The portico.
Here I watched the birds for augury. Aengus of the birds. They go, they come. Last night I flew. Easily flew. Men wondered. Street of harlots after. A cream-fruit melon he held to me. In. You will see.

Here Stephen is unconsciously exercising the prophetic faculty which Irish tradition attributes to all bards, whether of Avon or of Erin. There was an earlier allusion to this dream in Stephen's 'Proteus' monologue. Stephen apparently takes little or no notice of Mr Bloom, though the latter, a wise 'father', observes Stephen with such marked interest as to elicit a lewd jest from the irrepressible Buck. The quiet, almost unnoticed entry and departure of Mr Bloom, protagonist of *Ulysses*, the father whom Japhet-Stephen seeks, and the small *apparent* effect of his passage on the symposium of Dublin *littérateurs* rapt in the pure ecstasy of literary exhibitionism, adds a touch of dramatic irony to the episode.

It is as if a company of eminent politicians were discussing round a London dinner-table some burning topic – say, the career and statesmanship of Lenin. They argue the pro and the con with rising excitement as the argument tightens about a nucleus, the crux of their debate. There is a sudden lull in the conversation – is it twenty past the hour, or are they merely pausing to take breath? An apologetic knock is heard at the door; a waiter enters and in guttural accents asks if he can take away the plates. The host nods impatiently. They recommence their discussion with renewed ardour; they have not even noticed the man's discreet entry and soundless exit. Yet that waiter was a budding Lenin, the next 'Messiah' – and they knew him not!

Thus, for Stephen and the others, absorbed in their discussion of *Hamlet* and the mystical estate of fatherhood, that mystery 'founded like the world, macro- and microcosm, upon the void', Mr Bloom (Odysseus unrecognized by Telemachus), to whose atonement with his Second Person the huge, cosmic movement of *Ulysses* is tending, is merely a vague, importunate visitor who wants to consult the *Kilkenny People*, goodness knows why. Stephen is unaware of the link which unites him with prosaic Mr Bloom – indeed, at no time does his conscious self avow the union; it is, rather, Bloom, nearer to the earthmother, to the instinctive, who grasps, dimly albeit, the creator's purpose regarding their complementary interrelation. Nevertheless, Stephen is clairvoyant enough to feel that there is 'something in the air';[1] he perceives Bloom with the inward eye, as Hamlet his father's spirit, but without Hamlet's recognition. 'A dark back went before them. Step of a pard, down, out by the gateway, under portcullis barbs.' The episode ends on that trancelike 'calm of earth and heaven' which, according to Plotinus, is an antecedent condition of the 'ecstasy' in which the Alone communes with the Alone.

Kind air defined the coigns of houses in Kildare street. No birds. Frail from the housetops two plumes of smoke ascended, pluming, and in a flaw of softness softly were blown.

1. The Bloom 'aura', perhaps, 'fine like what do you call it gossamer, fine as anything' (*Ulysses*, page 357).

Cease to strive. Peace of the druid priests of Cymbeline, hierophantic: from wide earth an altar.

> Laud we the gods
> And let our crooked smokes climb to their nostrils
> From our bless'd altars.

The allusion to augury ('Here I watched the birds. ... No birds.') is one of the many links between *Ulysses* and the *Portrait*, and illustrates the way in which ideas, once they have formed an association in Stephen's mind, ever after reappear together. In the earlier scene, standing on the steps of the Library, under the portico, on a late March evening, he watched the flight of the birds and counted their number: 'Six, ten, eleven: and wondered were they odd or even in number. Twelve, thirteen: for two came wheeling down from the upper sky.'

Their cry was shrill and clear and fine and falling like threads of silken light unwound from whirring spools. ...

And for ages men had gazed upward as he was gazing at birds in flight. The colonnade above him made him think vaguely of an ancient temple and the ashplant on which he leaned wearily of the curved stick of an augur. A sense of fear of the unknown moved in the heart of his weariness, a fear of symbols and portents, of the hawklike man whose name he bore soaring out of his captivity on osierwoven wings, of Thoth, the god of writers, writing with a reed upon a tablet and bearing on his narrow ibis head the cusped moon.

Thus, in *Ulysses*, in this scene at the Library, he muses: 'coffined thoughts around me, in mummycases, embalmed in spice of words. Thoth, god of libraries, a birdgod, moony-crowned. And I heard the voice of that Egyptian high priest.[1] *In painted chambers loaded with tile-books.*' (The birdgod Thoth thus serves as mediator between the ideas *literature-library* and *birds-augury*.)

The legends of Daedalus, the hawklike man, and of Icarus, also, are recalled by Stephen in the course of this episode.

Fabulous artificer, the hawklike man. You flew. Whereto? Newhaven-Dieppe, steerage passenger. Paris and back. Lapwing. Icarus. *Pater, ait.* Seabedraggled, fallen, weltering. Lapwing you are. Lapwing he.

The allusion here is to Stephen's hurried return from Paris in obedi-

---

1. A reminiscence of John F. Taylor's speech, quoted in the 'Aeolus' episode. There is a touch of the birdgod Thoth in Aeolus-Crawford, as there is a touch of literature in journalism.

ence to his father's telegram: *mother dying come home father*. It is one of many links between this and the 'Proteus' episode (the art of philology is naturally associated with that of literature), in which, as here, we find Egyptian motifs employed and references to the 'Hamlet' side of Stephen Dedalus, as, for example, 'in the moon's midwatches I pace the path above the rocks, in sable silvered, hearing Elsinore's tempting flood'. The words 'You flew', besides their reference to the flight of Daedalus (and Stephen's from Paris), are a preparation for Stephen's dreamflight and the watching of the auspices.

Such are a few of the numerous cross-correspondences and allusions, literary, legendary, or personal to Stephen Dedalus, which abound in this episode, many-headed and elusive as the monster Scylla herself. It remains to consider the general import of this quasi-Platonic dialogue, in which Stephen plays the role of a Socrates, and of the curious conclusion to which the young symposiarch leads his reluctant elders along a dialectic tightrope. Briefly, this conclusion is that in the play of *Hamlet* the author identifies himself rather with Hamlet *père* than with Hamlet *fils*, and that, therefore, the groundling in his opinion of the personality of Shakespeare is clean abused. It must, however, be noted that Stephen never takes himself quite seriously in his role of dialectician. Thus at one moment he asks himself:

> What the hell are you driving at?
> I know. Shut up. Blast you! I have reasons.
> *Amplius. Adhuc. Iterum. Postea.*
> Are you condemned to do this?

When the symposium is over John Eglinton takes Stephen to task. '"You are a delusion. You have brought us all this way to show us a French triangle. Do you believe your own theory?"'

'No,' Stephen said promptly.

For Stephen, in fact, it is the intellectual interest, the aesthetic value of the dialogue that counts, rather than the truth of its conclusion. Indeed, to his mind one conclusion is as good as another – provided, only, it be fitting. There is an aesthetic validity, acceptable to the spirit, and that is the only absolute.

The discussion opens with a platitude from John Eglinton: 'Our young Irish bards have yet to create a figure which the world will set beside Saxon Shakespeare's Hamlet.' Stephen, before replying to this dictum, an opening gambit after Socrates' heart, carefully composes the setting of his stage.

Composition of place. Ignatius Loyola, make haste to help me! ...

'It is this hour of a day in mid June,' Stephen said. ... 'The flag is up on the playhouse by the bankside. The bear Sackerson growls in the pit near it, Paris garden. Canvasclimbers who sailed with Drake chew their sausages among the groundlings. ...

'The play begins. A player comes on under the shadow, made up in the cast-off mail of a court buck [a suggestive analogy is here established: Stephen is wearing Buck Mulligan's cast-off shoes], a wellset man with a bass voice. It is the ghost, the king, a king and no king, and the player is Shakespeare. ...

Hamlet, I am thy father's spirit. ...

'To a son he speaks, the son of his soul, the prince, young Hamlet and to the son of his body, Hamnet Shakespeare, who has died in Stratford that his namesake may live for ever.

'Is it possible that that player Shakespeare, a ghost by absence, and in the vesture of buried Denmark, a ghost by death, speaking his own words to his own son's name (had Hamnet Shakespeare lived he would have been prince Hamlet's twin) is it possible, I want to know, or probable that he did not draw or foresee the logical conclusion of those premises: you are the dispossessed son: I am the murdered father: your mother is the guilty queen. Ann Shakespeare, born Hathaway?'

Ann's character is now discussed and John Eglinton cruelly likens her to Xantippe. From her Socrates learnt his dialectic, 'and from his mother how to bring thoughts into the world'. Yet all the lore he learnt from women could not save him from 'the archons of Sinn Fein and their naggin of hemlock'.

'He had a good groatsworth of wit,' Stephen said, 'and no truant memory. He carried a memory in his wallet as he trudged to Romeville[1] whistling *The girl I left behind me.* ... That memory, *Venus and Adonis*, lay in the bedchamber of every light-of-love in London. Is Katharine the shrew ill-favoured? Hortensio calls her young and beautiful. Do you think the writer of *Anthony and Cleopatra*, a passionate pilgrim, and his eyes in the back of his head ...? Good: he left her and gained the world of men. But his boywomen are the women of a boy.

1. Romeville: cant word for 'London'. In the 'Proteus' episode, seeing the 'ruffian and his mort, spoils slung at her back', trudging up the sand, Stephen recalled the line of the jargon song: *Bing awast to Romeville then.* ...

Their life, thought, speech are lent them by males. He chose badly? He was chosen, it seems to me. If others have their will Ann hath a way. By cock, she was to blame. She put the comether on him, sweet and twentysix.'

John Eglinton points out that Shakespeare's later plays breathe a spirit other than that of bitterness – the spirit of reconciliation.

'There can be no reconciliation,' Stephen said, 'if there has not been a sundering. ...

'If you want to know what are the events which cast their shadow over the hell of time of *King Lear*, *Othello*, *Hamlet*, *Troilus and Cressida*, look to see when and how the shadow lifts. What softens the heart of a man, shipwrecked in storms dire, Tried, like another Ulysses, Pericles, prince of Tyre?'[1]

Head, redconecapped, buffeted, brineblinded.

'A child, a girl placed in his arms, Marina.' ...

'Marina,' Stephen said, 'a child of storm, Miranda, a wonder, Perdita, that which was lost. What was lost is given back to him: his daughter's child. *My dearest wife*, Pericles says, *was like this maid*. Will any man love the daughter if he has not loved the mother?'

But, if he was touched by the appeal of his own image in his daughter's child, belief in himself had none the less been untimely killed. 'Assumed dongiovannism', London, where 'life ran high in those days', cannot save him. There was in him 'a new passion, a darker shadow of the first, darkening even his own understanding of himself'. Like King Hamlet's, his soul has been stricken mortally, poison poured in the porch of a sleeping ear.

The poisoning and the beast with two backs that urged it king Hamlet's ghost could not know of were he not endowed with knowledge by his Creator. That is why the speech is always turned elsewhere, backward. ... He goes back weary of the creation he has piled up to hide him from himself, an old dog licking an old sore. But, because loss is his gain, he passes on towards eternity in undiminished personality, untaught by the wisdom he has written or by the laws he has revealed. His beaver is up. He is a ghost, a shadow now, the wind by Elsinore's rocks or what you will, the sea's voice, a voice heard only in the heart of him who is the substance of his shadow, the son consubstantial with the father.

There follows a creed: 'He Who Himself begot. ... Who let Him

1. An imitation of Shakespeare's rhymed endings. This is one of the rare mentions of the name 'Ulysses' in the text.

bury, stood up, harrowed hell, fared into heaven and there these nine-teen hundred years sitteth on the right hand of His Own Self. ...' in-dicating the *rapprochement* which is gradually being made throughout this episode between Shakespeare and the Creator.

'A father [Stephen continues] is a necessary evil. He wrote the play in the months that followed his father's death. If you hold that he, a greying man with two marriageable daughters, with thirtyfive years of life, *nel mezzo del cammin di nostra vita*, with fifty of experience is the beardless undergraduate from Wittemberg then you must hold that his seventyyear old mother is the lustful queen. No. The corpse of John Shakespeare does not walk the night. From hour to hour it rots and rots. He rests, disarmed of fatherhood, having devised that mystical estate upon his son. Boccaccio's Calandrino was the first and last man who felt himself with child. Fatherhood, in the sense of conscious begetting, is unknown to man. It is a mystical estate, an apostolic succession, from only begetter to only begotten. On that mystery and not on the madonna which the cunning Italian intellect flung to the mob of Europe the church is founded and founded irremovably because founded, like the world, macro- and microcosm, upon the void. Upon incertitude, upon unlikelihood. *Amor matris*, subjective and objective genitive, may be the only true thing in life. Paternity may be a legal fiction. ...'

Judge Eglinton summed up.

'The truth is midway,' he affirmed. 'He is the ghost and the prince. He is all in all.'

'He is,' Stephen said. 'The boy of act one is the mature man of act five. All in all. In *Cymbeline*, in *Othello* he is bawd and cuckold. He acts and is acted on. Lover of an ideal or a perversion, like José he kills the real Carmen. His unre-mitting intellect is the hornmad Iago ceaselessly willing that the moor in him shall suffer.'

'Cuckoo! Cuckoo!' Buck Mulligan clucked lewdly. 'O word of fear!'

Dark dome received, reverbed.

'And what a character is Iago!' undaunted John Eglinton exclaimed. 'When all is said Dumas *fils* (or is it Dumas *père*?) is right.[1] After God Shakespeare has created most.'

The playwright who wrote the folio of this world [Stephen observes, in epilogue], and wrote it badly (He gave us light first and the sun two days later), the lord of things as they are whom the most Roman of catholics call *dio boia*, hangman god, is doubtless all in all in all of us, ostler and butcher. ...

1. This confusion of substance, of the Dumas *père-et-fils*, is a recall of Stephen's and Sabellius's hypothesis.

To the Dubliners who heard and argued with the young Socrates in their midst, Stephen's Shakespearian hypothesis seemed, doubtless, a juvenile paradox, and 'Judge' Eglinton's gloss a happy compromise. If, however, the texture of this dialogue and, especially, the import of the 'theolologicophilolological'[1] excursions of Stephen's argument be closely examined, it will be found that a good deal more is implied than the mere portrayal of Shakespeare as a *Cocu Magnifique* or the discovery of a new complex in Hamlet. The mystery of paternity, in its application to the First and Second Persons of the Trinity, to King Hamlet and the Prince, and, by implication, to the curious symbiosis of Stephen and Mr Bloom, is ever in the background of Stephen's Shakespearian exegesis. All through this chapter he is capturing in a net of analogies, is *symbolizing* (in the exact meaning of this word: *throwing together*), the protean manifestations of the creative force (one of whose dynamics in the animate world is the rite of procreation, paternity). God (Father and Son) – Shakespeare – Stephen Dedalus: all are vehicles of a like energy. And the artist himself, creator of the saga of Dublin, the Viking city, is by a subtle cross-allusion drawn into the net.

'Why', asks Stephen, 'is the underplot of *King Lear* in which Edmund figures lifted out of Sidney's *Arcadia* and spatchcocked on to a Celtic legend older than history?'

'That was Will's way,' John Eglinton defended. 'We should not now combine a Norse saga with an excerpt from a novel by George Meredith. *Que voulez-vous?* Moore would say. He puts Bohemia on the seacoast and makes Ulysses quote Aristotle.'

There is, it so happens – but not accidentally – in this very episode a phrase lifted out of Meredith: 'The sentimentalist is he who would enjoy without incurring the immense debtorship for a thing done.'

The motion is ended. Gravediggers bury Hamlet *père* and Hamlet *fils*. A king and a prince at last in death, with incidental music. ... If you like the epilogue look long on it: prosperous Prospero, the good man rewarded, Lizzie, grandpa's lump of love, and nuncle Richie, the bad man taken off by poetic justice to the place where the bad niggers go. Strong curtain.

'Nuncle Richie', here, is the third brother of William Shakespeare and is 'recorded in the works of sweet William' in the character of

1. Cf. Hamlet's 'tragical-comical-historical-pastoral scene' and Swift's 'histori-theophysiological account of zeal' (*A Tale of a Tub*).

Richard Crookback, that 'whoreson crookback', who 'makes love to a widowed Ann (what's in a name?), woos and wins her a whoreson merry widow. Richard the conqueror, third brother, came after William the conquered.' (The last words quoted here recall Manningham's story of the burgher's wife who 'bade Dick Burbage to her bed'; Shakespeare had overheard her invitation and forestalled the favourite, and, when the latter came knocking at the gate, cried through the door: *William the conqueror came before Richard III.*) Behind the Shakespearian allusions in Stephen's epilogue, there is here an undoubted recall of a passage[1] in the *Proteus* episode, where Stephen speaks of his own 'nuncle Richie' and his niece little Crissie, 'a lump of love': another subtle indication of the William Shakespeare–Stephen Dedalus correspondence.

*

Scylla is one of the few place-names used in the *Odyssey* which have persisted unchanged till the present day. At the entry to the Straits of Messina, the city of Scylla, perched on a cliff 'that beetles o'er his base into the sea', still dominates the treacherous strip of water separating Sicily from the mainland. The city suffered severely in the earthquake of 1783 and the tip of the promontory on which it stands was detached. A cavern, opening to the west, 'turned to Erebus', once existed in the side of the cliff; it collapsed in the earthquake. 'The rock is smooth and sheer,' Homer tells us, 'as it were polished. And in the midst of the cliff is a dim cave turned to Erebus, towards the place of darkness. ... And therein dwelleth Scylla, yelping terribly.' Such 'yelping' caverns are frequently found on the coast. Sometimes their clamour is caused by the passage of wind through a narrow opening, sometimes by the flux and reflux of waves along the rocky base. The name 'Scylla' is derived from a Semitic word *skoula*, a rock, and the full title of the promontory was Skoula Krat'a, the sheer rock. Preferring, as usual, an anthropomorphic interpretation of Phoenician toponomy, Homer makes Scylla the daughter of Kratais, 'which bore her a bane to mortals', and yielding to the temptation of making a pun on the exotic word *Skoula*, attributes to Scylla the voice of a little Greek bitch, *skulax*.

Opposite Scylla lies the whirlpool of Charybdis, who 'sucks down her black water and thrice a day she spouts it forth'. The name Charybdis

1. page 35.

has no signification in Greek; Lewy finds in it the transliteration of a Semitic name, which actually existed in Syria, *Khar oubed*, meaning 'the hole of ruin'; this meaning is reproduced in the Homeric epithet ὀλοὴ applied to Charybdis, 'deadly'. Spallanzani gives an interesting description of the insidious perils of the strait.

When the wind is against the current and an inexperienced or imprudent navigator shortens sail to pass the narrows, his ship, the prey of opposing forces, is shattered against the rock of Scylla or wrecked on the shoals. For this reason twenty-four sturdy and courageous seamen keep watch night and day on the Messina shore. At the first sound of the warning cannon they man their light boats and hasten to tow off the ship in distress. The current does not extend right across the strait but follows a winding course and our mariners, aware of its deviations, can come to the rescue of the ship. But if the steersman refuse or forget to ask for their succour, for all his skill, he can hardly escape disaster. In the midst of whirlpools and the cross-seas stirred up by the violence of current and wind he cannot take soundings, nor can he cast anchor, for the seabed is rocky and affords no purchase. No skill in navigation will avail him; his only hope of safety lies in the courage and skill of the rescue-party from Messina.

The motifs of the sheer, steadfast rock of Scylla and the restless whirlpool of Charybdis, a sea of troubles, are utilized in a symbolic sense in this episode. The stability of Dogma, of Aristotle, and of Shakespeare's Stratford is contrasted with the whirlpool of Mysticism, Platonism, the London of Elizabethan times. Shakespeare, Jesus, and Socrates, like Ulysses, the man of balanced genius, pass bravely out, though not unscathed, from between these perils of the soul. 'A man passed out between them, bowing, greeting.' The departure of Mr Bloom from the metaphysical twilight of the library into a 'shattering daylight of no thoughts' symbolizes such an escape. This idea of evasion pervades the closing pages of the *Portrait* and was already associated in Stephen's mind with the conditions of Irish thought – the mystic school of the Celtic twilight[1] and over against it the sheer dogmatism of Jesuits and nationalists. 'When the soul of a man is born in this country there are

---

1. It is noteworthy that the only explicit reference, in this episode, which deals with the art of literature, to the Irish literary movement (elsewhere in *Ulysses* almost completely ignored) is placed in the mouth of ribald Buck Mulligan and wedged between ten lines of doggerel and the concluding 'harlequinade', Mulligan's obscene playlet, the cast of which is not (as he seems to claim) original. The 'ruined Pole' and most of his companions were known to Oxford men of the

nets flung at it to hold it back from flight. You talk to me of nationality, language, religion. I shall try to fly by those nets.'

'Elizabethan London lay as far from Stratford as corrupt Paris lies from virgin Dublin.' Stephen, escaping, flew to Paris: Shakespeare to London; but each was destined to return to 'that spot of earth where he was born'.

In the dizzy whirl of Charybdis Shakespeare was long enthralled.

Twenty years he lived in London and, during part of that time, he drew a salary equal to that of the Lord Chancellor of Ireland. His life was rich. His art, more than the art of feudalism, as Walt Whitman called it, is the art of surfeit. Hot herring-pies, green mugs of sack, honeysauces, sugar of roses, marchpane, gooseberried pigeons, ringocandies. Sir Walter Raleigh, when they arrested him, had half a million francs on his back including a pair of fancy stays. ... Twenty years he dallied there between conjugal love and its chaste delights and scortatory love and its foul pleasures. [But] ... the note of banishment, banishment from home, sounds repeatedly from the *Two Gentlemen of Verona* onward till Prospero breaks his staff, buries it certain fathoms in the earth and drowns his book. ... Man delights him not nor woman either. He returns after a life of absence to that spot of earth where he was born, where he has always been, man and boy, a silent witness and there, his journey of life ended, he plants his mulberry tree in the earth. Then dies. The motion is ended.

The idea of possible shipwreck between paired perils, of the constraint of a dilemma, manifests itself under various aspects. In the opening lines of the episode the quaker librarian purrs: 'And we have, have we not, those priceless pages of *Wilhelm Meister*? A great poet on a great brother poet. A hesitating soul taking arms against a sea of troubles, torn by conflicting doubts. ... The beautiful, ineffectual dreamer who comes to grief against hard facts [Scylla – 'the rock].'

Stephen sees himself between 'the Saxon smile and yankee yawp'. His allegiance is claimed both by 'corrupt Paris' and 'virgin Dublin'. We are reminded of the former by the comparatively frequent use of French words in this episode – as, for example, the references to Hamlet *père et fils*. A French poster is mentioned:

Hamlet

ou

Le Distrait

Pièce de Shakespeare

'It's so French, the French point of view. *Hamlet ou ...*'
'The absent-minded beggar,' Stephen ended.

And Stephen is ever aware of the perils that beset him from his hearers – the 'bane of miscreant eyes, glinting stern under wrinkled brows', steadfast John, Scylla: and, on the other hand, Charybdis, the suavity of 'beautifulinsadness Best'; he is aware, too, of the perils inherent in his theme and in his dialectic skilfully steers a course between the maelstrom of metaphysics and reef of realism.

The organ of the body to which this episode is related is the brain, cruellest of all the instruments that man has forged for his own undoing. We feel a tensity of cerebration that is almost pain in Stephen's dialectical progress towards a paradoxical conclusion, the cul-de-sac of a mystery. On that mystery the book *Ulysses*, all religion, and every explanation of the universe is founded – 'upon the void. Upon incertitude, upon unlikelihood.' This spirit of incertitude is materialized in the 'Circe' episode, where phantoms of the 'feast of pure reason'[1] – Shakespeare among them – gesticulate mechanically, inane puppets, in a *danse macabre*. Like the writhing seaweed watched by Stephen on the Dublin foreshore, 'lifted, flooded, and let fall. ... To no end gathered: vainly then released, forth flowing, wending back'.

Joyce's work [Professor Curtius has remarked in a penetrating article on *Ulysses*[2]] springs from a revolt of the spirit and leads to the destruction of the world. With implacable logic he presents in his walpurgisnight, amid larvae and lemurs, a vision of the end of the world. A metaphysical nihilism is the substance of Joyce's work. The world, macro- and microcosm, is founded upon the void. ... All this wealth of philosophical and theological knowledge, this power of psychological and aesthetic analysis, this culture of a mind schooled in all the literatures of the world, all these gifts serve but to spend themselves, to refute themselves in a world-conflagration, a flaming welter of metallic iridescence. What is left? An odour of ashes, the horror of death, sorrow of apostasy, pangs of remorse – Agenbite of Inwit.[3]

1. *Ulysses*, page 566.
2. *Neue Schweizer Rundschau, Heft* 1, January 1929.
3. But all these are excellent aesthetic material for the artist. I cannot help thinking that the learned critic overestimates the pessimism of *Ulysses*, and, perhaps, does not sufficiently bear in mind the fact that its author is an Irishman. Both Stephen and Bloom have their consolations – Stephen in his art, Bloom in his keen interest in material details. And both (Bloom especially) have a sense of humour.

10. THE WANDERING ROCKS

SCENE	The Streets
HOUR	3 p.m.
ORGAN	Blood
ART	Mechanics
SYMBOL	Citizens
TECHNIC	Labyrinth

THE structure of this episode is curious, and unique in *Ulysses*. It consists of eighteen short scenes followed by a *coda* describing a viceregal passage through Dublin. All these scenes take place in the streets of Dublin between the hours of 3 and 4 p.m., and their synchronism is indicated by the insertion in each fragment of one or more excerpts from other fragments, which serve to fix the correspondence in time. In its structure and its technic ('labyrinth') this episode may be regarded as a small-scale model of *Ulysses* as a whole. The first, and longest, of the eighteen sections describes the peregrinations of Father Conmee, the Jesuit rector of Clongowes Wood College, 'the decentest rector that was ever at Clongowes' (see *A Portrait of the Artist*). Other sections describe the movements of Stephen Dedalus, of Mr Bloom, of a one-legged sailor (who receives alms from Mrs Bloom), a meeting between Mr Dedalus and his daughter Dilly, a conversation between Buck Mulligan and Haines in a tearoom, the purchase of fruit by Blazes Boylan as an offering to Mrs Bloom and the wanderings of several minor personages, who reappear in the course of *Ulysses*.

In the second section we see Corny Kelleher, the undertaker, lounging in his doorway, chewing a blade of hay. 'Corny Kelleher sped a silent jet of hayjuice arching from his mouth while a generous white arm from a window in Eccles Street flung forth a coin.' In the next section we see the patriotic minstrelsy of the one-legged sailor rewarded. 'The blind of the window was drawn aside. A card *Unfurnished Apartments* slipped from the sash and fell. A plump and generous arm shone, was seen, held forth from a white petticoatbodice and taut shift-straps. A woman's hand flung forth a coin over the area railings.' In the ninth section Lenehan is describing to M'Coy (the husband of the singer, Mrs Bloom's rival) an annual dinner-party presided over by the mayor, Val Dillon, which Mrs Bloom graced by her presence.

'I know,' M'Coy broke in. 'My missus sang there once.'
'Did she?' Lenehan said.
A card *Unfurnished Apartments* reappeared on the window-sash of No. 7 Eccles Street.
He checked his tale a moment but broke out in a wheezy laugh.
'But wait till I tell you,' he said. ...

Lenehan proceeds to tell the story of his drive home at 'blue o'clock the morning after the night before' beside Mrs Bloom, 'a gamey mare and no mistake', with Bloom on the other side of the jaunting car pointing out and naming 'all the stars and comets in the heavens'.

The cometary gesture of Mrs Bloom thus serves to fix exactly the synchronism of these three sections.

This method, abruptly used, is apt to produce a confusing effect (that this confusion is purposive and relevant will be seen in the commentary which follows). Thus a section which describes Boylan's typist at work begins:

Miss Dunne hid the Capel Street library copy of *The Woman in White* far back in her drawer and rolled a sheet of gaudy notepaper into her typewriter.

Too much mystery business in it. Is he in love with that one, Marion? Change it and get another by Mary Cecil Haye.

The disk shot down the groove, wobbled a while, ceased and ogled them: six.

Miss Dunne clicked on the keyboard:

'16 June 1904.'

(One is tempted to surmise that Miss Dunne is none other than 'Martha Clifford', the typist with whom Mr Bloom, or, rather, 'Henry Flower', is carrying on a *poste restante* flirtation. The allusions to 'mystery business' and 'Marion' give colour to this theory; but these are, perhaps, some of the many false clues scattered through this episode, which, like wrecker's beacons, are intended – for reasons which will be given later – to take the reader off his course.)

The third sentence of this extract is incomprehensible till the reader arrives at the ninth section, wherein is described an invention of Tom Rochford, of the 'booky's vest' – a mock Greek turn – for indicating to patrons of a music-hall which turns are over and which is now in progress on the stage.

'See?' he said. 'Say it's turn six. In here, see. Turn Now On.'

He slid it into the left slot for them. It shot down the groove, wobbled a while, ceased, ogling them: six.

(This description of the 'ogling disks' is, perhaps, to be interlocked with references to the ogling minstrel, Eugene Stratton – his poster is one of the 'seamarks' in this episode – who might be called to the stage in obedience to them.)

Again, at the close of the first section, Father Conmee, walking on his way to Artane, encounters 'a flushed young man', accompanied by a young woman coming from a gap of hedge.

The young woman bent and with slow care detached from her light skirt a clinging twig.

Father Conmee blessed both gravely and turned a thin page of his breviary. *Sin: Principes persecuti sunt me gratis:*[1] *et a verbis tuis formidavit cor meum.*

The quotation is from Psalm 119, which, like this episode, is divided into brief sections, each being headed with a Hebrew letter. According to the Kabbalists the letter *Sin* or *Schin* corresponds to all *vegetable substances*, each Hebrew letter being held to indicate either an attribute of the Divine Name or a celestial or mundane quality of the universe, as well as a number. Here, as so often in *Ulysses*, behind the obvious relevance of a citation, we discover an occult innuendo.

In the eighth section Ned Lambert conducts a visitor over the ancient site of the council chamber of Saint Mary's Abbey, 'the most historic spot in all Dublin', where Silken Thomas proclaimed himself a rebel in 1534 and the Jews once held their synagogue. (Mr Bloom refers to this later, on page 649.)

Ned Lambert

stood to read the card in his hand.

'The Reverend Hugh C. Love, Rathcoffey. Nice young chap he is. He's writing a book about the Fitzgeralds he told me. He's well up in history, faith.'

The young woman with slow care detached from her light skirt a clinging twig.

'I thought you were at a new gunpowder plot,' J. J. O'Molloy said.

1. The words *principes persecuti sunt me gratis* are here symbolical of the role of Father Conmee in this chapter; as will be shown later, he is pitted against the counter-subject of the episode, the Viceroy, as the Irish Catholic Church against British rule, Christ against Caesar.

Mr Bloom, in the course of his wanderings, visits the bookshop whence he procures the 'curious' literature beloved by his wife, and, on this occasion, takes for her, after inspecting *The Awful Disclosures of Maria Monk*, Aristotle's *Masterpiece* (a work known to Mrs Bloom as 'The Aristocrat's Masterpiece' and containing lurid illustrations of embryonic growth), and *Fair Tyrants* by James Lovebirch, a luscious (?American) pornographic work entitled *Sweets of Sin*. He reads a passage from this erotic thriller, which, as remembered phrases from it frequently crop up in his silent monologue, must be quoted *in extenso*.

All the dollarbills her husband gave her were spent in the stores on wondrous gowns and costliest frillies. For him! For Raoul! ...

Her mouth glued on his in a luscious voluptuous kiss while his hands felt for the opulent curves. ...

'You are late,' he spoke hoarsely, eyeing her with a suspicious glare. The beautiful woman threw off her sabletrimmed wrap, displaying her queenly shoulders and heaving embonpoint. An imperceptible smile played round her perfect lips as she turned to him calmly.

At the same moment, perhaps, Stephen Dedalus, too, is examining books, on a huckster's bookcart.

'Twopence each,' the huckster said. 'Four for sixpence.'

Tattered pages. *The Irish Beekeeper. Life and Miracles of the Curé of Ars. Pocket Guide to Killarney.*

I might find here one of my pawned schoolprizes. *Stephano Dedalo, alumno optimo, palmam ferenti.*

Father Conmee, having read his little hours, walked through the hamlet of Donnycarney, murmuring vespers.

Binding too good probably, what is this? Eighth and ninth book of Moses. Secret of all secrets. Seal of King David. Thumbed pages: read and read. Who has passed here before me? ... How to win a woman's love. For me this. Say the following talisman three times with hands folded:

Se el yilo nebrakada femininum! Amor me solo! Sanktus! Amen.

Who wrote this? Charms and invocations of the most blessed abbot Peter Salanka to all true believers divulged. As good as any other abbot's charms, as mumbling Joachim's. Down, baldynoddle or we'll wool your wool.[1]

'What are you doing here, Stephen?'

Dilly's high shoulders and shabby dress.

Shut the book quick. Don't let see.

1. A recall of a passage in the 'Proteus' episode (page 36): '*Descende calve, ut ne nimium decalveris.*'

'What are you doing?' Stephen said.

A Stuart face of nonesuch Charles lank locks falling at its sides. It glowed as she crouched feeding the fire with broken boots. I told her of Paris. Late lieabed under a quilt of old overcoats, fingering a pinchbeck bracelet, Dan Kelly's token *Nebrakada Femininum*.

'What have you there?' Stephen asked.

'I bought it from the other cart for a penny,' Dilly said, laughing nervously. 'Is it any good?'

My eyes they say she has. Do others see me so? Quick, far and daring.[1] Shadow of my mind.

He took the coverless book from her hand. Chardenal's French Primer.

'What did you buy that for?' he asked. 'To learn French?'

She nodded, reddening and closing tight her lips.

Show no surprise. Quite natural.

'Here,' Stephen said. 'It's all right. Mind Maggy doesn't pawn it on you. I suppose all my books are gone.'

'Some,' Dilly said. 'We had to.'

She is drowning. Agenbite. Save her. Agenbite. All against us. She will drown me with her, eyes and hair. Lank coils of seaweed hair around me, my heart, my soul. Salt green death.

We.

Agenbite of inwit. Inwit's agenbite.

Misery! Misery!

*

The brief reference to the Wandering Rocks in the *Odyssey* is contained in the friendly counsel given to Odysseus by Circe for his safe return to Ithaca. After passing the Sirens there were, she said, alternative ways to take.

I will not tell thee fully which path shall thenceforth be thine, but do thou thyself consider it, and I will speak of both ways. On the one side[2] there are beetling rocks, and the great wave of the dark-eyed Amphitrite thunders against them for ever. These, ye must know, are they the blessed gods call the Rocks Wandering. By this way even winged things may never pass, nay, not even the cowering doves that bear ambrosia to Father Zeus, but the sheer rock evermore takes one of these away, and the Father sends in another to make up

1. The 'quickness' and wide range of Stephen's thoughts are in striking contrast with the slow tempo and provincialism of Mr Bloom's silent monologue.

2. 'On the one *course*' would be the more correct translation. Also the correctness of 'wandering' is doubtful; the name of these rocks, the Planctae, more probably derives from πλήσσω and means 'the Clashers'.

the tale. ... Only one ship of all that fare by sea hath passed that way, even Argo ... and Hera sent her by for the love of Jason.

The alternative route was between Charybdis and Scylla, and this was the course chosen by Odysseus. Thus, in this episode, Mr Bloom excels his great precursor, for he accepts a supplementary adventure which the latter declined. It is only in the Argonautic records, the exploits of Jason in quest of the Golden Fleece, that a full description of that peril of eastern seas, the Clashers or Wandering Rocks, is available. Jason sent out a dove to lead the way, and, choosing its moment, it flew between the clashing rocks and lost only the tip of its tail. The Argonauts followed its example and passed through unscathed, but for some damage to the stern of the *Argo*.

The most probable explanation of this legend is that which explains the 'wandering' or clashing of the rocks as an optical illusion. To mariners carried off their course by a swift, though imperceptible, current, these rocks, projecting above the surface of the sea, would seem to be changing their position all the time. One may picture an archipelago, a labyrinth of such rocks, a calm sea and favouring breeze. Nothing would seem simpler to the oarsmen, aided by an Aeolus in friendly mood, than to set their course midway between the reefs. But these would appear to be moving towards them, to be closing in on them, as the current bore the ship in their direction. The story of the dove that lost its tail is, perhaps, a reminder of the damage likely to be suffered in such a maze – the loss of a ship's rudder, despite the efforts of the rowers to pull away from the 'approaching' rock.

The Homeric description of these rocks, clashing together at regular intervals, girt about with 'storms of ruinous fire', is in striking contrast to the anthropomorphic treatment accorded to other natural phenomena – the somewhat similar dyad of dangers, for instance, personified by Scylla and Charybdis. Here we have one of the rare cases where the Greeks seem to have seen blind mechanism at work; where Homer fails to personify a peril of the sea. The 'art' of this episode, 'mechanics', is thus a deliberate allusion to this aspect of the legend of the Wandering Rocks. Rochford's mechanical invention with its twin columns of wobbling disks has already been mentioned; there are many other references to mechanical movement in this episode. Thus Kelleher 'spins a coffinlid on its axle', Artifoni 'trotted on stout trousers' (he seems rather to progress like one of H. G. Wells's Martians than as an ordinary human biped); there are allusions to a bicycle race, to the explosion on the *General Slocum* (shipwreck *plus* mechanical breakdown), to 'Mickey Anderson's all times ticking watches'.

The whirr of flapping leathern bands and hum of dynamos from the power-house urged Stephen to be on. Beingless beings. Stop! Throb always without you and the throb always within. Your heart you sing of. I between them. Where? Between two roaring worlds where they swirl, I.

Shatter them, one and both. But stun myself too in the blow. Shatter me you who can. Bawd and butcher were the words. I say! Not yet awhile. A look around.

Yes, quite true. Very large and wonderful and keeps famous time. You say right, sir. A Monday morning, 'twas so indeed.

Here Stephen, scared by his own blasphemy (as, later, in the 'Oxen of the Sun', by the thunder-clap), apologizes to the Creator and begs for time. He artfully praises the mechanical punctuality of the universe, that all times ticking watch, not Mickey Anderson's, and, the better to bluff omniscience, follows up with a Shakespearian formula – Hamlet's pretence that he is carrying on an innocent conversation (with Rosencrantz) when Polonius (that other ancient, not unlike the white-bearded and sententious deity of our youth's veneration) appears, *unberufen*, on the scene.

There is something mechanically neat in Haines's gesture, 'sinking two lumps of sugar deftly longwise, through the whipped cream of his *mélange*' – the slick transit of a motor-launch through a narrow, foaming fairway – and, in the last section, we find young Dignam struggling with that detestable modern invention, a collar-stud, which, too small for the button-hole, persists in slipping past the fissure, like Jason's dove from between the clashing rocks. Indeed, the whole structure of this episode and the manner in which its eighteen parts interlock like a system of cog-wheels or the linked segments of an endless chain, may be described as 'mechanical', for all the vital humanity of the fragments of Dublin life portrayed. Here, again, we see a reason for regarding this episode as the microcosm of the universe of *Ulysses*, inspired by its creator with the breath of life, yet fashioned by the practised hand of an artificer, maker of labyrinths: a living labyrinth.

A mariner, adrift in the archipelago of Wandering Rocks, that mobile tangle of illusions, found himself bewildered, lost as in a maze. Many forms of mirage are illustrated in this episode and, unless he advance with prudence, the reader is apt to lose his way. Thus we read that Cashel Boyle O'Connor Fitzmaurice Tisdall Farrell 'strode past Mr Bloom's dental windows', a statement which might easily mislead the reader into thinking that Mr Bloom was concerned with dentistry. This would be an error due to false analogy; Mr Bloom, the dentist, is quite another person. Another sunken rock of which the reader must be wary in threading his way through the corkscrew strait of this episode is the interlocking device already described, whereby fragments from one section are inserted in another.

Thus, in the section where the Rev. Hugh C. Love visits the 'most historic spot in all Dublin', conducted by Ned Lambert, we read:

> In the still faint light he [Ned Lambert] moved about, tapping with his lath the piled seedbags and points of vantage on the floor.
> From a long face a beard and gaze hung on a chessboard.
> 'I'm deeply obliged, Mr Lambert,' the clergyman said. ...

A reader who seeks to fit the 'long face' to one of the persons present at the 'historic spot' will lose his bearings. The sentence 'From a long face, etc.,' is 'lifted' from the sixteenth section, where we see John Howard Parnell playing chess in a tea-shop.

Counterbalancing the danger of false analogy (as illustrated in the case of 'dental Mr Bloom') there is the risk of failing to recognize the identity of person under difference of title. Thus, while Gerty Mac-Dowell refers to the Viceroy of Ireland as 'the lord lieutenant', Mr Kernan sees 'His Excellency'. Long John Fanning, Dublin's mayor-maker, ironically punctilious, announces the passage of 'the lord lieutenant general and general governor of Ireland', whereas two igno-rant old women, all at sea, halt 'to view with wonder the lord mayor and lady mayoress without his golden chain'. The Rev. Hugh C. Love, who has failed to get out of the labyrinth and, like so many prisoners of circumstance, consoles himself by looking backward, walks as in a dream, 'attended by Geraldines[1] tall and personable', towards the Thol-sel beyond the Ford of Hurdles, and to him the Viceroy is a 'lord deputy' of yore, holder of rich advowsons. Poor Mr Breen makes a characteristic *faux pas*, for, after being nearly knocked down by the outriders, he salutes by mistake the A.D.C. in attendance.

1. The feminine air of the name 'Geraldine' is another false clue. The Geraldines were the descendants of the Fitzgerald family, famous in Irish history.

The personages who figure in this episode are themselves victims of illusion, and many forms of mistake are illustrated, arising out of inattention, false inference, optical illusion, malidentification, etc. Young Dignam notices the announcement of a boxing match and plans to 'do a bunk on ma' to see it. 'When is it? May the twenty-second. Sure, the blooming thing is all over.' Boody Dedalus, seeing a pot aboil on the range, expects a meal; the pot, however, proves to contain shirts; appearances have deceived her – a false analogy. Mr Power watches 'Long John Fanning ascend towards Long John Fanning in the mirror', but is not the dupe of appearances. Mr Kernan, on the other hand, believes his eyes and is, at first, deceived.

Is that Lambert's brother over the way, Sam? What? Yes. He's as like it as damn it. No. The windscreen of that motorcar in the sun there. Just a flash like that. Damn like him.

He recalls the burial of Emmet at Glasnevin.

Corpse brought in through a secret door in the wall. Dignam is there now. Went out in a puff. Well, well. Better turn down here. Make a detour.

The ideas of detour or a reversal of direction, of only partial achievement (the Argonauts passed the perilous Symplegades but only with the loss of some part of the stern of the ship *Argo*), of positive failure (shipwreck), of 'just missing' something, recur in the course of this episode. Mr Bloom, for instance, before hitting upon *The Sweets of Sin*, explores other pornographic possibilities. Nosey Flynn, examining Rochford's invention, asks him exactly how it works, but we just miss the explanation. Dilly Dedalus tries to get a florin from her father but gets only a shilling; her father leaves her abruptly and walks off. Mr Kernan hurries to see the viceregal cavalcade. 'Too bad. Just missed that by a hair. What a pity!' The perils of Dublin pavements are recalled by the gesture of M'Coy who 'dodged a banana peel with gentle pushes of his toe from the path to the gutter. Fellow might damn easy get a nasty fall there coming along tight in the dark.' The expedient of complete reversal of direction, inevitable sometimes for one who is puzzling his way through a maze, is illustrated by the movements of Mr Farrell, who 'walked as far as Mr Lewis Warner's cheerful windows, then turned and strode back along Merrion square, his stickumbrelladustcoat dangling'.

The group of rocks which gave rise to the legend of the Symplegades is generally situated in the Bosphorus, between the European and Asiatic coasts. The Dubliners who figure in each of the sections, wandering in groups, each about his own business or pleasure, may be likened to the archipelago of the Wandering Rocks. There is a contrast, obviously intended, between the first section of the episode, which describes the journey of Father Conmee on foot and by tram from his presbytery to Artane, and the final section, or coda, describing a vice-regal progress from the Lodge to Mirus Bazaar, which the Viceroy was to inaugurate in aid of funds for Mercer's hospital. The Viceroy represents the European bank, the pomps of this world, the *imperium britannicum*; the priest stands for the Asiatic bank, the *rive gauche*, the spiritual antithesis of material glory. Between the two flows the Liffey, replacing the Bosphorus; in the labyrinth of wandering rocks and rest-less movement, Anna Liffey alone infallibly finds her way. Father Conmee feels his ankles 'tickled by the stubble of Clongowes field'; this is yet another possible source of illusion, for he is really on the way to Artane and only in imagination does he traverse the distant playing-fields of Clongowes Wood College (an English reader will realize the appropriate sense of *égarement* if he pictures the Rector walking on the outskirts of London, substituting, for Conmee, Arnold and, for Clon-gowes, Rugby). In imagination, too, he hears 'the joybells ringing in gay Malahide'. But the Viceroy cannot hear this music of the heart; his ears are deafened by a real band of 'highland laddies... blaring and drum-thumping' *My Girl's a Yorkshire Girl*. Each receives homage from those he encounters on his way; Father Conmee 'gravely blesses'; His Excel-lency (the late Lord Dudley) 'punctually acknowledges salutes'. Each has a silent accolade from the poster of Mr Eugene Stratton, who 'grins with thick nigger-lips' at the priest, and bids the Viceroy welcome with 'blub lips agrin'. We learn nothing of the Viceroy's thoughts, for his progress is mere pageantry, but Father Conmee's musings are those of a kindly humanist. Thus Eugene Stratton recalls to him the lot of the unbaptized heathen. 'Those were millions of human souls created by God in His Own Likeness to whom the faith had not (D.V.) been brought. But they were God's souls created by God. It seemed to Father Conmee a pity that they should all be lost, a waste, if one might say.' Such con-trasting of the material and the spiritual is frequently to be seen in the work of Joyce. In *Finnegans Wake* he situates the conflict in the ecclesiastical camp itself, and, in the fable of the Mookse and the Gripes, opposes His Holiness the Roman Pope (the Mookse) to *Sa Béatitude* of the Eastern Church, the Gripes of Orthodoxy.

Throughout the episode we follow the long voyage seaward, between blue Symplegades, of a miniature *Argo*, deviously drifting down the Liffey. Nearly five hours earlier Mr Bloom received a 'throwaway', *Elijah is coming*, which he dropped among the gulls wheeling above the river. 'Elijah thirtytwo feet per sec is coming. The ball bobbed unheeded on the wake of swells, floated under by the bridge piers.' The fourth section of this episode ends: 'a skiff, a crumpled throwaway, Elijah is coming, rode lightly down the Liffey, under Loopline bridge, shooting the rapids where water chafed round the bridgepiers, sailing eastward past hulls and anchorchains, between the Customhouse old dock and George's quay'. In the twelfth section (Mr Kernan's hour): 'North Wall and Sir John Rogerson's quay, with hulls and anchorchains, sailing westward, sailed by a skiff, a crumpled throwaway, rocked on the ferrywash, Elijah is coming.' Finally, at the close of the sixteenth section, we have last tidings of this eastward-bound argosy. 'Elijah, skiff, crumpled throwaway, sailed eastward by flanks of ships and trawlers, amid an archipelago of corks, beyond new Wapping Street past Benson's ferry, and by the threemasted schooner *Rosevean* from Bridgwater with bricks.'

11. THE SIRENS

SCENE	The Concert Room
HOUR	4 p.m.
ORGAN	Ear
ART	Music
SYMBOL	Barmaids
TECHNIC	*Fuga per canonem*

ONE of the most remarkable features of Dublin life in the hey-day of Mr Bloom was the boundless enthusiasm of all classes of citizens for music, especially of the vocal and operatic varieties. This passion is illustrated by their cult of the divo,[1] carried to a degree unknown even in Italy. All the great singers came to Dublin, and the names of Campanini, Joe Maas, Mario, Piccolomini (creator of 'Violetta' in *Traviata*), Tietjens, Giuglini, Trebelli-Bettini, and many others were household words. Their memories went back even to the legendary Lablache (the Chaliapin of his time), who was born (of an Irish mother and French father) in the eighteenth century. Other well-known vocalists of Irish blood were Catherine Hayes, William Ludwig (*né* Ledwidge), and Foli (*né* Foley). The personalities and careers of such artists were an unfailing theme of conversation – the tragic *finali*, for example, of Giuglini and of Ilma de Murska, and the curious appearance and supposed royal descent of Mario, Cavaliere de Candida (who had flourished sixty years before and was, for the Irish 'king's sons', the *Prince of Candia*). At the beginning of the 'Aeolus' episode, watching Mr Brayden mount the staircase of the *Freeman* office, Mr Bloom observes that he is 'like Mario the tenor' (it was then some thirty years since the death of Mario). Red Murray, the foreman, agrees, adding: 'Mario was said to be the picture of Our Saviour.' To both of them the appearance of this tenor was evidently as familiar as is still to Londoner or New Yorker the aspect of the latest deceased film-star. When Trebelli was singing at the Old Royal, the Dubliners were wont to unhorse her carriage and draw her in state to her hotel. The first interpreter of the roles of Basilio and Don Curzio was Michael Kelly, and many of the greatest modern singers

1. Second only to their adulation of that other histrion, the political leader.

(John Sullivan, regarded by some Italians as the most remarkable dramatic tenor since the death of Tamagno, John MacCormack, Margaret Sheridan, for example) are Irish.

Dublin is still, as far as *bel canto* is concerned, one of the most musical cities in the world. The famous Palestrina choir founded by Edward Martyn (the 'Dear Edward' of George Moore's trilogy) still flourishes. Dubliners can still wax enthusiastic over 'discoveries' of vocal talent in unlikely quarters and any day you may hear one saying to another, over a pint of Guinness: 'There's a young bricklayer lives down Bull Alley and I tell you he'd put all other tenors in the world into the shade only for the brickdust he gets down his throat!' Like Odysseus at the performance of the divine singer Demodocus, the Dubliner is keenly susceptible to the voice of one to whom 'the gods have given minstrelsy as to none else'.

All through *Ulysses* we find references to famous singers, to music and the fascination of music; the book itself is constructed on a musical pattern and has much of the formal intricacy of a fugue.

James Joyce himself, had he not chosen literature, would (as all who have heard him sing are convinced) have made his mark as a singer. The 'gift of minstrelsy' was in his blood. His father was reputed to have the best tenor voice in Ireland; his great-aunts, pupils of Michael Balfe (see the story 'The Dead' in *Dubliners*), trilled and warbled in a Dublin church up to the age of seventy, and his son is carrying on the family tradition. Until his death the first question Dubliners of his generation asked about the author of *Ulysses* was apt to run: 'Books? Yes, of course he has written some books. But – *how is his voice?*' The story of Joyce's abandonment of this career, much to the chagrin of his Italian teacher, who heard in him the promise of a future de Rezke, remains yet to be written.

His earliest work, the book of poems, *Chamber Music* (published over forty years ago), has been set to music by all classes of composers over and over again; one of the poems no less than seven times. In fact, the musical basis of Joyce's style, specifically illustrated in the episode of the 'Sirens', is one of the several factors distinguishing it from the work of any other writer. Even the difficult passages of the *Anna Livia Plurabelle* section of *Finnegans Wake* became lucid, pellucid as running water, when read aloud[1] in the appropriate rhythm and intonation by the

1. A gramophone record (H.M.V.) exists of Joyce's reading of this fragment.

author. In fact, rhythm is one of the clues to the meaning of the *Wake*, for each of the polymorphous personages of the work has his appropriate rhythm and many cross-correspondences can be verified by reference to the rhythm of the prose.

This résumé of the musical proclivities of the Dubliners in general and of the author of *Ulysses* in particular seemed not unnecessary as an approach to this chapter, the 'Sirens', which both in structure and in diction goes far beyond all previous experiments in the adaptation of musical technique and timbre to a work of literature.

*

The episode of the 'Sirens' opens with two pages of brief extracts from the narrative which follows. These fragmentary phrases appear almost meaningless[1] to the reader till he has perused the chapter to its end; nevertheless, they should not be skipped. They are like the overtures of some operas and operettas, in which fragments of the leading themes and refrains are introduced to prepare the hearer's mood and also to give him, when these truncated themes are completed and developed in their proper place, that sense of familiarity which, strangely enough, enhances for most hearers their enjoyment of a new tune.

Speaking of this episode, after a careful analysis of the overture, Professor Curtius observed:[2]

these two pages of seemingly meaningless text form in reality a carefully thought out composition, which can only be understood when the reader has perused the whole chapter, and studied it with the greatest attention. The literary technic here employed is an exact transposition of the musical treatment of the *leitmotif*, the Wagnerian method. But there is this difference, that the musical *motif* is complete in itself and aesthetically satisfying; I can hear a Wagnerian *leitmotif* with enjoyment, even though I cannot place its allusion (Valhalla theme? Walsungen theme?). But the *word-motif*, unintelligible in itself, acquires a meaning only when I relate it to its context. Of 'Horrid! And gold flushed more', I can make nothing. Joyce has deliberately ignored this essential difference between sounds and words, and, for this reason, his experiment is of questionable value.

1. So curious is the language of this episode that, when it was sent by the author from Switzerland to England during the First World War, the Censor held it up, suspecting that it was written in some secret code. Two English writers (it is said) examined the work and came to the conclusion that it was not 'code' but literature of some eccentric kind.

2. *Neue Schweizer Rundschau, Heft* 1, January 1929.

An answer to this objection (besides the justification for Joyce's technique which I have already suggested, the pleasure of musical reminiscence) is that the first notes of themes, for instance the intimations of the *Preislied*, are equally fragmentary; their meaning and beauty can only be apprehended when Walther sings the complete song. The clipped phrases give as much pleasure relatively to the completed phrase as does the *leitmotif*.

The two barmaids at the Ormond Restaurant, Miss Lydia Douce and Miss Mina Kennedy, are, when the episode opens, watching 'the vice-regal hoofs go by, ringing steel'. Miss Douce is convinced that the 'fellow in the tall silk' in the second carriage has observed her and, of course, fallen victim to her charms.

Her wet lips tittered:
'He's killed looking back.'
She laughed:
'O wept! Aren't men frightful idiots?'
With sadness.
Miss Kennedy sauntered sadly from bright light, twining a loose hair behind an ear. Sauntering sadly, gold no more, she twisted twined a hair. Sadly she twined in sauntering gold hair behind a curving ear.
'It's them has the fine times,' sadly then she said.

Presently Mr Dedalus strolls into the Ormond. Long practice and a natural propensity for philandering have made him expert in the little language of the bar and, opposite him, Miss Douce plays her Siren role of fascination. After the manner of her profession, she soon brings her victim to the drinking point.

'And what did the doctor order today?'
'Well now,' he mused, 'whatever you say yourself. I think I'll trouble you for some fresh water and a half glass of whiskey.'
Jingle.
'With the greatest alacrity,' Miss Douce agreed.

The 'jingle' here is the distant sound of Blazes Boylan's jaunting-car. On his way to keep his assignation for four o'clock with Mrs Bloom, he calls at the Ormond for a glass of sloe-gin. As the car approaches we hear it 'jingling on supple rubbers' and, later, when Mr Bloom is eating a belated lunch, he hears, in reality at first, afterwards with the inner ear of imagination, the jingle of the jaunting hero's car on its way to Eccles Street.

Lenehan, the humorous parasite, enters the bar and tries to flirt with the barmaids, but is snubbed. For Lenehan is one who 'never has it', as the Dubliners say. Meanwhile Mr Bloom, on his way to the Ormond, stops to buy some notepaper for his reply to Martha's letter.

Two sheets cream vellum paper one reserve two envelopes when I was in Wisdom Hely's wise Bloom in Daly's Henry Flower bought. Are you not happy in your home? Flower to console me and a pin cuts lo. Means something, language of flow. Was it a daisy? Innocence that is. Respectable girl meet after mass. Tanks awfully muchly. Wise Bloom eyed on the door a poster, a swaying mermaid smoking mid nice waves. Smoke mermaids, coolest whiff of all. Hair streaming: lovelorn. For some man. For Raoul. He eyed and saw afar on Essex bridge a gay hat riding on a jaunting car. It is. Third time. Coincidence.

Jingling on supple rubbers it jaunted from the bridge to Ormond quay. Follow. Risk it. Go quick. At four. Near now. Out.

'Twopence, sir,' the shopgirl dared to say.

'Aha ... I was forgetting ... Excuse.'

'And four.'

At four she. Winsomely she on Bloohimwhom smiled. Bloo smi qui go. Ternoon. Think you're the only pebble on the beach? Does that to all. For men.

In this *staccato* passage of Mr Bloom's monologue three themes may be observed which haunt his musing throughout the episode: Martha's letter (in which a flower was enclosed), the erotic book he has in his pocket (*The Sweets of Sin*), and the impending interview between Boylan and Mrs Bloom. He tends to associate that other conqueror, Raoul of *The Sweets of Sin* ('All the dollarbills her husband gave her were spent in the stores on wondrous gowns and costliest frillies. For him! for Raoul!'), with the seductive Blazes.

Boylan arrives at the Ormond and is hailed by his sycophant.

See the conquering hero comes. ...

He touched to fair Miss Kennedy a rim of his slanted straw. She smiled on him. But sister bronze outsmiled her, preening for him her richer hair, a bosom and a rose.

Miss Kennedy for the allurement of the hero's eyes performs the bar-parlour trick of *sonnez-la-cloche*. Boylan watches her gestures with some approval but he is 'boylan with impatience' to be off to his rendezvous. It is four o'clock and the lady waits. The ringing smack of 'nipped elastic garter smackwarm' against a shapely leg – *sonnez la cloche* – is a mere prompter's callbell for the undress rehearsal of *Love's Old Sweet Song* over which he will soon preside at No. 7 Eccles Street.

Meanwhile Mr Bloom, accompanied by Richie Goulding (Stephen's 'nuncle Richie'), has entered the restaurant.

Jingle a tinkle jaunted.

Bloom heard a jing, a little sound. He's off. Light sob of breath Bloom sighed on the silent bluehued flowers. Jingling. He's gone. Jingle. Hear....

Pat served uncovered dishes. Leopald cut liverslices. As said before he ate with relish the inner organs, nutty gizzards, fried cods' roes while Richie Goulding, Collis, Ward ate steak and kidney, steak then kidney, bite by bite of pie he ate Bloom ate they ate.

Bloom with Goulding, married in silence, ate. Dinners fit for princes.

While they eat, Ben Dollard (the 'bass barreltone'), Simon Dedalus, and 'Father Cowley' are providing musical entertainment at the piano (it has just been tuned by the blind youth to whom Mr Bloom played the good Samaritan earlier in the day). Mr Bloom's mood as usual responds quickly to the ambiance and his silent monologue is throughout the remainder of this episode impregnated with musical reminiscences and allusions.

The harping chords of prelude closed. A chord longdrawn, expectant drew a voice away.

'*When first I saw that form endearing.*'

Richie turned.

'Si Dedalus' voice,' he said.

Braintipped, cheek touched with flame, they listened feeling that flow endearing flow over skin limbs human heart soul spine. Bloom signed to Pat, bald Pat is a waiter hard of hearing, to set ajar the door of the bar. That will do. Pat, waiter, waited, waiting to hear, for he was hard of hear by the door.

'*Sorrow from me seemed to depart.*'

Through the hush of air a voice sang to them, low, not rain, not leaves in murmur, like no voice of strings of reeds or whatdoyoucallthem dulcimers, touching their still ears with words, still hearts of their each his remembered lives. Good, good to hear: sorrow from them each seemed to from both depart when first they heard. When first they saw, lost Richie, Poldy, mercy of beauty, heard from a person wouldn't expect it in the least, her first merciful lovesoft oftloved word....

Martha it is. Coincidence. Just going to write. Lionel's song. Lovely name you have. Can't write. Accept my little pres. Play on her heartstrings pursestrings too. She's a. I called you naughty boy. Still the name: Martha. How strange! Today.

The lovesong from *Martha*, Martha's letter and a memory of that romantic *soirée* when first he saw the form endearing of Marion Tweedy are mingled in Mr Bloom's soliloquy.

'*Each graceful look* ...'

First night when I saw her at Mat Dillon's in Terenure. Yellow, black lace she wore. Musical chairs. We two the last. Fate. After her. Fate. Round and round slow. Quick round. We two. All looked. Halt. Down she sat. All ousted looked. Lips laughing. Yellow knees.

'*Charmed my eyes* ...'

Singing. *Waiting* she sang. I turned her music. Full voice of perfume of what perfume does your lilactrees. Bosom I saw, both full, throat warbling. First I saw. She thanked me. Why did she me? Fate, Spanishy eyes....

'*Come!*'

It soared, a bird, it held its flight, a swift pure cry, soar silver orb it leaped serene, speeding, sustained, to come, don't spin it out too long long breath he breath long life, soaring high, high resplendent, aflame, crowned, high in the effulgence symbolistic, high, of the etherial bosom, high, of the high vast irradiation everywhere all soaring all around about the all, the endlessnessness....

The listeners in the concert-room applaud.

Bravo! Clapclap. Goodman. Simon. Clappyclapclap. Sound as a bell. Bravo, Simon. Clapclopclap. Encore, enclap, said, cried, clapped all.

In this passage, perhaps, we may hear an echo of Blake's *Dr Clash and Signior Falalasole*, a satire on the prevalent taste for exotic music,[1] the final stanza of which is, as Mr Foster Damon has remarked, 'an entire concert in itself, from the entrance of the conductor to the terminal applause'.

> *Gentlemen, Gentlemen!*
> *Rap, rap, rap,*
> *Fiddle, Fiddle, Fiddle,*
> *Clap, Clap, Clap.*

1. Thus to the Dubliners music was an essentially *Italian* art and they always liked to allude to songs by their Italian names, even though the opera whence they came was by a non-Italian composer and usually sung in English. Thus one would ask the other, 'How did he sing the *Dio possente?*' (*Even bravest hearts may swell*), or, as in this episode, demand *M'appari* (*When first I saw* ...).

Mr Bloom begins his letter to Martha, doing his best to conceal what he writes from the gaze of Richie Goulding.

Hope he's not looking, cute as a rat. He unfurled his *Freeman*. Can't see now. Remember write Greek ees. Bloom dipped. Bloo mur: dear sir. Dear Henry wrote: dear Mady. Got your lett and flow. Hell did I put? Some pock or oth. It is utterl imposs. Underline *imposs*. To write today.

As he writes, the sound of the piano and the thoughts it evokes are interwoven with memories of Martha's letter and of the servant next door ('whacking a carpet on the clothes line: the way her crooked skirt swings at each whack'); as he strings together his false pearls of sentiment for Martha's benefit, he murmurs aloud, for Richie's ('Answering an ad?' 'Yes.') benefit, the clichés of his business.

Bloom mur: best references. But Henry wrote: it will excite me. You know now. In haste. Henry. Greek ee. Better add postscript. What is he playing now? Improvising intermezzo. P.S. The rum tum tum. How will you pun? You punish me? Crooked skirt swinging, whack by. Tell me I want to. Know. O. Course if I didn't I wouldn't ask. La la la ree. Trails off there sad in minor. Why minor sad? Sign H. They like sad tail at end. P.P.S. La la la ree. I feel so sad today. La ree. So lonely. Dee.

The last item of this impromptu concert at the Ormond is Ben Dollard's 'trenchant rendition' of *The Croppy Boy*.

'*Bless me father,*' Dollard the croppy cried. '*Bless me and let me go.*'
Tap.
Bloom looked, unblessed, to go. Got up to kill: on eighteen bob a week. Fellows shell out the dibs. Want to keep your weathereye open. Those girls, those lovely. By the sad sea waves. Chorusgirl's romance. Letters read out for breach of promise. From Chickabiddy's own Mumpsypum. Laughter in court. Henry. I never signed it. The lovely name you.
Low sank the music, air and words. Then hastened. The false priest rustling soldier from his cassock. A yeoman captain. They know it all by heart. The thrill they itch for. Yeoman cap.
Tap. Tap.

The jingle of Boylan's car has ceased; he has arrived at Mrs Bloom's. A new motif makes itself heard in the closing pages of the episode – the blind tuner tapping his way back to the Ormond to recover the tuning-fork[1] which he left on the piano.

1. In the midst of the musical enthusiasm, the dialogue of melody and accompaniment, there is one instrument, trustiest of all, an Odysseus with his ears open

By rose, by satiny bosom, by the fondling hand, by slops, by empties, by popped corks, greeting in going, past eyes and maidenhair, bronze and faint gold in deepseashadow, went Bloom, soft Bloom. I feel so lonely Bloom.

Tap. Tap. Tap.

Pray for him, prayed the bass of Dollard. You who hear in peace. Breathe a prayer, drop a tear, good men, good people. He was the croppy boy.

Mr Bloom tramps out of the Ormond to the rhythm of a marching song and the echo of remembered streetcries.

Instruments. A blade of grass, shell of her hands, then blow. Even comb and tissue paper you can knock a tune out of. Molly in her shift in Lombard street west, hair down. I suppose each kind of trade made its own, don't you see? Hunter with a horn. ... *Cloche. Sonnez la.* Shepherd his pipe. Policeman a whistle. Locks and keys! Sweep! Four o'clock all's well! ... Drum? Pompedy. Wait, I know. Towncrier, bumbailiff. Long John. Waken the dead. Pom. Dignam. Poor little *nominedomine*. Pom. It is music. I mean of course it's all pom pom pom very much what they call *da capo*. Still you can hear. As we march we march along, march along. Pom.

*

The two Sirens, seated in a flowery mead,[1] 'bewitch all men' and 'enthrall them with their clear singing'. The Sirens are not mere *cantatrices*, they are also magicians who 'bind' men with their spells. The Semitic roots *sir-en*, in combination, signify the 'song of enthralment'. The two mermaids of the bar, bronze Miss Douce and gold Miss Kennedy, practise their arts of fascination on all who approach them. Miss Douce gaily polishes a tumbler trilling (for Mr Dedalus's benefit):

O Idolores, queen of the eastern seas.[2]

on the perilous voyage past the Sirens' isle, that does not play – the tuning-fork, the conscience of the episode. An emblem, this, of Mr Bloom; among these eccentrics, enthusiasts, patriots, braggarts, he alone stands for the norm of humanity, *homo* would-be *sapiens*.

1. As M. Bérard points out, the word here translated 'mead' is the Greek version of the Semitic root *abel* and is used also to describe the 'soft meadow of violets and parsley' which surrounded Calypso's home. The rocks of the Sirens, a group of islands near Capri, are covered with low herbs and meadows of narcissus. The Sirens, like Calypso, had a λειμῶν᾽ ἀνθεμοεντα. In this connexion, Mr Norman Douglas's *Siren Land* is not only fascinating reading but a mine of Siren lore. He has much to say about the habits and habitats of the Sirens, and agrees with M. Bérard as to their Phoenician origin.

2. The correct version of this line (from Leslie Stuart's *Florodora*, a musical comedy which had a great vogue at the beginning of the century) is '*Oh, my*

Like the Sirens' meadow, the Ormond dining-tables are adorned
with flowers; one of the humorous catches of the episode is 'Blue
Bloom is on the rye', a recall, perhaps, of the fate of Shakespeare who
was (as Stephen told us) 'overborne in a rye-field' by a boldfaced
Stratford wench.

> Between the acres of the rye
> Those pretty countryfolk would lie.

The Homeric correspondences in this episode are, generally speaking,
rather literal than symbolic. The Siren barmaids 'cowered under their
reef of counter', bronze by gold. Miss Douce tells Mr Dedalus that she
has been at the seaside 'lying out on the strand all day'. 'That was
exceedingly naughty of you,' Mr Dedalus remarks, pressing her hand.
'Tempting poor simple males.' She is wearing a rose, set off by maidenhair, at her breast. Mr Dedalus, filling his pipe, 'fingered shreds of hair,
her maidenhair, her mermaid's, into the bowl'. We see a Siren again
in the poster, 'a swaying mermaid smoking mid nice waves. Smoke
mermaid, coolest whiff of all. Hair streaming: lovelorn.' There is hung
in the music-room a dusty seascape: *A Last Farewell*. 'A headland, a
ship, a sail upon the billows. Farewell. A lovely girl, her veil awave
upon the wind upon the headland, wind around her.' The bar itself is
described in terms of a seascape. Miss Douce lowers the drop-blind.
'She drew about her bronze ... slow cool dim seagreen sliding depth of
shadow, *eau de Nil*.' 'The pined in depth of ocean shadow, gold by the
beerpull, bronze by maraschino.'

Douce now. Douce Lydia. Bronze and rose.

She had a gorgeous, simply gorgeous, time. And look at the lovely shell she
brought.

To the end of the bar to him she bore lightly the spiked and winding seahorn
that he, George Lidwell, solicitor, might hear....

Bloom through the bardoor saw a shell held at their ears. He heard more
faintly that that they heard, each for himself alone, then each for other, hearing
the plash of waves, loudly, a silent roar.

Bronze by a weary gold; anear, afar, they listened.

Her ear too is a shell, the peeping lobe there. Been to the seaside. Lovely seaside girls. Skin tanned raw.... Hair braided over: shell with seaweed....

Dolores', etc. Miss Douce, 'Idolores, a queen, Dolores', who, like the Sirens, sings
by ear, not by the score, has made a happy slip. The fate of the Croppy Boy is,
later, associated with this refrain: 'At Geneva barrack that young man died.
Dolor! O he dolores!'

The sea they think they hear. Singing. A roar. The blood is it. Souse in the ear sometimes. Well, it's a sea. Corpuscle islands.[1]

The language and content of this episode (its technique is the *fuga per canonem*) are throughout handled in a characteristically musical manner. The theme is rarely simple; there are generally two, three, or four overlapping *parts*, which, synchronized by intertwinement in the same sentence, or closely juxtaposed, produce the effect of a chord of music. He who reads such passages as certain cultured concert-goers prefer to hear a fugue – with the parts kept mentally distinct in four, or less, independent horizontal lines of melody – will miss much of the curious emotive quality of Joyce's prose in this episode. For most of the sensuous value of music, the enthralment of the Sirens' song, is missed by the musical 'high-brow' who forces himself to analyse the sounds he hears and separate the music into independent lines of horizontal parts.[2] To enjoy to the full the emotion of symphonic music the hearer should be aware of it as a sequence of chords, listen *vertically* as well as horizontally. And this holds good not only for the romantics such as Beethoven and Wagner, who (especially the latter) 'think in chords', but also, though in a somewhat less degree, for contrapuntal fuguists like Bach.

The various themes are introduced in the fugal manner: the first, the *Subject*, is obviously the Sirens' song: the *Answer*, Mr Bloom's entry and monologue; Boylan is the *Counter-Subject*. The *Episodes* or *Divertimenti* are the songs by Mr Dedalus and Ben Dollard. The Episodes, Subject, Answer, and Counter-Subject are often bound together contrapuntally in the narrative or in the texture of Mr Bloom's monologue (as illustrated in several of the extracts already given).

The effect of this technique is to thicken the texture of the narrative and, especially, the silent monologue. Certain passages (one of these was quoted and analysed in an introductory chapter), while they flatter the ear by the richness of their rhythms, demand the exercise of a keen

1. Cf. Stephen's monologue in the 'Proteus' episode: 'tides, myriadislanded within her, blood not mine, *oinopa ponton*, a winedark sea'. This is one of many passages in the early episodes of *Ulysses* which prepare the reader's mind for the meeting of Stephen with Bloom, forecasting of their mystical 'at-onement'.

2. I anticipate the retort: *De te fabula*. But I refer to the concert-goer when he is actually listening to the music. If he study the score outside the concert-room, he loses nothing and may find his pleasure enhanced by the knowledge he thus acquires.

memory and intuition for their complete understanding. Words are truncated, augmented, anastomosed. Phrases are clipped, interlocked.

'Goulding, a flush struggling in his pale, told Mr Bloom, face of the night Si, in Ned Lambert's, Dedalus house, sang *'Twas rank and fame.'* The technic is explained with humorous precision in the next sentence.

He, Mr Bloom, listened while he, Richie Goulding, told him, Mr Bloom, of the night he, Richie, heard him, Si Dedalus, sing *'Twas rank and fame* in his, Ned Lambert's, house.

By the separation of the adjective *pale* from its noun *face* a curiously significant amphibology is contrived.

Again, Mr Bloom, after writing his letter to Martha, says to himself: 'Blot over the other so he can't read. Idea prize titbit. Something detective read off blottingpad. Payment at the rate of guinea per col. Matcham often thinks of the laughing witch. Poor Mrs Purefoy. U.p.: up.'

The process of modulation which leads from first to last word in this fragment is typical. That morning, in the privy, Mr Bloom read in *Tit-Bits* the prize tit-bit, 'Matcham's Masterstroke', which begins 'Matcham often thinks of the masterstroke by which he won the laughing witch who now …' The author's name was Philip Beaufoy. Mr Bloom wonders if he, too, could earn a guinea or two by writing a prize tit-bit. Later in the morning he meets Mrs Breen in the street and asks her if she ever sees anything of 'Mrs Beaufoy'.

'Mina Purefoy?' she said.
Philip Beaufoy I was thinking. Matcham often …
'Yes.'

An association is thus formed between Mina[1] Purefoy, the friend who is 'three days bad' in the Lying-in Hospital and Philip Beaufoy. 'Poor Mrs Purefoy!' Just before telling Mr Bloom of Mrs Purefoy's condition, Mrs Breen showed him the anonymous postcard her husband had received, 'U.p.: up.' Thus the thought of Mrs Purefoy is associated with Mr Breen's postcard.

1. This allusion to *Mina* Purefoy, the christian-namesake of the barmaid *Mina* Kennedy, serves to draw attention to the nomenclature of the latter. The name 'Mina' is pronounced in Ireland with the *i* as in *minor*. Of the two barmaids, Miss Kennedy is in the *minor*; she has less to say, is softer, less provocative than her colleague, the 'hypomixolydian' Miss Lydia Douce, whose 'relative minor' she is.

Of the hundreds of musical forms verbally reproduced in the course of this episode I select a few to illustrate the lines on which Joyce has set his Canto of the Sirens to unheard music 'of some eccentric kind'.

Mr Bloom thinks of the days to come when Marion's lovers will have abandoned beauty in decay. 'Leave her: get tired. Suffer then. Snivel. Big Spanishy eyes goggling at nothing. Her wavyavyeavyheavyeavy-evyevy hair un comb:'d.' The last phrase here is a *trillando*, and the word *uncombed* is written exactly as a singer might have to enounce it at the close of a cadence.

'Will? You? I. Want. You. To' is a *staccato* effect; 'luring, ah, allur-ing' an *appoggiatura* (an ornamentation of the basic word *luring*). The triumphant knock of Boylan, the 'cock o' the roost', sounds *martellato*: 'One rapped on a door, one tapped with a knock, did he knock Paul de Kock, with a loud proud knocker, with a cock carracarracarra cock. Cockcock.'[1] Miss Mina Kennedy bending across the counter whispers *sordamente* to the 'gentleman with the tankard' that the singer is Ben Dollard. There are several *portamento* or *glissando* effects, the words slide on into one another, as in 'Rain. Diddle, iddle, addle, oodle, oodle'. There is the rhythm, sound, and form of a rondo in the passage: 'From the saloon a call came, long in dying. That was a tuningfork the tuner had that he forgot that now he struck. A call again. That now he poised that it now throbbed. You hear? It throbbed, pure, purer, softly and softlier its buzzing prongs. Longer in dying call.'

The devices of suspension and resolution are frequently employed, as in the passage: 'Upholding the lid he (who?) gazed in the coffin (coffin?) at the oblique triple (piano!) wires.' (Intellection is suspended till the last word resolves the mystery.) Examples of the 'hollow fifth' (*quinto vuoto*) are such words as 'Blmstup', where the 'thirds', the letters *oo* and *ood* (*Bloom stood up*) are omitted, and such sentences as 'Why did she me?' and 'Milly no taste', where the central verb is omitted between subject and object. Thus the hearer of an 'empty fifth'

---

1. Boylan's cockcrow is doubtless an allusion to that curious fowl the caracara, described by Buffon. 'I thus name (Caracara) this handsome bird from the Antilles. Père du Tertre says of him: "This pheasant is a very handsome bird, bulky as a capon, but taller, with a peacock's legs. ... His neck and breast plumage are of a fine gleaming blue, as picturesque as peacock's feathers; his back is brownish-grey, his wings and tail, which are rather short, are black. When this bird is domesti-cated, he behaves as if he were the master in the house. Easily tamed, he grows so familiar in his ways that he will tap at the door with his beak to gain admission." '

instinctively fills up the gap with a major third. There is a *fermata* effect (a note held beyond its normal duration), the aftermath of an *affrettando* passage (already quoted), in the 'held' word *endlessnessnessness* ...

The closing sentence of the following passage illustrates the 'polyphonic' treatment of words in this episode.

It was the only language Mr Dedalus said to Ben. He heard them as a boy in Ringabella, Crosshaven, Ringabella, singing their barcaroles. Queenstown harbour full of Italian ships. Walking, you know, Ben, in the moonlight with those earthquake hats. Blending their voices. God, such music, Ben. Heard as a boy. Cross Ringabella haven mooncarole.

The gradual augmentation of a chord is paralleled in such sequences as 'inexquisite contrast, contrast inexquisite nonexquisite' and 'vast manless moonless womoonless marsh'.

There is an obvious final cadence – dominant, tonic (twice repeated) – in 'Big Benaben. Big Benben. Big Benben'. (Dominant seventh followed by two perfect chords.)

Molly Bloom stands intuitively for what would be in music a sense of 'absolute pitch'. 'With look to look: songs without words. Molly that [Italian] hurdygurdy boy. She knew he meant the monkey was sick. ... Understand animals too that way. Solomon did. Gift of nature.'

The bringing together of all the persons at the bar, under abridged names, and of fragments of thematic material from preceding pages, in a swift simultaneous clink of libation, is clearly the *stretto* of the fugue.

Near bronze from anear near gold from afar they chinked their clinking glasses all, brighteyed and gallant, before bronze Lydia's tempting last rose of summer, rose of Castille. First Lid, De, Cow, Ker, Doll, a fifth: Lidwell, Si Dedalus, Bob Cowley, Kernan and Big Ben Dollard.

Not only is this episode composed on musical lines, the terminology also is rich in musical allusions. 'Miss Kennedy with manners transposed the teatray down to an upturned lithia crate, safe from eyes, low.' 'Backache he (Richie Goulding). Next item on the programme. Paying the piper. ... Stave it off awhile.' 'Callous: all for his own gut.' 'All trio laughed.' 'Want to listen sharp.' 'Rift in the lute.' 'Tenors get women by the score.' 'Fit as a fiddle.' 'In a giggling peal young goldbronze voices blended. ... They threw young heads back, bronze gigglegold, to let freefly their laughter ... signals to each other, high piercing notes.' 'Harmony Avenue, Donnybrook.' The climax of the song from

Martha is rendered in almost technical terms. 'Quitting all languor Lionel cried in grief, in cry of passion dominant to love to return with deepening yet rising chords of harmony.' After the *dominant* comes inevitably the *return*. Thus Stephen[1] expounds the perfection of the octave. 'The fundamental and the dominant are separated by the greatest possible interval which ... is the greatest possible ellipse consistent with the ultimate return.'

In no other episode, perhaps, of *Ulysses* has Joyce attained such a complete 'atonement' between subject-matter and form. To Professor Curtius the experiment appeared 'of questionable value', and, if it were a mere *tour de force*, an artificial grafting of musical on verbal idiom, musicoliteral virtuosity, his doubt would be well-founded. But here the musical rhythm, the sonority and counterpoint of the prose, are evocative of the theme itself, the Sirens' 'song of enthralment'. This episode differs from most examples of 'musical prose' in that the meaning does not lose but is, rather, intensified by the combination of the two arts; sense is not sacrificed to sound but the two are so harmonized that, unless his ears, like the Achaeans', are sealed with wax against the spell, the reader, hearkening to 'the voice sweet as the honeycomb and having joy thereof, will go on his way the wiser'.[2]

1. *Ulysses*, page 479.
2. *Odyssey*, XII: 186–8.

> οὐ γάρ πώ τις τῇδε παρήλασε νηὶ μελαίνῃ,
> πρίν γ' ἡμέων μελίγηρυν ἀπὸ στομάτων ὄπ' ἀκοῦσαι,
> ἀλλ' ὅ γε τερψάμενος νεῖται καὶ πλείονα εἰδώς.

12. THE CYCLOPS

SCENE	The Tavern
HOUR	5 p.m.
ORGAN	Muscle
ART	Politics
SYMBOL	Fenian
TECHNIC	Gigantism

THE setting of this episode is Barney Kiernan's, one of Dublin's most famous public houses at the turn of the century. Situated near the Green Street Courthouse, it was much patronized by those connected in one way or other with the law. Kiernan's hobby was the collection of exhibits connected with crime, counterfeit coins (which he nailed to his counter), weapons that had been used in murders, a piece of rope which had bound the Sheares brothers, the glass of the hangman who hanged them, and other hangmen's glasses. 'On my first visit to Barney Kiernan's about 1929,' writes Mr Roger McHugh in the witty and informative article[1] from which these facts are culled,

I had seen an impressive row of them (i.e. hangmen's glasses), all dusty, cobwebbed and garnished with spiders. The low-ceilinged bar was very dark, but one could see exhibits ranging from handcuffs and horse-pistols to a sugar-cone and faded prints of the Parnellite period. By 1939 the pub ... was obviously approaching the end of a decline that probably started about 1920 with the transfer of most legal business from Green Street to the Four Courts. Perhaps the most serious symptom of the decline was a large notice in the snug which said: 'A Bird is Known by its Song, a Man by his Language.' Today there is little to remind you that Barney Kiernan's ever existed.'

The appropriateness of this setting to the conversation in the Dublin Cyclops' den, and particularly to the incident of the hangman's letter, is obvious.

The story, here, is told by a simple and bibulous Dubliner, a nondescript, in the highly coloured idiom of the profane vulgar, and his

1. In *Envoy*, No. 1, Dublin, December 1949. I record my gratitude to Mr McHugh and the Editor for their kind permission to incorporate some of the information given in this article, and to quote from it.

simple periods are punctuated by Our Lady's adjective. Since *Pygmalion* and the Georgian novelists, however, that word, once unprintable, has ceased to alarm, and no excuse is needed for its frequent appearance in the course of the following pages. It occurs thrice in the first paragraph of the episode and this average is well kept up throughout the remainder. The narrator uses 'bloody' both in its pejorative sense and as a mere intensive, the latter usage being, strange to say, etymologically the more exact.

I was just passing the time of day with old Troy of the D.M.P. at the corner of Arbour hill there and be damned but a bloody sweep came along and he near drove his gear into my eye. I turned round to let him have the weight of my tongue when who should I see dodging along Stony Batter only Joe Hynes.

'Lo, Joe,' says I. 'How are you blowing? Did you see that bloody chimney-sweep near shove my eye out with his brush?'

Joe and the narrator, after a short conversation, decide to enter Barney Kiernan's, where they find a fierce Sinn Feiner, dubbed 'the citizen', having 'a great confab with himself' and an equally aggressive mongrel named Garryowen. Joe stands drinks and produces a sovereign in payment.

Begob the sight nearly left my eyes when I saw him land out a quid. O, as true as I'm telling you. A goodlooking sovereign.

'And there's more where that came from,' says he.

'Were you robbing the poorbox, Joe?' says I.

'Sweat of my brow,' says Joe. ''Twas the prudent member gave me the wheeze.'

The 'prudent member' is Mr Bloom who (see the 'Aeolus' episode) reminded Mr Hynes earlier in the day that he had money to draw at the *Freeman* office, in the hope (unrealized) that Hynes would at last repay a loan of three shillings.

The Citizen declaims against the *Irish Independent* which he is reading, 'founded by Parnell to be the workingman's friend'. The *soi-disant* patriotic organ specializes in notices of births and deaths which have occurred in England. 'How's that for a national press, eh, my brown son? How's that for Martin Murphy, the Bantry jobber?'

Little Alf Bergan popped in round the door and hid behind Barney's snug, squeezed up with the laughing, and who was sitting up there in the corner that I hadn't seen snoring drunk, blind to the world, only Bob Doran. I didn't know what was up and Alf kept making signs at the door. And begob what was it only that bloody old pantaloon Denis Breen in his bath slippers with two bloody big books tucked under his oxter and the wife hotfoot after him, unfortunate wretched woman trotting like a poodle. I thought Alf would split.

'Look at him,' says he. 'Breen. He's traipsing all round Dublin with a post-card someone sent him with u.p.: up on it to take a li ...'

And he doubled up.

'Take a what?' says I.

'Libel action,' says he, 'for ten thousand pounds.'

Presently Mr Bloom approaches.

Old Garryowen started growling again at Bloom that was skeezing round the door.

'Come in, come on, he won't eat you,' says the citizen.

So Bloom slopes in with his cod's eye on the dog and he asks Terry was Martin Cunningham there.

Alf Bergan produces a bundle of 'hangmen's letters' from his pocket for the entertainment of the company and Joe reads one out.

> 7 *Hunter Street*
> *Liverpool*

To the High Sheriff of Dublin,
  Dublin.

Honoured sir i beg to offer my services in the abovementioned painful case i hanged Joe Gann in Bootle jail on the 12 of February 1900 and i hanged private Arthur Chace for fowl murder of Jessie Tilsit in Pentonville prison and i was assistant when Billington executed the awful murderer Toad Smith i have a special nack of putting the noose once in he can't get out hoping to be favoured i remain, honoured sir, my terms is five ginnese.

> *H. Rumbold*
> *Master Barber*

The Citizen brings the conversation round to his favourite topic, politics, and Mr Bloom suffers himself to be drawn into an argument. 'And the citizen and Bloom having an argument about the point, the brothers Sheares and Wolfe Tone beyond on Arbour Hill and Robert Emmet and die for your country, the Tommy Moore touch about Sara Curran and she's far from the land.'

'The memory of the dead,' says the citizen taking up his pintglass and glaring at Bloom.

'Ay, ay,' says Joe.

'You don't grasp my point,' says Bloom. 'What I mean is ...'

'*Sinn Fein!*' says the citizen. '*Sinn fein amhain!* The friends we love are by our side and the foes we hate before us.'

Presently Mr Bloom explains that he has come in the hope of meeting Martin Cunningham, to arrange for payment of Dignam's insurance to the widow. But, for all his goodheartedness, Mr Bloom is odious to the Boeotian narrator.

He starts all confused mucking it up about the mortgagor under the act like the lord chancellor giving it out on the bench and for the benefit of the wife and that a trust is created but on the other hand that Dignam owed Bridgeman the money and now if the wife or the widow contested the mortgagee's right till he near had the head of me addled with his mortgagor under the act. He was bloody safe he wasn't run in himself under the act that time as a rogue and vagabond only he had a friend in court. Selling bazaar tickets or what do you call it royal Hungarian privileged lottery. True as you're there. O, commend me to an israelite! Royal and privileged Hungarian robbery.

With each round of drinks the Citizen becomes more and more patriotic. 'Off they started about Irish sport and shoneen games the like of the lawn tennis and about hurley and putting the stone and racy of the soil and building up a nation once again and all to that.' Joe inquires about the concert tour, organized by Blazes Boylan, in which 'Mrs B. is the bright particular star'.

Hoho begob, says I to myself, says I. That explains the milk in the cocoanut and absence of hair on the animal's chest. Blazes doing the tootle on the flute. Concert tour. Dirty Dan the dodger's son of Island bridge that sold the same horses twice over to the government to fight the Boers. ... That's the bucko that'll organise her, take my tip. 'Twixt me and you Caddereesh.

Messrs O'Molloy and Lambert enter and the conversation now turns to Mr Breen's famous libel action. The Citizen observes that Mrs Breen is to be pitied for marrying a half and half.

'How half and half?' says Bloom. 'Do you mean that he ...'
'Half and half I mean,' says the citizen. 'A fellow that's neither fish nor flesh.'
'Nor good red herring,' says Joe.
'That's what I mean,' says the citizen. 'A pishogue, if you know what that is.'
Begob I saw there was trouble coming.

The talk veers round to the Jewish problem whereon Mr Deasy gave wise counsel to Stephen earlier in the day.

'Those are nice things,' says the Citizen, a Nestor come to judgement, 'coming over here to Ireland filling the country with bugs.'

John Wyse Nolan and Lenehan join the party; the latter is depressed, for the results of the Ascot Gold Cup are out; *Throwaway*, an outsider, won the race.

Twenty to one. Such is life in an outhouse. Takes the biscuit and talking about bunions. Frailty, thy name is *Sceptre*.

The Citizen continues his fulminations; now, the variation on his perennial theme is a homily on the brutality of punishments in the navy. Bloom, as usual, takes the moderate view.

'But,' says Bloom, 'isn't discipline the same everywhere? I mean wouldn't it be the same here if you put force against force?'

Didn't I tell you? As true as I'm drinking this porter if he was at his last gasp he'd try to downface you that dying was living.

'We'll put force against force,' says the citizen. 'We have our greater Ireland beyond the sea. They were driven out of house and home in the black 47. Their mudcabins and their shielings by the roadside were laid low by the battering-ram. ... But those that came to the land of the free remember the land of bondage. And they will come again with a vengeance, no cravens, the sons of Granuaile, the champions of Kathleen ni Houlihan.'

'Perfectly true,' says Bloom. 'But my point was ...'

For the moment they do not let him state his point, but, presently, not without courage, Mr Bloom returns to the attack.

'Persecution,' says he, 'all the history of the world is full of it. Perpetuating national hatred among nations.'

'But do you know what a nation means?' says John Wyse.

'Yes,' says Bloom.

'What is it?' says John Wyse.

'A nation?' says Bloom. 'A nation is the same people living in the same place.'

'By God, then,' says Ned, laughing, 'if that's so I'm a nation for I'm living in the same place for the past five years.'

So of course everyone had a laugh at Bloom and says he, trying to muck out of it:

'Or also living in different places.'

'That covers my case,' says Joe.

'What is your nation if I may ask?' says the citizen.

'Ireland,' says Bloom. 'I was born here. Ireland.'[1]

The citizen said nothing only cleared the spit out of his gullet and, gob, he spat a Red bank oyster out of him right in the corner.

'Are you talking about the new Jerusalem?' says the citizen.

'I'm talking about injustice,' says Bloom.

'Right,' says John Wyse. 'Stand up to it then with force like men.'

That's an almanac picture for you. Mark for a softnosed bullet. Old lardy-face standing up to the business end of a gun. Gob, he'd adorn a sweepingbrush, so he would, if he only had a nurse's apron on him. And then he collapses all of a sudden, twisting round all the opposite, as limp as a wet rag.

'But it's no use,' says he. 'Force, hatred, history, all that. That's not the life for men and women, insult and hatred. ...'

Mr Bloom decides to go round to the court to see if Cunningham is there. Lenehan surmises

'... the courthouse is a blind. He had a few bob on *Throwaway* and he's gone to gather in the shekels.'

'Is it that whiteeyed kaffir?' says the citizen, 'that never backed a horse in anger in his life.'

'That's where he's gone,' says Lenehan. 'I met Bantam Lyons going to back that horse only I put him off it and he told me Bloom gave him the tip. Bet you what you like he has a hundred shillings to five on. He's the only man in Dublin has it. A dark horse.'

It will be recalled that earlier in the day (see the 'Lotus-eaters' episode) Bantam Lyons asked Mr Bloom to show him the racing column in his paper and Mr Bloom replied that he was just going to *throw* it *away*.

'What's that?'

'I say you can keep it,' Mr Bloom answered. 'I was going to throw it away that moment.'

The unconscious utterance of this omen by Mr Bloom and Lyons' manner of retailing it spell trouble for the former on his return to Barney Kiernan's (where, meanwhile, Martin Cunningham has arrived). To drunkenness and chauvinism the third ingredient of a perfect

1. Such arguments – as to what is a man's 'fatherland' – were familiar to the Greeks, as Samuel Butler has pointed out (*The Authoress of the Odyssey*, page 146). Thus a character in Aristophanes suggests that a man's fatherland is any place where he is making money, and another (in Euripides) that it is any land that will feed him. The reasons why such problems should have a special appeal to Greeks and Dubliners alike are suggested in Chapter 4 of my Introduction.

pogrom – a mistake of fact – is now added. The thirsty patriots expect
that Mr Bloom will pay a winner's tribute – drinks all round. But
Mr Bloom cannot understand their hints.

'Come on boys,' says Martin, seeing it was looking blue. 'Come along now.'
'Don't tell anyone,' says the citizen, letting a bawl out of him. 'It's a secret.'
And the bloody dog woke up and let a growl.
'Bye bye all,' says Martin.
And he got them out as quick as he could. ...
But begob I was just lowering the heel of the pint when I saw the citizen get-
ting up to waddle to the door, puffing and blowing with the dropsy and he
cursing the curse of Cromwell on him, bell, book and candle in Irish, spitting
and spatting out of him and Joe and little Alf round him like a leprechaun try-
ing to pacify him.
'Let me alone,' says he.
And begob he got as far as the door and they holding him and he bawls out
of him:
'Three cheers for Israel!'

A crowd collects and Martin tells the jarvey of his jaunting-car to
drive ahead; the Citizen bawls, a loafer starts singing 'If the man in the
moon was a jew, jew, jew'.

Mr Bloom retorts.

'Mendelssohn was a jew and Karl Marx and Mercadante and Spinoza. And
the Saviour was a jew and his father was a jew. Your God.'
'He had no father,' says Martin. 'That'll do now. Drive ahead.'
'Whose God?' says the citizen.
'Well, his uncle was a jew,' says he. 'Your God was a jew. Christ was a jew
like me.'

The Citizen is beside himself with fury.

'I'll brain that bloody jewman for using the holy name. ... I'll crucify him so
I will. Give us that biscuitbox here.'
As luck would have it the jarvey got the nag's head round the other way and
off with him.
'Hold on, citizen,' says Joe. 'Stop!'
Begob he drew his hand and made a swipe and let fly. Mercy of God the sun
was in his eyes or he'd have left him for dead.

Thus Mr Bloom, escaping the blind fury of the Sinn Feiner, survives
to fulfil his self-imposed errand of mercy.

*

The adventure of Odysseus with the 'monster Polypheme' reflects but little credit on the vaunted sagacity of the hero; he had, indeed, a regrettable habit of looking for trouble, and only proved himself 'rich in counsel' when escape from the consequences of an imprudence had to be contrived. No doubt he was wary enough at first, and concealed his fleet in the bay of an islet near the land of the Cyclopes, where there was an hospitable cave ringed with tall poplars and abundance of water and goats, whereon he and his men feasted to their hearts' content. But the spirit of adventure urged him to 'make proof of these Cyclopes, what manner of folk they are' – the same spirit that led Mr Bloom, unwisely wise, to make proof of the humanity of the loafers assembled in Kiernan's bar. Odysseus came to the outer court of the monster's den, 'built with stones, deep bedded, and with tall pines and oaks with high crown of leaves'. With twelve men he entered the cave, carrying a skin of dark wine for its owner (temporarily absent), that 'monstrous thing'. Homer gives us a detailed inventory of the contents of the cave, the baskets well laden with cheeses, the milk-pails and bowls, the folds thronged with lambs and kids, 'each kind penned by itself, the firstlings apart, and the summer lambs apart, apart too the younglings of the flock'. (It will be observed that there are several inventories or catalogues in the Homeric manner in the course of this episode.) Presently the Cyclops came home and questioned the wanderers, answering their polite and pious plea for hospitality with blasphemous invective. Then the sturdy patriot broke the heads of two of the Achaean immigrants and made his supper of them, eating 'like a lion of the hills'. Odysseus, 'prudent member', resisted an impulse to attack the monster. Next day, still prisoner in the cave, he contrived a means of escape, sharpening a club to a point and hardening it in the fire. At nightfall the guest played the part of host, offering copious bowls of unmixed wine to the giant, who was greatly mollified: 'Give me it again of thy grace and tell me of thy name.' 'Noman is my name,' Odysseus replied, 'and Noman they call me, my father and my mother and all my fellows.' Presently, when the Cyclops was sunk in drunken sleep, Odysseus, having heated the sharp end of the club in the fire, drove it into the giant's eye. The Cyclopes, his kinsmen of the hills, awakened by his cries for help, asked who harmed him. 'No man is slaying me by guile nor at all by force,' he replied. Our brother is delirious, they thought, and slept again.

At dawn Odysseus and his men escaped by a stratagem and embarked on their ship. The Cyclops hurled a rock at the fugitives, but, blinded as he was, missed his target. Odysseus, despite the admonitions of his ship's company, shouted a challenge, and the giant riposted with another rock which fell behind the rudder and drove the ship forward to safety.

Thus the negation contained in his pseudonym delivered Odysseus; for 'Odysseus' (Οδυσσεύς) is formed from two roots – Noman-Zeus (Οὖτις-Ζεύς).

What universal binomial denominations would be his as entity and nonentity?[1]

Assumed by any or known to none. Everyman or Noman.[2]

The structure of this episode presents several features of exceptional interest, for the appreciation of which it is necessary to examine the historical foundation of the Cyclops legend. Homer gives an indication of the habitat of the one-eyed giants when, speaking of the Phaeacians, he mentions that 'of old they dwelt in spacious Hypereia', whence they fled to escape the Cyclopes' persecution. *Hypereia* is 'the high town' and its Semitic equivalent is *Cumae*; similarly the Semitic name given to that region, *Oinotria*, corresponds to the Greek *Cyclopia*. The root *oin* signifies 'the eye', and *otar* 'the circle'; in combination we have 'the circle of the eye' (i.e. Cyclopia). The land of the Cyclopes may safely be located in the vicinity of Naples, round the bay of Cumae.[3] The

---

1. It may here be noted that from the Semitic point of view, anonymity may be identified with nonentity. In *La Civilisation phénicienne* (page 108) Dr Contenau observes: '*On remarquera que la plupart des noms divins sont une périphrase* [an example of such a periphrasis occurs towards the close of this episode]: *Melquart est "le roi de la ville"; d'autres nommés mon seigneur (adon), baal de tel endroit, dieu (el), ne révèlent point par leur nom leur identité. Cela tient à un point fondamental de la philosophie des peuples de l'Asie occidentale ancienne: une chose n'existe que si elle a un nom. La dénomination implique l'existence de l'objet et s'identifie à lui: nommer une chose c'est la créer, nommer un acte c'est déjà l'accomplir. Si l'on connaît le nom d'un dieu, le proférer c'est évoquer le dieu. Et comme venir à l'appel de son nom est obéir, il s'ensuit que l'homme peut se rendre maître du dieu dans une certaine mesure. La façon de parer à un tel inconvénient est de cacher le nom du dieu sous une périphrase.... C'est ce qu'ont fait les Hébreux pour qui le nom de Dieu était ineffable.*' Illustrations of the use of ritual periphrasis will be found in the course of my analysis of this episode.

2. page 688.

3. For these derivations and the account of Cyclopias which follow I am indebted to M. Bérard's *Les Phéniciens et l'Odyssée*, Tome II, pages 114–79 of the first edition.

Greeks, puzzled by the name Oinotria, believed that this country was vineland, the land of wine (*oinos – vinum*), but that the derivation suggested above is the more exact is evident from the fact that the first Greek settlers in that tract of the south-west coast of Italy described the natives as the Opikoi (i.e. the people of the eyes).

The coastline of the bay is studded with the extinct craters of volcanoes, and, near its eastern spur (in the direction of Naples), there is a small island, an extinct crater, with a narrow neck of sea where the wall of the crater has fallen in. Inside there is exactly the harbour described by Homer, 'where there is no need of moorings, either to cast anchor or to fasten hawsers'. Cyclopia is 'the land of the eyes', these *eyes* being the volcanic craters of the region. The Cyclops himself is an obvious personification of a volcano in eruption, one-eyed, vomiting rocks and lava with hideous clamour, 'like a wooded peak of the towering hills, which stands out alone apart from the others' (the characteristic appearance of a volcano). Thus the tables are turned on the anthropomorphist; to describe the giant who personifies a towering hill he has to use the similitude of the hill itself!

The Citizen is persistently clamorous and fulminant; the more liquid he absorbs, the greater his eruptive violence. He has a patriotic fixed idea; he will not brook the presence in his land of foreigner, Jew, or Sassenach, just as the Cyclopes, 'men exceeding proud', harried the more civilized Phaeacians till the latter were obliged to leave their colony in high Hypereia. The Citizen's method is to 'send to the right-about' all who are not members of his clan or do not see eye to eye with him. He is second to none in the eminently volcanic sport of 'putting the shot'. He fumes against 'half-and-halfs', *pishogues*. Thus even in historical times the Opikoi were the terror of their neighbours. The history of Cumae-en-Opikois, a town founded by the Peoples of the Sea, was, M. Bérard tells us, 'one long martyrdom; Dionysius of Halicarnassus has related the struggles of the Cumaeans against these savage barbarians, second to none in the arts of warfare. ...' The Greek hoplites alone could impose some sort of restraint on these giants of the coast; as for the 'Semitic businessman, little versed in violent sports and the perils of war, he preferred to avoid, or to flee before, the onslaught of the coastmen'. In like manner Mr Bloom is forced to beat a retreat before the weight-putter. To mollify the intransigent People of the Eyes, Greek and Roman travellers usually made offerings of wine – the surest way to the heart of all primitive peoples. Odysseus prudently brought with him a provision of wine when he entered the monster's cave, but Mr Bloom omitted to stand his round of drinks, with dire results.

There are many allusions to the *eye* in the course of the episode and it will be noticed that in each of the examples cited the word *eye* is in the singular; a precise homage to the monocular Polypheme. 'You should have seen Long John's eye.' 'There was not a dry eye in that record assemblage.' Garryowen has his 'eye all bloodshot from the drouth is in it'. The narrator refers to Mr Bloom as 'old cod's eye', to certain 'flash toffs with a swank glass in their eye', to 'a loafer with a patch over his eye'. J. J. O'Molloy, as a tentative defence to the Citizen's indictment of the British nation and all their works, 'puts in a word about one story was as good till you heard another and blinking facts and the Nelson policy putting your blind eye to the telescope and drawing up a bill of attainder to impeach a nation and Bloom trying to back him up moderation and botheration and their colonies and their civilization.

'Their syphilisation, you mean,' says the citizen. 'To hell with them!'

Not less outrageously spoke the Man of the Eye to Odysseus.

'The Cyclopes pay no heed to Zeus nor to the blessed gods' – in the mouth of the Cyclops this '*blessed*' is surely ironic, as in 'you're a *blessed* nuisance' – 'for verily we are better men than they.'

When the Citizen was hurling the biscuit tin at Mr Bloom, 'mercy of God the sun was in his eyes'. (In Cant jargon a person who is drunk is said to have 'the sun in his eyes'.)

There are many allusions to blindness – the boxer 'whose right eye was nearly closed', the narrator's desire, happily suppressed, to kick Garryowen 'where it wouldn't blind him', and we hear of that occult sewer, the 'blind intestine'. The first remark, indeed, of the narrator – an imprecation of the sweep who 'near drove his gear into my eye' – is an obvious recall of the blinding of the giant, and the huge club of olive wood sharpened and heated in the fire by Odysseus for that purpose, has its pigmy caricature in Mr Bloom's 'knockmedown cigar'.

Odysseus owed his escape from the Cyclops to a prudent change of name, a denial of personality which permitted his ghostlike evasion from durance. In this episode the idea of anonymity or misnomer is suggested under many aspects. Mr Bloom himself, we are reminded, is a Virag by birth. The name of the loquacious narrator is never stated, nor is the Citizen ever called by his name. At one moment the dog Garryowen[1] is rechristened Owen Garry. There is a reference to 'our greatest living phonetic expert (wild horses shall not drag it from us)', to a poet who uses the pseudonym *Little Sweet Branch*, to the false name given by O'Molloy when pawning his watch, to the writer of a letter to the *United Irishman* who signs himself 'P' ('"And a very good initial too," says Joe'). The characters rarely address each other by their surnames and express themselves metonymically whenever possible. There are instances of the shirking of names, allusions to a change of name accompanying a change of religion, enlistment, or marriage; to the metamorphosis of plain Mr Breen into Signor Brini, the papal zouave; to the uncertainty of the narrator as to the correct name of one Crofton or Crofter, 'the Orangeman or presbyterian', and, finally, we find a substitute for the divine name, the 'ineffable tetragrammaton', in *Abba Adonai*.

A curious feature of the last seven pages of the episode is that any reference to Mr Bloom by name is carefully evaded. In such phrases as 'He got them out as quick as he could, Jack Power and Crofton or whatever you call him and him in the middle of them', the suppression of Mr Bloom's name is too marked to be merely accidental. Like all apparent anomalies in *Ulysses* this omission is certainly deliberate and has, perhaps, a ritually symbolic bearing. In the 'bidding prayers' of the Catholic Good Friday service the priest prays for a long series of specified persons, calling on the congregation to 'bend their knees' (*Flecta-mus genua*). But when, last of all, he prays for the Jews – *Oremus et pro perfidis Judaeis* (How aptly that *et* falls into place!) – he omits the call to genuflexion, because the Jews bent the knee to Christ in mockery. The deliberate refusal to name Mr Bloom in the closing pages of the episode, his degradation to nomanhood, to nonentity, may be taken to symbolize the commination of Jewry implied in catholic ritual; further justification for this *rapprochement* may be found in the markedly reli-

---

1. Garryowen is (at page 337) mentioned as 'grandpapa Giltrap's lovely dog Garryowen that almost talked'. But the innominate Citizen is *not* to be identified with 'grandpapa Giltrap'. He walks out with the 'bloody old towser', but the animal is not his.

gious trend of the argument in these pages, Mr Bloom's 'blasphemous' homily on the parentage of the Saviour and the vision of an ascent into heaven on which the episode ends.

This episode is, moreover, a perfect *locus classicus* of the various ways in which to name (or, rather, misname), and accept the offer of a drink (needless to say, the case of a refusal does not present itself), and to propose the health of the company.

> 'Give it a name, citizen,' says Joe.
> 'Wine of the country,' says he.
> 'What's yours?' says Joe.
> 'Ditto MacAnaspey,' says I.
> 'Three pints, Terry,' says Joe. ...
> 'Health, Joe,' says I. 'And all down the form.'

(This is a formula used at Irish *wakes*, where the mourners, carousers, I should say, sit on long benches, like Homeric oarsmen.)

> 'The memory of the dead,' says the citizen taking up his pintglass and glaring at Bloom. ...
> 'Could you make a hole in another pint?'
> 'Could a duck swim?' says I.
> 'Same again, Terry,' says Joe. (To Mr Bloom) 'Are you sure you won't have anything in the way of liquid refreshment?' says he. ...
> '*Slan leat*,' says he.
> 'Fortune, Joe,' says I. 'Good health, citizen.' ...
> 'God save you,' says the citizen.
> 'Save you kindly,' says J. J. 'What'll it be, Ned?'
> 'Half one,' says Ned. ...
> 'What will you have?'
> 'An imperial yeomanry,' says Lenehan, 'to celebrate the occasion.'
> 'Half one, Terry,' says John Wyse, 'and a hands up.' ...[1]
> 'Will you try another, citizen?' says Joe.
> 'Yes, sir,' says he. 'I will.'
> 'You?' says Joe.
> 'Beholden to you, Joe,' says I. 'May your shadow never grow less.'
> 'Repeat that dose,' says Joe. ...[2]

1. i.e. Allsop, the bottles of which have on them a figure with an uplifted hand. 'Imperial Yeomanry' is a synonym, barbed with a nationalist sneer at the supposed conduct of that corps in the Boer War.
2. Cf. the Cyclops' way of asking for more. 'Give it me again of thy grace.'

'Here you are, citizen,' says Joe. 'Take that in your right hand and repeat after me the following words.' ...

'Have you time for a brief libation, Martin?' asks Ned.

'Only one,' says Martin. 'J. J. and S.' ...

'Well,' says Martin, rapping his glass. 'God bless all here is my prayer.'

'Amen,' says the citizen.

'And I'm sure he will,' says Joe.

'And so say all of us,' says Jack.

The parliamentary custom of avoiding reference to a member by name is illustrated by a passage between nationalist members and the Speaker. This dialogue also exemplifies the roundabout official way of evading a plain answer. 'Has the right honourable gentleman's famous Mitchelstown telegram inspired the policy of gentlemen on the treasury bench? (O! O!).'

The answer is in the negative.

('O, rocks!' practical Penelope would say, impatient of the eternal childishness of political man. 'Tell us in plain words!')

In this sense – but this sense only – the language of the group in the bar may be said to be parliamentary. Their speech suffers also from the disease of language styled catachresis, a preference for the *mot injuste*.

The truth, the whole truth and nothing but the truth, so help you Jimmy Johnson. ...

Don't you cast your nasturtiums on my character. ...

I beg your parsnips. ...

Show us the entrance out.

A Dubliner can, it seems, give points even to the Cockney in this form of badinage.

The technic of the episode, *gigantism*, at first produces the impression of a series of merely parodic effects. At intervals the narration is taken out of the mouth of the nondescript vulgarian and becomes mock-heroic, Gargantuan, pseudo-scientific, or antiquarian in style. This technic often amounts to parody, but it is parody of a special and appropriate kind. The method here is the inflation of certain themes to bursting-point, or the projection of Cyclopean shadows of human forms on the sides of a cavern. Thus an early allusion to the appearance of the Citizen is followed by the 'gigantic' description of him, distended to monstrous dimensions.

The figure seated on a large boulder at the foot of a round tower was that of a broadshouldered deepchested stronglimbed frankeyed redhaired freely freckled shaggybearded widemouthed largenosed longheaded deepvoiced barekneed brawnyhanded hairylegged ruddyfaced sinewyarmed hero. From shoulder to shoulder he measured several ells and his rocklike mountainous knees were covered, as was likewise the rest of his body wherever visible, with a strong growth of mountain gorse (*Ulex Europeus*).[1] The widewinged nostrils, from which bristles of the same tawny hue projected, were of such capaciousness that within their cavernous obscurity the fieldlark might easily have lodged her nest. The eyes in which a tear and a smile strove ever for the mastery were of the dimensions of a goodsized cauliflower. A powerful current of warm breath issued at regular intervals from the profound cavity of his mouth while in rhythmic resonance the loud strong hale reverberations of his formidable heart thundered rumblingly, causing the ground, the summit of the lofty tower and the still loftier walls of the cave to vibrate and tremble.

A patriotic outburst of the Citizen, lamenting the deforestation of Ireland, leads to the detailed description, as a provincial reporter would have written it, of a wedding in the family of the M'Conifer of the Glands at the church of Saint Fiacre *in Horto*. The numerous persons attending the wedding all bear arboreal names: Miss Blanche Maple, Miss Virginia Creeper, Miss Timidity Aspenall, Mrs Liana Forest, etc. (In the Homeric narrative there is an unusually precise description of the poplars on the island and of 'the tall pines and oaks with high crown of leaves' which encircled the cave of the Cyclops.) Mr Bloom, deprecating the Citizen's rancour, preaches the gospel of universal love. There follows a little homily on love's sweet ubiquity.

Love likes to love love. Nurse loves the new chemist. Constable 14A loves Mary Kelly. Gerty MacDowell loves the boy that has the bicycle. M.B. loves a fair gentleman. Li Chi Han lovey up kissy Cha Pu Chow. Jumbo, the elephant, loves Alice, the elephant. Old Mr Verschoyle with the ear trumpet loves old Mrs Verschoyle with the turnedin eye. The man in the brown macintosh loves a lady who is dead. ... You love a certain person. And this person loves that other person because everybody loves somebody but God loves everybody.

The elaborate description of the Citizen's handkerchief, 'a much-treasured and intricately embroidered ancient Irish face-cloth', 'the acme of art', depicting 'on the emanatory field' a number of lifelike

1. A prototype of H.C.E., hero of the *Wake*, one of whose avatars is the hirsute Hill of Howth.

scenes, brings to our mind Homer's detailed description of the golden baldric of Hercules (*Odyssey* XI: 609–14), 'whereon wondrous things were wrought', scenes of hunting and war. This implied analogy emphasizes the Herculean strength of the ferocious Dubliner.

The flinging of the biscuit tin at Mr Bloom leads to an earthquake.

The catastrophe was terrific and instantaneous in its effect. The observatory of Dunsink registered in all eleven shocks, all of the fifth grade of Mercalli's scale, and there is no record extant of a similar seismic disturbance in our island since the earthquake of 1534, the year of the rebellion of Silken Thomas. The epicentre appears to have been that part of the metropolis which constitutes the Inn's Quay ward and parish of Saint Michan covering a surface of fortyone acres, two roods and one square pole or perch. All the lordly residences in the vicinity of the palace of justice were demolished and that noble edifice itself, in which at the time of the catastrophe important legal debates were in progress, is literally a mass of ruins beneath which it is to be feared all the occupants have been buried alive.

Finally, in the 'gigantic' version of Mr Bloom's departure, we find the 'Elijah' motif, developed *maestoso*, soaring to height celestial, to crash at last, like Icarus, into sudden bathos.

You never saw the like of it in all your born puff. ... The jarvey saved his life as sure as God made Moses. ... And he let a volley of oaths after him.

'Did I kill him,' says he, 'or what?'

And he shouting to the bloody dog:

'After him, Garry! After him, boy!'

And the last we saw was the bloody car rounding the corner and old sheepsface on it gesticulating and the bloody mongrel after it with his lugs back for all he was bloody well worth to tear him limb from limb. ...

When, lo, there came about them all a great brightness and they beheld the chariot wherein He stood ascend to heaven. And they beheld Him in the chariot, clothed in the glory of the brightness, having raiment as of the sun, fair as the moon and terrible that for awe they durst not look upon Him. And there came a voice out of heaven, calling: *Elijah! Elijah!* And he answered with a main cry: *Abba! Adonai!* And they beheld Him even Him, ben Bloom Elijah, amid clouds of angels ascend to the glory of the brightness at an angle of fortyfive degrees over Donohoe's in Little Green Street like a shot off a shovel.

13. NAUSICAA

SCENE	The Rocks
HOUR	8 p.m.
ORGAN	Eye, nose
ART	Painting
COLOUR	Grey, blue
SYMBOL	Virgin
TECHNIC	Tumescence–detumescence

THE summer evening had begun to fold the world in its mysterious embrace. Far away in the west the sun was setting and the last glow of all too fleeting day lingered lovingly on sea and strand, on the proud promontory of dear old Howth guarding as ever the waters of the bay, on the weed-grown rocks along Sandymount shore and, last but not least, on the quiet church whence there streamed forth at times upon the stillness the voice of prayer to her who is in her pure radiance a beacon ever to the stormtossed heart of man, Mary, star of the sea.

Here, after the volcanic rages of the Cyclops' den and a miraculous escape from seismic catastrophe, rest comes at last to the stormtossed heart of Mr Bloom. By this way Stephen Dedalus passed on his morning walk along the foreshore; it was here that he noticed the two midwives, with their bag, coming down the shelving shore; 'flabbily their splayed feet sinking in the silted sand'. The scene of this episode is Sandymount shore, and perhaps over these very rocks lay Stephen's shadow ('Why not endless till the farthest star?'), manshape ineluctable, captor of Proteus, as he scribbled on his improvised 'tablets' *mouth to her mouth's kiss*, and mused: 'Touch me. Soft eyes. Soft soft soft hand. I am lonely here. O touch me soon, now. What is that word known to all men? I am quiet here alone. Sad too. Touch, touch me.' Seeds of vague desire strewn in the bright air of morning, their emanations linger yet, pervading the sunset dreams of tired Mr Bloom and Miss Gertrude MacDowell, lonely virgin of the rocks. Mr Bloom, too, has sentimental memories of dear old Howth. 'Hidden under wild ferns on Howth. ... Pillowed on my coat she had her hair, earwigs in the heather scrub, my hand under her nape, you'll toss me all. O wonder!'[1]

1. *Ulysses*, page 167.

In such an ambiance of sentiment Gerty MacDowell, 'gazing far away into the distance', dreams of loves forgotten, love to be. In such a night as this Nausicaa heard in dream Athena's summons to the Phaeacian beach, where a certain godlike wanderer was sleeping, snug in fallen leaves like a seed of fire within black embers. Gerty's girl friends, Cissy Caffrey and Edy Boardman, seated beside her on the rock, jealous creatures of grosser clay, strike, it must be admitted, a jarring note. And Tommy and Jacky Caffrey, the curly-headed twins, for all their tender years, are no better than they should be. They have built a round tower – a little *omphalos* of their own – on the Cape Mortella model, and theirs is the spirit of Corsican brotherhood.

Boys will be boys and our two twins were no exception to this golden rule. The apple of discord was a certain castle of sand which Master Jacky had built and Master Tommy would have it right go wrong that it was to be architecturally improved by a frontdoor like the Martello tower had. But if Master Tommy was headstrong Master Jacky was selfwilled too and, true to the maxim that every little Irishman's house is his castle, he fell upon his hated rival and to such purpose that the wouldbe assailant came to grief and (alas to relate!) the coveted castle too.

Baby Boardman in his pushcar, though too young to fight, manages to make a nuisance of himself in his own small way.

'Say papa, baby. Say pa pa pa pa pa pa pa.'

And baby did his level best to say it for he was very intelligent for eleven months everyone said and big for his age and the picture of health, a perfect little bunch of love, and he would certainly turn out to be something great they said.

'Haja ja ja haja.'

Cissy wiped his little mouth with the dribbling bib and wanted him to sit up properly and say pa pa pa but when she undid the strap she cried out, holy saint Denis, that he was possing wet and to double the half blanket the other way under him. Of course his infant majesty was most obstreperous at such toilet formalities and he let everyone know it.

'Habaa baaaahabaaa baaaa.'

And two great big lovely tears coursing down his cheeks. It was all no use soothering him with no, nono, baby, no and telling him about the geegee and where was the puffpuff but Ciss, always readywitted, gave him in his mouth the teat of the sucking bottle and the young heathen was quickly appeased.

It is a relief to turn to Gerty, 'as fair a specimen of winsome Irish girlhood as one could wish to see'.

The waxen pallor of her face was almost spiritual in its ivory-like purity though her rosebud mouth was a genuine Cupid's bow, Greekly perfect. Her hands were of finely veined alabaster with tapering fingers and as white as lemon juice and queen of ointments could make them though it was not true that she used to wear kid gloves in bed or take a milk footbath either. Bertha Supple told that once to Edy Boardman, a deliberate lie, when she was black out at daggers drawn with Gerty (the girl chums had of course their little tiffs from time to time like the rest of mortals) and she told her not to let on whatever she did that it was her that told her or she'd never speak to her again. No. Honour where honour is due. There was an innate refinement, a languid queenly *hauteur* about Gerty which was unmistakably evidenced in her delicate hands and high-arched instep. Had kind fate but willed her to be born a gentlewoman of high degree in her own right and had she only received the benefit of a good education Gerty MacDowell might easily have held her own beside any lady in the land and have seen herself exquisitely gowned with jewels on her brow and patrician suitors at her feet vying with one another to pay their devoirs to her. Mayhap it was this, the love that might have been, that lent to her softlyfeatured face at whiles a look, tense with suppressed meaning, that imparted a strange yearning tendency to the beautiful eyes, a charm few could resist.

Yet her love affair with young Reggy Wylie, a boy of her own age, seemed likely to end, like Nausicaa's, by a *nolle prosequi*.

He was undeniably handsome with an exquisite nose and he was what he looked, every inch a gentleman, the shape of his head too at the back without his cap on that she would know anywhere something off the common and the way he turned the bicycle at the lamp with his hands off the bars and also the nice perfume of those good cigarettes and besides they were both of a size and that was why Edy Boardman thought she was so frightfully clever because he didn't go and ride up and down in front of her bit of a garden.

Her ideal is changing; he who would win her love must be

a manly man with a strong quiet face who had not found his ideal, perhaps his hair slightly flecked with grey, and who would understand, take her in his sheltering arms, strain her to him in all the strength of his deep passionate nature and comfort her with a long long kiss. It would be like heaven. For such a one she yearns this balmy summer eve. With all the heart of her she longs to be his only, his affianced bride for riches for poor, in sickness in health, till death us two part, from this to this day forward.

She will make a tender, loving little wifie; 'they would have a beautifully appointed drawingroom with pictures and engravings and the photograph of grandpapa Giltrap's lovely dog Garryowen that almost talked'. (Garryowen will be recognized as the 'old towser', loaned by grandpapa as boon companion to a 'blood and ouns champion'.)

Tommy and the baby meanwhile are quarrelling about a ball which Tommy claims for his.

O, he was a man already was little Tommy Caffrey since he was out of pinnies. Edy told him no, no and to be off now with him and she told Cissy Caffrey not to give in to him.

'You're not my sister,' naughty Tommy said. 'It's my ball.'

But Cissy Caffrey told baby Boardman to look up, look up high at her finger and she snatched the ball quickly and threw it along the sand and Tommy after it in full career, having won the day.

'Anything for a quiet life,' laughed Ciss.

And she tickled tiny tot's two cheeks to make him forget and played here's the lord mayor, here's his two horses, here's his gingerbread carriage and here he walks in, chinchopper, chinchopper, chinchopper chin. But Edy got cross as two sticks about him getting his own way like that from everyone always petting him.

'I'd like to give him something,' she said, 'so I would, where I won't say.'

'On the beetoteetom,' laughed Cissy merrily.

Gerty MacDowell bent down her head and crimsoned at the idea of Cissy saying an unladylike thing like that out loud she'd be ashamed of her life to say, flushing a deep rosy red, and Edy Boardman said she was sure the gentleman opposite heard what she said. But not a pin cared Ciss.

Presently Master Jacky kicks the ball as hard as ever he can towards the seaweedy rocks. A gentleman in black sitting there intercepts the ball and throws it up towards Cissy, but it rolls back down the slope and stops right under Gerty's skirt. Cissy tells her to kick it away and Gerty gives a kick, but misses. The other girls laugh.

'If you fail try again,' Edy Boardman said.

Gerty smiled assent and bit her lip. A delicate pink crept into her pretty cheek but she was determined to let them see so she just lifted her skirt a little but just enough and took good aim and gave the ball a jolly good kick. ... Pure jealousy of course it was nothing else to draw attention on account of the gentleman opposite looking. She felt the warm flush, a danger signal always with Gerty MacDowell, surging and flaming into her cheeks. Till then they had only exchanged glances of the most casual but now under the brim of her new hat she ventured a look at him and the face that met her gaze there in the twilight wan and sadly drawn, seemed to her the saddest that she had ever seen.

Observing the lonely gentleman, she reads the story of a haunting sorrow written on his face.

He was looking up so intently, so still, and he saw her kick the ball and perhaps he could see the bright steel buckles of her shoes if she swung them like that thoughtfully with the toes down. She was glad that something told her to put on the transparent stockings thinking Reggy Wylie might be out but that was far away. Here was that of which she had so often dreamed. It was he who mattered and there was joy on her face because she wanted him because she felt instinctively that he was like no-one else. The very heart of the girlwoman went out to him, her dreamhusband, because she knew on the instant it was him. If he had suffered, more sinned against than sinning, or even, even, if he had been himself a sinner, a wicked man, she cared not. Even if he was a protestant or methodist she could convert him easily if he truly loved her.

Meanwhile the dusk has fallen and Gerty's companions are thinking of going home. But Gerty is in no hurry to move; the gentleman's eyes are fixed on her, 'literally worshipping at her shrine'. The Mirus Bazaar fireworks begin and the others run down the strand so as to see over the houses and the church. Gerty is left to her lovedreams and the rapt regard of Mr Bloom – for it is he, the sombre gentleman with the haunting sorrow. She 'senses' the mute appeal of his adoring eye; inapprehensible, she clutches to her compassion the aching void of the Bloomish heart.

Perhaps it was an old flame he was in mourning for from the days beyond recall.[1] She thought she understood. She would try to understand him because men were so different. The old love was waiting, waiting with little white hands stretched out, with blue appealing eyes. Heart of mine! She would follow her dream of love, the dictates of her heart told her he was her all in all, the only man in all the world for her for love was the master guide. Nothing else mattered. Come what might she would be wild, untrammelled, free.

Gerty swings her buckled shoe, transparent stockings, faster and yet faster. She leans back, far, further, too far back, while Mr Bloom follows her movements with the enraptured eyes of love-at-first-sight. And, since apostrophe befits this tender, old-world theme, let us pause, gentle reader, to acclaim the 'flappers' of Bloomsday, happy indeed, *sua si bona norint*, before the evil days befell of abridged skirts, when man no longer delights in any girl's legs. The consolations of a rainy day or

1. 'The dear, dead days beyond recall.' *Love's Old Sweet Song.*

rugged beach have gone the way of all flesh and left the exhibitionist no better off than a commoner. Leopold Bloom is *aux anges*.

And then a rocket sprang and bang shot blind blank and O! then the Roman candle burst and it was like a sigh of O! and everyone cried O! O! in raptures and it gushed out of it a stream of rain gold hair threads and they shed and ah! they were all greeny dewy stars falling with golden, O so lovely! O so soft, sweet, soft!

But now Cissy Caffrey vulgarly whistles to call Gerty, who knows that her golden hour is over. But first she makes a gesture of benediction, token that Love's Sweet Evensong is ended.

> *Though the heart be weary,*
> *Sad the day and long,*
> *Still there comes at twilight*
> *Love's Old Sweet Song.*

Gerty had an idea, one of love's little ruses. She slipped her hand into her kerchief pocket and took out the wadding and waved in reply of course without letting him and then slipped it back. Wonder if he's too far to. She rose. ... She drew herself up to her full height. Their souls met in a last lingering glance and the eyes that reached her heart, full of a strange shining, hung enraptured on her sweet flowerlike face. She smiled at him wanly, a sweet forgiving smile, a smile that verged on tears, and then they parted.

... She walked with a certain quiet dignity characteristic of her but with care and very slowly because, because Gerty MacDowell was ...

Tight boots? No. She's lame! O!

Now Mr Bloom sits alone, darkling, in a mood of calm reaction, of afterthoughts on love and woman's ways, embodied in a long silent monologue. But each phase is rounded by a thought of Marion, his wife, for he is faithful in his mild infidelity.

Wait. Hm. Hm. Yes. That's her perfume. Why she waved her hand. I leave you this to think of me when I'm far away on the pillow. What is it? Heliotrope? No. Hyacinth? Hm. Roses, I think. She'd like scent of that kind. Sweet and cheap: soon sour. Why Molly likes opoponax. Suits her with a little jessamine mixed. Her high notes and her low notes. At the dance night she met him, dance of the hours. Heat brought it out. She was wearing her black and it had the perfume of the time before. Good conductor, is it? Or bad? Light too. Suppose there's some connection. For instance if you go into a cellar when it's dark. Mysterious thing too. Why did I smell it only now? Took its time in coming like herself, slow but sure. Suppose it's ever so many millions of tiny grains blown across. Yes, it is. Because those spice islands, Cinghalese this morning, smell them leagues off. Tell you what it is. It's like a fine veil or web they have all over the skin, fine like what do you call it gossamer and they're always spinning it out of them, fine as anything, rainbow colours without knowing it. Clings to everything she takes off. Vamp of her stockings. Warm shoe. Stays. Drawers: little kick, taking them off. Byby till next time. Also the cat likes to sniff in her shift on the bed. Know her smell in a thousand. Bathwater too. Reminds me of strawberries and cream.

The sultry day has reached its sleepy close. Bats are bawking through the velvet sky. 'Short snooze now if I had. ... Just close my eyes a moment. Won't sleep though. Half dream. It never comes the same.'

A bat flew. Here. There. Far in the grey a bell chimed. Mr Bloom with open mouth, his left boot sanded sideways, leaned, breathed. Just for a few.

As Mr Bloom half dreams, his inner voice murmurs an epilogue of the day's memories and encounters, a jumble of words, disjointed yet associative – metempsychosis, Martha's letter, Raoul, and the 'heaving embonpoint' of *The Sweets of Sin*, dark, 'Spanish' Marion and her earliest lover, returned sailors 'smelling the tailend of ports', melonfields of Agendath Netaim. ... 'we two naughty Grace darling she him half past the bed met him pike hoses frillies for Raoul to perfume you wife black hair heave under embon *senorita* young eyes Mulvey plump years dreams return tail end Agendath swoony lovey showed me her next year in drawers return next in her next her next'.

It is interesting to compare this summer night's dream of Mr Bloom with another night-piece, those famous last lines of the 'Anna Livia Plurabelle' section of *Finnegans Wake*, where two garrulous old washerwomen, metamorphosed into a tree and a stone, are fixed in an ageless dream, beside the dark waters of the Anna Liffey:

Can't bear with the waters of. The chittering waters of. Flittering bats, fieldmice bawk talk. Ho! Are you not gone ahome? What Thom Malone?[1] Can't hear with bawk of bats, all thim liffeying waters of. Ho, talk save us! My foos won't moos. I feel as old as yonder elm. A tale told of Shaun or Shem? All Livia's daughtersons. Dark hawks hear us. Night! Night! My ho head halls. I feel as heavy as yonder stone. Tell me of John or Shaun? Who were Shem and Shaun the living sons or daughters of? Night now! Tell me, tell me, tell me,

---

1. Their voices grow blurred and indistinct as they call to each other across the turmoil of 'hitherandthithering waters'.

elm! Night, night! Tellmetale of stem or stone. Beside the rivering waters of,
hitherandthithering waters of. Night!

*

The Phaeacians were a seafaring race and their wealth came to them in
ships. The name of Nausithoos, founder of their city, as well as that of
the princess Nausicaa, marks their nautical turn of mind. On the Phaeacian strand there was 'a goodly temple of Poseidon, furnished with
heavy stones deep bedded in the earth'. The 'Nausicaa' episode of
Ulysses opens with the mention of a similar shrine. 'The Abbey of
Howth is situated on a delightful spot overhanging the ocean. Tradition states that its foundation was laid in 1235, on the removal of the
prebendal church from Ireland's Eye. It was dedicated to the Blessed
Virgin, and hence styled St Mary's. Over the western door is a ruined
belfry, and at the opposite end a triplet window.'[1] One of the bells,
removed from the Abbey to Howth Castle, bears the inscription:

SANCTA:MARIA:ORA:PRO:NOBIS:AD:FILIUM

The symbol of this episode is 'virgin' and one of its colours is blue,
and it is fitting that the romance-without-words of Gerty MacDowell
and Mr Bloom should develop under the patronage of Mary, Star of
the Sea, moist realm no longer Neptune's. For Star has vanquished
Trident, our Lady of the Sacred Heart the Shaker of the Earth. Even
in Corfu, Nausicaa's isle, the Poseideion has crumbled to dust and on
its site there stands a shrine dedicated to Saint Nicholas, patron of sea-
faring men.

One of the many virtues of a seamanly folk is the cult of cleanliness.
The necessity of keeping a ship in apple-pie order and an immunity
from that hydrophobia which afflicts many inland races are factors
making for personal immaculateness and frequent laundering; seablue
and spotless white are the sailor's – and virgin's – colours. Thus
Nausicaa begs Alcinous: 'Father, dear, couldst thou not lend me a high
waggon with strong wheels, that I may take the goodly raiment to the
river to wash, so much as I have lying soiled? Yea and it is seemly that
thou thyself when among the princes in council should have fresh raiment to wear. Also, there are five dear sons of thine in the halls, two
married, but three are lusty bachelors, and these are always eager for

1. Black's *Guide to Ireland*.

new-washen garments wherein to go to the dances, for all these things I have taken thought.' 'When they had washed and cleansed all the stains, they spread all out in order along the shore of the deep, even where the sea, in beating on the coast, washed the pebbles clean.'

The cleanliness of the Phaeacians [M. Bérard observes] was the wonder of the Achaeans, as that of the Dutch was the admiration of the eighteenth century and that of the English is admirable to contemporaries. Once on shore, sea-faring men are eager for white shirts, patent-leather shoes, a change of linen, a new rig-out in which to go to dances. Inland folk are not so particular. I picture the Achaeans as similar to the Albanians, gloriously dirty, decorated with gold, embroidery and grease-stains, redolent of stale oil and goat's butter – as the traveller encounters them at the Corfu jetties or embarking on European boats, whose cleanness appals them. They are clad in felt or woollen fabrics which last a lifetime. The Phaeacians wear white linen, well-laundered, starched, ironed, frilled, which calls for frequent washing.

Gerty is a true Phaeacian.

As for undies they were Gerty's chief care and who that knows the fluttering hopes and fears of sweet seventeen (though Gerty would never see seventeen again) can find it in his heart to blame her? She had four dinky sets, with awfully pretty stitchery, three garments and nighties extra, and each set slotted with different coloured ribbons, rose-pink, pale blue, mauve and peagreen, and she aired them herself and blued them when they came home from the wash and ironed them and she had a brickbat to keep the iron on because she wouldn't trust those washerwomen as far as she'd see them scorching the things.

As an Irish girl Gerty can claim to be of blood royal, and the wonders of the palace of Alcinous are faintly reproduced by the 'artistic standard designs' of Catesby's cork lino (in which her father deals), 'fit for a palace, gives tiptop wear and always bright and cheery in the home'. Gerty loves lovely things. She has a beautiful almanack picture of halcyon days (she found out in Walker's pronouncing dictionary about halcyon days, what they meant), a young gentleman offering a bunch of flowers to his ladylove. The latter was 'in a soft clinging white in a studied attitude', and the gentleman looked a thorough aristocrat. 'She often looked at them dreamily ... and felt her own arms that were white and soft like hers with the sleeves back.' Nausicaa λευκώλενος, of the white arms.

The famous game of ball which Nausicaa plays with her young com-panions has an obvious counterpart in the game which led to Mr

Bloom's observation of Gerty and his interception of the ball amid the lusty cries of the players. 'So then the princess threw the ball at one of her company; she missed the girl, and cast the ball into a deep eddying current, whereat they all raised a piercing cry. Then the goodly Odysseus awoke and sat up, pondering in his heart and spirit.' 'Yes, it was her he was looking at and there was meaning in his look. His eyes burned into her. ...'

A rising tide of sentiment and emotion lifts the narrative to the high-watermark of intensity when the rocket bursts in a shower of gold hair and the hour of adieu has struck for both. The soar of the rocket and its fall symbolize the technic of this episode: 'tumescence-detumescence', a quiet opening, a long crescendo of turgid, rhapsodic prose towards a climax, a pyrotechnic explosion, a dying fall, silence. The last firework fades out in a single white spark, *stella maris*, against the blue. 'A lost long candle wandered up the sky ... and broke, drooping, and shed a cluster of violet but one white stars.'

Like Gerty, Nausicaa had a maidenly hope regarding the godlike stranger; 'would that such an one might be called my husband, dwelling here; and that it might please him here to abide'. Gerty hoped for 'a nice snug and cosy little homely house, every morning they would both have brekky, simple but perfectly served, for their own two selves ... '. Nausicaa enjoyed the brief triumph of leading her *trouvaille* to the paternal palace and hearing him tell the tale of his adventures in manly hexameters before he sailed away to his Penelope, whereas poor Gerty had to return alone to her linolean 'palace', leaving the hero lonely on the shore.

A sentimental pair, Gerty and Nausicaa, over-ready to fall for the fascination of any 'dark stranger'. Yet they typify an ineradicable instinct of girlhood. Even in the 'Palaces' *dernier cri* of the Riviera, where the blue flower is no longer sported, you will observe that, despite the cavils of outraged nordics, the dark stranger has but to rise to conquer. Gerty's luscious prose – for, though her tale is told in the third person, I see in Gerty the true narrator of the first part of this episode (as Samuel Butler saw in Nausicaa the 'authoress of the *Odyssey*') – is a potpourri of everlastings from the garden of *jeunes filles en fleurs*.

Nausicaa's father, King Alcinous, was a hospitable man who kept a good cellar. The barman Pontonous 'mixed the gladdening wine' (Homer's 'mixed' has, surely, a very modern tinkle!) and it was not till they had 'drunken to their hearts' content' that Alcinous 'made harangue'. His speech was brief, and briefer still his guest's reply, and, forthwith, there was another drinking to their hearts' content – they were convivial folk, those Phaeacians. Gerty's father too, true scion of the Nausithous stock, 'exceeded', much to Gerty's distress. 'Had her father only avoided the clutches of the demon drink, by taking the pledge or the drink habit cured in Pearson's Weekly, she might now be rolling in her carriage second to none.' Her soul-communion with Mr Bloom is accompanied by an anthem of men's voices and the sound of the organ pealing out from the simple fane beside the waves, where a men's temperance retreat, conducted by the Rev. John Hughes, s.j., is in progress. With no less zeal, we may be sure, did good queen Arete (the master-spirit in the royal household) sermonize the king for his too frequent calls on the services of Pontonous. Through Gerty's musings, across the vibrant intensity of Mr Bloom's gaze, there runs a cross-current of sacred song, a waft of fragrant incense and fragrant names; 'spiritual vessel, pray for us, vessel of singular devotion, pray for us, mystical rose. ...' Thus, too, the hearts of the Phaeacians were uplifted and Odysseus was moved even to tears by the lay of divine Demodocus, to whom the gods gave minstrelsy as to none else to make men glad in what way soever his spirit stirred him to sing.

Far out at sea the anchored lightship twinkled, winked at somnolent Mr Bloom. 'Life those chaps must have out there. Penance for their sins.' Not otherwise did Poseidon penalize the Phaeacians who con-veyed Odysseus to Ithaca, for the too notorious swiftness of their ships,[1] a challenge to his might. For the gods love not those who would persistently exceed the proper rhythm of progress – as the modern world is discovering to its cost.

Now Poseidon went on his way to Scheria, where the Phaeacians dwell. There he abode awhile: and lo! the seafaring ship drew very near, being lightly sped; and nigh her came the shaker of the earth, and he smote her into a stone, and rooted her far down below with the downstroke of his hand.

Then one to another they spake winged words, the Phaeacians of the long oars, mariners renowned. And thus they would speak, looking each man to his neighbour:

1. '*Leur spécialité, leur gloire, c'est d'avoir dompté l'Adriatique et, par un service de messageries extra-rapides, supprimé ce grand abîme de mer.*' *Les Phéniciens et l'Odyssée*, Tome I, page 584.

'Ah me! who is this that hath bound our swift ship on the deep as she drave homewards? Even now she was clear in sight.'

Even so they would speak; but they knew not how these things were ordained.

Mr Bloom's *'penance for their sins'* may be a dim recall of past experience, of 'how these things were ordained': an ancient dream fluttering bat-like from the gate of horn. Again, looking out to sea, he evokes a picture[1] of the perils of them that go down to the sea in ships: an old fresco in Akâsa retouched by a modern hand.

The anchor's weighed. Off he sails with a scapular or a medal on him for luck. Well? And the tephilim no what's this they call it poor papa's father had on his door to touch. That brought us out of the land of Egypt and into the house of bondage. Something in all those superstitions because when you go out never know what dangers. Hanging on to a plank or astride of a beam for grim life, lifebelt round him, gulping salt water, and that's the last of his nibs till the sharks catch hold of him. Do fish ever get seasick?

Then you have a beautiful calm without a cloud, smooth sea, placid, crew and cargo in smithereens, Davy Jones' locker. Moon looking down. Not my fault, old cockalorum.

But the daughter of Cadmus marked him, Ino of the fair ankles ... and sat upon the well-bound raft and spake: 'Hapless one, wherefore was Poseidon, shaker of the earth, so wondrous wroth with thee? ... Take this veil divine and wind it about thy breast; then there is no fear that thou suffer aught or perish. But when thou hast laid hold of the main land with thy hands, loose it off from thee and cast it into the wine-dark deep.' ... As when a great tempestuous wind tosseth a heap of parched husks and scattereth them this way and that, even so did the wave scatter the long beams of the raft. But Odysseus bestrode a single plank as one rideth on a courser, and fell prone in the sea. ... But Athene, daughter of Zeus, turned to new thoughts. She bound up the courses of the other winds and charged them all to cease and be still; but she roused the swift North and brake the waves before him. ... So for two nights and two days he was wandering in the swell of the sea, and much his heart boded of death. But when at last the fair-tressed dawn brought the full light of the third day, thereafter the breeze fell and lo! there was a breathless calm, and with a quick glance ahead he saw the land very near.

1. The 'art' of this episode is 'painting'; Mr Bloom's monologue here is a sequence of mental pictures, rarely meditative. Gerty, too, visualizes her memories and aspirations.

14. THE OXEN OF THE SUN

SCENE	The Hospital
HOUR	10 p.m.
ORGAN	Womb
ART	Medicine
COLOUR	White
SYMBOL	Mothers
TECHNIC	Embryonic Development

THE scene of this episode is the Lying-in Hospital in Holles Street, where Mrs Purefoy is waiting to be delivered of a child.[1] Mr Bloom (as we have heard in the 'Lestrygonians') received news of the impending event from Mrs Breen earlier in the day and, in the course of his meditations after the eclipse of Nausicaa, decided to call at the hospital for news of the lady who, Mrs Breen had told him, was having a 'very stiff birth'. In the hospital common-room he comes upon a group of medical students carousing with Stephen Dedalus. Buck Mulligan and Haines presently join them. The conversation is ribald and fertile in obstetric allusion. The young men debate birth-control, the question whether, when that fatal dilemma arises, the life of the mother or of the child should be saved, and various other aspects of procreation. While they so discourse the child is born and, soon after, the company adjourns to Burke's public house where they continue their potations. This meeting with Stephen in the halls of the Sun-god, the quickener, brings to the foreground of Mr Bloom's mind the vague craving for paternity which has all day been latent in his soliloquies. There is a passage (in fifteenth-century prose) which suggests an association in Mr Bloom's mind between his dead son Rudy and Stephen.

And she (Marion Bloom) was wondrous stricken of heart for the evil hap and for his burial did him on a fair corselet of lamb's wool, the flower of the flock, lest he might perish utterly and lie akeled (for it was then about the midst

1. This hospital is to be distinguished from the Mater Misericordiae in Eccles Street, the hospital patronized by Mr Bloom when he was attacked and wounded by a bee, here referred to as 'a horrible and dreadful dragon'. Most Catholic funerals pass the Mater Misericordiae on their way to the neighbouring cemetery. The Lying-in Hospital, the house of life, now patronized by Stephen, is more cheerfully situated, on the road leading to the Dublin horse show.

of the winter) and now sir Leopold that had of his body no manchild for an heir looked upon him his friend's son and was shut up in sorrow for his fore-passed happiness and sad as he was that him failed a son of such gentle courage (for all accounted him of real parts) so grieved he also in no less measure for young Stephen for that he lived riotously with those wastrels and murdered his goods with whores.

Mr Bloom plays here a ripely paternal role as he sits, humdrum, among these harum-scarums, genuinely shocked by their callousness. Still, when they try to draw him, he answers with a discretion worthy of his prototype, 'as astute if not astuter than any man living'. Stephen, on the other hand, enters, in appearance at least, into the spirit of the medicos and, thanks to his command of words and dialectic, is able to outpace even these experts in the obstetric and the obscene on their own terrain of pseudo-medical bawdry. After the symposium he invites them to Burke's public house and, as he has money in his pocket, lacks not a following. More drinks at Burke's complete his intoxication and, fuddled beyond reason, he embarks, accompanied by Lynch, one of the carousers, for the isle of Circe. Bloom, prudent as ever, has drunk only a little too much; if he, too, in the next episode yields to the ambiance of hallucination, it is as much the effect of weariness and the red miasma of Walpurgisnacht as of the liquor he has absorbed.

*

This episode has been described as a chapter of parodies and that is, doubtless, the first impression that it gives. It is obvious that one section is in the Carlyle manner, in another there are echoes of *The Pilgrim's Progress*, elsewhere of the *Opium Eater*. But, if the texture of the prose be carefully examined, it will be seen that, though in some passages the style is probably meant to satirize the original (as where an *Ars Amatoria* is expounded in the manner of a Bunyan parable), the greater part seems to be devoid of satiric intention; that wilful exaggeration of mannerisms which points a parody is absent and the effect is rather of pastiche than of travesty.

The rationale of this sequence of imitations lies in the theme. The technic and the subject of this episode are both 'embryonic development' and the styles of prose employed follow an exact historical order. It begins with a set of three incantations, in the manner of the *Fratres Arvales*, each thrice repeated:

Deshil Holles Eamus. Deshil Holles Eamus. Deshil Holles Eamus.

Send us, bright one, light one, Horhorn, quickening and wombfruit. Send us, bright one, light one, Horhorn, quickening and wombfruit. Send us, bright one, light one, Horhorn, quickening and wombfruit.

Hoopsa, boyaboy, hoopsa! Hoopsa, boyaboy, hoopsa! Hoopsa, boyaboy, hoopsa!

The first of these formulas means simply: 'Let us go south to Holles Street.' The second is an invocation to the Sun, Helios, personified by Sir Andrew Horne, the head of the Lying-in Hospital, the 'House of Horne'. The third is the triumphant cry of the midwife as, elevating the new-born, she acclaims its sex.

Trinacria (Sicily), the triangular island,[1] was dedicated to Helios. His seven herds of sacred oxen were guarded by his daughters, Phaethusa and Lampetie, to whom correspond, in this episode, the two nurses, 'white[2] sisters in ward sleepless ... for Horne holding wariest ward'. The landing-place of Odysseus was (M. Bérard suggests) probably near the ancient Tauromenium and the colony of Naxos, where there was an altar to Apollo Archegetes. Another cult observed at Naxos was that of Aphrodite whose *Aphrodision* was famous for its γέρρα Ναξια (phallic and triangular), sexual emblems of Phoenician origin. The Oxen of the Sun are symbols of fertility.[3] The frequent references to the procreative function in this episode are thus in harmony with the symbolism of the Homeric legend.

To get the full effect of the literary artifice employed in the text which follows this prelude, the reader probably needs a fairly intimate acquaintance with the literary landmarks which cast their shadow upon it, but even without precise knowledge he cannot but feel, as he reads

1. The apotheosis of the triangle, a sign upon the forehead of Taurus, in a passage quoted hereafter, is significant.

2. 'White' is the colour related to this episode: the white daughters of the Sun, daylight itself, 'seeds of brightness', the white house of life contrasted with the 'tenebrosity' of the nether world.

3. That Mr Bloom's encounter with the bee, twice mentioned in this episode, is apposite to the general theme, is suggested by a passage in Porphyry's *Cave of the Nymphs*. 'The priestesses of Ceres, as being initiated into the mysteries of the terrene Goddess, were called by the ancients *bees*, and Proserpine herself was denominated by them *honied*. The moon, likewise, who presides over generation, was called by them a bee, and also a bull. And Taurus is the exaltation of the moon. But bees are ox-begotten. And this application is also given to souls proceeding into generation. The God, likewise, who is occultly connected with generation, is a stealer of oxen.' (Trans. Thomas Taylor.)

on, that under the protean transformations a constant evolution is un-folding itself, that the changes of style are purposeful and progressive. The process of development begins in a murk of chaos, recalling the opening phase of the Creation: 'the earth was without form and void, and darkness was upon the face of the deep.'

Universally that person's acumen is esteemed very little perceptive concern-ing whatsoever matters are being held as most profitably by mortals with sapience endowed to be studied who is ignorant of that which the most in doctrine erudite and certainly by reason of that in them high mind's ornament deserving of veneration constantly maintain when by general consent they affirm that other circumstances being equal by no exterior splendour is the prosperity of a nation more efficaciously asserted than by the measure of how far forward may have progressed the tribute of its solicitude for that proliferent continuance which of evils the original if it be absent when fortunately present constitutes the certain sign of omnipollent nature's incorrupted benefaction.

This appalling sentence reads like the literal translation of a tract on child welfare written in medieval Latin – reminiscent of the *Epistolae obscurorum virorum*, for instance – by a demented German *Docent*.[1]

Bloom's entry into the hospital is described in a hotchpotch of early Anglo-Saxon, a monosyllabic tramp of lumpish assonance like the thudding of the hoofs of oxen. For the delineation of this early stage of embryonic growth the author, it may be noted, does not coin new word-forms or use uncouth constructions; the language is bare and primitive but always English and historically authentic.

In ward wary the watcher hearing come that man mildhearted eft rising with swire ywimpled to him her gate wide undid. Lo, levin leaping lightens in eye-blink Ireland's westward welkin! Full she dread that God the Wreaker all man-kind would fordo with water for his evil sins. Christ's rood made she on breast-bone and him drew that he would rather infare under her thatch. That man her will wotting worthful went in Horne's house.

1. In a letter to Mr Frank Budgen, quoted by Mr A. M. Klein in his brilliant and detailed analysis of the 'Oxen of the Sun' (in *Here and Now*, January 1949), Joyce wrote that this episode is 'introduced by a Sallustian-Tacitean prelude (the unfertilized ovum)'. But no style could be further than this from the concision of Sallust and the epigrammatic brilliancy of Tacitus. A comparison of this letter, written while Joyce was working on the episode, with the printed version shows that he made some changes in his programme, and this is one of them. Doubtless he saw that the style of a highly sophisticated writer like Tacitus would have been out of place in this context and amended the introduction accordingly.

In this passage Bloom symbolizes the male element; the nurse and, by extension, the hospital vestibule, the ovum. Bloom's gesture in taking off his hat has, I believe, its significance for the biologist. The nurse who opens the door is an old friend of Mr Bloom. 'On her stow he ere was living with dear wife and lovesome daughter that then over land and seafloor nine years had long outwandered.' The storm which soon is to burst in a single and prodigious clap of thunder broods in the offing.

The growth of an embryo is not uniform; one part, stealing a march on the others, may prematurely reach a higher stage of development; an eye, for instance, may develop out of its turn. Thus, in the passage which follows, there is an anticipation of an early Church style which is in advance of its context in the episode.

Therefore, everyman, look to that last end that is thy death and the dust that gripeth on every man that is born of woman for as he came naked forth from his mother's womb so naked shall he wend him at the last for to go as he came.

The description of the dining-table, knives and forks, a tin of sardines[1] is given in the style of Mandeville.

And in the castle was set a board that was of the birchwood of Finlandy and it was upheld by four dwarfmen of the country but they durst not move more for enchantment. And on this board were frightful swords and knives that are made in a great cavern by swinking demons out of white flames that they fix in the horns of buffaloes and stags that there abound marvellously. And there were vessels that are wrought by magic of Mahound out of seasand and the air by a warlock with his breath that he blares into them like to bubbles. ... And there was a vat of silver that was moved by craft to open in the which lay strange fishes withouten heads though misbelieving men nie that this be possible thing without they see it natheless they are so. And these fishes lie in an oily water brought there from Portugal land because of the fatness that therein is. ...

The passage beginning 'This meanwhile this good sister stood by the door' recalls Thomas Malory. One sentence in it, that which describes Mr Bloom's hesitation whether to stay and look after Stephen or follow his wiser judgement and go quietly home, is a reversion to the early,

1. The companions of Odysseus, during their sojourn on the isle of the Sun, were driven by hunger to catch and eat fish, a food for which the Homeric heroes had an ingrained aversion. In the end, despite their oath to Odysseus, they slaughtered and ate the sacred oxen of the Sun, rather than persist in such an irksome diet.

alliterative style. 'Ruth red him, love led on with will to wander, loth to leave.' On the following page there is a further allusion to Mr Bloom's solicitude for Stephen ('he was the most drunken that demanded still more of mead'). The obstetric jests of the students distress him.

Sir Leopold was passing grave maugre his word by cause he still had pity of the terror causing shrieking of shrill women in their labour and as he was minded of his good lady Marion that had borne him an only manchild which on his eleventh day on live had died and no man of art could save so dark is destiny.

Stephen denounces 'birth-control' – 'those Godpossibled souls that we nightly impossibilize, which is the sin against ... the Giver of Life'. Here there is an allusion to the Sun-god and his oxen, symbols of fertility. The crime of Odysseus's companions (the 'fraud' of the Malthusians) was the slaying of the sacred kine, 'flocks of a dread god, even of Helios'. No long while after Odysseus had left the triangular island punishment overtook the sinners: 'came the shrilling West with the rushing of a great tempest. ... Zeus thundered and càst his bolt upon the ship, and she reeled all over stricken by the bolt of Zeus and was filled with sulphur.' Thus presently there comes 'a black crack of noise in the street' (God is for Stephen a 'noise' or a 'shout in the street'). 'Loud on left Thor thundered: in anger awful the hammer-hurler.'

The style moves on towards the seventeenth century. In the passage which follows the language is reminiscent of Sir Thomas Browne and the Authorized Version; the structure and theme recall the *Improperia* of the Catholic liturgy for Holy Week.

Remember, Erin, thy generations and thy days of old how thou settedst little by me and by my word and broughtest in a stranger to my gates to commit fornication in my sight and to wax fat and kick like Jeshurum. Therefore thou hast sinned against the light and hast made me, thy lord, to be the slave of servants. Return, return, Clan Milly: forget me not O Milesian. Why hast thou done this abomination before me that thou didst spurn me for a merchant of jalaps and didst deny me to the Roman and the Indian of dark speech with whom thy daughters did lie luxuriously? Look forth now, my people, upon the land of behest, even from Horeb and from Nebo and from Pisgah and from the Horns of Hatten unto a land flowing with milk and money. But thou hast suckled me with a bitter milk: my moon and my sun hast thou quenched for ever. And thou hast left me alone for ever in the dark ways of my bitterness: and with a kiss of ashes thou hast kissed my mouth.

Of the *Improperia* Dom Fernand Cabriol, o.s.b., in *My Missal* writes as follows:

The cultus of the Cross is very ancient and found expression most naturally on Good Friday. The verses, antiphons and responsories which are sung during the adoration of the Cross are called *Improperia* or reproaches (addressed by Christ to the Jewish people). They form one of the most tragic episodes of this Friday service which is a real drama and suggested the medieval Passion plays.

*Popul
 meus, quid feci tibi? aut in quo contristavi te? responde mihi. Quia eduxi te de terra Aegypti: parasti crucem Salvatori tuo.*

O my people, what have I done to thee? or in what have I grieved thee? answer me. Because I led thee out of the land of Egypt, thou hast prepared a cross for thy Saviour.

Quid ultra debui facere tibi et non feci? Ego quidem plantavi te vineam meam speciosissimam: et tu facta es mihi nimis amara: aceto namque sitim meam potasti; et lancea perforasti latus Salvatori tuo.

What more ought I to have done for thee that I have not done? I planted for thee my fairest vineyard and thou hast turned exceeding bitter to me; for thou gavest me vinegar to drink in my thirst, and pierced with a lance thy Saviour's side.

Ego dedi tibi sceptrum regale: et tu dedisti capiti meo spineam coronam.

I gave thee a royal sceptre: and thou gavest a crown of thorns to my head.

Ego te exaltavi magna virtute: et tu me suspendisti in patibulo crucis.

I lifted thee up with great power and thou didst hang me upon the gibbet of the Cross.

This passage of *Ulysses* is undoubtedly personal, a remonstration in which, perhaps, many another artist out of Ireland might join. There is no blasphemy here, only a great sorrow which, in solitude,[1] invokes its greatest prototype. It is no new theme in the work of Joyce. In the *Portrait* he bitterly attacks the disloyalty of his country to her great men. 'Ireland is the old sow that eats her farrow.' In the last words of this passage, 'with a kiss of ashes hast thou kissed my mouth', Stephen for

1. It is notable that the name Sikelia (Sicily) is derived from a Semitic word *sikoulim, sekoul,* which describes the lot of a man who is alone, forsaken by all. M. Bérard points out that the theme of *solitude* plays an important part in Odysseus's adventure in the island of the Sun. Odysseus *alone* is against landing, he walks *alone* in the island, and, finally, all his men are lost in the tempest and he continues on his way *alone*. Stephen may seem at home in the company of the drunken medicos, but he knows, and they know, that he is a man apart; at closing-time, when they can no longer swill at his expense, they unanimously forsake him.

a moment likens his country to his dead mother. 'In a dream, silently, she had come to him ... her breath bent over him with mute secret words, a faint odour of wetted ashes.' Each asked of him something he could not give, an obedience he refused to render. When, in the next episode, the phantom of his mother appears to him and bids him repent, he cries '*Ah non, par exemple!* ... With me all or not at all. *Non serviam!*' He 'will not serve'.

When the crash of thunder comes, Bloom seeks to reassure Stephen by talk of a 'natural phenomenon'. This leads to a passage in the manner of Bunyan, where Phenomenon personifies the God of this world.

But was young Boasthard's fear vanquished by Calmer's words? No, for he had in his bosom a spike named Bitterness which could not by words be done away. And was he then neither calm like the one nor godly like the other? He was neither as much as he would have liked to be either. But could he not have endeavoured to have found again as in his youth the bottle Holiness that then he lived withal? Indeed not, for Grace was not there to find that bottle. Heard he then in that clap the voice of the god Bringforth or, what Calmer said, a hubbub of Phenomenon? Heard? Why, he could not but hear unless he had plugged up the tube Understanding (which he had not done). For through that tube he saw that he was in the land of Phenomenon where he must for a certain one day die as he was like the rest a passing show.

Next, the company present are described in the Pepys–Evelyn manner, with a characteristic reference to Mrs Purefoy's coming delivery:

should be a bullyboy from the knocks they say, but God give her soon issue. 'Tis her ninth chick to live, I hear, and Lady day bit off her last chick's nails that was then a twelvemonth and with other three all breastfed that died written out in a fair hand in the king's bible. Her hub fifty odd and a methodist but takes the Sacrament and is to be seen any fair sabbath with a pair of his boys off Bullock harbour dapping on the sound with a heavybraked reel or in a punt he has trailing for flounder and pollock and catches a fine bag, I hear.

The verbal allusions to the Homeric paradigm of this episode, in 'bullyboy' and 'Bullock (harbour)', are characteristic. Thus, in this same 'Pepys' paragraph Bannon refers to Milly Bloom as a 'a skittish heifer ... beef to the heel'.[1] The theme is developed at length in the

1. Milly, the 'photo girl', wrote to her father: 'We did great biz yesterday. Fair day and all the beef to the heels were in.' (She worked for a photographer at Mullingar.) 'Mullingar heifers', 'beef to the heel', are slang terms for girls with thick ankles. A traveller passing through Mullingar, the *Slang Dictionary* relates,

next imitation. Mr Deasy's letter has, thanks to Stephen's efforts, appeared in the evening paper and a conversation is now engaged, first in the Defoe manner, then in the Swiftian, on the foot-and-mouth disease and, by a natural transition, on bulls, Irish, papal, and others. Dixon speaks of the

bull that was sent to our island by farmer Nicholas,[1] the bravest cattle breeder of them all with an emerald ring in his nose. ... He had horns galore, a coat of gold and a sweet smoky breath coming out of his nostrils so that the women of our island, leaving doughballs and rolling pins, followed after him hanging his bulliness in daisychains.

Lord Harry (Henry VIII), too, 'discovered in himself a wonderful likeness to a bull and on picking up a blackthumbed chapbook that he kept in the pantry he found sure enough that he was a lefthanded descendant of the famous champion bull of the Romans, Bos Bovum, which is good bog Latin for boss of the show'. (A parliament convened in Dublin in 1536 declared the king spiritual head of the Church.) Dixon's bovine fantasia on a critical period of Irish history is in the manner of Swift, with whose discourse on bulls in *A Tale of a Tub* it may be compared.

But of all Peter's rarities he most valued a certain set of bulls, whose race was by great fortune preserved in a lineal descent from those that guarded the golden fleece. ... Whether by secret connivance or encouragement from their master, or out of their own liquorish affection to gold, or both, it is certain they were no better than a sort of sturdy, swaggering beggars; and where they could not prevail to get an alms would make women miscarry, and children fall into fits, who, to this very day, usually call sprites and hobgoblins by the name of bull-beggars.[2]

The paragraphs which follow are in the style of Addison in the *Tatler* and the Addison–Steele combination in the first years of the eighteenth century. Next, Lynch tells the company of an *amour*, in the manner of Sterne.

---

was so struck by this local peculiarity in the women that he asked a Mullingar girl: 'May I inquire if you wear hay in your shoes?' 'Faith an' I do,' she replied, 'and what then?' 'Because', said the traveller, 'that accounts for the calves of your legs coming down to feed on it.'

1. Nicholas Brakespear, when he became Pope Hadrian IV, 'conferred the lordship of the Island (Ireland) on Henry II, in order, as his bull states, "to extirpate the vices which had there taken root" '. *Haliday*.

2. *A Tale of a Tub*, section IV.

Ah, Monsieur, had you but beheld her as I did with these eyes at that affecting instant with her dainty tucker and her new coquette cap (a gift for her feast day as she told me) in such an artless disorder, of so melting a tenderness, 'pon my conscience, even you, Monsieur, had been impelled by generous nature to deliver yourself wholly into the hands of such an enemy or to quit the field for ever. I declare, I was never so touched in my life.

Nurse Callan enters and informs Dixon, the junior surgeon, that Mrs Purefoy has given birth to a son. Costello, 'a low fellow who was fuddled', speaks coarsely of the nurse. Dixon, in the Goldsmith manner, rebukes him.

I want patience with those who, without wit to enliven or learning to instruct, revile an ennobling profession which, saving the reverence due to the Deity, is the greatest power for happiness upon the earth. I am positive when I say that if need were I could produce a cloud of witnesses to the excellence of her noble exercitations which, so far from being a byword, should be a glorious incentive in the human breast. I cannot away with them. What? Malign such an one, the amiable Miss Callan, who is the lustre of her own sex and the astonishment of ours and at an instant the most momentous that can befall a puny child of clay? Perish the thought!

Bloom, sincerely sharing Dixon's affected indignation, is prudent enough to leave his homily (in the language of Burke) unspoken.

It was now for more than the middle span of our allotted years that he had passed through the thousand vicissitudes of existence and, being of a wary ascendancy and self a man of a rare forecast, he had enjoined his heart to repress all motions of a rising choler and, by intercepting them with the readiest precaution, foster within his breast that plenitude of sufferance which base minds jeer at, rash judgers scorn and all find tolerable and but tolerable. To those who create themselves wits at the cost of feminine delicacy (a habit of mind which he never did hold with) to them he would concede neither to bear the name nor to herit the tradition of a proper breeding.

But the indelicacy of Mr Bloom in presuming to criticize, even in unuttered thought, his betters, is rebuked in a Junian apostrophe. The following passage, in which the staff of the hospital are referred to as the secretary of state for domestic affairs and members of the privy council, recalls the gravity of Gibbon's prose (the imitation of his use of paired words, 'silent in unanimous exhaustion and approbation', 'the length and solemnity of their vigil', is notable) and is intercalated with

an example of nineteenth-century scientific jargon (premature development of a part of the embryo).

The apparition of Haines is gruesomely depicted – shades of the
Castle of Otranto.

Which of us did not feel his flesh creep? He had a portfolio full of Celtic literature in one hand, in the other a phial marked *Poison*. Surprise, horror, loathing
were depicted on all faces while he eyed them with a ghastly grin. I anticipated
some such reception, he began with an eldritch laugh, for which, it seems,
history is to blame.

This is a recall of Haines's remark in the first episode: 'We feel in
England that we have treated you rather unfairly. It seems history is to
blame.'

Meanwhile Mr Bloom has been 'ruminating, chewing the cud of
reminiscence' in the manner of Charles Lamb at his most sentimental.

He is young Leopold, as in a retrospective arrangement, a mirror within a
mirror (hey, presto!), he beholdeth himself. That young figure of then is seen,
precociously manly, walking on a nipping morning from the old house in Clam-
brassil street to the high school, his booksatchel on him bandolierwise, and in it
a goodly hunk of wheaten loaf, a mother's thought. Or it is the same figure, a
year or so gone over, in his first hard hat (ah, that was a day!), already on the
road, a fullfledged traveller for the family firm, equipped with an orderbook,
a scented handkerchief (not for show only), his case of bright trinketware (alas,
a thing now of the past!), and a quiverful of compliant smiles for this or that
halfwon housewife reckoning it out upon her fingertips or for a budding
virgin shyly acknowledging (but the heart? tell me!) his studied baisemoins.

Not otherwise did some Phoenician merchant-traveller of Homeric
times, roaming far across the inland sea, even to the Pillars of the West,
Calypso's home, offer, with ingratiating oriental smirks, his trinketware
from Sidon or from Tyre to a housewife of the western isles; not otherwise did the simple islander reckon out on her fingers the price to pay
in baskets of olives, capering kids, or skins of black wine.

The passage in the de Quincey manner which follows is built up from
memories of Simon Dedalus's song in the Ormond music-room, of
Boylan's refrain *Those lovely seaside girls, Your head it simply swirls*
(which has been running in Mr Bloom's head all day), of his daughter
Milly ('Oh, Milly Bloom, you are my darling!'), of that mystic word
parallax, whose meaning he has forgotten (if he ever knew it), of the

Agendath Netaim advertisement, and the immediate aspect of a bottle of Bass's beer which confronts him. The protean skill of the creator has adapted these unpromising materials to the texture of an apocalyptic vision.

The voices blend and fuse in clouded silence: silence that is the infinite of space: and swiftly, silently the soul is wafted over regions of cycles of cycles of generations that have lived. A region where grey twilight ever descends, never falls, on wide sagegreen pasturefields, shedding her dusk, scattering a perennial dew of stars. She follows her mother with ungainly steps, a mare leading her fillyfoal. ... They fade, sad phantoms: all is gone. Agendath is a waste land, a home of screechowls and the sandblind upupa. Netaim, the golden, is no more. And on the highway of the clouds they come, muttering thunder of rebellion, the ghosts of beasts. Huuh! Hark! Huuh! Parallax stalks behind and goads them, the lancinating lightnings of whose brow are scorpions. ... Ominous, revengeful zodiacal host! They moan, passing upon the clouds, horned and capricorned, the trumpeted with the tusked, the lionmaned, the giantantlered, snouter and crawler, rodent, ruminant and pachyderm, all their moving moaning multitude, murderers of the sun.[1]

Onward to the dead sea they tramp to drink, unslaked and with horrible gulpings, the salt somnolent flood. And the equine portent grows again, magnified in the deserted heavens, nay to heaven's own magnitude it looms, vast, over the house of Virgo.[2] And, lo, wonder of metempsychosis, it is she, the everlasting bride, harbinger of the daystar, the bride, ever virgin. It is she, Martha, thou lost one, Millicent, the young, the dear, the radiant. How serene does she now arise, a queen among the Pleiades, in the penultimate antelucan hour, shod in sandals of bright gold, coifed with a veil of what do you call it gossamer! It floats, it flows about her starborn flesh and loose it streams emerald, sapphire, mauve and heliotrope, sustained on currents of cold interstellar wind, winding, coiling, simply swirling, writhing in the skies a mysterious writing till after a myriad metamorphoses of symbol, it blazes, Alpha, a ruby and triangled sign upon the forehead of Taurus.

In the chastened style of a Landor the encounter of Father Conmee with 'a flushed young man and a young woman'[3] is now narrated by the young man in question. There follows a paragraph in the scientific

1. Thus, after the murder of the oxen of the Sun by the companions of Odysseus, 'the skins were creeping, and the flesh bellowing upon the spits, both the roast and the raw, and there was a sound as the voice of kine'.

2. In astrology, the constellation Virgo governs the womb; the organ of the body to which this episode is related is the womb.

3. *Ulysses*, page 212.

style (containing certain interesting allusions to embryogenesis), another in the manner of Macaulay, followed by a return to the scientific style (here chronologically in place – i.e. not a 'premature development'). There is a pretty-pretty picture of the mother and babe, as Dickens might have written it.

> She had fought the good fight and now she was very very happy. Those who have passed on, who have gone before, are happy too as they gaze down and smile upon the touching scene. Reverently look at her as she reclines there with the motherlight in her eyes, that longing hunger for baby fingers (a pretty sight it is to see) ...

Passages in the manner of Newman, Pater, and Ruskin follow. The description of a game of bowls has an 'Epicurean', gemlike preciosity.

> A shaven space of lawn one soft May evening, the wellremembered grove of lilacs at Roundtown, purple and white, fragrant slender spectators of the game but with much real interest in the pellets as they run slowly forward over the sward or collide and stop, one by its fellow, with a brief alert shock.

The embryo has now attained maturity and it is convenient here to consider in retrospect the technical devices employed by Joyce in this episode, apart from the historico-literary progression already described. Readers of this episode who have some acquaintance with embryology will find many allusions which mark the changes of the embryo, month by month, as it grows to perfection in the womb. Thus, in the first month, it is wormlike, a 'punctus', in the second it has a (relatively) big head, webbed fingers, is eyeless, mouthless, sexless. The mention of fishes 'withouten head' in 'oily water' is a reference to the first month: the vermiform shape and the amniac fluid. Later, Stephen tells how 'at the end of the second month' a human soul is infused and, soon after, we see Mr Bloom 'lay hand to jaw'; the formation of the jawbone is a feature of the third month. At that stage the embryo has a distinct tail – hence the mutation of 'Oxford' into 'Oxtail'.[1] The reference to 'visual organs commencing to exhibit signs of animation'[2] marks the seventh month. There are many more such correspondences to be detected by the reader of *Ulysses* who, unlike the writer of this study, has more than a superficial acquaintance with the facts of prenatal development.

As elsewhere, the metaphors are coloured by the art of the episode,

1. *Ulysses*, page 375.　　　　　2. page 398.

'medicine', and especially the art of obstetrics. Such expressions as 'a pregnant word', 'this tenebrosity of the interior', 'biggish swollen clouds', 'embryo philosopher', 'every phase of the situation was successively eviscerated', etc., exemplify this anastomosis of style and subject.

In a curious esoteric tract named *Vénus Magique*[1] there is a passage describing the 'magical' view of embryonic growth.

Dans la première nuit de sa conception, l'embryon est comme une eau chaotique; dans les six suivantes, cette eau devient opaque: elle prend une forme sphérique dans la deuxième semaine. En un mois l'embryon acquiert de la consistance; en deux la tête se forme; au troisième mois, les pieds; au quatrième, l'estomac et les reins; au cinquième, la colonne vertébrale; au sixième, le nez, les yeux et les oreilles; au septième, il reçoit le souffle de vie; au huitième il se complète; au neuvième il se recouvre de sa peau.

Dans le neuvième mois, l'esprit entre dans sa nouvelle résidence élémentaire; il y connait par une profonde contemplation le Mot indestructible.

This association of a mystic Word with the culmination of the embryonic stage is grotesquely introduced in the antepenultimate phase of this episode (in the manner of Ruskin).

Enter that antechamber of birth where the studious are assembled and note their faces. Nothing, as it seems, there of rash or violent. ... But as before the lightning the serried storm-clouds, heavy with preponderant excess of moisture, in swollen masses turgidly distended, compass earth and sky in one vast slumber, impending above parched field and drowsy oxen and blighted growth of shrub and verdure till in an instant a flash rives their centres and with the reverberation of the thunder the cloudburst pours its torrent, so and not otherwise was the transformation, violent and instantaneous, upon the utterance of the Word.

The 'word' is 'Burke's': the name of a public house whither Stephen invites the company for further drinks at his expense. (The style is now Carlyle's.)

Burke's! Outflings my lord Stephen, giving the cry, and a tag and bobtail of all them after, cockerel, jackanapes, welsher, pilldoctor, punctual Bloom at heels with a universal grabbing at headgear, ashplants, bilbos, Panama hats and scabbards, Zermatt alpenstocks and what not.

There follows a roaring panegyric of Theodore Purefoy, the polyphiloprogenitive.

1. Chamuel, Éditeur. Paris, 1897.

Thou art, I vow, the remarkablest progenitor barring none in this chaffering allincluding most farragineous chronicle. [An apt description of *Ulysses*, this!] A truce to threnes and trentals and jeremies and all such congenital defunctive music. Twenty years of it, regret them not. With thee it was not as with many that will and would and wait and never do. Thou sawest thy America, thy lifetask, and didst charge to cover like the transpontine bison. How saith Zarathustra? *Deine Kuh Trübsal melkest Du. Nun trinkest Du die süsse Milch des Euters. ... Per deam Partulam et Pertundam nunc est bibendum!*

The last pages of this episode are a pandemonium of ejaculations in every form of dialect, jargon, slang, ancient and modern. The young men, gloriously methelated, have felt the gift of tongues descend on them. Any language, the worse the better, is apt to their impolite conversation.

Waiting, guvnor? Most deciduously.[1] Bet your boots on. Stunned like seeing as how no shiners is acoming. Underconstumble?[2] He's got the chink *ad lib.* Seed near free poun on un a spell ago a said war hisn. Us come right in on your invite, see? Up to you, matey. Out with the oof. Two bar and a wing.[3] You larn that go off they there Frenchy bilks? Won't wash here for nuts nohow.[4] Lil chile velly solly. Ise de cutest colour coon down our side. Gawds teruth, Chawley. We are nae fou. We're nae tha fou. Au reservoir, Moosoo. Tanks you. ...

You move a motion? Steve boy, you're going it some. More bluggy drunkables? Will immensely splendiferous stander permit one stooder of most extreme poverty and one largesize grandacious thirst to terminate one expensive inaugurated libation? Give's a breather. Landlord, landlord, have you good wine, staboo? Hoots, mon, we drap to pree. Cut and come again. Right Boniface! Absinthe the lot. *Nos omnes biberimus viridum toxicum diabolus capiat posteriora nostra.*[5]

The episode closes in the manner of a dithyrambic American super-hot-gospeller canvassing conversion with a punch in it.

1. In the next episode the Yews, their leaves falling, lisp this affirmative.
2. Cf. Miss Notable's 'I underconstumble you, gentlemen', in Swift's *Polite Conversation*.
3. Half a crown (slang).
4. Stephen, lately returned from Paris, forgets the rule of Irish bars – Cash on Delivery.
5. Such puppy-latin seems always to have been popular with Dublin undergraduates. Examples are found in the *Tripos*, a college magazine to which Swift is believed to have contributed, and Stephen and his friends speak it, on occasion (see *A Portrait of the Artist as a Young Man*).

Come on, you winefizzling ginsizzling booseguzzling existences! Come on, you dog-gone, bullnecked, beetlebrowed, hogjowled, peanutbrained, weasel-eyed fourflushers, false alarms and excess baggage! Come on, you triple extract of infamy! Alexander J. Christ Dowie that's yanked to glory most half this planet from 'Frisco beach to Vladivostock. ... You'll need to rise precious early, you sinner there, if you want to diddle the Almighty God. Pflaaaap! Not half. He's got a coughmixture with a punch in it for you, my friend, in his back-pocket. Just you try it on.

Thus, after long labour, from precedent to precedent, the mountains have brought forth – a grinning golliwog, *enfant terrible*, the language of the future.

Hoopsa, boyaboy, hoopsa!

15. CIRCE

SCENE	The Brothel
HOUR	12 midnight
ORGAN	Locomotor Apparatus
ART	Magic
SYMBOL	Whore
TECHNIC	Hallucination

THE last episode closed with the orgy of Stephen and the medical students at Burke's public house, culminating, just on closing-time, with a round of absinthe. Mr Bloom, determined to watch over Stephen, is faithful to the end, though unwanted and jeered at by the company of young men who are having a 'gorgeous drunk' at Stephen's expense. 'Vel, I ses, if that aint a sheeny nachez, vel, I vil get misha mishinnah.' Prudent Mr Bloom, declining absinthe, has confined himself to 'Rome booze', a glass of wine. Quite exhausted, he is yet nearly sober, but Stephen who has been 'mixing' is far gone. From closing-time till the opening of 'Circe' (midnight), there is a blank period of one hour; what happened in the interval can be pieced together from fragments in other episodes. Mulligan and Haines, no more drinks being forthcoming, 'euchred' (as Mr Bloom puts it) Stephen at the Westland Row Station. Mr Bloom has the gravest suspicions of 'the Buck'. 'It wouldn't occasion me the least surprise to learn that a pinch of tobacco or some other narcotic was put in your drink for some ulterior object.' Stephen, abandoned by all but Lynch,[1] jumps into a loopline train determined to make a night of it. Mr Bloom precipitately follows.

Wildgoose[2] chase this. Disorderly houses. Lord knows where they are gone. Drunks cover distance double quick. Nice mixup. Scene at Westland row. Then

---

1. Lynch is one of Stephen's oldest friends. It was with him that Stephen held the remarkable dialogue on aesthetics (recorded in the *Portrait*) from which I have so often had occasion to quote.

2. The word 'wildgoose' is appropriate here not only because it is an 'animal' metaphor and, so, apt to the 'Circe' episode, but also because Stephen is a 'wild-goose', as the Irish use the word – an Irishman who will not stay in his own country but migrates to foreign parts: for example, 'Trieste-Zürich-Paris'.

jump in first class with third ticket. Then too far. Train with engine behind. Might have taken me to Malahide or a siding for the night or collision. Second drink does it. Once is a dose. What am I following him for? Still, he's the best of that lot.

It is a misty night after the downpour and Mr Bloom loses sight of Stephen at the entrance of the nighttown. He presses on resolutely through the mist, past spectral shadows, drunken harpies, rowdy soldiers, lurching workmen, and finally comes upon Stephen in the house of Mrs Bella Cohen in Tyrone Street. Stephen and Lynch, in the company of the prostitutes Zoe, Flora, and Kitty,[1] are engaged in a rambling discourse on the philosophy of music; Stephen is strumming 'empty fifths' on the brothel piano. Mrs Bella Cohen demands her fees; Stephen, with fuddled generosity, exceeds the tariff, but Bloom comes to the rescue.

BLOOM [*quietly lays a half sovereign on the table between Bella and Florry*]: Allow me. [*He takes up the poundnote.*] Three times ten. We're square.

BELLA [*admiringly*]: You're such a slyboots, old cocky. I could kiss you. ...

BLOOM [*quietly*]: You had better hand over that cash to me to take care of. Why pay more?

STEPHEN [*hands him all his coins*]: Be just before you are generous.

BLOOM: I will, but is it wise? [*He counts.*] One, seven, eleven, and five. Six. Eleven. I don't answer for what you may have lost.

Lynch hands Zoe two pennies to insert in the slot of the piano, which strikes up *My Girl's a Yorkshire Girl*, and the young men and girls dance together. Stephen whirls giddily, faster ever faster, in a frenzy of drunken *tripudium*.[2]

FLORRY [*points to Stephen*]: Look! He's white.

BLOOM [*goes to the window to open it more*]: Giddy.

At the climax of his ecstasy he smashes the gas chandelier and rushes out into the darkness. Mr Bloom stays behind to settle for the damage to the lamp. Hurrying out, he finds Stephen involved in a brawl with two soldiers, who imagine that he has insulted their girl.

1. Female creature, flower, virgin ore: animal, vegetable, mineral.

2. *Salios ancilia ferre ac per urbem ire canentes carmina cum tripudiis sollenique saltatu jussit* (Liv. I, 20). This idea of a *ritual* dance is, for reasons which will be given hereafter, appropriate to the 'Circe' episode. Stephen, crying 'Quick! Quick! Where's my augur's rod?', runs to the piano and takes his ashplant, 'beating his foot in tripudium'. This allusion was prepared for in the *Proteus* episode (*Ulysses*, page 46).

PRIVATE CARR [*breaks loose*]: I'll insult him.

[*He rushes towards* STEPHEN, *fists outstretched, and strikes him in the face.* STEPHEN *totters, collapses, falls stunned. He lies prone, his face to the sky, his hat rolling to the wall.* BLOOM *follows and picks it up.*]

Stephen lies unconscious on the ground with Mr Bloom solicitously watching over him, whispering in his ear. A couple of policemen arrive and start taking names. The undertaker, Corny Kelleher, who is conducting a party of 'commercials' round the brothel quarter, appears out of the darkness. With his aid the policemen are pacified (Corny is a popular Dublin figure) and the episode ends as Stephen is gradually recovering consciousness, watched over by loyal Mr Bloom.

*

'Brothels are built with the bricks of religion.' Blake's paradox may afford some explanation of the curious fact that Dublin, the great Catholic city of northern Europe, should have had a recognized 'red-light quarter'. The Catholic religion, upholding the inviolable sanctity of marriage, accepts no compromise, and condemns the ostrich morality of those hybrid creeds which, burying their heads in the sands of seemliness, refuse recognition of the weakness of the flesh. Thus it is written of that great saint, Vincent Ferrer, that 'an ancient tradition assures us that he drew up a code of regulations for the *maisons de tolérance*'.[1] The man who, passing under the red beacon of ill fame, visits a 'regulated' brothel cannot but know that he is committing deadly sin; no compromise with conscience is possible, none of the callow pity which condones fornication or adultery as a romantic necessity or unpremeditated lapse. Nor, of course, are the modern devices of quick divorce and free love, promiscuity in fact, compatible with the existence of brothels. In such an ambiance the prostitute disappears; in a world of competent amateurs the professional has no place. But the Catholic religion, relentlessly logical, sets in sharp contrast virtue on the one side, vice on the other; white light of heaven, red of hell; the Holy Eucharist and the Black Mass. Stephen Dedalus enters the brothel chanting an *Introit* and at the climax, just before the drunken soldier fells him with a blow, participates in a Black Mass. The episode of 'Circe' is, in fact, 'built with the bricks of religion'.

1. Fage, *Sermons*, Tome II, pages 305, 198. (This, it may be noted, is a religious, *not* a rationalist work.)

The tale of Circe is a legend of black magic. Under the Monte Circeo (this is one of the rare Homeric place-names which have persisted through the ages) is still the cave of the sorceress, *Grotta della maga*. Here Odysseus and his comrades landed after their adventure with the Lestrygonians, and a party of twenty-two set out towards the interior to spy out the land.

In the forest glades they found the halls of Circe builded, of polished stone, in a place with a clear prospect. And all around the palace wolves of the hills and lions were roaming, whom she herself had bewitched with evil drugs that she gave them. Yet the beasts did not set on my men, but lo, they ramped about them and fawned on them, wagging their long tails.

M. Bérard points out that, at the foot of the high Monte Leano which dominates the swampy, thickly wooded region behind the Mount of Circe, there was once a famous temple of Feronia, goddess of wild beasts. After the beginning of June 'the swamps dry up and the pools are dry. The children tremble with fever.' Wild boars and wolves infested these malarial swamps. The 'Circe' episode has all the feverish instability, the luminous intensity which (as all who have lived in the Far East know to their cost) characterize the hallucinations of malaria.

The Achaeans entered the palace of Circe.

She led them in and set them upon chairs and high seats, and made them a mess of cheese and barley-meal and yellow honey with Pramnian wine, and mixed harmful drugs with the food to make them utterly forget their own country.[1] Now when she had given them the cup and they had drunk it off, she smote them presently with a wand, and shut them up in the styes of the swine.

Odysseus, apprised by the sole survivor of this metamorphosis, hurried to the rescue. On his way he met Hermes of the golden wand, who gave him a magic herb wherewith to counteract the drugs of Circe. 'It was black at the root, but the flower was like to milk. The gods call it moly,[2] but it is hard for mortal men to dig; howbeit with the gods all things are possible.'

1. Thus Mr Bloom suspects that Stephen has been 'doped'.
2. M. Bérard sees in 'moly' the *Atriplex halimus*, a yellow-flowering shrub which is found in that region. Another view is that garlic is meant. I suspect that opium is intended, paradoxical though this may seem. The opium poppy has a white flower and is cultivated in Asia Minor as well as the Far East. In its dried commercial form it looks like a root, and the Greeks may well have believed it to be such. The Phoenician opium-growers naturally would not undeceive them; if a Greek,

Armed with the magic plant, Odysseus boldly drank of Circe's golden cup.

Now when she had given it and I had drunk it off and was not bewitched, she smote me with her wand and spake and hailed me:
'Go thy way now to the stye, couch thee there with the rest of thy company.'
So spake she, but I drew my sharp sword from my thigh and sprang upon Circe, as one eager to slay her. But with a great cry she slipped under, and laid hold of my knees.

Circe, recognizing Odysseus, bade him to her bed and, at his behest, set his comrades free.

Circe passed out through the hall with the wand in her hand, and opened the doors of the stye, and drave them forth in the shape of swine of nine seasons old. There they stood before her, and she went through their midst, and anointed each one of them with another charm. And lo! from their limbs the bristles dropped away, wherewith the venom had clothed them, which Circe gave them. And they became men again, younger than before and goodlier far, and taller to behold.

The domain of Feronia, goddess of forests and fauna, to this day abounds in boars and pigs; since a remote past neighbouring towns have borne the names of Setia and Suessa (pigtown). Thus Zoe, in reply to Mr Bloom's question 'Where are you from?' glibly replies, 'Hog's Norton where the pigs plays the organs.'

The art of this episode is 'magic' and its technic 'hallucination'. Inanimate objects, unuttered thoughts, take life, speak and move as independent, zoomorphic beings. Spectres rise from the dead, the squalid brothel parlour is transformed in a bewildering sequence of scenic changes. In fact, the background of this episode, the most 'theatrical' of *Ulysses*, is a series of transformation scenes. All these hallucinations, however, are amplifications of some real circumstance, they have a logic of their own and are not mere empty visions descending from a cuckoocloudland of befuddlement and exhaustion. *Ex nihilo nihil fit*; even the magician Circe could only transform, not create. One of the most interesting aspects of this episode, as engrossing as the pursuit

---

having vainly tried to extract opium from the root, sought counsel from the oriental, the latter would doubtless reply: 'it is hard for mortal men to dig. We alone know the secret.' Opium is known to travellers as a valuable preventive against the deadly fevers of the evergreen jungles of the Burma hills.

of clues in a well-knit detective story, is the detection of the thing, word, or thought whence the hallucination has grown. Here too, despite the pandemoniac welter of apparitions, the artist keeps a tight rein on the tigers of wrath which draw his chariot through this new inferno.

In all metamorphosis there is a stage of clumsy, trammelled movement. The butterfly, newly emerged from the pupa and floundering her way up a branch to dry her limp, bedraggled wings, cuts as ungainly a figure as a *nouveau riche* at his first dinner-party. The companions of Odysseus, after Circe had made pigs of them, though their mind may have been, as Homer tells us, 'steadfast as before', must have been very unsteady at first on their four legs as they trotted about the stye. In this episode there are many passages where the clumsiness of larval movements is portrayed. Thus, when Bloom is about to enter the brothel, 'he trips awkwardly'.

ZOE [*her lucky hand instantly saving him*]: Hoopsa! Don't fall upstairs.
BLOOM: The just man falls seven times. [*He stands aside at the threshold.*] After you is good manners.
ZOE: Ladies first, gentlemen after.
　[*She crosses the threshold. He hesitates. She turns and, holding out her hands, draws him over. He hops.*]

The mind and thoughts of Mr Bloom (and, in a less degree, of Stephen) undergo a feral metamorphosis. His inchoate desires take form and realize themselves before him. All that he secretly willed to do, to see, to suffer, the obscure perversions, obscene imaginations of the dweller below the threshold, more beast than man, all these caper, gibbering, about the brothel parlour. 'Hell is empty, and all the devils are here.' Bloom's visions are generally erotic and perverse, Stephen's are grotesque or tragic. However, in the last pages of the episode Bloom redeems himself, with the wistful vision of his dead son Rudy.

It was, I believe, Mr Middleton Murry who first baptized the 'Circe' episode (sometimes mistakenly assimilated with the *Hades* episode of the *Odyssey*) the '*Walpurgisnacht*' of *Ulysses*, and the fitness of this title, adopted by many subsequent writers, is obvious.[1] But there is another

1. For example, we see in the opening scenes of both a glow of distant fires and will-o'-the-wisp signals. (The feast of Saint Walburga falls on 1 May, Beltane Eve the night of fire.) A Huckster-Witch offers Faust her curious wares – a dagger stained in fratricide, a poisoner's cup, etc. Here Rumbold, Demon Barber, proffers a length of hangman's rope. The Brocken is '*zaubertoll*', mad with magic; so, here,

rapprochement (suggested by Mr Wyndham Lewis in *Time and Western Man*) perhaps equally appropriate. In Flaubert's *Tentation de Saint Antoine* we find a similar conjuring up of spectres from the catacombs of consciousness, we witness like processions of grotesque symbolic figures streaming across the desert and there, too, animals, real or mythical (notably the saint's faithful pig), renew the miracle of Baalam's ass. Generally, however, in the *Tentation*, the phantoms arise automatically, as it were, out of the inane, whereas Circe's 'temptations' are always prepared, the logical amplification of some real object, glosses of some silent or uttered thought. Occasionally, however, Flaubert's technique anticipates that of Joyce, for example in the passage where the saint strives to fix his attention on the Holy Book.

> Ah! ... cela me fait du bien ... ma tête se dégage! ... pour voir ceux qui tondaient ses brebis. ...
> *Un bêlement part de l'horizon.*

Or, again, when he muses on his youth:

> ... quand je courais sur les montagnes après les cerfs légers. ...
> *Il tombe en rêverie.*
> Et la voix des chiens m'arrivait avec le bruit des torrents et le murmure du feuillage.
> *Deux lévriers accouplés passent leurs museaux par les branches, tout en tirant sur la corde que retient du doigt une jeune femme court-vêtue.*

In these passages the bleating of sheep and the leashed greyhounds are hallucinations directly springing from what the saint is reading or thinking – but such cases are exceptional in the *Tentation*.

There is a curious similarity between Bloom's vision of his wife as a handsome woman in Turkish costume, standing 'beside her mirage of datepalms', and Saint Anthony's vision of the Queen of Sheba. Mrs Bloom is attended by an obsequious camel.

> On her feet are jewelled toerings. Her ankles are linked by a slender fetterchain. Beside her a camel, hooded with a turreting turban, waits. A silk ladder of innumerable rungs climbs to his bobbing howdah. He ambles near with disgruntled hindquarters. Fiercely she slaps his haunch, her goldcurb wristbangles

---

is the witch's parlour whither a mephistophelian youth leads his faustian father, the spirit Al-Kohol their meteor-guide. Goethe's first *Walpurgisnacht* is life soaked in magic; here we have a *Walpurgisnacht* itself soaked again in an even more potent magic.

angriling, scolding him in Moorish. ... The camel, lifting a foreleg, plucks from a tree a large mango fruit, offers it to his mistress, blinking, in his cloven hoof, then droops his head and, grunting, with uplifted neck, fumbles to kneel!

Flaubert thus describes the arrival of the Queen of Sheba.

Les bêtes haletantes se couchent. Les esclaves se précipitent sur les ballots, pour en dénouer les cordes avec leurs dents. On déroule des tapis bariolés, on étale par terre des choses qui brillent. Un éléphant blanc, caparaçonné d'un filet d'or, accourt en secouant le bouquet de plumes d'autruches attaché à son frontal. Sur son dos, parmi des coussins de laine bleue, jambes croisées, paupières à demi closes et se balançant la tête, il y a une femme si splendidement vêtue qu'elle envoie des rayons tout autour d'elle. ... L'éléphant plie les genoux, et la reine de Saba, se laissant glisser de son épaule, descend sur les tapis et s'avance vers saint Antoine. ... Elle secoue son parasol, dont toutes les clochettes tintent. Douze négrillons crépus portent la longue queue de sa belle robe, dont un singe tient l'extrémité qu'il soulève de temps à autre pour regarder dessous.

These last lines are echoed in Stephen's vision of himself as Cardinal Dedalus, Primate of All Ireland. 'Seven dwarf simian acolytes, also in red, cardinal sins, uphold his train, peeping under it.' This allusion is deliberate, and intended to suggest a parallel between the pomps and vanities of the Church and the luxury of the Queen of Sheba.

In his introduction to the *Première Tentation de Saint Antoine* (from which version the above quotations are taken), certain observations of M. Louis Bertrand are as apposite to Joyce's work as to Flaubert's.[1]

As in medieval miracle plays, the theme of *Saint Anthony* is, generally speaking, the triumph of Faith over Error, of Vice over Virtue [sic], and, especially, that problematic triumph, the salvation of a soul. Despite his temptations and the flux of suggestions which assails him, will the hermit be saved? As a matter of fact, Flaubert does not answer this question and offers no *dénouement* to his drama. And this because his philosophy goes even further than that of Spinoza. Flaubert is an *absolute* sceptic. Spinoza believes in Science, in the future of scientific knowledge, but Flaubert mistrusts these, as he mistrusts all possible explanations of the universe. ... 'I see passing on the walls as it were vague shadows and I am afraid.'[2] Those vague shadows are the vast unknown, all that

1. The reception of the *Tentation* was generally hostile. 'Le bon Flaubert l'avouait lui-même, non sans un certain orgueil: "J'ai le don", disait-il, "d'ahurir la critique."' Joyce, too, had that gift – witness the early press criticisms of *Ulysses*, and, subsequently, of *Finnegans Wake*.

2. Thus Stephen (in the *Portrait*) says: 'I imagine that there is a malevolent reality behind those things I say I fear.'

will for ever elude the grasp of science, all that perturbs him despite his will to ignore the mystery.

Nor has Flaubert any faith in Reason. As the devil says to Saint Anthony: 'Supposing the absurd were the true?'

Thus his book leads to no conclusion. In accordance with a fixed principle of his he forbade himself a conclusion.[1] The artist should stand to his work as God to His creation. God has never imposed a conclusion, or revealed His final plan.

The 'atmosphere' of the episode is created in the opening stage direction – mist, squalor, impeded speech and movement, *stunted* creatures, a pigmy woman, a Caliban growling in bestial slumber, a Sycorax returning to her lair. (In the extracts which follow it will be noted that the gestures and acts of the personages are frequently described in terms of the animal world.)

The Mabbot street entrance of nighttown, before which stretches an uncobbled tram-siding set with skeleton tracks, red and green will-o'-the-wisps and danger signals. Rows of flimsy houses with gaping doors. Rare lamps with faint rainbow fans. Round Rabaiotti's halted ice gondola stunted men and women squabble. They grab wafers between which are wedged lumps of coal and copper snow. Sucking, they scatter slowly. Children. The swancomb of the gondola, highreared, forges on through the murk, white and blue under a lighthouse. Whistles call and answer.

THE CALLS: Wait, my love, and I'll be with you.

THE ANSWERS: Round behind the stable.

[*A deafmute idiot with goggle eyes, his shapeless mouth dribbling, jerks past, shaken in Saint Vitus' dance. A chain of children's hands imprisons him.*]

THE CHILDREN: Kithogue! Salute.

THE IDIOT [*lifts a palsied left arm and gurgles*]: Grhahute!

THE CHILDREN: Where's the great light?

THE IDIOT [*gobbing*]: Ghaghahest.

[*They release him. He jerks on. A pigmy woman swings on a rope slung between the railings, counting. A form sprawled against a dustbin and muffled by its arms and hat moves, groans, grinding growling teeth, and snores again. On a step a gnome totting among a rubbishtip crouches to shoulder a sack of rags and bones. A crone standing by with a smoky oil lamp rams the last bottle in the maw of his sack. He heaves his booty, tugs askew his peaked cap and hobbles off mutely. The crone makes back for her lair swaying her lamp. A bandy child, asquat on the doorstep with a papershuttlecock, crawls sidling after her in spurts, clutches her skirt, scrambles up. A drunken navvy grips with both hands the railings of an area, lurching heavily. At a corner two night watch in shoulder capes, their hands upon*]

1. Cf. *A Portrait of the Artist.* 'The artist, like the God of creation, remains within or behind or beyond or above his handiwork, invisible ... indifferent.'

their staffholsters, loom tall. A plate crashes; a woman screams; a child wails. Oaths of a man roar, mutter, cease. Figures wander, lurk, peer from warrens. In a room lit by a candle stuck in a bottleneck a slut combs out the tatts from the hair of a scrofulous child.....]

Through this inferno Stephen advances, followed at a distance by Bloom unseen.

[STEPHEN, *flourishing the ashplant in his left hand, chants with joy the introit for paschal time.* LYNCH, *his jockey cap low on his brow, attends him, a sneer of discontent wrinkling his face.*]

STEPHEN: *Vidi aquam egredientem de templo a latere dextro. Alleluia.*

[*The famished snaggletusks of an elderly bawd protrude from a doorway*].

THE BAWD [*her voice whispering huskily*]: Sst! Come here till I tell you. ... Sst.

STEPHEN [*altius aliquantulum*]: *Et omnes ad quos pervenit aqua ista....*

STEPHEN [*triumphaliter*]: *Salvi facti i sunt.*

[*He flourishes his ashplant shivering the lamp image, shattering light over the world. A liver and white spaniel on the prowl slinks after him growling.* LYNCH *scares it with a kick.*]

The vapours thicken into elemental forms.

'Snakes of river fog creep slowly. From drains, clefts, cesspools, middens arise on all sides stagnant fumes. A glow leaps in the south beyond the seaward reaches of the river.' There is a 'big blaze' somewhere. The words remind Mr Bloom of the odious Boylan and he gleefully surmises 'Might be his house', humming: 'London's burning, London's burning! On fire, on fire!' He has been running to catch up Stephen, and now suddenly he bends to one side and groans: 'Stitch in my side. Why did I run?' (Mr Bloom's 'side-stitch' is an example of the 'impeded movement' motif in this episode. Cf. Caliban's 'old cramps'.)

Bloom hurries on and is nearly run over by two cyclists who 'swim by him' in the mist and, again, by a pugnosed tramdriver, perhaps the same who 'balked him' in the morning 'with that horsey woman' (see the 'Lotus-eaters'). He trickleaps to the curbstone.

This narrow escape from accident (another characteristic example is Bloom's near fall as he enters the brothel) introduces a symbolic interpretation of Homer's *moly*, which is several times suggested in this episode; for Joyce the moly represents the element of chance or luck, whose vagaries play so large a part in every Odyssey. Chance is a white flower springing from a dark root; 'it is hard for mortal men to dig, howbeit with the gods all things are possible'. To omniscience and to such mortal men as are good delvers both the flower and its hidden roots are apprehensible. Even the winning number at the roulette table[1] could be predicted by one who could discern all the dark roots of the event.

As Mr Bloom advances through the murk he is followed by a dog whose transformations remind us of the proteiform dog watched by Stephen in the morning. The dog, 'a liver and white spaniel', slinking after Stephen, is kicked by Lynch; it reappears as a retriever sniffing after Bloom, later as terrier, bulldog, beagle. Trudging wearily on in quest of Stephen, Mr Bloom is confronted by phantom forms which rise from the shadows on his path. Old Rudolph Bloom admonishes him in Yiddish-English: 'What are you making down this place?' His mother shrilly laments an accident of his youth. Bloom has bought a 'crubeen' (pig's foot) and a sheep's trotter and, as he is bestowing these in his pockets, Marion suddenly appears before him – doubtless evoked by a thought of the face-lotion, ordered by her, which his pockets should, but do not, contain.

A VOICE [*sharply*]: Poldy!
BLOOM: Who? [*He ducks and wards off a blow clumsily*] At your service.[2]
[*He looks up. Beside her mirage of datepalms a handsome woman in Turkish costume stands before him. Opulent curves fill out her scarlet trousers and jacket slashed with gold. A wide yellow cummerbund girdles her. A white yashmak violet*

1. We see in this episode a hobgoblin (homunculus), evoked by a mention of the end of the world, playing roulette with the planets. 'His jaws chattering, he capers to and fro, goggling his eyes, squeaking, kangaroohopping, with outstretched clutching arms, then all at once thrusts his lipless face through the fork of his thighs. *Il vient! C'est moi! L'homme qui rit! L'homme primigène!* He whirls round and round with dervish howls. *Sieurs et dames, faites vos jeux!* He crouches juggling. Tiny roulette planets fly from his hands. *Les jeux sont faits.* The planets rush together, uttering crepitant cracks. *Rien n'va plus.* The planets, buoyant balloons, sail swollen up and away.'

2. It is noteworthy that both Calypso (Marion) and Circe (Bella Cohen) are presented in this episode as masterful women and Bloom not only accepts but obviously enjoys their domination. *À propos* of masterly women Samuel Butler has an amusing tale to tell in his *Authoress of the Odyssey*. 'Calypso is the master mind, not Ulysses; and be it noted, that neither she nor Circe seem to have a manservant on their premises. I was at an inn once and asked the stately landlady if I could see the landlord. She bridled up and answered, "We have no landlord, sir, in this house; I cannot see what use a man is in a hotel except to clean boots and windows." Thus spoke Circe and Calypso, but neither of them seems to have made even this much exception in man's favour.'

in the night covers her face, leaving free only her large dark eyes and raven hair.]

BLOOM: Molly!

MARION: Welly? Mrs Marion from this out, my dear man, when you speak to me. [*Satirically*] Has poor little hubby cold feet from waiting so long?

BLOOM [*shifts from foot to foot*]: No, no. Not the least little bit.

[*He breathes in deep agitation, swallowing gulps of air, questions, hopes, crubeens for her supper, things to tell her, excuses, desire, spellbound. ...*]

Mr Bloom, 'harking back in a restrospective arrangement', now conjures up an *amour* of his youth, Mrs Breen, 'her roguish eyes wide-open, smiling in all her herbivorous buckteeth'.

MRS BREEN: Mr Bloom! You down here in the haunts of sin! I caught you nicely! Scamp!

BLOOM [*hurriedly*]: Not so loud my name. Whatever do you think me? Don't give me away. Walls have hears. How do you do? It's ages since I. You're looking splendid. Absolutely it. Seasonable weather we are having this time of year. Black refracts heat. Short cut home here. Interesting quarter. Rescue of fallen women. Magdalen asylum. I am the secretary. ...

Now Mr Bloom engages in a spectral flirtation with the sometime 'prettiest deb in Dublin', culminating in a 'pigeon kiss'.

[*She fades from his side. Followed by the whining dog he walks on towards hells-gates. ... Outside a shuttered pub a bunch of loiterers listen to a tale which their broken-snouted gaffer rasps out with raucous humour. An armless pair of them flop wrestling, growling, in maimed sodden playfight.*]

THE GAFFER [*crouches, his voice twisted in his snout*]: And when Cairns came down from the scaffolding in Beaver Street what was he after doing it into only into the bucket of porter that was there waiting on the shavings for Derwan's plasterers.

THE LOITERERS [*guffaw with cleft palates*]: Oh jays!

[*Their paintspeckled hats wag. Spattered with size and lime of their lodges they frisk limblessly about him.*]

The allusion to Beaver Street has transformed the loiterers into a troop of clumsy animals (*die Unbehilflichen*), spattered with the debris of their 'lodges'.[1]

1. There is a perpetual interplay of human and bestial forms. The personages growl and grunt, twitter and croak. 'Circe' resembles a medieval 'bestiary'. Cf. also *Comus*, in which one of the stage directions runs: 'COMUS *enters, with a charming-rod in one hand, his glass in the other; with him a rout of monsters, headed like*

Mr Bloom passes on. 'Gaudy dollwomen loll in the lighted doorways, in window embrasures, smoking birdseye cigarettes. The odour of the sicksweet weed floats towards him in slow round ovalling wreaths.' (Cf. Circe's magic philtres.) The sight of two 'raincaped watch' approaching evokes in his guilty conscience the spectres of past and present misdemeanours – by intention with the typist Martha Clifford, in act with the servant Mary Driscoll.

He surprised me in the rere of the premises, your honour, when the missus was out shopping one morning with a request for a safety pin. He held me and I was discoloured in four places as a result.

Certain ladies of importance whom he has desired from afar, but not chastely, rise up to denounce him before the court of conscience.

[*His Honour, sir Frederick Falkiner, recorder of Dublin, in judicial garb of grey stone rises from the bench, stonebearded.*[1] *He carries in his arms an umbrella sceptre. From his forehead arise starkly the Mosaic ramshorns.*]

THE RECORDER: I will put an end to this white slave traffic and rid Dublin of this odious pest. Scandalous! [*He dons the black cap.*] Let him be taken, Mr Subsheriff, from the dock where he now stands and detained in custody in Mountjoy prison during His Majesty's pleasure and there be hanged by the neck until he is dead and therein fail not at your peril or may the Lord have mercy on your soul. Remove him. [*A black skullcap descends upon his head.*]

The hangman Rumbold appears and Bloom lamely protests 'I was at a funeral'.

FIRST WATCH [*draws his truncheon*]: Liar!
        [*The beagle lifts his snout, showing the grey scorbutic face of* PADDY DIGNAM. *He has gnawed all. He exhales a putrid carcasefed breath. He grows to human size and shape. His dachshund coat becomes a brown mortuary habit. His green eye flashes bloodshot. Half of one ear, all the nose and both thumbs are ghouleaten.*]
PADDY DIGNAM [*in a hollow voice*]: It is true. It was my funeral. Doctor Finucane pronounced life extinct when I succumbed to the disease from natural causes.
        [*He lifts his mutilated face moonwards and bays lugubriously.*]

---

sundry sorts of wild beasts, but otherwise like men and women, their apparel glistering. They come in making a riotous and unruly noise, with torches in their hands.' Analogies with the 'Circe' episode are obvious, Stephen's ashplant playing the part of the charming-rod, the navvy's 'flaring cresset' that of a torch, etc.

1. There is here an allusion to the 'stony effigy', the *Moses* of Michelangelo. Sir Frederick Falkiner was '*le bon juge Magnaud*' of Dublin.

BLOOM [*in triumph*]: You hear?
PADDY DIGNAM: Bloom, I am Paddy Dignam's spirit. List, list, O list!

Bloom's quest is nearly ended; he pauses before a lighted house, whence kisses, winging from their bowers, fly about him, twittering, warbling, cooing.

THE KISSES [*warbling*]: Leo! [*Twittering*] Icky licky micky sticky for Leo! [*Cooing*] Coo coocoo! Yummyumm Womwom! [*Warbling*] Big comebing! Pirouette! Leopopold! [*Twittering*] Leeolee! [*Warbling*] O Leo!
  [*They rustle, flutter upon his garments, alight, bright giddy flecks, silvery sequins.*]

There is here a recall of the close of the 'Nestor' episode: 'the sun flung spangles (upon Mr Deasy's shoulders), dancing coins.'
Bloom has reached Mrs Bella Cohen's house,[1] the palace of Circe, where Stephen and Lynch are seated, talking to the three young witches. Zoe feels in Bloom's pocket and extracts a 'black shrivelled potato' – a literal recall, this, of the black root of moly.

  [*She puts the potato greedily into a pocket, then links his arm, cuddling him with supple warmth. He smiles uneasily. Slowly, note by note, oriental music is played. He gazes in the tawny crystal of her eyes, ringed with kohl. His smile softens.*]
ZOE: You'll know me the next time.
BLOOM [*forlornly*]: I never loved a dear gazelle but it was sure to …
  [*Gazelles are leaping, feeding on the mountains. Near are lakes. Round their shores file shadows black of cedargroves. Aroma rises, a strong hair growth of resin. It burns, the orient, a sky of sapphire, cleft by the bronze flight of eagles. Under it lies the womancity, nude, white, still, cool, in luxury. A fountain murmurs among damask roses. Mammoth roses murmur of scarlet winegrapes. A wine of shame, lust, blood exudes, strangely murmuring.*]
ZOE [*murmuring singsong with the music, her odalisk lips lusciously smeared with salve of swinefat and rosewater*]: Schorach ani wenowach, benoith Hierushaloim.[2]

Zoe mocks Bloom's pompous phrases. 'Go on. Make a stump speech out of it.' In a flash the scene changes to a public ceremony where Bloom is hailed as 'the world's greatest reformer', and anointed King of Ireland. He is applauded by John Howard Parnell, Tom Kernan,

1. The Ulyssean pilgrim will seek in vain this cloud-capped palace, No. 82 Lower Tyrone Street; it has gone up into thin air, like so many landmarks of our *vieux ports – où sont les bouges d'antan?* – in the Beltane fires of social 'progress'.
2. 'I am black but comely, O ye daughters of Jerusalem.'

John Wyse Noland, and many others. The 'mystery man' from 'Hades' alone is dissentient.

THE MAN IN THE MACINTOSH: Don't you believe a word he says. That man is Leopold M'Intosh, the notorious fireraiser. His real name is Higgins.

BLOOM: Shoot him! Dog of a christian! So much for M'Intosh!

[*A cannonshot. The man in the macintosh disappears.* BLOOM *with his sceptre strikes down poppies. The instantaneous deaths of many powerful enemies … are reported. Bloom's bodyguard distribute Maundy money, commemoration medals, loaves, and fishes, temperance badges, expensive Henry Clay cigars, free cow-bones for soup, … readymade suits, porringers of toad in the hole, bottles of Jeyes' Fluid, purchase stamps, 40 days' indulgences, spurious coins, dairyfed pork sausages, theatre passes, season tickets available for all tram lines, coupons of the royal and privileged Hungarian lottery, penny dinner counters, cheap reprints of World's Twelve Worst Books: Froggy and Fritz (politic), Care of the Baby (infantilic), 50 Meals for 7s. 6d. (clinic), Was Jesus a Sun Myth? (historic), Expel that Pain (medic), Infant's Compendium of the Universe (cosmic), Let's All Chortle (hilaric), Canvasser's Vade Mecum (journalic), Loveletters of Mother Assistant (erotic), Who's Who in Space (astric), Songs that Reached Our Heart (melodic), Pennywise's Way to Wealth (parsimonic). A general rush and scramble. Women press forward to touch the hem of Bloom's robe.*]

But now a priest rises to denounce him and (as it was with Parnell) the mob turns against him. Various doctors are called to testify to Bloom's infirmities, and this they do at length in the jargon of their art, differing from each other after the manner of experts. Thus, while Dr Mulligan declares the accused a *virgo intacta*, Dr Dixon appeals for clemency 'in the name of that most sacred word our vocal organs have ever been called upon to speak. He is about to have a baby'. (This is the dramatization of a passage in the 'Lestrygonians', where Bloom imagines himself suffering the pains of childbirth.)

But the medical witnesses are unable to exonerate him. 'All the people cast soft pantomime stones at Bloom. Many bonafide travellers and ownerless dogs come near him and defile him.' Finally, an officer of the Fire Brigade sets him on fire and 'a choir of a hundred voices, conducted by Mr Vincent O'Brien, sings the Alleluia chorus, accompanied on the organ by Joseph Glynn. Bloom becomes mute, shrunken, carbonized'.

ZOE: Talk away till you're black in the face.

For a moment the phantoms vanish. The prostitute invites Bloom in to see the new pianola. 'With little parted talons she captures his hand, her forefinger giving to his palm the passtouch of secret monitor, luring him to doom.' (There are a number of such 'masonic' allusions in this episode; I shall comment on these later.) Bloom is drawn by her 'lion reek' and he has a vision of the male brutes, Circe's victims, who have enjoyed her, 'faintly roaring, their drugged heads swaying to and fro'.

Bloom follows Zoe into the brothel. After a while Stephen turns and sees him, murmuring 'A time, times and half a time'.

'Along an invisible tightrope taut from zenith to nadir the End of the World whirls through the murk' and 'Elijah's voice, harsh as a corncrake's, jars on high' – a recall of the Dowie throwaway, which Mr Bloom was given in the forenoon. Elijah invites the company to join in a 'buck joyride to heaven'. 'The hottest stuff that ever was. It's the whole pie with the jam in. It's just the cutest snappiest line out. It is immense, supersumptuous. It restores. It vibrates.'

A *cortège* of phantoms passes: the medical students, the debaters in the library, Mananaan. Suddenly Lipoti Virag (Bloom's grandfather) chutes down the chimney. 'He is sausaged into several overcoats and wears a brown macintosh under which he holds a roll of parchment. ... On his head is perched an Egyptian pshent. Two quills project over his ears.' Virag is one of the oddest of the spectral denizens of Circe's palace.[1] He strikes a series of epileptic poses, some of which seem exact reproductions of the grotesque gargoyles round Notre Dame at Paris. His speech bristles with sharp interjections and he has a trick of ending his declamations with a queer-sounding word. 'Hippogriff. Am I right?' 'Parallax! (*With a nervous twitch of his head.*) Did you hear my brain go snap?[2] Polysyllabax!' In a jargon of insane exactness he classifies the charms of the three prostitutes. He admires item number three, so 'obviously mammal'.

Such fleshy parts are the product of careful nurture. When coopfattened their livers reach an elephantine size. Pellets of new bread with fennygreek and gumbenjamin swamped down by potions of green tea endow them during their brief existence with natural pincushions of quite colossal blubber. That suits

---

1. Like the Medusa in the Brocken scene, he has a detachable head, which, when he is about to go, he 'unscrews in a trice' and carries off under his arm.

2. One of Mrs Piper's frequent remarks when 'coming out' of trance was, 'Did you hear something snap in my head?' and nervous twitchings accompanied the process. There is much of the atmosphere of a mediumistic séance in 'Circe'.

your book, eh? Fleshhotpots of Egypt to hanker after. Wallow in it. Lycopodium. (*His throat twiches.*) Slapbang! There he goes again.

A moth, flying round and round the gasjet, blundering into the shade, recalls some panic fear in Virag's metallic brain. '*Dans une mort d'insecte on voit tous les désastres. ...*'

VIRAG [*head askew, arches his back and hunched wingshoulders, peers at the moth out of blear bulged eyes, points a horning claw and cries*]: Who's Ger Ger? Who's dear Gerald? O, I much fear he shall be most badly burned. Will some pleashe pershon not now imediment so catastrophics mit agitation of firstclass tablenumpkin? [*He mews*] Luss puss puss puss! [*He sighs, draws back and stares sideways down with dropping underjaw*] Well, well. He doth rest anon.

> I'm a tiny tiny thing
> Every flying in the spring
> Round and round a ringaring.
> Long ago I was a king.
> Now I do this sort of thing
> On the wing, on the wing!
> Bing!

[*He rushes against the mauve shade flapping noisily*] Pretty pretty pretty pretty pretty pretty petticoats.

Fleeting allusions evoke Ben Jumbo Dollard, nakkering castanet bones (as in the 'Sirens'), Henry Flower (Bloom's double), the Nurses, daughters of the Sun. Florry tells Stephen he must be a 'spoiled priest' and 'His Eminence Stephen Cardinal Dedalus, Primate of All Ireland', appears in the doorway, imparts the Easter kiss, and doubleshuffles off.

[*The door opens.* BELLA COHEN, *a massive whoremistress, enters. ... On her left hand are wedding and keeper rings. Her eyes are deeply carboned. She has a sprouting moustache. Her olive face is heavy, slightly sweated and fullnosed, with orange-tainted nostrils. She has large pendant beryl eardrops.*]

In the passage between Bloom and Bella which follows, the metamorphosis of Bloom, tapped by Bella's fan (the wand), to utter animalism is achieved. With each change of scene we plunge deeper into the miasma of the Feronian swamps. Bloom is tortured, becomes a light woman,[1] and is sold by auction. Bella is changed to a male brute who

---

1. Compare the change of sex in the *Attis* poem of Catullus (LXIII), in which, as here, the ritual dance of the *tripudium* is mentioned. (*My Girl's a Yorkshire Girl* is in three-time, a *tripudium*.)

bestrides Bloom. 'Gee up! A cockhorse to Banbury cross. I'll ride him for the Eclipse stakes.' At a command from Bello, 'On the hands down!', Bloom sinks to her swinish self. 'With a piercing epileptic cry she sinks on all fours, grunting, snuffling, rooting at his feet, then lies, shamming dead with eyes shut tight, trembling eyelids, bowed upon the ground in the attitude of most excellent master.' Bello 'trains' her and she becomes a houri, a sadist's victim from the pages of some erotic thriller.

The Sins of the Past rise to divulge Bloom's most secret infamies and Bello gloats over his victim's shame. Bloom bows: 'Master! Mistress! Mantamer!' and, as he lifts his arms, his bangle bracelets fall. At last he breaks down and clasping his head cries 'My will power! Memory! I have sinned! I have suff ...' Bello sneers: 'Crybaby! Crocodile tears!' He dies and darkshawled figures of the circumcised throng around him wailing in pneuma: '*Shema Israel Adonai Elohenu Adonai Echad.*'

[*From the suttee pyre the flame of gum camphire ascends. The pall of incense smoke screens and disperses. Out of her oak frame a nymph with hair unbound, lightly clad in teabrown art colours, descends from her grotto and, passing under interlacing yews, stands over* BLOOM.]

THE YEWS [*their leaves whispering*]: Sister. Our sister. Ssh.

The *Photo Bits* picture of a Nymph, that 'splendid masterpiece in art colours', which hangs over Mr and Mrs Bloom's bed, has come to life. The yews are a transmutation of the brothel wallpaper, 'of yew-fronds and clear glades', the Circean forest. The action now moves in a pastoral setting. The Halcyon Days (a memory of 'Nausicaa') call to Bloom, a schoolboy now, 'Live us again.' Bloom cheers feebly: 'Hurray for the High School!' and Echo answers 'Fool!' The nymph and the yews discourse of the boyish infamies of Bloom. A nannygoat passes high on Ben Howth through the rhododendrons where Mr Bloom in

---

'Quo nos decet citatis celerare tripudiis.'
Simul haec comitibus Attis cecinit, notha mulier. ...

Bloom, too, is here a *notha mulier*, a mock-woman. The Attis poem is, it may also be noted, concerned with the worship of Cybele, Tellus, the Great Mother (see the episode of 'Penelope' for the assimilation of Mrs Bloom with this goddess), the characteristics of whose rites were frenzied excitement and self-castration, in which the votary made himself the serving-woman, handmaid of the goddess, 'ministra et Cybeles famula',

his courting days lay 'ravished, full lips full open, kissed her mouth'.[1] The nymph coldly rebukes him for the sights she has had to endure as presiding deity of his bedroom. 'We', she says, 'are stonecold and pure. We eat electric light.' (In an earlier episode Bloom pictured the nymph 'doing Pygmalion and Galatea', and wondered how she would like a tanner lunch after 'quaffing nectar at mess with gods, golden dishes, all ambrosial. ... Nectar, imagine it drinking electricity.') But Mr Bloom resents this cold douche on his visionary fervour. 'If there were only ethereal', he taunts her, 'where would you all be, postulants and novices? Shy but willing. ...'

THE YEWS [*their silverfoil of leaves precipitating, their skinny arms ageing and swaying*]: Deciduously!

(The 'silverfoil' here is the wrapping from a chocolate which Bloom has handed to Zoe and she is 'nibbling'.)

At last the nymph, assaulted by Bloom, takes to flight, followed by his taunts. 'As if you didn't get it on the double yourselves. ... Eh! I have sixteen years of black slave labour behind me. And would a jury give me five shillings alimony tomorrow, eh? Fool someone else, not me.' The hallucination passes. Bella Cohen stands before him, demanding her fees.

Zoe begins to read Stephen's hand.

ZOE [*she takes his hand*]: Blue eyed beauty. I'll read your hand. [*She points to his forehead*] No wit, no wrinkles. [*She counts*] Two, three, Mars, that's courage. [*Stephen shakes his head*] No kid.

LYNCH: Sheet lightning courage. The youth who could not shiver and shake. [*To Zoe*] Who taught you palmistry?

ZOE [*turns*]: Ask my... [*To Stephen*] I see it in your face. The eye, like that. [*She frowns with lowered head.*]

LYNCH [*laughing, slaps Kitty behind twice*]: Like that. Pandy bat.
    [*Twice loudly a pandybat cracks, the coffin of the pianola flies open, the bald little round jack-in-the-box head of* FATHER DOLAN *springs up.*]

FATHER DOLAN: Any boy want flogging? Broke his glasses? Lazy idle little schemer. See it in your eye.
    [*Mild, benign, rectorial, reproving, the head of* DON JOHN CONMEE *rises from the pianola coffin.*]

DON JOHN CONMEE: Now, Father Dolan! Now I'm sure that Stephen is a very good little boy.

1. *Ulysses*, page 167.

These are apparitions from Stephen's schooldays – an incident described in the *Portrait*. Stephen, having broken his glasses, could not do his lessons. The prefect of studies, Father Dolan, makes his round inspecting the 'lazy idle little schemers', as he calls the boys. 'See it in your eye' is a pet phrase of his. He notices that Stephen is not working – 'Lazy little schemer. I see schemer in your face' – and, despite Stephen's terrified explanation, bids him hold out his hand, touches it for a moment at the fingers to steady it (this touch of the prefect's soft, firm fingers leaves a vivid impression on the boy's mind) and 'pandies' him. Stephen complains to the Rector, Father Conmee, of the injustice, and is consoled by the Rector's sympathy. Here the touch of Zoe's fingers on his and her 'I see it in your face' have sufficed to materialize the whole incident before Stephen's eyes.

Two of the girls start whispering together and giggling. Bloom has a vision of the interview between Marion and Blazes Boylan; he sees himself, a flunkey with a powdered wig, attending on their amorous frolics, hears their theroid sighs of ecstasy, and masochistically applauds the conqueror. Bella and her three disgraces begin to laugh.

LYNCH [*points*]: The mirror up to nature. [*He laughs.*] Hu hu hu hu hu hu.
  [STEPHEN *and* BLOOM *gaze in the mirror. The face of* WILLIAM SHAKE-SPEARE, *beardless, appears there, rigid in facial paralysis, crowned by the reflection of the reindeer antlered hatrack in the hall.*]
SHAKESPEARE [*in dignified ventriloquy*]: 'Tis the loud laugh bespeaks the vacant mind. [*To Bloom*] Thou thoughtest as how thou wastest invisible. Gaze. [*He crows with a black capon's laugh*] Iagogo! How my Oldfellow chokit his Thursdaymomum. Iagogogo!

Lynch's 'the mirror up to nature' has evoked this grotesque hallucination, Shakespeare's beardless, paralysed face and stuttering speech (impeded movement). It is significant, in view of the 'confusion of persons' hinted at in the episode of 'Scylla and Charybdis', that Stephen and Bloom, looking *together* into the glass, should see the face of Shakespeare there.

Stephen entertains the company with an imitation of a French guide vaunting in broken English the attractions of *Paris la nuit*: 'how much smart they are on things love and sensations voluptuous'. He recalls his dream – of the melon, the street of harlots ('It was here!') and the red carpet spread (a dream-memory, perhaps, of the Queen of Sheba's carpet outspread, in the *Tentation*) – followed by the dream of flight. 'No, I flew. My foes beneath me. And ever shall be. World without end. ... *Pater!* Free!' The *Pater!* here is a recall of the 'Scylla and Charybdis' episode (as well, of course, as the tale of Daedalus's flight in the *Metamorphoses*): 'Fabulous artificer, the hawklike man. You flew. ... Lapwing. Icarus. *Pater, ait.*' Here Stephen dramatizes the flight of Icarus and (this is, perhaps, rather strange coming from Stephen) sees his father in the role of the artificer Daedalus.

STEPHEN: Break my spirit, will he? *O merde alors!* [*He cries, his vulture talons sharpened*] Hola! Hillyho!
  [SIMON DEDALUS' *voice hilloes in answer, somewhat sleepy but ready.*]
SIMON: That's all right. [*He swoops uncertainly through the air, wheeling, uttering cries of hearkening, on strong ponderous buzzard wings*] Ho, boy! Are you going to win? Hoop! Pschatt! Stable with those halfcastes. Wouldn't let them within the bawl of an ass. Head up! Keep our flag flying! An eagle gules volant in a field argent displayed. Ulster king at arms! hai hoop! [*He makes the beagle's cry giving tongue*] Bulbul! Burblblbrurblbl! Hai, boy![1]
  [*The fronds and spaces of the wallpaper file rapidly across country. ...*]

The scene now changes to a race-meeting (a dramatization of Stephen's day-dream as he observed the pictures of race-horses in Mr Deasy's study) and 'a dark horse riderless bolts like a phantom past the winningpost, his mane moonfoaming, his eyeballs stars'. (This is an echo from the 'Proteus' episode, an allusion to the houyhnhnm Swift, who ran to the wood of madness, 'his mane foaming in the moon, his eyeballs stars'.)

The brothel pianola, with changing lights, begins to play the waltzsong *My Girl's a Yorkshire Girl* (we have already heard this tune blared and drumthumped by a Highland band, at the close of the 'Wandering Rocks'). The dancing-master Maginni suddenly appears from between curtains; with a deft kick he sends his top hat spinning to his crown and 'jauntyhatted skates in' to act as the *Maître de Cérémonies*. The lights change, glow, fade: gold, rose, violet.

---

1. Here we have probably a recall of Homer's famous simile (*Odyssey*, XXII: 302–6), likening Telemachus and his father slaughtering of the suitors to 'vultures of crooked claws and curved beak, that came forth from the mountains and dash upon smaller birds, and these scour low in the plain, stooping in terror from the clouds, while the vultures pounce on them, and slay them and there is no help nor way of flight and men are glad at the sport',

THE PIANOLA:

> Two young fellows were talking about their girls, girls, girls,
> Sweethearts they'd left behind ...

[*From a corner the morning hours run out, goldhaired, slim, in girlish blue, wasp-waisted, with innocent hands. Nimbly they dance, twirling their skipping ropes. The hours of noon follow in amber gold. Laughing linked, high haircombs flashing, they catch the sun in mocking mirrors, lifting their arms.*]

MAGINNI [*clipclaps glovesilent hands*]: Carré! Avant deux! Breathe evenly! Balance!

[*The morning and noon hours waltz in their places, turning, advancing to each other, shaping their curves, bowing vis à vis.* CAVALIERS *behind them arch and suspend their arms, with hands descending to, touching, rising from their shoulders.*]

HOURS: You may touch my ...
CAVALIERS: May I touch your?
HOURS: O, but lightly!
CAVALIERS: O, so lightly!

This dance of the hours is a recall of the close of the 'Calypso' episode. 'Morning after the bazaar dance when May's band played Ponchielli's dance of the hours. Explain that morning hours, noon, then evening coming on, then night hours. ... Evening hours, girls in grey gauze. Night hours then black with daggers and eyemasks. Poetical idea pink, then golden, then grey, then black.'

[*The night hours steal to the last place. Morning, noon and twilight hours retreat before them. They are masked, with daggered hair and bracelets of dull bells. Weary, they curchycurchy under veils.*]

THE BRACELETS: Heigho! Heigho! ...

[*Arabesquing wearily, they weave a pattern on the floor, weaving, unweaving, curtseying, twisting, simply swirling.*]

All this passage is built up of recalls from earlier pages. The pattern on the floor, woven and unwoven (like Penelope's veil) by the feet of the Hours,[1] is a sublimation of the oilcloth mosaic of jade and azure and cinnabar rhomboids on the brothel floor. 'Footmarks are stamped

---

1. Circe's home is in the isle Aeaean, 'where are the dwellings of Dawn, the child of darkness, and the dancing-grounds and rising of the Sun'. The curious term 'dancing-grounds', χοροί, is explained by M. Bérard as being of Egyptian origin. The Sungod Ra had four manifestations – as the god of spring and dawn, of summer and morning, of autumn and afternoon, of winter and night. Ra daily performed a *danse en rond*, passing through each of these avatars as he moved from room to room of his palace. Here the dance of the hours is a recall of the ritual dance of the sungod.

over it in all senses, heel to heel, heel to hollow, toe to toe, feetlocked, a morris of shuffling feet without body phantoms, all in a scrimmage higgledypiggledy' (an apt Circean epithet, this last word). The Hours (as important personages in *Ulysses* as in the work of Proust) are associated with the 'morris' (moorish) dancers with their 'caps of indices', numbered like the hours. The dull bells of the bracelets are an echo of the 'dark iron' of the bells of Saint George's church, heard by Mr Bloom while he was dramatizing in imagination Ponchielli's dance. 'Simply swirling' is a recall of the song of the 'seaside girls' and the vision of the queen of the Pleiades (in the 'Oxen of the Sun'), 'coifed with a veil of what do you call it gossamer ... sustained on currents of cold interstellar wind, winding, coiling, simply swirling'.

The music swells *crescendo*. Kitty cries 'O, they played that on the hobbyhorses at the Mirus bazaar', and, running to Stephen, dances with him. 'A screaming bittern's harsh high whistle shrieks. Groangrousegurgling Toft's cumbersome whirligig turns slowly the room right roundabout the room.' The orgy grows wilder; now all the whores are dancing, and with them Bloom. Bloom's partner is Bella (an avatar, perhaps, of the 'Old Witch', Mephistopheles's partner, in the Walpurgis ball).

[*All wheel, whirl, waltz, twirl. Bloombella, Kittylynch, Florryzoe, jujuby women.*[1] STEPHEN *with hat ashplant frogsplits in middle highkicks with skykicking mouth shut hand clasp part under thigh, with clang tinkle boomhammer tallyho hornblower blue green yellow flashes. Toft's cumbersome turns with hobbyhorse riders from gilded snakes dangled, bowels fandango leaping spurn soil foot and fall again.*]

THE PIANOLA:

> Though she's a factory lass
> And wears no fancy clothes.

[*Closeclutched swift swifter with glareblueflare scudding they scootlootshoot lumbering by. Baraabum!*] ...

STEPHEN: Dance of death.

[*Bang fresh barang bang of lacquey's bell, horse, nag, steer, piglings, Conmee on Christass lame crutch and leg sailor in cockboat armfolded ropepulling hitching stamp hornpipe through and through. Baraabum! On nags, hogs, bellhorses, Gadarene swine, Corny in coffin. Steel shark stone onehandled Nelson, two trickies Frauenzimmer plumstained from pram falling bawling. Gum, he's a champion. Fuseblue peer from barrel rev. evensong Love on hackney jaunt Blazes blind cod-*]

---

1. In *jujuby* there is, perhaps, a punning allusion to African magic.

doubled bicyclers Dilly with snowcake no fancy clothes. Then in last wiswitchback
lumbering up and down bump mashtub sort of viceroy and reine relish for tub-
lumber bumpshire rose. Baraabum!]

[*The couples fall aside.* STEPHEN *whirls giddily. Room whirls back. Eyes closed,*
he totters. Red rails fly spacewards. Stars all around suns turn roundabout.
Bright midges dance on the wall. He stops dead.]

The materials used in this *crescendo* are nearly all themes which have
been previously stated. Through them 'drumthumps' the percussive
tripudium of the *Yorkshire Girl*: 'Yorkshire through and through',
'Gum, he's a champion', 'wears no fancy clothes', 'I've a sort of a
relish for My little Yorkshire rose. Baraabum!'

The lacquey's bell is the handbell at Dillon's auction-room, heard by
Dilly Dedalus at 3 p.m.;[1] the onelegged sailor received alms from Mrs
Bloom at about the same time;[2] 'Corny in Coffin' is another echo of
the 'Wandering Rocks'.[3] The 'steel shark' is a battleship, an allusion
to the 'Nausicaa' episode. 'Onehandled Nelson' and the plumstained
Frauenzimmer figure in Stephen's Parable of the Plums.[4] The 'pram' is a
recall of the Boardman baby ('Nausicaa'). 'Fuseblue' is a reference to
Kevin Egan's 'blue fuse' match;[1] 'peer from barrel'[5] (probably) to
Guinness's Brewery;[6] the Rev. Love is the antiquarian enamoured of
Geraldines;[7] the 'coddoubled bicyclers' have coasted down from the
poster of a cycle race seen by Mr Bloom, 'cyclist doubled up like a cod
in a pot';[8] 'mashtub' is a recall of 'I thinks of my old mashtub down
Limehouse way'.[9] This confounding together of Stephen's and Bloom's
memories and experiences (personal or assimilated, by a kind of clair-
voyance, each from each) in a swirling vortex of movement on Toft's
roundabout has a curious analogy with Flaubert's *Song of the Poets and
Mummers* (in the first version of the *Tentation*).

Nous chantons, nous crions, nous pleurons, nous bondissons sur la corde,
avec de grands balanciers. L'orchestre bruit, la baraque en tremble, des miasmes
passent, des couleurs tournent, l'idée se bombe, la foule se presse, et, palpitants,
l'oeil au but, absorbés dans notre ouvrage, nous accomplissons la singulière
fantaisie, qui fera rire de pitié ou crier de terreur. ... Tournons, tournons sur nos
chevaux de manège qui galopent sans trêve et ruent du sable à la face du peuple
applaudissant.

Suddenly the movement ceases; there is dead silence in the room.

1. *Ulysses*, page 224.   2. page 212.   3. page 212.
4. page 138.   5. page 40.   6. page 71.
7. page 218.   8. page 78.   9. page 295.

[*Stephen's mother, emaciated, rises stark through the floor in leper grey with a wreath of faded orange blossoms and a torn bridal veil, her face worn and noseless, green with grave mould. Her hair is scant and lank. She fixes her bluecircled hollow eyesockets on Stephen and opens her toothless mouth uttering a silent word. A choir of virgins and confessors sing voicelessly.*]

THE CHOIR:

> Liliata rutilantium te confessorum ...
> Iubilantium te virginum ...

[*From the top of a tower* BUCK MULLIGAN, *in particoloured jester's dress of puce and yellow and clown's cap with curling bell, stands gaping at her, a smoking buttered split scone[1] in his hand.*]

BUCK MULLIGAN: She's beastly dead. The pity of it! Mulligan meets the afflicted mother. [*He upturns his eyes.*] Mercurial Malachi.

THE MOTHER [*with the subtle smile of death's madness*]: I was once the beautiful May Goulding. I am dead.

STEPHEN [*horrorstruck*]: Lemur, who are you? What bogeyman's trick is this?

BUCK MULLIGAN [*shakes his curling capbell*]: The mockery of it! Kinch killed her dogsbody bitchbody. She kicked the bucket. [*Tears of molten butter fall from his eyes into the scone.*] Our great sweet mother! *Epi oinopa ponton.*

THE MOTHER [*comes nearer, breathing upon him softly her breath of wetted ashes*]: All must go through it, Stephen. More women than men in the world. You too. Time will come.

STEPHEN [*choking with fright, remorse and horror*]: They said I killed you, mother. He offended your memory. Cancer did it, not I. Destiny.

This passage derives from Mulligan's remark that Stephen's mother was 'beastly dead',[2] and his allusion to Stephen as a poor 'dogsbody' (the inversion of divine substance). 'More women than men in the world' recalls Mr Bloom's soliloquy at the funeral of Dignam:[3] 'Wise men say. There are more women than men in the world', a fragment of a comic song which continues:

> That's why some girls
> Are single all their lives,
> Six women to every man,
> Say, girls, say if you can,
> Why can't every man
> Have six wives?

1. Mulligan, the 'lubber jester', is the clown in the 'Circus of the Idea'. The 'split scone' is a recall of the scene in the 'D.B.C.' tea-shop (page 235). 'Kinch' is one of Mulligan's nicknames for Stephen.

2. *Ulysses*, page 6.   3. page 94.

This uttering by the phantom of Stephen's mother of words which were in Mr Bloom's mind earlier in the day (other instances of such recalls follow) suggests a momentarily complete fusion of their personalities, of 'fatherless' son and sonless father.

Again, the mother says to Stephen, 'I pray for you in that other world'. 'That other world' is one of the phrases which have haunted Mr Bloom's soliloquies throughout the day. It is a fragment from Martha's letter: 'I do not like that other world' ('word', she meant to typewrite). The deliberate bathos of these citations is characteristic of Joyce's handling of tragic moments.

Stephen grows pale and Bloom opens the window more.

THE MOTHER [*with smouldering eyes*]: Repent! O, the fire of hell!

STEPHEN [*panting*]: The corpsechewer! Raw head and bloody bones!

THE MOTHER [*her face drawing near and nearer, sending out an ashen breath*]: Beware! [*She raises her blackened, withered right arm slowly towards Stephen's breast with outstretched fingers.*] Beware! God's hand! [*A green crab with malignant red eyes sticks deep its grinning claws in Stephen's heart.*] ...

STEPHEN: *Nothung!*

[*He lifts his ashplant high with both hands and smashes the chandelier. Time's livid final flame leaps and, in the following darkness, ruin of all space, shattered glass and toppling masonry.*]

THE GAS JET: Pwfungg!

Stephen's exclamation 'Raw head and bloody bones!' is an echo of Bloom's disgust at the sights of the Lestrygonian butcher's shop.[1] 'Butcher's buckets wobble lights. Give us that brisket off the hook. Plup. Raw head and bloody bones.' Here, as elsewhere, Stephen sees in the Deity a Lord of Death, *dio boia*, hangman god, a ghoul, a butcher.

'Stephen, abandoning his ashplant, his head and arms thrown back stark, beats the ground and flees from the room ...' Bloom lifts the ashplant towards the lamp to prove to Bella that only the paper shade has suffered. Bella (as Circe, when Odysseus raised his sword against her, and 'with a great cry she slipped under') shrinks away screaming 'Don't!' He settles with a shilling and hurries after Stephen, whom he finds attempting to engage in a philosophical discussion with two drunken soldiers. Stephen is still hallucinated by the fumes of intoxication. 'My centre of gravity is misplaced. I have forgotten the trick. ... (*He taps his brow*) But in here it is I must kill the priest and the king.'

1. *Ulysses*, page 159.

The soldiers believe that, after insulting their girl, he is now insulting their king, and defy him to 'say it again'. Grotesque partisans intervene in the phantom conflict, Dolly Gray to cheer the soldiers on, Old Gummy Granny (the old milk-woman of the first episode, 'poor old Ireland', the 'King of Spain's daughter'), seated on a 'midnight mushroom', admonishing Stephen: 'Remove him, acushla.' A composite Irish 'wild goose', one of those expatriate Irishmen who have made their name in the service of foreign states,[1] Don Emile Patrizio Franz Rupert Pope Hennessy, speaking in a mixture of many tongues, urges Stephen to overthrow the pigs of 'johnyellows'. 'Werf those eykes to footboden, big grand porcos of johnyellows todos covered of gravy!'

The soldiers are no less truculent; such language, indeed, as they use in this passage of words had probably never appeared in print before. There is a cry of 'Police!' and distant voices call: 'Dublin's burning! Dublin's burning! On fire! On fire!' Amid a *Götterdämmerung* of brimstone fires and the booming of guns, the dead arise, a chasm opens, it rains dragon's teeth, armed heroes spring up from the furrows, and the Irish clans joust together.

A Black Mass is celebrated, a blasphemous parody of the Sacrament, where the voices of Adonai and the Damned, reversing the holy words,[2] call, in antiphone with the Blessed, *Dooooooooooog!* and *Htengier Tnetopinmo Dog Drol eht rof, Aiulella!*[3]

The hallucination passes. Despite Bloom's efforts at reconciliation, Private Carr fells Stephen to the ground. Corny Kelleher appears out of darkness in the nick of time (another example of the white flower of luck that springs from a dark root) to pacify the officious night-watch. Bloom is left standing alone over the prostrate body of Stephen, who, gradually coming to, murmurs fragments of Yeats's *Countess Cathleen.*

STEPHEN [*groans*]: Who? Black panther vampire. [*He sighs and stretches himself, then murmurs thickly with prolonged vowels*]

Who ... drive ... Fergus now.
And pierce ... wood's woven shade? ...

1. For example, MacMahon in France, O'Donnell, Duke of Tetuan, in Spain, Taafe in Austria.

2. Cf. the Kabalistic axiom: *Daemon est Deus inversus.*

3. The cry *Alleluia!*, as M. Bérard observed, has a curiously Greek resonance. 'Le mot *ololuxan*, ὀλόλυξαν, dont le poète désigne les cris des Achéennes (*Odyssey*, III: 450–2), me semble bien voisin de ces alleluias, que vont répétant nos fidèles, sans savoir qu'ils parlent hébreu.'

[*He turns on his left side, sighing, doubling himself together.*]

BLOOM: Poetry. Well educated. Pity. [*He bends again and undoes the buttons of Stephen's waistcoat.*] To breathe. [*He brushes the wood shavings from Stephen's clothes with light hands and fingers.*] One pound seven. Not hurt anyhow. [*He listens*] What!

STEPHEN [*murmurs*]:

> ... shadows ... the woods.
> ... white breast ... dim ...

[*He stretches out his arms, sighs again and curls his body.* BLOOM *holding his hat and ashplant stands erect. A dog barks in the distance.* BLOOM *tightens and loosens his grip on the ashplant. He looks down on Stephen's face and form.*]

BLOOM [*communes with the night*]: Face reminds me of his poor mother. In the shady wood. The deep white breast. Ferguson, I think I caught. A girl. Best thing could happen him ... [*He murmurs*] ... swear that I will always hail, ever conceal, never reveal, any part or parts, art or arts... [*He murmurs*] in the rough sands of the sea ... a cabletow's length from the shore ... where the tide ebbs ... and flows ...

[*Silent, thoughtful, alert, he stands on guard, his fingers at his lips in the attitude of secret master. Against the dark wall a figure appears slowly, a fairy boy of eleven, a changeling, kidnapped, dressed in an Eton suit with glass shoes and a little bronze helmet, holding a book in his hand. He reads from right to left inaudibly, smiling, kissing the page.*]

BLOOM [*wonderstruck, calls inaudibly*]: Rudy!

RUDY [*gazes unseeing into Bloom's eyes and goes on reading, kissing, smiling. He has a delicate mauve face. On his suit he has diamond and ruby buttons. In his free left hand he holds a slim ivory cane with a violet bowknot. A white lambkin peeps out of his waistcoat pocket.*]

There have been hints in previous episodes that Mr Bloom is a Freemason, and several masonic terms and ritual formulas are employed in this, the 'magic' episode of *Ulysses*.[1] Here Mr Bloom, hearing Stephen's broken whispers (which, however, he misunderstands), murmurs to himself fragments of the masonic oath of secrecy.

In the vision of Rudy, Mr Bloom's dead son, a tranquil close after the bestiality, the pandemonium, the cataclysms of the 'Circe' pantomime, we have a moment of almost Dickensian tenderness. Bloom, gazing at Stephen, remembers Rudy in his tiny coffin of white deal, glass-lidded, clamped with bronze, 'a dwarf's face mauve and

---

1. 'The fraternity [of the freemasons] originated in magic and amongst alchemists and magicians.' A. E. Waite, *The Occult Sciences*.

wrinkled',[1] clad in a little corselet of lamb's wool, his mother's last gift lest he should feel cold in the grave.[2] From the mists of memory he conjures up an elfin boy of eleven (Rudy's age, had he lived) with the trappings of death transmuted into a sparkling panoply of fairyland, a changeling, than any earthborn child 'goodlier far', like the Achaean heroes released from the rough magic of a Circean stye.

The motion is ended.

This calm that follows a hurricane of passions is other than the druid peace of *Cymbeline* which concluded the turmoil of ideas in the 'Shakespearian' episode; it is, rather, the physical appeasement of a wave-worn mariner who, riding out a tempest mad with magic, has made at last the haven where he would be.

> These our actors,
> As I foretold you, were all spirits, and
> Are melted into air, into thin air:
> And, like the baseless fabric of this vision,
> The cloud-capp'd towers, the gorgeous palaces,
> The solemn temples, the great globe itself,
> Yea, all which it inherit, shall dissolve,
> And, like this insubstantial pageant faded,
> Leave not a rack behind.

1. *Ulysses*, page 88.
2. 'I suppose I oughtn't to have buried him in that little woolly jacket I knitted crying as I was.'

16. EUMAEUS

SCENE	The Shelter
HOUR	1 a.m.
ORGAN	Nerves
ART	Navigation
SYMBOL	Sailors
TECHNIC	Narrative (old)

PREPARATORY to anything else Mr Bloom brushed off the greater bulk of the shavings and handed Stephen the hat and ashplant and bucked him up generally in orthodox Samaritan fashion, which he very badly needed. His (Stephen's) mind was not exactly what you would call wandering but a bit unsteady and on his expressed desire for some beverage to drink Mr Bloom, in view of the hour it was and there being no pumps of Vartry water available for their ablutions, let alone for drinking purposes, hit upon an expedient by suggesting, off the reel, the propriety of the cabman's shelter, as it was called, hardly a stonesthrow away near Butt Bridge, where they might hit upon some drinkables in the shape of a milk and soda or a mineral. But how to get there was the rub.

It is now well after midnight and no vehicle is to be found. Mr Bloom, indignant at the manner in which Stephen's companions have all deserted him, is determined to play the 'orthodox Samaritan' to the end. As they walk slowly on, he profits by the occasion and the taciturnity of his companion to deliver a verbose homily on the dangers of nighttown and the providential appearance of Corny Kelleher, failing whom Stephen might have ended the night in the lock-up.

You frittered away your time, he very sensibly maintained, and health and also character besides which the squandermania of the thing, fast women of the *demimonde* ran away with a lot of £ s. d. into the bargain and the greatest danger of all was who you got drunk with though, touching the much vexed question of stimulants, he relished a glass of choice old wine in season as both nourishing and bloodmaking and possessing aperient virtues (notably good burgundy which he was a staunch believer in) still never beyond a certain point where he invariably drew the line as it simply led to trouble all round to say nothing of your being at the tender mercy of others practically.

On their way to the shelter they pass the sentrybox of a corporation watchman, whom, by an effort, Stephen recognizes as one Gumley, 'a quondam friend of his father's', now on the rocks. A 'figure of middle height', prowling in the darkness, now salutes Stephen, and Mr Bloom, seeing Stephen stop to speak with the dark unknown, has an anxious moment. 'Although unusual in the Dublin area, he knew that it was not by any means unknown for desperadoes who had next to nothing to live on to be about waylaying and generally terrorising peaceable pedestrians by placing a pistol at their head in some secluded spot out-side the city proper.' The nightbird turns out to be 'Lord' John Corley, whose

genealogy came about in this wise. He was the eldest son of Inspector Corley of the G Division, lately deceased, who had married a certain Katherine Brophy, the daughter of a Louth farmer. His grandfather, Patrick Michael Corley, of New Ross, had married the widow of a publican there whose maiden name had been Katherine (also) Talbot. Rumour had it, though not proved, that she des-cended from the house of the Lords Talbot de Malahide in whose mansion, really an unquestionably fine residence of its kind and well worth seeing, his mother or aunt or some relative had enjoyed the distinction of being in service in the washkitchen. This, therefore, was the reason why the still comparatively young though dissolute man who now addressed Stephen was spoken of by some with facetious proclivities as Lord John Corley.

This Corley's appearance was described in the tale of 'Two Gallants' (*Dubliners*). 'His head was large, globular and oily; it sweated in all weathers; and his large round hat, set upon it sideways, looked like a bulb which had grown out of another. Whenever any job was vacant a friend was always ready to give him the hard word.' According to his habit, he asks Stephen 'where in God's earth he could get something, anything at all to do'. Stephen replies that there will be a job tomorrow or the next day at Mr Garrett Deasy's school at Dalkey. Corley recites a tale of woe. 'Though this sort of thing went on every other night or very near it still Stephen's feelings got the better of him in a sense though he knew that Corley's brandnew rigmarole, on a par with the others, was hardly deserving of much credence.' He feels in his pockets for money and fishes out what he believes to be pennies. Corley loyally – the Talbot de Malahide touch – points out to Stephen his error, but accepts one of the half-crowns. Stephen rejoins Mr Bloom who has been cruising in the offing and the latter resumes consideration of the problem where Stephen is to sleep, now that his friends have 'ratted'.

After passing an ice-cream car where some Italians are exchanging obscene abuse they at last enter the cabman's shelter, kept, the story went, by Fitzharris the 'Invincible', popularly known as Skin-the-Goat.[1] The company consists of jarvies or stevedores and a 'redbearded bibulous individual, a portion of whose hair was greyish, a sailor, probably'.[2] Mr Bloom, having ordered a cup of coffee and bun for Stephen, discourses on the beauty of the Italian language ('*Bella Poetria!* it is so melodious and full. *Belladonna voglio*'), the correct pronunciation of which is one of his preoccupations, doubtless because the repertoire of 'Madame Marion Tweedy' is partly drawn from Italian opera. Stephen observes that sounds are impostures; the Italians were merely haggling over money.

The rufous mariner, learning that Stephen's name is Dedalus, remarks that he has heard of Stephen's father.

'He's Irish,' the seaman bold affirmed … 'All Irish.'
'All too Irish,' Stephen rejoined.

The sailor explains that 'a matter of ten years ago' (a Trojan memory) he saw Mr Dedalus shoot two eggs off bottles over his shoulder, left-handed, at Stockholm, in Hengler's Royal Circus. 'Curious coincidence,' Mr Bloom unobtrusively confides to his young convoy.

Encouraged by Skin-the-Goat, the sailor, after asking and receiving from one of the navigators of the streets a quid of tobacco, launches out on a series of tall tales.

'I seen a crocodile bite the fluke of an anchor same as I chew that quid.'
He took out of his mouth the pulpy quid and, lodging it between his teeth, bit ferociously.
'Khaan! Like that. And I seen maneaters in Peru that eats corpses and the livers of horses. Look here. Here they are. A friend of mine sent me.'
He fumbled out a picture postcard from his inside pocket, which seemed to be in its way a species of repository, and pushed it along the table. The printed matter on it stated: *Choza de Indios. Beni, Bolivia.*

1. The 'Invincibles' were the gang which on 6 May 1882, in broad daylight, murdered the Chief Secretary, Lord Frederick Cavendish, and an Under-Secretary, Mr Thomas Burke, in Phoenix Park. The murderers were detected and hanged; other Invincibles were condemned to penal servitude. The Phoenix Park murders are mentioned in the 'Aeolus' episode.
2. All these persons, it will be noted, are concerned with navigation, urban or maritime. The art of this episode is 'navigation'.

All focussed their attention on the scene exhibited, at a group of savage women in striped loincloths ... outside some primitive shanties of osier.

'Chews coca all day long,' the communicative tarpaulin added. 'Stomachs like breadgraters.' ...

'Know how to keep them off?' he inquired genially.

Nobody volunteering a statement, he winked, saying:

'Glass. That boggles 'em. Glass.'

Mr Bloom, without evincing surprise, unostentatiously turned over the card to peruse the partially obliterated address and postmark. It ran as follows: *Tarjeta Postal, Señor A. Boudin, Galeria Becche, Santiago, Chile.* There was no message evidently, as he took particular notice. Though not an implicit believer in the lurid story narrated (or the eggsniping transaction for that matter despite William Tell and the Lazarillo–Don Cesar de Bazan incident depicted in *Maritana* on which occasion the former's ball passed through the latter's hat) having detected a discrepancy between his name (assuming he was the person he represented himself to be and not sailing under false colours after having boxed the compass on the strict q.t. somewhere) and the fictitious addressee of the missive which made him nourish some suspicions of our friend's *bona fides* nevertheless it reminded him in a way of a longcherished plan he meant to one day realize some Wednesday or Saturday of travelling to London *via* long sea not to say that he had ever travelled extensively to any great extent but he was at heart a born adventurer though by a trick of fate he had consistently remained a landlubber except you call going to Holyhead which was his longest.

Our perforce sedentary Ulysses now boxes the compass of imaginary circular tours and, coming back as usual to thoughts of his Penelope, considers the possibilities of arranging an extensive concert-tour for her with an 'all-star Irish cast'. He reviews the 'beauty-spots' of Ireland – Poulaphouca (the Circean waterfall),

... Wicklow, rightly termed the garden of Ireland, an ideal neighbourhood for elderly wheelmen, so long as it didn't come down, and in the wilds of Donegal where, if report spoke true, the *coup d'oeil* was exceedingly grand, though the last-named locality was not easily getatable ... while Howth with its historic associations and otherwise,[1] Silken Thomas, Grace O'Malley, George IV, rhododendrons several hundred feet above sealevel was a favourite haunt with all sorts and conditions of men, especially in the spring when young men's fancy, though it had its own toll of deaths by falling off the cliffs by design or accidentally, usually, by the way, on their left leg. ...

Meanwhile the ancient mariner continues his yarn-spinning; the

1. See *Ulysses*, pages 167, 359 and 516.

Chinese 'cooks rats in your soup', he says; they have 'little pills like putty' that open in water and every pill is something different, a house, a ship, a flower.

'And I seen a man killed in Trieste by an Italian chap. Knife in his back. Knife like that.'

Whilst speaking he produced a dangerous looking claspknife, quite in keeping with his character, and held it in the striking position.

'In a knockingshop it was count of a tryon between two smugglers. Fellow hid behind a door, come up behind him. Like that. *Prepare to meet your God*, says he. Chuck! It went into his back up to the butt.'

Mr Bloom attempts to divert the stream of maritime reminiscence towards Gibraltar and Europa Point, scenes of Marion's youth, but without success.

Our *soi-disant* sailor munched heavily awhile, hungrily, before answering.

'I'm tired of all them rocks in the sea,' he said, 'and boats and ships. Salt junk all the time.'

Tired, seemingly, he ceased. His questioner, perceiving that he was not likely to get a great deal of change out of such a wily old customer, fell to woolgathering on the enormous dimensions of the water about the globe. Suffice it to say that, as a casual glance at the map revealed, it covered full three-fourths of it and he fully realized accordingly what it meant, to rule the waves.

The seaman drags his shirt open 'so that, on top of the mariner's hope and rest, they had a full view of the figure 16 and a young man's sideface looking frowningly rather'. By stretching the skin he persuades the tattoo-man (Antonio, by name) to gape in a sort of smile.

'Ay, ay,' sighed the sailor, looking down on his manly chest. 'He's gone too. Ate by sharks after. Ay, ay.' ...

'And what's the number for?' loafer number two queried.

'Eaten alive?' a third asked the sailor.

'Ay, ay,' sighed again the latter personage, more cheerily this time, with some sort of a half smile, for a brief duration only, in the direction of the questioner about the number. 'A Greek he was.'

For a moment the wandering prostitute, with a 'face like dip', seen by Mr Bloom earlier in the day, when he was putting off from Siren Island, peers into the tavern. Mr Bloom charitably comments on her unhappy lot.

'Unfortunate creature! Of course, I suppose some man is ultimately responsible for her condition. Still no matter what the cause is from ...'

Stephen had not noticed her and shrugged his shoulders, merely remarking:

'In this country people sell much more than she ever had and do a roaring trade. Fear not them that sell the body but have not power to buy the soul. She is a bad merchant. She buys dear and sells cheap.'

Mr Bloom maunders on about the 'necessary evil' such women are, till, the purport of Stephen's last observation having gradually penetrated his awareness, he asks Stephen point-blank if he believes in the existence of the soul and receives a characteristic reply.

'They tell me on the best authority it is a simple substance and therefore incorruptible. It would be immortal, I understand, but for possibility of its annihilation by its First Cause, Who, from all I can hear, is quite capable of adding that to the number of His other practical jokes, *corruptio per se* and *corruptio per accidens* being both excluded by court etiquette.'

This 'mystical finesse' is a bit out of Mr Bloom's sublunary depth but he feels bound to enter a sort of demurrer.

Simple? I shouldn't think that is the proper word. Of course, I grant you, to concede a point, you do knock against a simple soul once in a blue moon. But what I am anxious to arrive at is it is one thing for instance to invent those rays Röntgen did, or the telescope like Edison, though I believe it was before his time, Galileo was the man I mean. The same applies to the laws, for example, of a farreaching natural phenomenon such as electricity but it's a horse of quite another colour to say you believe in the existence of a supernatural God.

It is curious how, throughout this episode, these two complementary personages, at last united in intimate conversation, talk at cross-purposes. As Mr Bloom would say, it is a case of East is East and West is West. But that, perhaps, is the secret of true 'atonement'. *Ne rien comprendre c'est tout pardonner.*

Mr Bloom proceeds to discourse on the sad end of Antonio; by extension, on the wild ways of Italians and Spaniards in general, and, by intention, of the southern charms of Calpe's daughter in particular. 'All are washed in the blood of the sun.' The denizens of the shelter babble meanwhile of shipwrecks, of barratry and the like till Skin-the-Goat, who has a reputation to keep up, serves them the *crambe repitita* of Irish symposia, a diatribe on the grievances of Erin. Mr Bloom regards his prediction of England's impending downfall as 'egregious balderdash'. 'Pending that consummation devoutly to be or not to be wished for, he was fully cognisant of the fact that their neighbours across the channel, unless they were much bigger fools than he took them for, rather concealed their strength than the opposite.' He considered it was 'highly advisable in the interim to try to make the most of both countries'. Skin-the-Goat's outburst reminds him of his passage at arms with the Cyclops and he asks Stephen's opinion of his gentle reminder that, after all, the founder of the Christian religion was a Jew.

'*Ex quibus*,' Stephen mumbled in a noncommittal accent, their two or four eyes conversing, *Christus* or Bloom his name is, or, after all, any other, *secundum carnem*.

Mr Bloom proclaims himself the adept of a vague socialism, picturing an earthly paradise 'where you can live well if you work'. 'Count me out,' Stephen says. Mr Bloom hastens to explain that he includes brain-workers in his ideal state. Brain and brawn are equally important.

'You suspect,' Stephen retorted with a sort of a half laugh, 'that I may be important because I belong to the *faubourg Saint Patrice* called Ireland for short.'
'I would go a step farther,' Mr Bloom insinuated.
'But I suspect,' Stephen interrupted, 'that Ireland must be important because it belongs to me.'[1]
'What belongs?' queried Mr Bloom, bending, fancying he was under some misapprehension. 'Excuse me. Unfortunately I didn't catch the latter portion. What was it you ...?'
Stephen, patently crosstempered, repeated and shoved aside his mug of coffee, or whatever you like to call it, none too politely, adding:
'We can't change the country. Let us change the subject.'

Meanwhile the general conversation has drifted round to that pet topic of such gatherings fifty years ago – the lost leader Parnell and the chances of his 'return'.

'There was every indication they would arrive at that,' Mr Bloom said.
'Who?' the other, whose hand by the way was hurt, said.
One morning you would open the paper, the cabman affirmed, and read *Return of Parnell*. He bet them what they liked. A Dublin fusilier was in that shelter one night and said he saw him in South Africa. Pride it was killed him.

1. Cf. Stephen's remark to the drunken soldiers: 'You die for your country, suppose. ... But I say: Let my country die for me.' Thus Plotinus, when he was asked to attend worship of the gods, arrogantly answered: 'It is for them (the spirits) to come to me.' (*Isis Unveiled*, 1, 489.)

He ought to have done away with himself or lain low for a time after Committee Room No. 15 until he was his old self again with no-one to point a finger at him. Then they would all to a man have gone down on their marrowbones to him to come back when he had recovered his senses. Dead he wasn't. Simply absconded somewhere. The coffin they brought over was full of stones. He changed his name to De Wet, the Boer general. He made a mistake to fight the priests. And so forth and so on.

Mr Bloom recalls an occasion when, in a brawl, Parnell's hat had been knocked off and he (Bloom) had handed it back to him.[1] Parnell merely said 'Thank you' but 'in a very different tone of voice from the ornament of the legal profession whose headgear Bloom also set to rights earlier in the course of the day,[2] history repeating itself with a difference'. (The last six words are an unconscious allusion to the Bloom–Ulysses correspondence.) Mr Bloom expounds his views as to the possibility and the desirability, or otherwise, of Parnell's return. He alludes to the woman who wrecked Parnell's career – 'if I don't greatly mistake, she was Spanish too' – and takes the opportunity of showing Stephen Mrs Bloom's photograph. Presently he wanders off into a muddled diatribe on the popular and journalistic attitude to matrimonial complications.

An awful lot of makebelieve went on about that sort of thing involving a lifelong slur with the usual splash page of letterpress about the same old matrimonial tangle alleging misconduct with professional golfer or the newest stage favourite instead of being honest and aboveboard about the whole business. How they were fated to meet and an attachment sprang up between the two so that their names were coupled in the public eye was told in court with letters containing the habitual mushy and compromising expressions, leaving no loophole, to show that they openly cohabited two or three times a week at some wellknown seaside hotel and relations, when the thing ran its normal course, became in due course intimate. Then the decree *nisi* and the King's Proctor to show cause why and, he failing to quash it, *nisi* was made absolute. But as for that, the two misdemeanants, wrapped up as they largely were in one another, could safely afford to ignore it as they very largely did till the matter was put in the hands of a solicitor, who filed a petition for the party wronged in due course.

It seemed a thousand pities to Mr Bloom that Stephen, with his brains, should waste his 'valuable time with profligate women'.

1. Cf. the opening line of this episode: 'Preparatory to anything else Mr Bloom … handed Stephen the hat and ashplant.' The *rapprochement* is, of course, deliberate.
2. See the 'Hades' episode.

In the nature of single blessedness he would one day take unto himself a wife when Miss Right came on the scene but in the interim ladies' society was a *conditio sine qua non* though he had the gravest possible doubts, not that he wanted in the smallest to pump Stephen about Miss Ferguson, as to whether he would find much satisfaction basking in the boy and girl courtship idea and the company of smirking misses without a penny to their names bi- or tri-weekly with the orthodox preliminary canter of complimentpaying and walking out leading up to fond lovers' ways and flowers and chocs. ... The queer suddenly things he popped out with attracted the elder man who was several the other's senior or like his father.

Mr Bloom learns that Stephen has had no dinner and his protective instinct as well as that subtler feeling of which he is hardly conscious impels him to invite Stephen to Eccles Street to spend the night at his house. They leave the jarvies and the mariner to yawn the night out in the shelter and, as Stephen is still 'a bit weak on his pins', Mr Bloom gives him an arm. They now converse of music; Mr Bloom speaks with approval of 'Mercadante's *Huguenots*', 'Meyerbeer's *Seven Last Words on the Cross*' and the 'immortal numbers' of Rossini's *Stabat Mater*. 'He had a penchant, though only with a surface knowledge, for the severe classical school such as Mendelssohn'. Stephen 'launched out into praises of Shakespeare's songs, at least of in or about that period', Dowland, Tomkins and John Bull; and Mr Bloom naturally inquired 'if it was John Bull the political celebrity of that ilk'. The episode ends with Mr Bloom's peripatetic dream of a brilliant musical career for his protégé who in a 'phenomenally beautiful tenor voice' is singing, as they fare towards the well-builded halls of Penelope, a 'retrospective sort of' song.

> Von der Sirenen Listigkeit
> Tun die Poeten Dichten.
>
> . . . .
> Und alle Schiffe brücken.

*

The technic of 'Eumaeus', first of the three episodes which compose the third and last part of *Ulysses*, corresponding to the '*Nostos*' ('Return') panel of the Homeric triptych, is 'narrative (old)'. It stands in counterpoise to the first episode of the first part ('Telemachus') whose technic is 'narrative (young)'. The personages in 'Telemachus' are, with one exception, young men; in 'Eumaeus' all save Stephen are old or middle-aged. In 'Telemachus' the time is early morning; 'warm sunshine merrying the sea'. On their way to the Eumaean tavern Mr Bloom and Stephen walk through dark, deserted streets, where the only vestiges of human occupation are forlorn vagrants who spring to uncertain life from dim archways, caves of darkness, and the 'scythed car' of the street-sweeper. Mr Bloom is weary and his thoughts no longer burn with a clear rubious flame, or indeed with any flame at all. He is too exhausted to achieve a logical ending to most of his periods. His fancies, irresolute and untended, wander away into murky culs-de-sac. The style seems to be paralysed by that sort of aphasia which the Germans aptly name *Hexenschuss*, an after-effect of Circe's bane. The silent monologue, utterly disintegrated, ramifies into the structure of an equally decrepit narrative, so that not only the meditations of Mr Bloom but descriptive passages, too, are clouded o'er with the dark cast of fatigue. Stephen has little to say for himself at first; his recovery from the *enfer artificiel* of Circe is gradual. Even what little he says, as the fumes slowly dissipate, seems almost unintelligible to Mr Bloom, who is no hand at following Daedalian flights of fancy.

The cabman's shelter kept by Skin-the-Goat corresponds to the steading of the swineherd Eumaeus, whither Odysseus fared, disguised as a beggar, on his return to Ithaca. This tavern was situated near the docks and frequented by a mixed European–Asiatic population, a suitable background for the beginning of an intimacy (as far as intimacy was possible) between Stephen and Mr Bloom. The false story told by Odysseus to Eumaeus – the rigmarole concerning his Cretan parentage, his journeys into Libya and Dulichium, his expedition to Egypt – finds a spokesman in the marine Munchausen, an Odysseus Pseudangelos sailing under false colours, who regales the gaping jarvies with his yarns.

One of the persons who accompanied Telemachus to Eumaeus's hut where, on his return from Pylos, he met his father and together they compassed the destruction of the suitors, was the seer Theoclymenos (already referred to in my notes on the 'Hades' episode). In 'Eumaeus' there is a passage of fifty-odd lines, akin to that where the 'mystery man', M'Intosh, appeared, wearing the same irrelevant air of an Homeric interpolation. This passage describes Stephen's brief encounter with 'Lord' John Corley, who appears from and returns to darkness, unwanted, insignificant. 'Lord' Corley has no relevance to the narrative, and one may picture some Martian scholiast of *Ulysses* three thousand years hence suggesting that this incident was interpolated by an obsequious editor to immortalize the family name of the Malahide Corleys. As in the Homeric texts an interpolation is placed between two more or less identical lines, so here Mr Bloom's monologue recommences, when Stephen has quitted Corley, at the point where it broke off, that is to say with the 'ratting' of his boon companions once they had succeeded in getting drunk at his expense. Corley, like Theoclymenos, came of a good family, as his genealogy suggests, though not without a certain *gaucherie*, so to speak; such 'left-handedness' is, for reasons given hereafter, a characteristic feature of the 'Eumaeus' episode. In much the same roundabout way the family-tree of Theoclymenos is set out in Book XV of the *Odyssey*.

The leading theme of this episode is the return of the wanderer home from sea after long absence, a favourite epic subject, like that of the son who roams the world over in quest of a father,[1] with which (as here) it is naturally allied. At the close of the 'Proteus' episode Stephen saw 'moving through the air high spars of a threemaster, her sails brailed up on the crosstrees, homing upstream, silently moving, a silent ship', and, two hours later, Mr Bloom's skiff Elijah, light crumpled throwaway, sailed eastward by the threemasted schooner *Rosevean* from Bridgwater with bricks. It was this very bark that bore the *soi-disant* wave-worn wanderer W. B. Murphy, A.B., and Pseudangelos, to his native shore.

'That's right,' the sailor said, 'Fort Camden and Fort Carlisle. That's where I hails from. My little woman's down there. She's waiting for me ... my own true wife I haven't seen for seven years now, sailing about.'

Mr Bloom could easily picture his advent on this scene – the homecoming to the mariner's roadside shieling after having diddled Davy Jones – a rainy night with a blind moon.[2] Across the world for a wife. Quite a number of stories

1. Thus in his *Untersuchungen über die Sagen vom Tod des Odysseus*, a treatise rich in suggestions for those who desire to study, beyond the scope of this commentary, the Joycean treatment of the Odysseus legend, the author (Albert Hartmann) remarks: '*Diese Untersuchung hat gezeigt, wie man das Motiv vom Sohn, der den fernen Vater sucht, im Lauf der Zeit durch alle Möglichkeiten hindurchvariiert hat. Dass ein Sohn nach dem fernen Vater in die Welt auszieht, ist bei Irrfahrtsagen eine denkbar naheliegende und einfache Erfindung; die verschiedenen Möglichkeiten des Ausgangs sich auszudenken, erfordert nicht viel mehr Erfindungsgabe.*'

2. Compare the story of Odysseus Pseudangelos in the fourteenth book of the *Odyssey*. 'For seven whole years I abode with their king, and gathered much

there were on that particular Alice Ben Bolt topic, Enoch Arden and Rip van Winkle and does anybody hereabouts remember Caoc O'Leary. ... Never about the runaway wife coming back, however much devoted to the absentee. The face at the window! Judge of his astonishment when he finally did breast the tape and the awful truth dawned upon him anent his better half, wrecked in his affections. You little expected me but I've come to stay and make a fresh start. There she sits, a grass widow, at the selfsame fireside. Believes me dead. ... No chair for father. Boo! The wind! Her brandnew arrival is on her knee, *post mortem* child. With a high ro! and a randy ro! and my galloping tearing tandy O! Bow to the inevitable. Grin and bear it. I remain with much love your brokenhearted husband, W. B. Murphy.

The 'Flying Dutchman' motif, first introduced in the episode of 'Proteus', reappears in 'Eumaeus'.

However, reverting to friend Sinbad and his horrifying adventures (who reminded him a bit of Ludwig, *alias* Ledwidge, when he occupied the boards of the Gaiety when Michael Gunn was identified with the management in the *Flying Dutchman*, a stupendous success, and his host of admirers came in large numbers, everyone simply flocking to hear him though ships of any sort, phantom or the reverse, on the stage usually fell a bit flat as also did trains), there was nothing intrinsically impossible about it, he conceded.

The tattoo mark on the sailor's chest, the number 16[1] beside Antonio's face – 'a Greek he was'[2] – can be historically associated with the 'homecoming' of a pretender, for tattoo marks have played an important part in the solution of such problems of identity as the Tichbourne case. Thus Lord Bellew, a schoolfellow of Roger Tichbourne, deposed that he had seen tattooed on the arm of the latter a cross, heart, and anchor and had himself added, in Indian ink, the letters R.C.T. The

---

substance among the Egyptians. ... But when we left Crete, and no land showed in sight but sky and sea only, even then the son of Cronos stayed a dark cloud over the hollow ship and the deep waxed dark beneath it.' Odysseus goes on to relate how, when the ship was smitten by a bolt of Zeus, the crew fell overboard 'and the god cut off their return', he alone was saved after nine days' peril on 'great rolling waves', clinging to 'the huge mast of the dark-prowed ship'.

1. '*Blasio vit à Naples une prostituée ayant sur le ventre une femme nue, sur la mamelle de laquelle on lisait les deux nombres 6 et 16 qui, dans l'argot napolitain, signifient deux formes de coit; au-dessous était écrit le nom de la femme, à côte de celui de l'amant qui avait dessiné le tatouage.' Les Tatouages*, Collection de Psychologie Populaire de Dr Jaf.

2. For a similar use of the word 'Greek', compare Mulligan's comment on Mr Bloom, whom he saw considering, *a posteriori*, the Museum statues: 'O, I fear me, he is Greeker than the Greeks. ... Venus Kallipyge.'

absence of such tattoo marks was conclusive proof of the falsity of the claim advanced by the homecoming Australian pretender. Mr Bloom, in the course of his rambling monologue, directly alludes to the Tichbourne case.

Still, as regards return, you were a lucky dog if they didn't set the terrier at you directly you got back. Then a lot of shillyshally usually followed. Tom for and Dick and Harry against. And then, number one, you came up against the man in possession and had to produce your credentials, like the claimant in the Tichbourne case, Roger Charles Tichbourne, *Bella* was the boat's name to the best of his recollection he, the heir, went down in, as the evidence went to show, and there was a tattoo mark too in Indian ink, Lord Bellew, was it? As he might very easily have picked up the details from some pal on board ship and then, when got up to tally with the description given, introduce himself with, Excuse me, my name is So-and-So or some such commonplace remark. A more prudent course, Mr Bloom said, to the not over effusive, in fact like the distinguished personage under discussion beside him, would have been to sound the lie of the land first.

Mr Bloom's 'got up to tally' may contain an allusion to another famous impostor, Vidocq, who, more fortunate than the Tichbourne claimant, personated one Auguste Duval, after having 'picked up the details' from a sailor formerly acquainted with the real Duval, who had died two years before at St-Pierre de Martinique. This Duval had tattoo marks on his left arm, an altar with a wreath above it, and the impostor's friend successfully reproduced these marks of identification on Vidocq's arm. The pseudo-Duval was promptly and positively 'recognized' by the Duval family. Thus even tattoo marks may, like sounds, be 'impostures'.

Mr Bloom's reflections on the reception Parnell would have if, as many supposed, he were not really dead, and returned to Ireland, are an extension of the 'Rip van Winkle' theme,[1] which, not unnaturally,

1. M. Marcel Brion in an interesting essay (in *Our Exagmination round his Factification for Incamination of Work in Progress*) on the time-factor in Joyce's work (which he compares with Proust's), observes that Joyce has 'broken through the too narrow restraints of time and space.' 'Certain thinkers have at times wondered if the essential difference existing between man and God were not a difference of time. ... We measure time but we do not know what it is. We often encounter in mystical literature the story of the monk or poet who has fallen asleep in the forest. When he awakes he no longer recognizes either men or the countryside. His meditation or slumber, which to him has appeared very short, has in reality lasted hundreds of years. But during the moment in which he has been snatched from the

recurs frequently in his thoughts and conversation,[1] along with other legends of a return to the domestic 'shell' 'wigwam' or 'fleshcase',[2] after long absence in a far land, or on another planet.

Mr Bloom, too, is a Wandering Jew, an exile, though only half desirous of repatriation, and the Agendath Netaim prospectus which he picked up at his compatriot, the butcher's shop, early in the morning meant more to him than a mere invitation to take a commercial interest in 'orangegroves and immense melonfields north of Jaffa'. But his common sense tells him that the delights of such a return, whether his or Parnell's or Enoch Arden's, are apt to prove a mere mirage, an idle dream.[3]

Looking back now in a retrospective kind of arrangement, all seemed a kind of dream. And the coming back was the worst thing you ever did because it went without saying you would feel out of place as things always moved with

---

tyranny of time he has caught a glimpse of the mysterious aspects of infinity, he has neared the laws of the Cosmos, the throne of God.' The structure of *Ulysses* (though to a less extent than that of the *Wake*) indicates that Joyce aspired to outsoar the category of time and see a simultaneous universe – to take, so to speak, a God's-eye view of the cosmos.

1. This allusion is also hinted at in Hauptmann's drama *Der Bogen des Odysseus* (Act III. *The interior of Eumaeus' hut*).

'ODYSSEUS: In eines Räuberschiffes
    Bauch lebt'ich fürchterliche Jahre, bis
    Ich alt und krank ward, und die Ruderknechte
    Mich ganz Enträfteten aussetzten. Schlafend
    Schleppten sie mich hierher an euren Strand
    Dies war ein wunderlicher Schlaf, o Greis,
    Und ein Erwachen wie aus tausend Toden.
LAERTES: Du sprichst nicht übel. Doch, wie meinst du das?
ODYSSEUS: Ich plappre nur so gradaus, was mir einfällt,
    Und weiss nicht was, und kann mich nicht erinnern.'

The earliest reference to this theme in *Ulysses* occurs in the 'Calypso' episode. 'Cold oils slid through his veins, chilling his blood: old age crusting him with a salt cloak.' Another is in 'Nausicaa', where Mr Bloom compares himself (the allusion to the 'cyclical' return of metempsychosis is significant in this connexion) to a 'circus horse walking in a ring. Rip van Winkle we played. Rip: tear in Henny Doyle's overcoat. Van: bread van delivering. Winkle: cockles and periwinkles. Then I did Rip van Winkle coming back. She leaned on the sideboard watching. Moorish eyes. Twenty years asleep in Sleepy Hollow. All changed. Forgotten. The young are old. His gun rusty from the dew.' The theme reappears in the 'Circe' and 'Ithaca' episodes, *q.v.*

2. See pages 38 and 180.

3. Even the 'godpossibled' *Nostos* of Moses was, as J. J. O'Molloy points out (in 'Aeolus'), a disappointment – for Moses himself. 'He died without having entered the land of promise.'

the times. Why, as he reflected, Irish town Strand, a locality he had not been in for quite a number of years, looked different somehow since, as it happened, he went to reside on the north side.

On the whole, Mr Bloom decides, Parnell's return from 'complete oblivion' would be 'highly inadvisable'. They would 'set the terrier against him'; Parnell had cooked his goose. A left-handed liaison with a married or divorced woman might just be tolerated in catholic clerical circles, but a subsequent marriage with her put the offender outside the pale.

> *Le scandale du monde est ce qui fait l'offense,*
> *Et ce n'est pas pécher que pécher en silence.*

Mr Bloom faces facts and has little of Stephen's aversion from their logic. He has reached that age when the survival value of conventions, even censorship, are appreciated. ('Where', old wisdom, a Nestor come to judgement, might ask, 'would genius be without Aunt Sally Grundy, the epicure without his *fruit défendu*?') A little latitude from time to time, if you like: *sub rosa*, nothing to talk about. Let not thy right hand know what thy left hand doeth.

There are frequent allusions in 'Eumaeus' to the left side; for instance, the left-handed descent of Corley, Mr Dedalus as a left-hand shot, the fact that persons falling from the Howth cliffs usually land on their left leg. Such references reinforce the theme of the lying messenger who sails under false colours. Mr Bloom, referring to Buck Mulligan's way of 'deprecating' Stephen in his absence, points out that this habit throws 'a nasty sidelight on that side of a person's character – no pun intended'. When Stephen and his pseudo-father together leave the cabman's shelter, the latter 'passed his left arm in Stephen's right', an unusual and symbolic gesture.

Every man has, like the moon, a hidden side, every family a bend sinister, however dexterously disguised, and *nostalgia* may, like *amor matris*,[1] have a bilateral meaning: sorrow for absence and sorrow of return. A *Nostos* must always prove, in some measure, a disappointment, a left-handed boon unhappy in its opportunity; it is in absence of mind, when he is up in the clouds or on his way to Cythera, that man achieves the energy of happiness.

---

1. '*Amor matris*, subjective and objective genitive, may be the only true thing in life.' (*Ulysses*, page 196.)

The whole climax of *Ulysses* [Mr Cyril Connolly has written[1]] is a single moment of intimacy, when Bloom, the comic character, rescues Stephen in a drunken brawl. Bloom had a son who died, Stephen a father who is alive; but for this instant of spiritual paternity all the swelter of that urban summer, all the mesembrian pub-crawls of Bloom and Stephen, the vermin and the scales and the serpents move into place.[2]

'Though they didn't see eye to eye in everything,' Mr Bloom reflects, 'a certain analogy there somehow was, as if both their minds were travelling, so to speak, in the one train of thought.' (This transitory intimacy 'in the one train of thought' was humorously prefigured in Mr Bloom's journey from Westland Row station. 'Nice mixup. Then jump in first class with third ticket. What am I following him for?')

The ultimate return, after 'the greatest possible ellipse', the octave, is an empty consonance; the interest lay in the modulations, the effort towards that goal. After the Circean whirligig of changing lights, the dark hesitant prose of 'Eumaeus' comes as an anticlimax; the scales of the serpent have moved into place and the sparkle has gone out of them.

1. *Life and Letters*, vol. II, No. II.
2. Mr Connolly is alluding to Mr Forster's denunciation of *Ulysses* as 'an epic of grubbiness and disillusion ... in which smaller mythologies swarm and pullulate, like vermin between the scales of a poisonous snake.'

17. ITHACA

SCENE	The House
HOUR	2 a.m.
ORGAN	Skeleton
ART	Science
SYMBOL	Comets
TECHNIC	Catechism (impersonal)

FROM this episode the flesh of sentiment and trappings of style have been stripped till it is little more than a skeleton. The incidents of the interview between Stephen and Mr Bloom in the kitchen of No. 7 Eccles Street, their differences and resemblances, the contents of Mr Bloom's house and of his mind are described meticulously in terms of natural phenomena: or, rather, they are not merely 'described', they are analysed and listed. One is, at times, reminded of the catalogue of some provincial auction-sale whither, a venerable great-aunt having died at last, young heirs have sent *en bloc* the stuffed birds, frayed rugs, gilded chairs, defunct marble clocks – all the long-hoarded treasures of a Victorian home.

The technic of this, the middle chapter of the final triptych ('Catechism, impersonal'), balances that of 'Nestor' ('old wisdom'), the middle chapter of the Telemachia. But while, there, the catechism was personal, informal, and humane, question and answer first between Stephen and his sleepy pupils, then between Mr Deasy and his young assistant, here we have a detailed analysis, precise as the *Summa theologiae*, and the ruthlessness of a theological inquisition. ('Ithaca', it may be mentioned, was Joyce's favourite episode.)

Such a treatment applied to the personages of *Ulysses*, to their aspirations, to the economy and simple equipment of Mr Bloom's home, has a more devastating effect on its object than any calculated gesture of scorn.

Consider the living Helen, queen of beauty, who never dies and once in a life, by Aphrodite's grace, reveals herself to Everyman, and see how she is made. Measure her nose, weigh her ears, and count the hairs of her eyelashes; suppute the number and secretion of her pores, subtract her quarts, pints, and gallons of ubiquitous liquid (ninety per cent of her, as we learn in this episode). Dehydrated, what would she be like? A pearl – or a pat of pigiron? Consider the hundredweights of butcher's meat ('Give us that brisket off the hook. Plup') that have gone to her making, and the spectres of carnage that haunt the court of beauty. And, lo, as in the vision of Theoclymenos, 'the walls and the fair spaces between the pillars are sprinkled with blood, and the porch is full of phantoms and full is the court ... and the sun has perished out of heaven, and an evil mist has overspread the world'. Observe closely, as Virag bade his grandson, 'the mass of oxygenated vegetable matter on her skull. What ho, she bumps!' Such analysis is seduction's surest antidote, a slaughter of the wooers of illusion. For we are now in the small hours of Friday, 17 June, and Friday (as Mr Bloom told us in 'Hades') is the Dublin 'killing day'.

Before the arrows of reason (Bloom bends the bow, but Stephen strings it with his logical method) scruples and false sentiment are scattered 'like a drove of kine that the flitting gadfly falls upon and scatters hither and thither in springtime, when the long days begin'. This massacre of the scruples which have been eating away the hearts of the protagonists is no less thorough, in its own way, than the Homeric slaughter of the Lords of the Isles.[1]

Even, as we shall see, the proud Eurymachus, that suitor who boldly raised his sword against the favoured of Athene – even Boylan the 'bester' falls at last.

In the same moment goodly Odysseus shot the arrow forth and struck him on the breast by the pap and drove the swift shaft into his liver. So he let the sword fall from his hands and grovelling over the table he bowed and fell, and split the food and the double cup on the floor. And in his agony he smote the ground with his brow, and spurning with both his feet he struck against the high seat, and the mist of death was shed upon his eyes.

Mr Bloom and Stephen advance 'at normal walking pace' – for everything in this episode is normal, all-too-normal – towards Eccles Street, the street with a Greek-sounding name, the street of meeting, within sound of the tolling hours of Saint George's Church, the only

1. It is, however, significant that Joyce, characteristically averse from scenes of carnage, compresses his counterpart for the section of Homer's *Odyssey* (a quarter of the entire poem) which deals with the slaughter of the suitors, into a single episode (less than a tenth of *Ulysses*).

church in Dublin with a Greek inscription (referred to in *Finnegans Wake* as 'St George-le-Greek'). And the number in Eccles Street of Mr Bloom's house is *seven*, the sacred number *par excellence* of the East, of the Homeric world.[1]

Mr Bloom finds he has forgotten his latchkey (Freudians please note!) and is doubly annoyed 'because he had forgotten and because he remembered that he had reminded himself twice not to forget'. He enters, as Odysseus revisited his palace, like a menial, by the service door and with the aid of a ruse.

A stratagem. Resting his feet on the dwarf wall, he climbed over the area railings, compressed his hat on his head, grasped two points at the lower union of rails and stiles, lowered his body gradually by its length of five feet nine inches and a half to within two feet ten inches of the area pavement, and allowed his body to move freely in space by separating himself from the railings and crouching in preparation for the impact of the fall.

Did he fall?

By his body's known weight of eleven stone and four pounds in avoirdupois measure, as certified by the graduated machine for periodical selfweighing in the premises of Francis Frœdman, pharmaceutical chemist of 19 Frederick street, north, on the last feast of the Ascension, to wit, the twelfth day of May of the bissextile year one thousand nine hundred and four of the christian era (jewish era five thousand six hundred and sixtyfour, mohammedan era one thousand three hundred and twentytwo), golden number 5, epact 13, solar cycle 9, dominical letters C B, Roman indication 2, Julian period 6617, MXMIV.

Having like a malefactor gained retarded access to the kitchen, he lights the gas (14 C.P.), climbs the stairs (by the light of a candle of 1 C.P.), lets Stephen in by the halldoor, and leads him down to the kitchen. After composing a pyre in the grate, he 'kindled it at three projecting points of paper with one ignited lucifer match, thereby

1. *Seven* was held to be a number of peculiar virtue by Chaldaeans, Phoenicians, Egyptians, and Greeks alike. Thus the Chaldaean towers had seven storeys, Anou seven messengers, Hell seven gates, Sinbad made seven voyages, the Nile has seven mouths, etc. 'We find in the *Odyssey*', M. Bérard observes, 'an alternation of septenary and quinary rhythms, and this system of enumeration is, like the Homeric toponomy, Graeco-semitic.' 'The number seven,' according to Hartmann, 'is the scale of nature, it is represented in all departments of nature from the sun whose light is broken by a dewdrop into the seven colours of the rainbow, down to the snowflake crystallizing in six points round the invisible centre.' 'Seven', as John Eglinton observed (*Ulysses*, page 173), 'is dear to the mystic mind.'

releasing the potential energy contained in the fuel by allowing its carbon and hydrogen elements to enter into free union with the oxygen of the air'.

The contents of the kitchen are minutely described; Bloom sets a saucepan on to boil. The Dublin water-supply system is now expounded as by a municipal engineer and the qualities of water are analysed in detail. Mr Bloom washes his hands 'with a partially consumed tablet of Barrington's lemonflavoured soap, to which paper still adhered (bought thirteen hours previously for fourpence and still unpaid for)'.

Through the greater Odyssey of Bloomsday there runs a 'Little Odyssey', a *Saponiad*, the wandering of the soap – a comic counterpart of the heroic tale. Mr Bloom[1] strolled out of the chemist's shop with the coolwrappered soap, 'sweet lemony wax', in his hand. On his way to the Hammam he folds his famous 'throwaway' newspaper into a square and lodges the soap in it; a few minutes later we observe him using the soap in the bath. As he is being jolted along in the cab, following Dignam's remains, the soap (now in his hip-pocket) adds to his discomfort: 'better shift it out of that'. When an occasion arises,[2] he transfers it 'paperstuck' to his inner handkerchief pocket. In the newspaper office[3] 'he took out his handkerchief to dab his nose. Citronlemon? Ah, the soap I put there. Lose it out of that pocket. Putting back his handkerchief he took out the soap and stowed it away, buttoned, into the hip pocket of his trousers.' At the close of the 'Lestrygonian' adventure, when he espies Blazes Boylan in the offing,[4] 'his hand looking for the where did I put it found in his hip pocket soap lotion have to call tepid paper stuck. Ah, soap there! Yes.' After the meal at the Sirens' restaurant,[5] 'Bloom stood up. Ow. Soap feeling rather sticky behind.' After 'Nausicaa' has left him, Mr Bloom sniffs first the air, then himself.[6] 'Almonds or. No. Lemons it is. Ah no, that's the soap.' As he approaches the palace of Circe,[7] some children run into him. 'Beware of pickpockets. Old thieves' dodge. Collide.' 'Bloom pats with parcelled hands watch, fobpocket, bookpocket, pursepocket, sweets of sin, potato, soap.' Presently, remembering for the nth time that he has forgotten his wife's face-lotion, he decides to get it first thing in the morning and we witness the apotheosis of the soap.[8]

1. *Ulysses*, page 177.   2. page 92.   3. page 114.   4. page 172.
5. page 272.   6. page 358.   7. page 417.   8. page 421.

[*He points to the south, then to the east. A cake of new clean lemon soap arises, diffusing light and perfume.*]

THE SOAP:

> We're a capital couple are Bloom and I;
> He brightens the earth, I polish the sky.

[*The freckled face of* SWENY, *the druggist, appears in the disc of the soapsun.*]

SWENY: Three and a penny, please.

Finally the hero of this Little Odyssey, a celestial *numen* now, is reverently invoked in the litany of the 'Daughters of Erin'.

Wandering Soap, pray for us.

Stephen declined Mr Bloom's suggestion that he should wash his hands, for 'he was hydrophobe, hating partial contact by immersion or total by submersion in cold water (his last bath having taken place in the month of October of the preceding year), disliking the aqueous substances of glass and crystal, distrusting aquacities of thought and language'. Presently the kettle boils and Mr Bloom prepares two cups of cocoa. 'Relinquishing his symposiarchal right to the moustache cup of imitation Crown Derby presented to him by his only daughter, Millicent (Milly), he substituted a cup identical with that of his guest and served extraordinarily to his guest and, in reduced measure, to himself, the viscous cream ordinarily reserved for the breakfast of his wife Marion (Molly).' Mr Bloom jocosely directed Stephen's attention to this mark of hospitality, the offering of ambrosia, usually reserved for a goddess, to his young guest, who accepted it seriously. 'They drank in joco-serious silence Epps's massproduct, the creature cocoa.' (Here the terminology emphasizes the ritualism of Mr Bloom's 'joco-serious' gesture.)

There follows a catechistic exposition of the hero's early years, his attempts at writing poetry, his kindness to old Mrs Riordan ('Dante' of the *Portrait*, a link between Stephen and Bloom), his scant athletic prowess. Neither alluded to their racial difference, but each was aware of it.

What, reduced to their simplest reciprocal form, were Bloom's thoughts about Stephen's thoughts about Bloom and Bloom's thoughts about Stephen's thoughts about Bloom's thoughts about Stephen?

He thought that he thought that he was a jew whereas he knew that he knew that he knew that he was not.

Bloom's scientific temperament (as opposed to Stephen's, the artistic) led him to plan (though not to execute) such inventions as 'astronomical kaleidoscopes exhibiting the twelve constellations of the zodiac', 'miniature mechanical orreries', and the like. He tried vainly to instruct Mrs Bloom, who 'forgot with ease': a Gaea-Tellus oblivious of her creatures' inventions, religions, ideologies, those toys men have contrived to avert their thoughts from her indifference. 'Unusual polysyllables of foreign origin she interpreted phonetically or by false analogy or by both: metempsychosis (met him pike hoses), *alias* (a mendacious person mentioned in sacred Scripture).'

After Stephen has repeated his Parable of the Plums, Mr Bloom cites three examples of 'postexilic eminence': Moses of Egypt, Moses Maimonides (these two 'seekers of pure truth' have been in Stephen's thoughts in the course of the day) and Moses Mendelssohn. They now compare the Hebrew and the Irish languages and history and (like the orator Taylor) discover points of similarity. Stephen chants in a modulated voice a strange legend on an allied theme – the ballad of *Hugh of Lincoln*, or rather an abridged variant, for we do not hear of the 'apple red and green' nor of the voice from the 'deep draw-well'. Stephen's comment on this tale of ritual crime, the murder of the little Christian by the Jew's daughter, is characteristic.

One of all, the least of all, is the victim predestined. Once by inadvertence, twice by design he challenges his destiny. It comes when he is abandoned and challenges him reluctant and, as an apparition of hope and youth, holds him unresisting. It leads him to a strange habitation, to a secret infidel apartment and there, implacable, immolates him, consenting.

Something similar, indeed, has befallen Stephen himself in the brothel, whither, abandoned by all but Judas, he has been seduced by a Jew's daughter (? Zoe). Even Lynch in the end abandoned Stephen, when the latter was involved in the altercation with the redcoats. As Lynch disappeared, Stephen pointed to him, saying: *Exit Judas. Et laqueo se suspendit.*

The early years of Milly Bloom are analysed and her affinities with the domestic cat expounded. Summing up, the catechist decides that 'in passivity, in economy, in the instinct of tradition, in unexpectedness, their differences were similar'.

Mr Bloom proposes that Stephen should stay the night, or what is left of it. Stephen promptly, inexplicably, with amicability, gratefully declines, but undertakes to inaugurate a 'course of vocal instruction' with Mrs Bloom and to engage in 'peripatetic intellectual dialogues' with his host.

What rendered problematic for Bloom the realization of these mutually self-excluding propositions?

The irreparability of the past: once at a performance of Albert Hengler's circus in the Rotunda, Rutland Square, Dublin, an intuitive particoloured clown in quest of paternity had penetrated from the ring to a place in the auditorium where Bloom, solitary, was seated and had publicly declared to an exhilarated audience that he (Bloom) was his (the clown's) papa. The imprevidibility of the future: once in the summer of 1898 he (Bloom) had marked a florin (2s.) with three notches on the milled edge and tendered it in payment of an account due to and received by J. and T. Davy, family grocers, 1 Charlemont Mall, Grand Canal, for circulation on the waters of civic finance, for possible, circuitous or direct, return.

Was the clown Bloom's son?
No.

Had Bloom's coin returned?
Never.

(Here we seem to have 'arrows' directed at the themes of *paternity* and *return*, to which there have been so many allusions in the course of *Ulysses*.)

Mr Bloom's belief in perfectibility, 'vital growth through convulsions of metamorphosis', is expounded and Stephen states his creed, if creed it can be called. 'He affirmed his significance as a conscious rational animal proceeding syllogistically from the known to the unknown and a conscious rational reagent between a micro- and macrocosm ineluctably constructed upon the incertitude of the void.'

The symposium is ended and Stephen leaves Bloom's house, his diaconal hat elevated on his augur's rod, the ashplant.

With what intonation *secreto* of what commemorative psalm?
The 113th, *modus peregrinus: in exitu Israel de Egypto: domus Jacob de populo barbaro.*

Together at the door they observe 'the heaventree of stars hung with humid nightblue fruit'.

With what meditations did Bloom accompany his demonstrations to his companion of various constellations?

Meditations of evolution increasingly vaster: of the moon invisible in incipient lunation, approaching perigee: of the infinite lattiginous scintillating uncondensed milky way, discernible by daylight by an observer placed at the lower end of a cylindrical vertical shaft 5000 ft deep sunk from the surface towards the centre of the earth: of Sirius (alpha in Canis Major) 10 lightyears (57,000,000,000,000 miles) distant and in volume 900 times the dimension of our planet: of Arcturus: of the precession of equinoxes: of Orion with belt and sextuple sun theta and nebula in which 100 of our solar systems could be contained: of moribund and nascent new stars such as Nova in 1901: of our system plunging towards the constellation of Hercules: of the parallax or parallactic drift of socalled fixed stars, in reality evermoving from immeasurably remote eons to infinitely remote futures in comparison with which the years, threescore and ten, of allotted human life formed a parenthesis of infinitesimal brevity.

Mr Bloom continues his astronomical discursions at length; the ironic influence of Stephen, however, is discernible in the passage where we are invited to consider:

the posited influence of celestial on human bodies: the appearance of a star (1st magnitude) of exceeding brilliancy dominating by night and day (a new luminous sun generated by the collision and amalgamation in incandescence of two non-luminous exsuns) about the period of the birth of William Shakespeare over delta in the recumbent neversetting constellation of Cassiopeia and of a star (2nd magnitude) of similar origin but lesser brilliancy which had appeared in and disappeared from the constellation of the Corona Septentrionalis about the period of the birth of Leopold Bloom and of other stars of (presumably) similar origin which had (effectively or presumably) appeared in and disappeared from the constellation of Andromeda about the period of the birth of Stephen Dedalus, and in and from the constellation of Auriga some years after the birth and death of Rudolph Bloom, junior, and in and from other constellations some years before or after the birth or death of other persons.

As for astrological influences on sublunary disasters, these seemed to Mr Bloom 'as possible of proof as of confutation and the nomenclature employed in selenographical charts as attributable to verifiable intuition as to fallacious analogy: the lake of dreams, the sea of rains, the gulf of dews, the ocean of fecundity'.

Saint George's clock strikes the hour. Stephen hears in the sound the prayer he always associates with his mother's death.

Liliata rutilantium. Turma circumdet.
Iubilantium te virginum. Chorus excipiat.

Mr Bloom hears *Heigho* (the bracelet-bells of the Hours) four times repeated.

Re-entering his house he finds his ingress of the front room suddenly arrested by a solid timber angle. During the day Mrs Bloom has been indulging one of her whims – the rearrangement of the furniture in the room, and Mr Bloom has impinged against the displaced walnut sideboard. 'Nature delights not in anything so much as to alter all things and present them under another form.' The chairs (a 'dull passive' easychair 'with stout arms extended', directly opposite a 'slender bright active' cane chair) and the piano (on which is *Love's Old Sweet Song*, open at the last page, 'with the final indications *ad libitum, forte*, pedal, *animato*, sustained, pedal, *ritirando*, close', which Boylan has – *inter alia* – been practising with Molly Bloom) are exactly described and attention is drawn to their 'significances of posture, of symbolism, of testimonial supermanence'.

Mr Bloom's library is catalogued and the various objects which attract his gaze defined. As he begins to undress his gestures and the sections of his anatomy consecutively revealed are graphically, cinematographically depicted. Now he pauses to meditate. 'It was one of his axioms that similar meditations or the automatic relation to himself of a narrative concerning himself or tranquil recollection of the past when practised habitually before retiring for the night alleviated fatigue and produced as a result sound repose and renovated vitality.'

We are now conducted over Mr Bloom's Ideal Home – 'Bloom Cottage or Saint Leopold's or Flowerville' – its garden and appurtenances, we learn the exact salaries of his (ideal) domestic personnel and visit even his 'lumbershed with padlock for various inventoried implements'.

As?

Eeltraps, lobsterpots, fishingrods, hatchet, steelyard, grindstone, clodcrusher, swatheturner, carriagesack, telescope ladder, 10 tooth rake, washing clogs, haytedder, tumbling rake, billhook, paintpot, brush, hoe and so on.

Various plans for making a quick fortune are worked out down to the smallest detail, and his chances of realizing these projects assessed. The contents of the first drawer of his writing-table are catalogued: a miscellaneous collection of photographs, documents, advertisements, his correspondence with Martha Clifford, and her transliterated name and address 'in reserved alphabetic boustrophedontic punctuated quadrilinear cryptogram (vowels suppressed) N. IGS./WI.UU.OX/W. OKS. MH/Y.IM'.[1] In the second drawer are various legal documents (specified), a press-cutting concerning the change by deedpoll of Rudolph Virag's name to Bloom, other family papers, a stock-certificate, etc.

A problem is now set. 'Reduce Bloom by cross multiplication of reverses of fortune, from which these supports protected him, and by elimination of all positive values to a negligible negative irrational unreal quantity.' In the answer which follows we see his gradual decline, stage by stage, to a mendicant befouled by unlicensed vagabond dogs, pelted by 'the infantile discharge of decomposed vegetable missiles, worth little or nothing or less than nothing'. Such a situation could be precluded 'by decease (change of state), by departure (change of place)'.

There follows the analysis of an hypothetical journey, a disappearance, which may be compared with the legends and speculations of certain post-Homeric writers as to the subsequent journeys of Odysseus after his return to Ithaca and destruction of the suitors. A second journey was, in fact, enjoined on Odysseus by Tiresias, an expedition far inland till he should come upon 'such men as know not the sea neither eat meat savoured with salt'. According to one account[2] Odysseus journeyed to Aetolia, married a princess and died there at an advanced age; another legend relates that Odysseus settled in Thesprotia, married queen Kallidike, and, after leading the Thesprotians to many victories, came to an honoured end in the country of his adoption. Thus Mr Bloom sees himself travelling to Jerusalem, to 'the land of the Eskimos (eaters of soap), the forbidden country of Thibet (from which no traveller returns), the bay of Naples (to see which was to die), the Dead Sea'. The consequences of such an eclipse are explored and we read the advertisement – £5 reward, lost, stolen, or strayed, etc. – whereby the grass widow would seek to regain her lost adventurer. We have an astronomical version of the 'return of the wanderer' motif (often alluded to in this commentary, and elsewhere illustrated by references to Sinbad, Rip van Winkle, the octave).

Would the departed never nowhere nohow reappear?
Ever he would wander, selfcompelled, to the extreme limit of his cometary

1. To solve superpose an alphabet from left to right on one from right to left. The second word, a secret name, is 'reserved'; the clue to this reservation may be found in the Black Mass of 'Circe'.
2. See Albert Hartmann, *Untersuchungen über die Sagen vom Tod des Odysseus.*

orbit, beyond the fixed stars and variable suns and telescopic planets, astronomical waifs and strays, to the extreme boundary of space, passing from land to land, among peoples, amid events. Somewhere imperceptibly he would hear and somehow reluctantly, suncompelled, obey the summons of recall. Whence, disappearing from the constellation of the Northern Crown he would somehow reappear reborn above delta in the constellation of Cassiopeia and after incalculable eons of peregrination return an estranged avenger, a wreaker of justice on malefactors, a dark crusader, a sleeper awakened, with financial resources (by supposition) surpassing those of Rothschild or of the silver king.

What would render such return irrational?

An unsatisfactory equation between an exodus and return in time through reversible space and an exodus and return in space through irreversible time.

What play of forces, inducing inertia, rendered departure undesirable?

The lateness of the hour, rendering procrastinatory: the obscurity of the night, rendering invisible: the uncertainty of thoroughfares, rendering perilous: the necessity for repose, obviating movement: the proximity of an occupied bed, obviating research: the anticipation of warmth (human) tempered with coolness (linen), obviating desire and rendering desirable: the statue of Narcissus, sound without echo, desired desire.

The happenings of Bloomsday are now summed up in ritual terms, for example: the preparation of breakfast (burnt offering); the bath (rite of John); the funeral (rite of Samuel); the altercation with a truculent troglodyte (holocaust); the visit to the disorderly house and subsequent brawl (Armageddon); nocturnal perambulation to and from the cabman's shelter, Butt Bridge (atonement).

The sight of the occupied bed, desirable and desired, molests the tender spot of Mr Bloom's consciousness, his awareness of the *bonne fortune* of Blazes Boylan; but, fortunately, Mr Bloom is a man who has seen and suffered much, a double first at what he likes to call 'the university of life'.

If he had smiled why would he have smiled?

To reflect that each one who enters imagines himself to be the first to enter whereas he is always the last term of a preceding series even if the first term of a succeeding one, each imagining himself to be first, last, only and alone, whereas he is neither first nor last nor only nor alone in a series originating in and repeated to infinity.

> *Der ganze Strudel strebt nach oben:*
> *Du glaubst zu schieben, und du wirst geschoben.*[1]

1. Goethe, in the 'Brocken Scene' of *Faust*.

(This passage has, of course, a far wider reference than the amorous vagaries of Molly Bloom, who, as I shall point out in the final chapter, in many of her aspects represents the Earth, Nature herself. Each man thinks he is 'first, last, only and alone' – this is, in fact, the 'life illusion' – but, we may suppose, the Demiurge smiles at such fatuity.)

With what antagonistic sentiments were his subsequent reflections affected? Envy, jealousy, abnegation, equanimity. ...

Equanimity?

As natural as any and every natural act of a nature expressed or understood executed in natured nature by natural creatures in accordance with his, her and their natured natures, of dissimilar similarity. As not as calamitous as a cataclysmic annihilation of the planet in consequence of collision with a dark sun. As less reprehensible than theft, highway robbery, cruelty to children and animals, obtaining money under false pretences, forgery, embezzlement, misappropriation of public money, betrayal of public trust, malingering, mayhem, corruption of minors, criminal libel, blackmail, contempt of court, arson, treason, felony, mutiny on the high seas, trespass, burglary, jailbreaking, practice of unnatural vice, desertion from armed forces in the field, perjury, poaching, usury, intelligence with the king's enemies, impersonation, criminal assault, manslaughter, wilful and premeditated murder. As not more abnormal than all other altered processes of adaptation to altered conditions of existence, resulting in a reciprocal equilibrium between the bodily organism and its attendant circumstances, foods, beverages, acquired habits, indulged inclinations, significant disease. As more than inevitable, irreparable.

For Mr Bloom has learnt that an 'unwritten law' is worth less even than the paper it is not written on, that the 'eternal triangle' is a mere geometrical figure. He completes the extinction of Eurymachus by considering:

the natural grammatical transition by inversion involving no alteration of sense of an aorist preterite proposition (parsed as masculine subject, monosyllabic onomatopoeic transitive verb with direct feminine object) from the active voice into its correlative aorist preterite proposition (parsed as feminine subject, auxiliary verb and quasimonosyllabic onomatopoeic past participle with complementary masculine agent) in the passive voice: ... the futility of triumph or protest or vindication: the inanity of extolled virtue: the lethargy of nescient matter: the apathy of the stars.

To Molly, who is lying awake, the returned wanderer narrates his adventures, but, like Odysseus, who omitted mention of Nausicaa, he prudently suppresses certain details. He makes 'Stephen Dedalus, professor and author', the salient point of his narration.

In what directions did listener and narrator lie?

Listener, S.E. by E.; Narrator, N.W. by W.: on the 53rd parallel of latitude N. and 6th meridian of longitude, W.: at an angle of 45° to the terrestrial equator.

In what state of rest or motion?

At rest relatively to themselves and to each other. In motion being each and both carried westward, forward and rereward respectively,[1] by the proper perpetual motion of the earth through everchanging tracks of neverchanging space.

In what posture?

Listener: reclined semilaterally, left, left hand under head, right leg extended in a straight line and resting on left leg, flexed, in the attitude of Gea-Tellus, fulfilled, recumbent, big with seed. Narrator: reclined laterally, left, with right and left legs flexed, the indexfinger and thumb of the right hand resting on the bridge of the nose, in the attitude depicted on a snapshot photograph made by Percy Apjohn, the childman weary, the manchild in the womb.

Womb? Weary?

He rests. He has travelled.

With?

Sinbad the Sailor and Tinbad the Tailor and Jinbad the Jailer and Whinbad the Whaler and Ninbad the Nailer and Finbad the Failer and Binbad the Bailer and Pinbad the Pailer and Mindbad the Mailer and Hinbad the Hailer and Rinbad the Railer and Dinbad the Kailer and Vinbad the Quailer and Linbad the Yailer and Xinbad the Phthailer.

When?

Going to dark bed there was a square round Sinbad the Sailor roc's auk's egg in the night of the bed of all the auks of the rocs of Darkinbad the Brightdayler.

Where?

*

This was the last word of the tale, when sweet sleep came speedily upon him, sleep that loosens the limbs of men, unknitting the cares of his soul.[2]

1. As we learn in 'Penelope', Mr and Mrs Bloom have a curious way of sleeping side by side; the latter is normally disposed, but Leopold lies with his feet towards the head of the bed.

2. *Odyssey*, XXIII: 342, 343.

18. PENELOPE

SCENE	The bed
HOUR	...
ORGAN	Flesh
ART	...
SYMBOL	Earth
TECHNIC	Monologue (female)

'SATIRE is a sort of glass, wherein beholders do generally discover everybody's face but their own.' And the comment of the average woman on this, the last episode of *Ulysses*, is apt to run: 'How true – of *that* class of woman, with which, thank goodness, *I* have nothing in common!' But the force of this long, unpunctuated meditation, in which a drowsy woman's vagrant thoughts are transferred in all their naked candour of self-revelation on to the written record, lies precisely in its universality.

The long unspoken monologue of Mrs Bloom which closes the book [Arnold Bennett wrote in *The Outlook*] (forty difficult pages, some twenty-five thousand words without any punctuation at all) might in its utterly convincing realism be an actual document, the magical record of inmost thought by a woman that existed. Talk about understanding 'feminine psychology'! ... I have never read anything to surpass it, and I doubt if I have ever read anything to equal it.

After her husband's return and his recital of the day's adventures, Mrs Bloom settles herself to sleep. But her mind is restless and, in her body too, there is unrest, a punctual flux of 'tides, myriadislanded within'. 'Murphy' (as Mr Bloom facetiously nicknames the dream-moulder) denies his gift. As the nighthours pass and, despite intermittent changes of position in the bed, she fails to achieve somniferous repose, her thoughts roam far afield, 'casting', as Mr Bloom observed of another lady of Spanish extraction, 'every shade of decency to the winds'. She sees herself again a 'flapper' at Gibraltar, she recalls the ways of her earliest lovers, her own simplicity, the hobbies of Major Brian Cooper Tweedy, her father, that ranker-officer and astute philatelist, warmth and sunlight of the south, the Rock 'standing up like a big giant'.[1] Two male 'subjects' recur persistently in this fantasia of reminiscence: 'Blazes' Boylan, ill-mannered and heartless (as she is fully aware), yet compelling her reluctant admiration by his rufous virility; 'Poldy', her unsatisfying, ageing husband, for whom, even in the more aggressive passages where she airs the classic grievances of the eternal feminine against its wedded male, she, nevertheless, displays a quasi-maternal affection, a tribute to that queer solidarity which fortifies the union, consecrated ritually and by habit, of even an ill-assorted couple. Towards the close, thoughts of a third male, Stephen Dedalus, usurp, for a while, the foreground of her monologue. Mr Bloom has described the young man to her and she welcomes the proposal that he should lodge with them. Mr Bloom's ideal nymph (of the *Photo Bits* picture) has, for Molly Bloom, a counterpart in the statuette of a naked boy: 'that lovely little statue he bought I could look at him all day long curly head and his shoulders his finger up for you to listen theres real beauty and poetry for you I often felt I wanted to kiss him all over'. In Stephen, perhaps, she may find that youth, 'real beauty and poetry' after which her maturity hankers.

Mr Bloom has prudently refrained from mentioning his encounter with Nausicaa, but his wife has a flair for such emotional indiscretions and suspects something. He has asked to have his breakfast in bed and at first she wonders if he is ill. If so, it would be much better for him to go to hospital, sick men are a nuisance,

theyre so weak and puling when theyre sick they want a woman to get well if his nose bleeds youd think it was O tragic and that dyinglooking one off the south circular when he sprained his foot at the choir party at the sugarloaf Mountain the day I wore that dress Miss Stack bringing him flowers the worst old ones she could find at the bottom of the basket anything at all to get into a mans bedroom with her old maids voice trying to imagine he was dying on account of her to never see thy face again though he looked more like a man with his beard a bit grown in the bed father was the same besides I hate bandaging and dosing when he cut his toe with the razor paring his corns afraid hed get blood poisoning but if it was a thing I was sick then wed see what attention only of course the woman hides it not to give all the trouble they do

No, it is probably the result of some casual encounter, 'anyway love its not or hed be off his feed thinking of her'. She remembers Mr

1. An anticipation, this, of the Anna Livia - Hill of Howth conjugation in *Finnegans Wake*.

Bloom's indiscreet benevolence towards a maid they had in palmier days, 'proposing she could eat at our table on Christmas if you please O no thank you not in my house stealing my potatoes and the oysters 2/6 per doz'.

But Molly Bloom's jealousy is mainly proprietary and economical; kissing-time with Poldy is 'done now once and for all'. 'Its only the first time after that its the ordinary do it and think no more about it why cant you kiss a man without going and marrying him first you sometimes love to wildly when you feel that way so nice all over you you cant help yourself.' 'A kiss long and hot down to your soul.' The word 'soul' fires a train of religious digressions, the attraction of priests (mentioned by Mr Bloom earlier in the day, 'the tree of forbidden priest'), a memory of the storms at Gibraltar, 'the thunder that woke me up as if the world was coming to an end[1] God be merciful to us I thought the heavens were coming down about us to punish ... and they come and tell you theres no God what could you do if it was running and rushing about nothing only make an act of contrition'.

The 'Boylan' theme recurs (Mrs Bloom spares us no detail of her afternoon's experiences), followed by a memory of Poldy's wooing and one of their earliest quarrels, a

standup row about politics he began it not me when he said about Our Lord being a carpenter at least he made me cry of course a woman is so sensitive about everything I was fuming with myself after for giving in only for I knew he was gone on me and the first socialist he said He was he annoyed me so much I couldnt put him into a temper still he knows a lot of mixed up things especially about the body and the insides I often wanted to study up that myself what we have inside us in that family physician I could always hear his voice talking when the room was crowded and watch him after that I pretended I had on a coolness with her over him because he used to be a bit on the jealous side whenever he asked who are you going to and I said over to Floey and he made me the present of Lord Byrons poems and the three pairs of gloves so that finished that

A good thing she did not, like her friend Josie Powell, marry a lunatic like old Breen who 'used to go to bed with his muddy boots on when the maggot takes him'. Poldy has his good points; he wipes his feet when he comes in and 'takes off his hat when he comes up the street

1. This mention of the 'end of the world' is one of several thematic links between the Odyssey proper, which has gone before, and this, its epilogue.

like that'. 'Of course some men can be dreadfully aggravating drive
you mad and always the worst word in the world what do they ask us
to marry them for if were so bad as all that comes to yes because they
cant get on without us.' She recalls her first sight of 'Blazes' Boylan,
his way of looking at her, and the tenor Bartell d'Arcy who kissed her
on the choirstairs ('tenors get women by the score', as Mr Bloom remarked earlier in the day). Her memories wander back to Lieut. Gard-
ner, an earlier lover, who was killed in the Boer War. Mrs Bloom has
that natural philosophy, which is (or used to be) the prerogative of her
sex, in her attitude to the wasteful and perverse pastimes of Man, that
incorrigible dreamer, the games of war and politics. 'I hate the mention of politics ... they could have made their peace at the beginning
or old oom Paul and the rest of the old Krugers go and fight it out between them instead of dragging on for years and killing any finelook-
ing men there were.' Herself a chimaera, woman does not hunt
chimaeras.

I don't care what anybody says itd be much better for the world to be
governed by the women in it you wouldn't see women going and killing one
another and slaughtering when do you ever see women rolling around drunk
like they do or gambling every penny they have and losing it on horses yes
because a woman whatever she does she knows where to stop

The next phase of her monologue, equally feminine, reveals her cult
of personal beauty and fine raiment and leads on to a characteristic
homily on the nuisance a husband can be when one goes out shopping.

I hate those rich shops get on your nerves nothing kills me altogether only he
thinks he knows a great lot about a womans dress and cooking mathering everything he can scour off the shelves into it if I went by his advices every blessed
hat I put on does that suit me yes take that thats alright the one like a wedding
cake standing up miles off my head he said suited me or the dishcover one coming
down on my backside on pins and needles about the shop girl in that place in
Grafton street I had the misfortune to bring him into and she as insolent as ever
she could be with her smirk saying Im afraid were giving you too much trouble
whats she there for but I stared it out of her

Mrs Bloom's reflections on her personal appearance lead her to a
comparison of male and female charms. 'The woman is beauty of
course thats admitted.' Instance 'those statues in the museum' – another
link with the wanderer who is sleeping beside her in the curious 'anti-
podean' position already described.

I suppose there isnt in all creation another man with the habits he has look at
the way hes sleeping at the foot of the bed how can he without a hard bolster its
well he doesn't kick or he might knock out all my teeth breathing with his hand
on his nose like that Indian god he took me to show one wet Sunday in the
museum in Kildare street all yellow in a pinafore lying on his side on his hand
with his ten toes sticking out that he said was a bigger religion than the jews
and Our Lords both put together all over Asia imitating him as hes always
imitating everybody I suppose he used to sleep at the foot of the bed too with
his big square feet up in his wifes mouth

A distant train passes and its rhythm is woven into the refrain of *Love's
Old Sweet Song*, which she is to sing on Boylan's concert tour.

frseeeeeeeefronnnng train somewhere whistling the strength those engines
have in them like big giants and the water rolling all over and out of them on
all sides like the end of Loves old sweet sonnnng the poor men that have to be
out all the night from their wives and families in those roasting engines stifling
it was today ... the rain was lovely just after my beauty sleep I thought it was
going to get like Gibraltar my goodness the heat there before the levanter came
on ... the poplars and they all whitehot and the mosquito nets and the smell of
the rainwater in those tanks watching the sun all the time weltering down on
you

Memories of Gibraltar follow, of a girl friend of hers there, of the
books she used to read, *Eugene Aram, Molly Bawn* – 'I dont like books
with a Molly in them like that one he brought me about the one from
Flanders a whore always shoplifting anything she could cloth and stuff
and yards of it' – the 'damn guns bursting and booming' on the
Queen's birthday or when some bigwig like General Ulysses Grant
visited the Rock. It was a dull life there – never any letters except the
'old few' she posted to herself to pass the time. Letter-writing reminds
her of

those long crossed letters Atty Dillon used to write to the fellow that was something in the four courts that jilted her after out of the ladies letterwriter when I
told her to say a few simple words he could twist how he liked not acting with
precipit precipitancy with equal candour the greatest earthly happiness answer
to a gentlemans proposal affirmatively my goodness theres nothing else its all
very fine for them but as for being a woman as soon as youre old they might as
well throw you out in the bottom of the ashpit

The first love-letter she received was from a young naval officer,

Lieut. Mulvey; it was brought to her in bed by their old housekeeper Mrs Rubio, a 'disobliging old thing' with a conscience.

I didnt run into mass often enough in Santa Maria to please her with her shawl up on her except when there was a marriage on with all her miracles of the saints and her black blessed virgin with the silver dress and the sun dancing 3 times on Easter Sunday morning and when the priest was going by with the bell bringing the vatican to the dying blessing himself for his Majestad

To tease Mulvey she informed him that she was engaged to the son of a Spanish nobleman, Don Miguel de la Flora: 'theres many a true word spoken in jest'. When he sailed away she climbed the hill to see the last of him through Captain Rubio's[1] telescope, 'the straits shining I could see over to Morocco almost the bay of Tangier white and the Atlas mountain with snow on it and the straits like a river so clear Harry Molly Darling I was thinking of him on the sea all the time after at mass when my petticoat began to slip down at the elevation'.

Another train in the distance rumbles an accompaniment to her murmured 'sweet ssoooooong', thoughts of her concert, of Kathleen Kearney[2]

skitting around talking about politics. ... Irish homemade beauties soldiers daughter am I ay and whose are you bootmakers and publicans I beg your pardon coach I thought you were a wheelbarrow

Her thoughts swing back to the present, Mr Bloom's late return – she hopes he is not being led astray – and thence on to the future, plans for a picnic *en famille*, with Boylan of the party.

not a bank holiday anyhow I hate those ruck of Mary Ann coalboxes out for the day Whit Monday is a cursed day too no wonder that bee bit him better the seaside but Id never again in this life get into a boat with him after him at Bray telling the boatman he knew how to row if anyone asked could he ride the steeplechase for the gold cup hed say yes then it came on to get rough the old thing crookeding about and the weight all down my side telling me to pull the

1. The names 'Mrs Rubio' and 'Captain Rubio' are recalls of the 'ruby' theme, a *leitmotif* persistently recurring, associated with Mr Bloom, throughout *Ulysses*. It is probably an allusion to the Phoenician prototype of Mr Bloom, for the Phoenicians were to the Hellenes (as their name implies) the 'Red-skins'. It may also be noted that Europa was the daughter of the red-gold Phoenix and great-grandmother of Minos, patron of the artificer Daedalus.

2. For further information regarding this talented and patriotic young accompanist, see the story 'A Mother' in *Dubliners*.

right reins now pull the left and the tide swamping in floods in through through the bottom and his oar slipping out of the stirrup its a mercy we werent all drowned he can swim of course me no theres no danger whatsoever keep yourself calm in his flannel trousers Id like to have tattered them down off him before all the people and give him what that one calls flagellate till he was black and blue

After the husband, the daughter; for a while maternal grievances occupy the foreground of Mrs Bloom's consciousness – the misdeeds of her daughter Milly. 'I couldnt turn round with her in the place lately unless I bolted the door first gave me the fidgets coming in without knocking ... then doing the loglady all day put her in a glasscase with two at a time to look at her'.

A malaise of womanhood diverts her attention to the inner world, evoking memories of her experiences with doctors, those professional exploiters of her *bêtes noires*, 'jawbreaking' technical terms. Disgusting creatures men are! And deceitful!

all their twenty pockets arent enough for their lies ...

Still, Mr Bloom has his good points even if, once in a while, he comes home in the small hours. 'Theyre not going to get my husband again into their clutches if I can help it making fun of him then behind his back I know well when he goes on with his idiotics because he has sense enough not to squander every penny piece he earns down their gullets and looks after his wife.' The drunken ways of the Dublin male turn her thoughts to Dignam, to Simon Dedalus who was always turning up at concerts 'half-screwed', then to Stephen Dedalus whose present age she calculates, cheerfully inferring 'I'm not too old for him'.

She contrasts Hugh Boylan with Stephen (as she pictures him in imagination). 'No thats no way for him has he no manners nor no refinement nor no nothing in his nature slapping us behind like that ... because I didn't call him Hugh the ignoramus that doesn't know poetry from a cabbage.' Presently she reverts to her grievances against 'Don Poldo de la Flora'. 'Lord knows what he does that I dont know and Im to be slooching around down in the kitchen to get his lordship his breakfast while hes rolled up like a mummy while I indeed did you ever see me running Id just like to see myself at it show them attention and they treat you like dirt.' A home without a woman in it falls to pieces.

'The hand that rocks the cradle ...', as sleeping Poldy would observe. That is why Stephen is 'running wild now out at night away from his books and studies and not living at home on account of the usual rowy house I suppose well its a poor case that those that have a fine son like that theyre not satisfied and I none'. She is reminded of the death of Rudy, the fairy boy. 'That disheartened me altogether I suppose I oughtnt to have buried him in that little woolly jacket I knitted crying as I was but give it to some poor child but I knew well Id never have another our 1st death too it was we were never the same since.' Grievances, yet again. Men 'have friends they can talk to weve none either he wants what he wont get or its some woman ready to stick her knife into you I hate that in women no wonder they treat us the way they do we are a dreadful lot of bitches I suppose its all the troubles we have makes us so snappy'.

A pity Stephen did not accept Poldy's invitation to stay the night.

I could have brought him his breakfast in bed with a bit of toast so long as I didnt do it on the knife for bad luck or if the woman was going her rounds with the watercress and something nice and tasty there are a few olives in the kitchen he might like I never could bear the look of them in Abrines I could do the criada the room looks all right since I changed it the other way you see something was telling me all the time Id have to introduce myself not knowing me from Adam very funny wouldnt it Im his wife or pretend we were in Spain with him half awake without a Gods notion where he is dos huevos estrellados senor Lord the cracked things come into my head sometimes itd be great fun supposing he stayed with us

As sleep approaches, her mood, with one interruption, softens. After all, she will give Poldy 'one more chance'; she will go out early marketing and bring him his breakfast in bed, play the faithful Penelope. But, if she is not faithful, it is his fault – and she will let him know it, 'tell him every scrap'. A wave of bitterness passes over her. 'Its all his own fault if I am an adulteress as the thing in the gallery said O much about it if thats all the harm ever we did in this vale of tears God knows its not much doesnt everybody only they hide it I suppose thats what a woman is supposed to be there for or He wouldnt have made us the way He did.' But this gust of defiance is quickly lulled and gentler thoughts prevail as she recalls, for the last time before her eyes close, the 'beautiful skies of Andalusia', and in an act of contrition mingles with these memories her Poldy's lovemaking, among the rhododendrons on the

Hill of Howth, that leapyear sixteen years past when she asked him with her eyes to ask again and yes she said Yes

*

Molly Bloom, daughter of Major Brian Cooper Tweedy and the Spanish Jewess with the 'lovely name', Lunita Laredo, regarded under her prototypal and symbolic aspects is a trinity of personages: Penelope, Calypso, and the Earth herself, Gaea-Tellus. The association of Penelope, paragon of faithful helpmates, with Mr Bloom's passionate bedfellow may at first surprise. There is, however, one respect in which the two are obviously in accord; Mrs Bloom, despite her unfaithfulness and with all her grievances, has, as we learn from her monologue, no real desire to change. Homer's Penelope, resisting the solicitations of lusty young aspirants of the Boylan type, remained faithful to the 'bald, middle-aged gentleman' (as Samuel Butler described him) who was her lawful husband, and Molly Bloom is, one may say, faithful too – in her fashion. Her lovers are to her mere toys, and her delinquencies of the nature, as Mr Bloom would say, of a natural phenomenon.

It is, of course, possible to account for the 'natural' incontinence of Molly Bloom by regarding it as the outcome of the 'Calypso' or earthier side of her character, but there is another, more plausible, interpretation, for which I am largely indebted to that *tour de force* in Homeric criticism, Samuel Butler's *Authoress of the Odyssey*. It may, first, be noted that Homer's account of the absolute fidelity of Penelope was not endorsed by later classical writers. Thus Herodotus relates that she became the mother of Pan by Hermes, or (as a Scholiast pleasantly suggests) by all the suitors together. According to another legend she married Telegonus (Odysseus's son by Circe), after Telegonus had slain Odysseus. Butler points out that, even in the Homeric version, she is not reported to have announced point-blank that she did not intend to marry again.

'She does not,' Telemachus says, 'refuse the hateful marriage, nor yet does she bring matters to an end.' Apparently not; but if not, why not? Not to refuse at once is to court courtship, and if she had not meant to court it she seems to have been adept enough in the art of hoodwinking men to have found some means of 'bringing the matter to an end'.

Sending pretty little messages to her admirers was not exactly the way to get rid of them. Did she ever try snubbing? Nothing of the kind is placed on record.

Did she ever say, 'Well, Antinous, whomever else I may marry, you may make your mind easy that it will not be you.' Then there was boring – did she ever try that? Did she read them any of her grandfather's letters? Did she sing them her own songs, or play them music of her own composition? I have always found these courses useful when I wanted to get rid of people. There are indeed signs that something had been done in this direction, for the suitors say that they cannot stand her high art nonsense and aesthetic rhodomontade any longer, but it is more likely she had been trying to attract them than to repel. Did she set them by the ears by repeating with embellishments what they had said to her about one another? Did she ask Antinous or Eurymachus to sit to her for her web – give them a good stiff pose, make them stick to it, and talk to them all the time? Did she find errands for them to run, and then scold them, and say she did not want them? or make them do commissions for her and forget to pay them, or keep on sending them back to the shop to change things, and they had given ever so much too much money and she wished she had gone and done it her-self? Did she insist on their attending family worship? In a word, did she do a single one of the thousand things so astute a matron would have been at no loss to hit upon if she had been in earnest about not wishing to be courted? With one touch of common sense the whole fabric crumbles to dust.

Even in her early days, Butler might have added, Penelope was a lady who habitually objected to making up her mind about the man she loved. Pausanias tells us that, when Odysseus won the hand of Penelope, he was asked by her father Icarius, a Lacedaemonian, to remain at Sparta but declined to do so. Icarius then insisted that his daughter should stay. When Odysseus asked her to decide she refused at first to give an answer; at length, modestly covering her face, she said she would follow Odysseus. Taking the ungallant view of a Butler, one might suspect a counter-attraction in Sparta as the cause of young Penelope's reluctance to leave her home-town; but, if so, her father clearly knew nothing of it, for, to commemorate her charming gesture, he erected a statue of Modesty on the spot. Will Dublin, one wonders, do as much some day for Molly Bloom?

Young Lieut. Mulvey, precursor of Odysseus, was the first wooer of the young nymph of Calpe. 'He didnt know what to make of me with his peaked cap on that he always wore crooked as often as I settled it straight H M S Calypso.' They climbed the Rock together ('I suppose it must be the highest rock in existence') and Molly told him all about the 'old Barbary apes they sent to Clapham without a tail careering all over the show on each others back'. She remembers 'Michaels cave …

Im sure thats the way down the monkeys go under the sea to Africa when they die'. The dying monkeys return to Apes Hill (Abila-Atlas) on the African coast, the 'father' of Calypso's isle.[1] 'He went to India he was to write the voyages these men have to make to the ends of the world and back its the least they might get a squeeze or two at a woman while they can going out to be drowned or blown up somewhere.' Not otherwise three thousand years before a certain Phoenician rover, cruising from Tyre or Carthage towards the pillars of the sky at the world's end, landed on that secret island, where in her hollow cave dwelt the nymph of the braided tresses, and round about there was a wood blossoming, alder and poplar and sweet-smelling cypress, and meadows of violets and parsley, and, after a squeeze or two at our lady of the veils, sailed back eastwards to securer seas.[2]

In her roles of Calypso and Gaea-Tellus Molly Bloom owns to a racial affinity with the gigantic, and much of the attraction she feels for Blazes Boylan is due to his gigantism – he is a 'Sir Lout'. As the nymph Calypso, she displays a pious admiration for her parent, Atlas, the huge upholder of the sky. 'The levanter came on black as night and the glare of the rock standing up in it like a big giant compared with their 3 Rock mountain they think is so great.' Throughout her monologue Mrs Bloom makes comparison of her past estate and grandeurs with the pettiness of the Irish scene and stay-at-home Dubliners. The realm of Calypso is a little isle, a mere 'boss' on the vast shield of waters, but it partakes of the eminence of her father, the 'highest rock in existence'. One of the many links between *Ulysses* and the legendary past (there were giants in those days) is the frequent reference to beings of superhuman stature. The boulders of the shore where Stephen walked in the forenoon are 'Sir Lout's toys. Mind you don't get one bang on the ear. I'm the bloody well gigant rolls all them bloody well boulders. ...' In the 'Cyclops', not only is there an elaborate description of a giant but the technique of the episode itself is, as we have seen, 'gigantism'. The belief that such monsters existed at an early stage of the world's development is common to the traditions of all nations

1. See my notes on the 'Calypso' episode.
2. The song of parting – *Good-bye, Dolly Gray, The Girl I Left Behind Me, Dolores* – is a natural concomitant of the 'Wanderer' theme in *Ulysses*. It was pictorialized in the 'Sirens', '*A Last Farewell*. A headland, a ship, a sail upon the billows. Farewell. A lovely girl, her veil awave upon the wind upon the headland, wind around her.'

and accepted, in some measure, by palaeontologists. It is also one of the starting-points of Vico's *Scienza nuova*, whose influence on Joyce's last work is well known. After the deluge the sole survivors were certain giants who roamed, lonely, each a law unto himself, on the mountain heights, till a sudden peal of thunder tamed their minds to reverence and obedience to the heavenly *numen*. Gradually, Vico tells us, under the influence of more civilized conditions,

their sons lost that monstrous stature and shrank to normal size. How admirable the ways of Providence, which ordained that in earlier days men should be giants, for they needed in those years of wandering a robust constitution to support the rude airs and violence of the seasons, and a superhuman force to thrust their way through the vast forest that covered the earth!

The cult of the gigantic is at once a filial instinct of the Atlantid, Molly Bloom (an instinct she shares with the Anna Livia of *Finnegans Wake*), and Earth's recall of the rude primal matter of the race of men, 'bloody well gigants' and Cyclopes 'like a wooded peak of the towering hills'.

But Mrs Bloom is not only a time-serving wife who weaves and unweaves a tangled web at home, awaiting the delayed return of a Rip van Winkle, not only an immortal nymph, ambrosia-fed, who hospitably intreats bold navigators of the wine-dark sea, she personifies something older and greater than these, Gaea-Tellus, the Great Mother, Cybele.[1] Gaea, the Earth, was, according to the Greeks, the first being that sprang from Chaos and by her son Uranus (the Sky) was the mother of a brood of giants.[2] *Mater omnipotens et alma*, she was the bountiful all-producer,[3] and patroness of marriages. The Romans worshipped her under the name of Tellus and invoked her by sinking their arms downwards towards the earth instead of, as for the other gods, uplifting them. Cybele was the greatest of Levantine gods and, since she was a divinity of the earth and the lion is the strongest and noblest of earth's creatures, was always attended by lions. Thus Molly Bloom compares Boylan to a lion as bedfellow, but, rather scornfully, adds. 'Im sure hed have something better to say for himself an old Lion would'. It is noteworthy that she honours the dean of beasts with a capital letter.

1. See Lucretius, II: 600.
2. The *gigantes* were, as their name implies, the 'earth-born'.
3. 'Terra mater est in medio quasi ouum corrotundata, et omnia bona in se habet tanquam fauus.' Petronius, *Satiricon*, XXXIX.

The tone of her monologue is unmistakably earthy, literally *terre à terre*, thoughts that, ignoring 'uplift', sink down towards the earth. When she heard some 'corner boys' declaiming an obscene doggerel 'it didnt make me blush why should it either its only nature'. Why indeed? Molly herself (they say these things better in France) is *très nature, on ne peut plus*. But though she calls things by their vulgar names (some of her nouns are, in fact, extremely vulgar) – a spade, a spade – she does not 'gloat', like certain modern pornosophers, and call a spade 'a bloody shovel'. She has (as a French writer said of Swift) *une sérénité dans l'indécence* which compels our admiration, something of that maternal longanimity which enables woman (*mater alma*) to play the ministering angel's part without a blush for even the most disgusting of infirmities. Throughout her monologue, except for occasional moments when she bethinks herself of her Catholic upbringing, she applies to her conduct but one test, simplicity itself – Is it natural? But she is not a degenerate modern playing at a 'return to nature', phallus-worship, the simple life, and what not; she is the voice of Nature herself, and judges as the Great Mother, whose function is fertility, whose evangel 'that exalted of reiterately procreating function ever irrevocably enjoined', whose pleasure is creation and the rite precedent.[1]

In the course of her long monologue there are many passages where, positively geotropic, full of the spirit of nature, she speaks with the voice of Genetrix, the Earth. 'I feel all fire inside me', 'I love flowers Id love to have the whole place swimming in roses'; observing the flowers of the wallpaper, she sees them 'like the stars'. She looks back to her youth 'like all through a mist makes you feel so old', remembers the old consul at Gibraltar 'that was there from before the flood', how

1. The 'Great Mother' was one of the two supreme rulers of the early Asiatic pantheon, the other being the bull-god (celebrated in the 'Oxen of the Sun'), a masculine principle. She was worshipped as Ishtar in Babylon; to the Phoenicians she was Astarte and to the Syrians Atargatis. Associated with the Mother and the Bull, we find a young god, Tammuz or Adonis, who is represented as the son of the Great Mother, or her lover, or both at once. In this connexion it is interesting to note how Molly feels herself drawn to the youthful Stephen, Mr Bloom's 'spiritual son', and tends to idealize, not to say idolize, this 'fine young man' in her reverie. With thoughts of Stephen she links the project of a visit to the market to see the vegetables and 'splendid fruits' come in. Adonis was the god of nature's rebirth in the spring. A Phoenician legend connected Adonis with the river of that name, whose waters at a certain period of each year flowed reddened as with blood into the sea near Byblos; signifying the 'death' of the young god, to be followed annually by the green magic of his reincarnation.

it was 'rotten cold that winter when I was only about ten was I yes I had the big doll with all the funny clothes' – her glacial epoch and its strange mastodons – how once she was 'in a swamp' and now has always 'to be slooching around', how one of her lovers 'crushed all the flowers on her bosom'. Such expressions as 'like nothing on earth', 'see it all round you like a new world', 'an unearthly hour', come naturally to her lips. She decides to rise early and watch the earth's produce come to market, 'to see all the vegetables and cabbages and tomatoes and carrots and all kinds of splendid fruits all coming in lovely and fresh who knows whod be the 1st man Id meet': an Eve before the Fall in quest of her Adam. She will be up and about with the first light of morning, escaping from the dark cave of Eccles Street; 'I'm sick of Cohens old bed' – this 'lumpy old jingly' antiquity is one of her aversions. But she is older than the bed on which she sleeps and, when she tries to remember her age, has to calculate by the dates of her marriage and the birth of her daughter; yet, even so, she fails – like the geologists – to reach a positive conclusion.

The movements of Molly Bloom's thoughts in this episode appear, at first sight, capricious and subject to no law. But a close examination shows that there are certain words which, whenever they recur, seem to shift the trend of her musings, and might be called the 'wobbling-points' of the monologue. Such words are 'woman', 'bottom', 'he', 'man'; after each of these there is a divagation in her thoughts, which, as a general rule, revolve about herself. To consider the movements of the earth – besides the continuous movement of rotation about her axis from west to east, there are no less than ten distinct movements, due principally to the attraction of other bodies. These are (a) Revolution about the sun along the plane of the ecliptic; (b) Precession: 'The axis of the earth does not preserve an invariable direction in space, but in a certain time it describes a cone, in much the same manner as the axis of a top spinning out of the vertical.'[1] This movement, the Precession of the Equinoxes, is a consequence of the Sun's and Moon's attraction on the Earth not being a single force through its centre of gravity. The Earth has a spheroidal form, an 'opulent curve' as Mr Bloom would say, and the equatorial band is more strongly attracted, the conse-quence being a tilting of the axis. Precession is of two kinds, lunar

1. This and the following quotations are extracted from the article on 'The Earth' in the *Encyclopedia Britannica*.

and solar; there are thus two distinct movements under this head; (c) *Nutation*: 'Irregularities in the attracting forces which occasion precession also cause a slight oscillation backwards and forwards, the pole tracing a wavy line or "nodding".' This movement also is of two kinds, solar and lunar; (d) *Planetary Precession*: the plane of the earth's orbit, the ecliptic, is subject to a motion due to the attractions of the planets on the earth; (e) *Secular, annual, diurnal motions*; (f) *Variation of Latitude*: the axis of rotation is not rigidly fixed within the earth; its polar extremities wander in a circle of about fifty feet in diameter.

The general movement of Molly Bloom's monologue is egocentric – she thinks of herself, her grievances, her youth. But it will be noticed that time after time she is aware of an outside force, the attraction of 'Poldy', her Apollo, round whom her thought, half reluctantly, turns. Occasionally, too, after the intervention of a wobbling-point, the movement is deflected; a lunar influence tilts her musings towards a woman, to Hester, for instance – a symbol of lunar precession. Thus, again,[1] the word 'bottom' induces a deviation towards the ruling planet of the moment, her lover Boylan. The words 'the bottom of the ashpit'[2] mark the end of a period and the tilt of a new digression towards Spanish memories, Mrs Rubio, and her 'black blessed virgin with the silver dress' – lunar nutation. 'Tides, myriadislanded, within her. Behold the handmaid of the moon.'[3]

'The determination of the figure of the Earth is a problem of the highest importance in astronomy, inasmuch as the diameter of the Earth is the unit to which all celestial differences must be referred.' Thus we find that Molly Bloom acts as the paradigm or *Massstab* of all the characters (or nearly all) in *Ulysses*. She sums them up in her monologue and in the light of her natural understanding we see their proportions reduced to a real scale of magnitudes. She takes their measure according to an ancient wisdom, the warmblooded yet unsentimental exigence of the life-force. This episode is limited, it will be observed, to no *time*, and illustrates no *art*; Gaea-Tellus is 'timeless' and 'artless'.

In her childhood, as she dimly remembers it, the influences were different; in those days she was half asleep, struggling against bitter cold without and fire within, an 'icy wind skeeting across from those mountains standing at the fire with the little bit of a short shift I had'. All through the monologue we observe her moving, growing, expand-

1. *Ulysses*, page 700.   2. page 718.   3. page 44.

ing, just as the child's vision gradually extends beyond the misty limits of infancy to a wider scope of experience, in increasing circles of intellection. She begins small, a very ordinary woman, the *petite bourgeoise* of Eccles Street, a humbler Madame Bovary, to end as the Great Mother of gods, giants, and mankind, a personification of the infinite variety of Nature as she has developed by gradual differentiation from the formless plasma of her beginning.

The concluding pages, a passage of vivid lyrical beauty (which I quote *in extenso*), are at once intensely personal and symbolic of the divine love of Nature for her children, a springsong of the Earth; it is significant for those who see in Joyce's philosophy nothing beyond a blank pessimism, an evangel of denial, that *Ulysses* ends on a triple paean of affirmation.

I love flowers Id love to have the whole place swimming in roses God of heaven theres nothing like nature the wild mountains then the sea and the waves rushing then the beautiful country with fields of oats and wheat and all kinds of things and all the fine cattle going about that would do your heart good to see rivers and lakes and flowers all sorts of shapes and smells and colours springing up even out of the ditches primroses and violets nature it is as for them saying theres no God I wouldnt give a snap of my two fingers for all their learning why dont they go and create something I often asked him atheists or whatever they call themselves go and wash the cobbles off themselves first then they go howling for the priest and they dying and why why because theyre afraid of hell on account of their bad conscience ah yes I know them well who was the first person in the universe before there was anybody that made it all who ah that they dont know neither do I so there you are they might as well try to stop the sun from rising tomorrow the sun shines for you he said the day we were lying among the rhododendrons on Howth head in the grey tweed suit and his straw hat the day I got him to propose to me yes first I gave him the bit of seedcake out of my mouth and it was leapyear like now yes sixteen years ago my God after that long kiss I near lost my breath yes he said I was a flower of the mountain yes so we are flowers all a womans body yes that was one true thing he said in his life and the sun shines for you today yes that was why I liked him because I saw he understood or felt what a woman is and I knew I could always get round him and I gave him all the pleasure I could leading him on till he asked me to say yes and I wouldnt answer first only looked out over the sea and the sky I was thinking of so many things he didnt know of Mulvey and Mr Stanhope and Hester and father and old captain Groves and the sailors playing all birds fly and I say stoop and washing up dishes they called it on the pier and the sentry in front of the governors house with the thing round his white helmet poor devil half roasted and the Spanish girls laughing in their shawls and their tall combs and the auctions in the morning the Greeks and the jews and the Arabs and the devil knows who else from all the ends of Europe and Duke street and the fowl market all clucking outside Larby Sharons and the poor donkeys slipping half asleep and the vague[1] fellows in the cloaks asleep in the shade on the steps and the big wheels of the carts of the bulls and the old castle thousands of years old yes and those handsome Moors all in white and turbans like kings asking you to sit down in their little bit of a shop and Ronda with the old windows of the posadas glancing eyes a lattice hid for her lover to kiss the iron and the wineshops half open at night and the castanets and the night we missed the boat at Algeciras the watchman going about serene[1] with his lamp and O that awful deepdown torrent O and the sea the sea crimson sometimes like fire and the glorious sunsets and the figtrees in the Alameda gardens yes and all the queer little streets and pink and blue and yellow houses and the rosegardens and the jessamine and geraniums and cactuses and Gibraltar as a girl where I was a Flower of the mountain yes when I put the rose in my hair like the Andalusian girls used or shall I wear a red yes and how he kissed me under the Moorish wall and I thought well as well him as another and then I asked him with my eyes to ask again yes and then he asked me would I yes to say yes my mountain flower and first I put my arms around him yes and drew him down to me so he could feel my breasts all perfume yes and his heart was going like mad and yes I said yes I will Yes.

1. Here the word 'vague' and, a few lines later, 'serene' may strike the reader as being too precious, and unlikely to be used by Molly Bloom. They are, as a matter of fact, echoes of common Spanish words she used to hear at Gibraltar; *vago*, a vagrant, and *sereno*, the night-watchman's cry as he goes his rounds, 'All's well – *sereno!*'

Index

*Some other Peregrine books
are described on the
following pages*

A CRITICAL HISTORY OF
ENGLISH POETRY

Herbert Grierson and J. C. Smith

This famous work was the result of the wartime collaboration of two Scottish scholars. Their tracing of the course of English poetry has been described by *The Times Literary Supplement* as a 'volume of masterly compression'. They deliberately spend most time on the greatest poets, believing that, significant as traditions and influences are, the great poet himself affects the spirit of his age and moulds the tradition he has inherited. At the same time, enough attention is paid to minor poets to make the book historically complete, and to fill in the most important links in the chain of poetic development. Thus Gower is here, as well as Chaucer; Patmore, as well as Browning. Both in scope and in detail *A Critical History of English Poetry* is a distinguished and valuable work.

'Alive with witty and just appreciation of the best that has been done in our tongue' — *Scotsman*

THE LITERATURE
OF THE SPANISH PEOPLE

Gerald Brenan

Y16

'In a single volume it surveys the literature of the Spaniards from its Latin beginnings to the writers born before 1890, and surveys it in a manner that will satisfy and stimulate those with a previous knowledge of the subject, give new ideas to students specializing in one or other aspects of Spanish literature, and convey a sense of excited sympathy in readers who have never read any of the Spanish authors under discussion' – *The Times Literary Supplement*

'Whether one turns to the pages on Cervantes, or on the dramatists, to the discussion of Arabic influences on the earliest poetry, or to the section devoted to that very great and neglected novelist Perez Caldos, one finds the evidence of a fine palate for literature and an easy familiarity with current scholarship. This should be the standard work on its subject for many years to come' – *Observer*

There is a full bibliography of texts and critical works for each chapter.

NOT FOR SALE IN THE U.S.A.